THE CLIMAX
OF THE COVENANT

THE CLIMAX
OF THE COVENANT

Christ and the Law in Pauline Theology

by

N. T. WRIGHT

FORTRESS PRESS
MINNEAPOLIS

THE CLIMAX
OF THE COVENANT

Christ and the Law in Pauline Theology

Library of Congress Cataloging-in-Publication Data
Wright, N.T. (Nicholas Thomas)
The climax of the convenant/by N.T, Wright — 1st Fortress Press ed.
p. cm.
Includes bibliographical references and indexes.
ISBN 0-8006-2632-X
1. Covenants — Biblical teaching. 2. Jesus Christ — History of doctrines — Early church, ca. 30-600. 3. Law (Theology) — Biblical teaching. 4. Bible. N. T. Epistles of Paul — Theology. I. Title. BS2655. C74W75 1992
231.7'6—dc20   91-28454 CIP

Manufactured in Great Britain   1-2632
95   94   93   92   1   2   3   4   5   6   7   8   9   10

For N.I.W. and R.W.

Contents

Contents

Preface

One task leads to another, and while working on a book on Pauline theology, as yet incomplete, I discover that I have spent a fair amount of my limited research time in recent years wrestling with the detailed exegesis of certain key Pauline passages. For a variety of reasons, these relate particularly to his view of Jesus Christ on the one hand and the Jewish law on the other. Some of these studies have already been published; others have been given as seminar papers in various places. For this new arrangement some of them have been extensively reworked, others less so. All of them reflect not only solitary study but the constant, and often frustrating, attempt to clarify Paul's thought and expression in tutorials, seminars and lectures. The reason for publishing them here is simply that, while they form part of the essential underpinning for arguments that I wish to advance about Pauline theology as a whole, they are too long and detailed to be included as they stand within a volume that already promises to be large. They nevertheless belong closely with the wider task: study of Paul involves work in exegesis as well as in theology, history of religion, and hermeneutics, and exegesis is sometimes in danger of being swamped—even in commentaries!—by the other three. And I venture to think that these studies also belong quite tidily with each other.

The overall title reflects my growing conviction that covenant theology is one of the main clues, usually neglected, for understanding Paul, and that at many points in his writings, several of which are discussed in this book, what he says about Jesus and about the Law reflects his belief that the covenant purposes of Israel's God had reached their climactic moment in the events of Jesus' death and resurrection. This suggestion, I am well aware, is controversial within the present climate of Pauline scholarship. I hope these essays will at least encourage colleagues who are used to reading Paul in other ways to consider this one more closely.

There can be no pretence of completeness about the book. Several passages of vital importance for understanding Paul's thought about Christ and the Law are not discussed, or only mentioned in passing. The letter to the Romans, in particular, begs to be included all over the place, but apart from a few appearances will have to wait for another occasion. Nor do the chapters dealing with whole passages or sections of Paul pretend to be detailed commentaries: they ask specific questions and try to answer them, leaving aside many matters that a commentary would have to tackle. The annotation varies in quantity and level, partly as a result of the different provenance of the various chapters, partly because the secondary literature on some issues (for instance, the meaning of Philippians 2.6, discussed in ch. 4) is itself arguably confused, and needs sorting out along with the issue of Paul's meaning itself, and partly because in the case of Romans (see chs. 2 and 10–13) we are now well served with commentaries that chronicle the recent scholarly hand-to-hand fighting. I have adopted the custom of referring to secondary literature by author's name and date, with full details in the Bibliography. Where the date of original publication is more than ten years or so before that of the edition or translation used, I have given the earlier date in brackets to avoid confusion. I have avoided abbreviations for the most part, leaving only the regular biblical, Jewish and classical ones.

Since the book has in some sense been growing slowly ever since the earliest article was written (chapter 11, originally written in 1977), there are several people who should be thanked for their help and encouragement on the way. Many of the chapters were first conceived while I was working in McGill University, Montreal, from 1981 to 1986, and I am grateful to the Faculty of Religious Studies there for a congenial and friendly environment for such work, as I am to my colleagues at Worcester College, Oxford, where the book has been completed. My secretary from 1987 to 1990, Jayne Cummins, and her husband, Tony Cummins, have helped in a great variety of ways, not least by keeping the weight of administration off my shoulders sufficiently to enable me to grab a few hours of research time here and there amidst the extraordinary schedule that university lecturers (not to mention College chaplains) now enjoy. Additional and very welcome help also came from Lucy Duffell; and Kathleen Miles has excelled in the numerous editorial and research tasks without which the completion of the book on time would have been impossible. For all this I must also thank the various friends around the world who have, to my astonishment, subscribed to a fund that provides me with secretarial and research assistance at a time when the academic world is required to produce more bricks with less straw (and to write reports on brickmaking while doing so). The thought that I would be able to produce camera-ready copy of the book myself would have been laughable a year ago; that it is now a reality I owe partly to the manufacturers of the superb *Nota Bene* software and partly to the generous advice and help of Craig Hill, Robert Webb and Rob Harnish. I am deeply grateful to the editors and staff of T. and T. Clark for accepting this book and steering it cheerfully on its way.

At a more personal level, my longsuffering wife and children have lived with Paul at one remove for a long time, and have shown much stamina and patience in the process. My dear friends Brian Walsh and Michael Lloyd have sustained, supported and encouraged me through good times and bad. Lis and Andrew Goddard have helped generously in numerous ways. Professor Charlie Moule has been an adopted mentor (after the tragically early death of my own teacher, Professor George Caird) for whose wise advice and encouragement I have constantly had reason to be grateful; his careful reading of, and shrewd comments upon, the typescript of this book is typical of many kindnesses. My colleagues in the Canadian Society of Biblical Literature (when I was working in Montreal) and in the Pauline Theology seminar of the Society of Biblical Literature have given me a great deal, listening to several of these chapters in earlier forms and engaging in a dialogue which is far from complete and always exciting. I am particularly grateful to my friend and former pupil Professor Frank Thielman, of the Beeson Divinity School at Samford University, Birmingham, Alabama, who read through what I had thought was a final version of the text and pointed out several things that needed adjusting. And, more than all, I must thank Professor Richard B. Hays, of Yale Divinity School. His friendship, wisdom, and encouragement have given me boldness to try to think Paul's thoughts after him in new and creative ways. My debate with him in the last chapter not only provides (I think) a fitting semi-colon at the end of these studies, but also reflects many happy hours discussing Pauline theology face to face.

The dedication reflects, though it can scarcely repay, my oldest human debt. The present book is in some ways a first-fruit of my doctoral thesis (1980), which was itself the culmination of a long educational process. Had it not been for the initiative, sacrifice and constant support of my parents, that process would have been unthinkable. Without wishing to embarrass them by speaking (*inter alia*) of their example of patience, hard work, and undemonstrative Christian witness, I nevertheless wish in this way to record my gratitude and love.

N.T. Wright
Worcester College, Oxford

St David's Day, 1991

Introduction

Chapter One

CHRIST, THE LAW, AND 'PAULINE THEOLOGY'

The present climate of Pauline scholarship is exciting, but often more than a little confused.[1] It will therefore be as well, before plunging into particular details, to reflect for a while on the nature of the wider task to which the present studies belong.[2] In this introductory chapter we shall look first at 'Pauline Theology' itself, and then at some of the specific questions which have been raised about Christ and the Law in Paul's writings.[3]

(i) What is 'Pauline Theology'?

Since those who look for nothing often find it, it may be as well to say briefly what this entity, 'Pauline Theology', may be conceived to be. I take the phrase to refer to that integrated set of beliefs which may be supposed to inform and undergird Paul's life, mission and writing, coming to expression in varied ways throughout all three. If we were to specify the content of this set of beliefs, it would be natural to begin with definitely Jewish categories, since Paul by his own admission continued to understand his work from the standpoint of one who had been a zealous Pharisaic Jew; and that would mean grouping them under the twin heads of Jewish theology, viz. monotheism and election, God and Israel.[4] Indeed, my underlying argument throughout my discussion of Paul, here and elsewhere, is that his theology consists precisely in the redefinition, by means of christology and pneumatology, of those two key Jewish doctrines. Those familiar with recent discussions may feel that the *form* of this conclusion is not far from J.C.

---

[1]For an assessment of the present state of Pauline studies see Neill and Wright 1988, 403–430.

[2]Sections (i)–(iii) of the present chapter correspond to the first part of my contribution to Bassler 1991, reproduced here by permission of Augsburg Fortress.

[3]I shall assume in this book that Colossians is Pauline, though not many of my arguments, even in ch. 4, hinge vitally on this.

[4]See, e.g., Schechter 1961, and other similar treatments.

1

Beker's 'coherence and contingency'; and in some senses, though not all, I shall suggest that my proposal is also not so far from his as might at first appear in terms of *substance*.[5] That is to say, what I see as Paul's redefinition, via Christ and the Spirit, of the Jewish doctrines of monotheism and election corresponds quite closely, when its eschatological implications are explored, to what Beker and others mean by his christological redefinition of apocalyptic.

There are two obvious problems, of course, about saying anything like this today. First, *are* Paul's beliefs really integrated? Second, are Paul's beliefs, whether integrated or not, the real heart and driving force of his writing and work? Several scholars, notably H. Räisänen, have recently answered 'no' to both questions, arguing some form of the thesis that Paul's theology is full of rank inconsistencies, best explained on the hypothesis that what appears to be theological argumentation in Paul is merely secondary rationalization of positions reached on quite other grounds.[6] These two charges must be dealt with at more length (sections (ii) and (iii) below). But before we turn to them specifically we may venture another observation which tells initially in a different direction.

Wayne Meeks has pointed out, on the basis of his sociological enquiry into the Pauline churches, that the boundary-marker of these early Christian communities was the confession which we find in 1 Corinthians 8.6: One God, one Lord.[7] This confession, as I have suggested elsewhere,[8] is itself a rewriting, whether by Paul or by some other early Christian, of the Jewish confession of faith, the *Shema*. This, in fact, I believe to be the heart of the Pauline doctrine of justification by faith: that the community of the people of God, those declared in the present to be δίκαιος, are those whose faith has precisely this content. They are marked off from pagan polytheists on the one hand by their firm monotheism (since the formula, in its context in 1 Corinthians 8, is clearly monotheistic in intent), and from Jews on the other hand by the radical and startling christological redefinition of that Jewish monotheism. Rather than move with Sanders to neologism, therefore, and use the noun 'faith' as a verb,[9] I would propose that we use the noun cognate with 'believe' to express the status of this confession within the Pauline communities: justification by *belief*, i.e. covenant membership demarcated by that which is believed.

If this suggestion is anywhere near the truth (I am well aware that it will be frowned on by many, despite my redefinition of what 'justification' thus

[5]See Beker 1980 and elsewhere.
[6]See Räisänen 1986a, 1986b.
[7]Meeks 1983, ch. 6.
[8]See below, ch. 6.
[9]See e.g. Sanders 1983, e.g. 143 'the community of those who faith in Christ'.

actually *means*), then a corollary follows. The nature of that faith (not in the sense of the analysis of the act of believing but in the sense of an analysis of the thing(s) believed or believed in), is of vital importance to Paul in his work. This is so, not because he is an Idealist (or simply an armchair theologian) wishing to achieve a coherence of abstract thought for its own sake, but because he is anxious about the boundary-markers of the communities he believes himself called upon to found and nurture. And, classically, he is anxious in negative and positive ways. On the one hand, the boundary-marker must be faith in Christ, and those whose behaviour or affirmations show that they do not have such faith are to be regarded as outside. On the other hand, the boundary-marker is faith in Christ and *not* Jewish race, with its badges of circumcision, kosher laws, sabbath observance and, in and through all, the possession of, or attempts to keep, Torah, so that racial background is irrelevant to membership in the people of God. Paul's theology thus has, if you like, a sociological cutting edge: it is precisely theology, that which is believed, which declares on the one hand that (only) those who *believe* in Christ belong to the community, and on the other that *all* those who believe in Christ, irrespective of racial background, belong. It therefore leads Paul into action in relation to his communities, just as modern study of those communities leads back inexorably—as in the case of Meeks—to the study of theology, of that which is believed and confessed.

Pauline Theology, then, may be regarded initially as a worthwhile and plausible object of study, integrated with (and not set over against) other ways of reading Paul.[10] But how are we to investigate it? It is not enough merely to consider the specific topics treated by Paul at various points in his letters. It is also important to ask questions about the underlying (or, equally metaphorically, over-arching) structure of his belief-system. What options were open to him at this level, and which (if any) did he take up? Here we have to do with issues too large to be seen frequently on the surface: questions of monism and dualism; of paganism, pantheism, polytheism; of monotheism, its types, alternatives and implications. Despite the almost total absence of such themes in recent writing on Paul,[11] it is my conviction that if we are really studying Paul's theology these issues must at least be on the table, if we are not to condemn ourselves ultimately to shallowness. In the last analysis, theology is all about the great wholes, the world-views which determine and dominate the day-to-day handling of varied issues. When all is said and done, most, perhaps all, great thinkers and writers can and should be studied at this level.

[10]Contrast Watson 1986.

[11]Notable exceptions are Wire 1974, Dahl 1977, 178-91 and Moxnes 1980; their suggestions have not noticeably been taken up in subsequent studies.

It thus becomes all the more important to ask: what about the supposed 'inconsistencies' in Paul?

(ii) Contradictions, Tensions, Inconsistencies, Antinomies and Other Worrying Things

(a) To call someone inconsistent seems today a somewhat two-edged compliment. Schechter's dictum is often quoted to the effect that, whatever faults the Rabbis may have had, consistency was not among them. It is implied that watertight consistency is the province of small minds, and that awareness of larger truth, or readiness to be open to different aspects of the situation, will lead inevitably to a healthy inconsistency which is a sign, not of mental laziness or sloppiness, but of continual growth in stature. Thus Paul is declared 'gloriously' inconsistent, and it is somehow implied that he ought to be pleased with the compliment. Who wants to be rigidly dogmatic?[12]

The appearance of inconsistency, nevertheless, presents a problem for students of any abstract thinker or writer. An apparent inconsistency in Plato, say, is a cause for scholarly questioning. Did he change his mind? Was he aware of the problem? Is there a third passage which reconciles the two? Are we forcing his ideas into the wrong mould? This problem increases when the text in question forms part of a corpus which some regard as in some sense authoritative—which is still the case among many Pauline scholars, including some who expose his apparent inconsistencies. Do we set up a scheme of textual surgery?[13] Or postulate development of thought?[14] Or situation ethics?[15] Or suggest using *Sachkritik*?[16] Or do we carefully expound the passages in question so that one set is allowed to dominate and the others apparently made to harmonize with it?[17] Or should we have part of the cake and eat the other part, dividing it up into 'coherence' and 'contingency'?[18] Or must we simply give up and say that Paul contradicts himself on major matters, that the impression of profundity is simply the

---

[12]The most recent example of this idea is Sanders 1991, 127 f.: 'Let us not put [Paul] entirely into the strait-jacket of logical arrangement... [He] did not reconcile his responses to these multifaceted problems with one another. ...must a religion, in addressing diverse problems, offer answers that are completely consistent with one another? Is it not good to have passionate hopes and commitments which cannot all be reduced to a scheme in which they are arranged in a hierarchical relationship?'

[13]O'Neill 1975.

[14]Drane 1975, Hübner 1984, and many others.

[15]Richardson 1980.

[16]Käsemann 1980.

[17]Cranfield 1975, 1979, giving priority to Romans; many Lutherans, making Galatians the yardstick.

[18]Beker 1980.

result of this confusion,[19] and that many of his arguments are not real arguments but psychologically explicable secondary rationalizations?[20] At this point the compliment seems to be wearing a little thin, but Paul is still left in the position of being unable to reply to the charges laid against him, since (it is implied) he ought to be flattered rather than threatened by them.

(b) It is of course pleasantly easy to produce apparent self-contradiction in almost any writer.[21] Ronald Knox had no difficulty in proving the existence of different hands in the Sherlock Holmes corpus, or in demonstrating that the second half of *Pilgrim's Progress* was written by a middle-aged Anglo-Catholic woman (Pseudo-Bunyan, of course).[22] If we imagine the sort of reply Bunyan himself would have made to this happy nonsense we may well be able to imagine also potential replies that Paul might make. The way to produce inconsistency is to ask a sharp question (especially on a subject not central to all the writings in question: try asking, for instance, what was Jane Austen's attitude to repentance) and to insist on a yes-or-no answer. Is Montreal a hot city, yes or no? Is Greek an easy language to learn, yes or no? Was Jane Austen in favour of repentance, yes or no? Is the Bible the word of God, yes or no? Is the Torah abolished, yes or no? We surely want to reply 'It all depends...', but the words are scarcely out of our mouths before our questioner interrupts: don't prevaricate, don't fob me off with cheap quibbles—I only asked a simple question. When we meet this sort of thing in real life, we smile and explain the problem, or simply change the subject. When we meet it in scholarship we allow ourselves to be browbeaten, to be threatened by the implied rebuke: if you manage to answer yes *and* no, you're just a harmonizer, a flattener out of Paul's craggy contours, denying the poor apostle the fun, and the scholarly prestige, of his own splendid inconsistency.

(c) If apparent harmonization is disallowed *a priori* as an objection in principle to the charge of Pauline self-contradiction, or at least (the softer version of the same point) inconsistency, a more philosophical counter-attack suggests itself. How could the charge of contradiction be either proved or falsified? If neither is possible, the charge hangs in the air as a fairly worthless hypothesis, creating a fog perhaps, but not deserving to arrest our forward progress. What will count as contradiction? What will count as a refutation of the charge? I suggest that we should operate with a fairly tight definition of contradiction: contradiction is present when two passages in which the same subject is being discussed make irreconcilable assertions on

---

[19]Sanders 1983, 80 f., 199.

[20]Räisänen 1986a.

[21]See Martin 1989, 40. Martin's criticisms of Sanders and Räisänen do not, in my view, have as much force as they might have done.

[22]R. Knox, *Essays in Satire*.

the same point. This of course leaves open the question whether the same subject, or the same point, is in fact at issue in the two passages in question, and for that matter what counts as irreconcilability; but these are matters of detail. Conversely, I suggest that the charge of contradiction can in principle be falsified by old-fashioned hypothesis and verification. Is there a larger category, preferably one which Paul somewhere spells out explicitly, which sets up a framework within which the two things thought of as irreconcilable are in fact held together? A good historical example of this kind of move would be the replies, by the early English reformers, to the charge that they, following Luther, were proposing a scheme in which faith and works were mutually exclusive. Their replies (I am thinking particularly of William Tyndale) consistently sketched a larger doctrine of salvation in which the respective places of faith and works were explicated and correlated. Whether or not they were successful is not my point; the method they used, of widening categories to show consistency between apparently opposed claims, is what is needed. I shall suggest in Part Two that the narrative substructure of Paul's theology offers a similar model within which the charge of inconsistency appears shallow and blinkered.

(d) Literary criticism (if one may generalize so sweepingly) would in general provide another possible line of counter-attack. In some recent writing on Paul, one gets the impression that he is contradictory until proved otherwise: the irreconcilable material is so obvious that one starts from the presupposition that nothing can be done about it, and then rejects, or scorns, all attempts to solve it. But the literary critic would be inclined to proceed in the opposite direction, to start with the assumption of coherence and only relinquish it when forced to do so, having tried all reasonable hypotheses to save the appearances. This method is taken in principle by, for instance, Ernst Käsemann in his commentary on Romans (p. viii): 'Until I have proof to the contrary I proceed on the assumption that the text has a central concern and a remarkable inner logic that may no longer be entirely comprehensible to us.'[23] Käsemann, of course, does not allow himself to be thereby prevented from using *Sachkritick* to relativize certain aspects of the letter; but in his hands *Sachkritik* is a method, not so much of exegesis, as of hermeneutics: this is how we find not only the 'real centre' of Paul's thought (though he would hope for that too) but the real centre of his message for the church. The same sort of move is made by C.H. Dodd: see his comment on Romans 9.20–1, 'Man is not a pot'.[24] For those who are not so concerned with making such a hermeneutical move the problem thereby solved is not so pressing. If we are interested in Paul simply as a historical figure of some importance for the history of first-century religion, we can leave him as

[23]Käsemann 1980, viii.
[24]Dodd 1959 <1932>, 171.

inconsistent or self-contradictory as we like. Indeed (though this is not so often noticed) to leave him self-contradictory may often be a subtle way of arguing that he is best left in his own century, and should not be allowed to roam free and weave his confusions in the modern world too. He must be kept in his place.[25]

(e) Within the attempt to find a hypothetical larger model (the attempt might, of course, prove futile sufficiently often for it to become arguable that *no* solution will ever be found), the softer categories of inconsistency, tension and antinomy may well find a place. Theologians love to point out the antinomy between waves and particles in physics: nobody doubts that both are in some sense true and important, but nobody can reconcile them within present models of understanding. Tensions are present in every interesting writer on every subject, and are indeed exploited deliberately by any good writer as a way of teasing the reader into thinking harder about the subject. Neither, then, is sufficient ground for predicating contradiction. Inconsistency is a slippery category, sometimes meaning 'apparent contradiction', implying that given time and/or more papyrus Paul could and perhaps would have reduced the apparent contradiction to a mere tension or antinomy. A further similar category would be incoherence, in which the implied assertion would be that Paul (or whoever) was struggling to say something clearly (and perhaps that we can say it more clearly on his behalf) but that he just failed to attain clarity in his actual expression. This charge, even more than the others, rebounds too often on its proposers for any cautious critic to be utterly happy about using it. I suggest that care be taken in discussing Paul lest we use these various words too loosely, or without sufficiently recognizing the baggage which some of them carry.

(f) I suggest further, to take one example of considerable importance for one of the subject-areas of this book, that Paul's treatments of Torah are in fact not self-contained, but that they form part of a larger whole, or indeed several larger wholes. They cannot be isolated from, for instance, his treatment of justification, his discussions of Israel, his christology and theology of the cross, his pneumatology, even his view of baptism. And it is my contention that, when even some of these contexts are taken seriously as the matrix of his various remarks about Torah, some at least of the contradictions (and other unpleasant things) which are often, and sometimes too gleefully, found in his writings will be discovered to be illusory. And when that happens we will be forced to think again about the nature of his theological method, which is often currently dismissed by the charge of 'rationalization'. What do such charges involve?

[25]See Watson 1986.

7

(iii) Proofs, Arguments, Assertions, Rationalizations and Excuses

(a) Scholars have often failed to think clearly about what precisely Paul is *doing* in any particular passage. 'Paul proves this point by an argument which...'; 'The apostle here argues that...'; 'Paul attempts to demonstrate...'; 'Paul rationalizes this by asserting...': such phrases, the stock-in-trade of writers about Paul, are often used almost interchangeably as a way simply of introducing the next verse under discussion. But there are, in fact, several quite different things which Paul does in his letters.[26] He is quite capable of arguing a point millimetre by millimetre, from first principles, but he certainly does not employ this method for all, or even most, of the time. Nor should he be criticized for illogicality if on occasion it can be shown that what he has done is not argue but assert, not prove but rationalize. Thus, for instance, he sometimes merely asserts a point, without attempting to argue it. 'The sting of death is sin, and the power of sin is the Torah' (1 Corinthians 15.56); Paul does in fact argue this fully in Romans 6–8, but in context it is a bald, and provocative, assertion. Sometimes he argues in regular syllogistic form: if a then b, if b then c: so if a then c. This regularly leads either to the conclusion 'and a is in fact true' (an assertion within an argument), 'and therefore c is also true' or a *reductio ad absurdum* 'and c is absurd, therefore a, which would have led to it, is untrue'. An example of the first would be Romans 8.9–11, analysed into its effective component stages:

> a. If you belong to Christ, the Spirit dwells in you:
> b. The Spirit is the one who raised Jesus from the dead:
> c. Therefore if you belong to Christ, the Spirit will raise you too.
> > Practical conclusion: since you do in fact belong to Christ (an assertion, here unsupported, within an argument), the Spirit will in fact raise you too.

Properly speaking, this requires a further premise, $b2$: the Spirit will do for Jesus' people, i.e. those who are in Christ, what he did for Jesus. Paul is able to assume this from his previous statements, e.g. those in ch. 6.

An example of the *reductio ad absurdum* would be Romans 6.15–23, similarly analysed:

> a. If you yield yourselves to sin, you become the slave of sin:
> b. Slavery to sin leads to death:
> c. Therefore yielding oneself to sin leads to death.
> > Practical conclusion: death is the wrong place to end up, therefore yielding oneself to sin is the wrong place to begin.

[26]So, rightly, Sanders 1991, 51 f.

It must be stressed that in syllogisms like these, or indeed in almost any form of argument, the terms of the syllogisms are not themselves argued for. While Paul is arguing from *a* and *b* to *c*, he is not usually at the same time arguing for the truth of *a* and *b* themselves. Confusion often arises at this point. Scholars frequently attempt to read Paul as if he were actually arguing for every line, as if (for instance) the sentence 'I through the law died to the law' in Galatians 2.19 were the result of, or even part of the flow of, a consecutive argument. It is in fact a fresh assertion introduced to bring a *new* point *into* an argument. It thus becomes part of the argument, but is not itself here argued *for*. (In this particular case, it could be suggested, or even argued, that Paul argues the point fully in Romans 7—the same place, in fact, where he argues fully the tendentious assertion of 1 Corinthians 15.56.)

A further variant on the syllogism may also be noted here. Paul sometimes reverses the order of minor premise and conclusion, *b* and *c*:

a. Torah, sin and death are the problem analysed in Romans 7:

c. Therefore there is no condemnation for those in Christ Jesus (8.1):

b. Because God has solved the problem of Romans 7 (8.2–11).

There are thus different, interlocking types of writing in Paul. Although we have customarily used the word 'argument' loosely, referring to almost anything that Paul says, we should (I suggest) restrict it more carefully to passages where Paul actually *is* arguing, and note carefully those sentences within an argument which are not themselves there argued for. This will have the effect of restricting the ambitions of exegesis, placing bounds on the desire to extract (say) a full doctrine of Torah from every passage in which it is mentioned. It will also, I believe, help in the task of identifying, in relation to my previous section, places where the charge of contradiction has even any initial plausibility.

One final kind of argument should be noted here in passing. In his stimulating monograph *The Faith of Jesus Christ*, Richard B. Hays suggests that we can trace a narrative substructure underneath Paul's argument at key points in Galatians 3–4, and that this substructure carries its own kind of narrative logic on the basis of which certain things can be regarded as proven, not by regular formal argument but by appeal to the known story. This possibility must at least be borne in mind as a useful, perhaps sometimes even necessary, tool for exegesis in certain passages (perhaps, e.g., Philippians 3.2–11); I explore its possible use in relation to a key passage in Romans in ch. 10 below.[27]

[27] See Hays 1983.

(b) What is a rationalization? An argument, presumably, designed to lead to a conclusion already reached by the writer or speaker on different grounds. (One of the greatest advantages, and temptations, of an academic education is the ability it gives one not only to produce cunning rationalizations of ideas, or courses of action, which one wants to assert or pursue for oneself, but also ruthlessly to expose those of others.) When put like that, 'rationalization' seems clearly a term of abuse, strong enough indeed to knock down an entire line of thought: 'you only say that because you want to remain a good Calvinist/Lutheran/liberal/conservative'. But this weapon has too light a trigger. Unless we are simply arational beings, in which case we might as well stop talking altogether, there will always be reasons for what we say, and having such reasons can hardly be in every case an argument against saying anything at all. One is reminded of C.S. Lewis' *reductio ad absurdum* for this sort of thing:

> 'Now tell me, someone, what is argument?'
> There was a confused murmur.
> 'Come, come,' said the jailor. 'You must know your catechisms by now. You, there, what is argument?'
> 'Argument is the attempted rationalization of the arguer's desires.'
> 'Very good,' replied the jailor, 'but you should turn out your toes and put your hands behind your back. That is better. Now: what is the proper answer to an argument proving the existence of the Landlord?' [i.e. God]
> 'The proper answer is, "You say that because you are a Steward."' [Priest]
> ...'Good. Now just one more. What is the answer to an argument turning on the belief that two and two make four?'
> 'The answer is, "You say that because you are a mathematician."'
> 'You are a very good boy,' said the jailor. 'And when I come back I shall bring you something nice...'[28]

Not only is the cry 'rationalization' likely to prove too much. It frequently invokes a quite unwarranted slur on an argument. If something is in fact true, it is likely *a priori* that there will be more than one valid argument by which it can be proved. Thus, if I wish to know the height of the fir-tree I can see from my study window, I have more than one option. I can climb the tree clutching a long piece of string attached to the ground, mark the height, return to the ground and measure the string. I can, alternatively, conduct comparatively sophisticated geometrical experiments with vertical poles placed some distance from the tree, measuring angles and poles instead of the tree itself. I can even take a reading of the ground-level height above sea

---

[28]Lewis 1943, 62–3. The 'jailor' is of course Freud.

level with an air-pressure gauge, fly in a helicopter to a point level with the treetop, take another reading, and subtract *a* from *b*. And—and this is the point that really matters for the study of Paul—there is no reason why the argument I give to demonstrate to someone else that the tree is, say, forty-five feet high should be any particular one of these; no reason, moreover, why it should be *the same argument by which I myself arrived at the information*. Wisdom suggests that I choose arguments likely to be understood,and seen to be valid, by the person whom I wish to convince. I may have arrived at the conclusion in the first instance by any one of a variety of routes. I may have guessed; I may have believed the guess of a friend with a practised eye; I may have compared the tree with the building next to it, whose height I happen to know for other reasons. Especially in the first case (the guess), there will be a need to provide what are in fact rationalizations: reasoned-out demonstrations of a point reached by other, perhaps even non-rational, means. *Such a process does not discredit the rationalizations. It actually requires them.* In Paul's case, it is clear that the resurrection of Jesus, which he came to believe in at the time of, or shortly after, his Damascus Road experience, was his actual starting-point; but, once having come to believe in Jesus as the risen Messiah, he was at liberty to see the scheme whole, with the resurrection as climax, not ground, and to start at any other point in a specific debate. He could, and did, choose his ground and direction not according to autobiography but according to the demands of his particular audience and argument.

There is, in fact, every likelihood that some people will find some sorts of arguments convincing, and others others. A good arguer will appeal to the ones deemed likely to convince the particular audience addressed. Thus, when Paul argues a point about the Torah, it is quite illegitimate to respond 'But, Paul, that's not how *you* came to your view'. Did he ever claim that it was? (Possible answer: no, but several of his interpreters have.)

If we look at other fields of enquiry, we will find the same thing. Almost every scientific argument, for instance, is a secondary rationalization designed to argue inductively for a conclusion reached originally by a leap of imagination. Nearer home, many well-accepted scholarly arguments in the biblical field are of this type. Consider, for instance, Wellhausen's own account of his instant acceptance of Graf's hypothesis about the lateness of P: 'Wellhausen tells us, when he heard of Graf's conclusion, in a private conversation with Albrecht Ritschl, he sensed immediately that it was right, even though he could not at the time examine Graf's reasons.'[29] That is, he reached in a flash of intuition (why?) an idea which was only subsequently filled out by the mass of detail which was then presented, and quite properly

[29]Clements 1976, 9.

so, as argument for the benefit of those who could not come by the intuitive leap—the Damascus Road experience in which the four sources appeared in glory—made by the master. Nearer home still, I am sceptical, in a friendly sort of way, of Cranfield's suggestion[30] that his theological essays at the end of the Romans commentary are to be seen as the result of the detailed exegesis that has preceded them. The fullest is in fact a reworking of his famous essay on Paul and the Law, first printed many years before in the *Scottish Journal of Theology*, which has at point after point influenced the actual course of exegesis. I do not say, influenced for the worse. I do not think, and this in fact is my main point here, that the detailed argument which provides reasons for an hypothesis is any the worse for having that status. If it is, Einstein falls along with Cranfield. Thus, while there is no need to doubt Räisänen's protestations that *he* did not come to *his* research with a fixed notion of the results he eventually found[31], there was in fact no need for him to be so sensitive about the possibility.

Why, then, have rationalizations had such a bad press? Why did Räisänen want to avoid the charge himself? Because, clearly, they are very often illegitimate as arguments in their own right, and Räisänen, who is about to use this as his principal charge against Paul, is obviously warding off in advance any chance of a *tu quoque*. But the charge is only worth making under the following circumstances. It is possible that a writer or speaker will advance, as a supposedly valid argument for a position he has reached on other grounds, a line of thought which is in fact *not* valid in itself, but which gains its apparent force simply from rhetorical skill or emotive pressure. When seen in the cold light of day, the argument turns out to be spurious, an *invalid* secondary rationalization of a position reached on other grounds. But it is the invalidity of the argument itself, not the fact that it is a secondary rationalization, which renders it null and void. A better word for such a process would be 'excuse', though even that does not of itself carry the negative force required; 'invalid excuse' would be better.

And it is only in such cases that the question of motive—of the psychological and sociological factors with which Räisänen makes so much play, which are to my mind the principal weaknesses of his book—even needs to be raised. If we can see that the argument is invalid, we are entitled to ask, why then did somebody who gives the appearance, if not necessarily of actually being rational, but at least of desiring to be thought so, advance it in the first place? I am not saying that we can give satisfactory answers to such questions. Psychologists and therapists have a hard enough time answering them when the patient is sitting still in the same room and co-operating.

[30]Cranfield 1975, 1.
[31]Räisänen 1986a, v.

12

How ancient historians can hope to have any success in the same process with fantastically small evidence is beyond my comprehension.

All of the above serves as a major premise to a syllogism of my own, whose minor, like some of Paul's, cannot for reasons of space be argued, but merely stated.

> *a*. Only some rationalizations are invalid:
> *b*. Räisänen (and others) argue as if all rationalizations are invalid:
> *c*. Therefore the question remains open whether Paul's actual arguments, even if demonstrably rationalizations, are in fact invalid.

I am not, of course, suggesting that there are no problems in Paul's arguments: only (here) that the problems do not lie just where they are commonly thought to. Most of this book will consist of particular studies of particular arguments, and the case will have to be made step by step.

What method, then, is it appropriate to use when dealing with questions of Pauline Theology? Unquestionably the right starting point is exegesis, and that is among the justifications for a book like this. But we cannot come to exegesis pretending to be neutral. We join the hermeneutical spiral, travelling (we may hope) in an upward direction as we go round from text to hypothesis, or vice versa, and back again. We need at least some preliminary questions to ask, and their choice is far from neutral. The questions I have to offer are the result of several trips round the spiral. I do not pretend that they are not, in the sense described above, part of a process of rationalization. I do claim that they are advanced genuinely as questions. One of the tests of whether a rationalization is valid or invalid is whether, in the course of making it, its proponent is prepared to modify the position being rationalized. If so, then the scientific model of hypothesis and verification is being followed, and there is no need to grumble.

(iv) The Preliminary Questions

I have suggested that Paul's Jewish background makes it natural for us to approach him with certain theological questions in mind. These are not, actually, the ones we normally bring to him, culled from later dogmatic theology, but rather include the following: What was his view of God and the people of God? Monotheism and election served, in the Judaism of Paul's day, not so much as abstract beliefs, mere propositions to which intellectual assent should be given by the thinking Jew, but as truths to be celebrated, as boundary markers round the community, as symbols of national and racial solidarity.[32] It is natural to ask, then: what, if anything, did Paul do with these beliefs? Did they change through his becoming Christian, and if so in what way? Could we, from what we know of first-century Pharisaism, have 'predicted' (in the scientific sense) these modifications? If we take care when setting up the issues, we will be less likely to end up begging the questions that really matter.

Let us therefore pursue these vital issues a bit further. It seems clear on the one hand that Paul is consistently undermining the traditional Jewish view of election, and establishing a new view of the people of God (some have denied even this bare statement, but we will deal with that a little later). Yet he does these things without, apparently, going the whole way into (what we have come to call) a Marcionite position. The new is in some sort of continuity with the old, as well as some sort of discontinuity. It is the precise shape of this continuity and discontinuity that poses our problem. This is the problem to which, in fact, Marcionism, whether the original variety or in some more modern guise, is one of the best-known solutions: God has simply abandoned and abolished the Torah and 'Israel' altogether, in order to establish something new. At the other end of the spectrum is the modern two-covenant theory, which may perhaps have its own ancient antecedents: this view holds that God has no particular fault to find with Israel or the Torah, and is happy that Jews should continue to follow their ancestral religion without modification, while Christianity offers a way of salvation intended, primarily at least, for non-Jews. Advocates of both these positions attempt from time to time to read their positions back into Paul, with mixed success, failure often being disguised with a comment about the unsystematic and inconsistent nature of Paul's writing. The critique of Israel, however, emerges constantly in Paul, both in sustained arguments and in frequent 'asides' or allusions; though the former are clearly the primary evidence, the latter should not be ignored, since they frequently give insights into a whole suppressed train of thought (see the example already mentioned, that of 1 Corinthians 15.56–57 in relation to Romans 6–8). One need only think of Paul's frequent mention of the flesh and its weakness, particularly in relation to Israel; of the inability of the Torah to do what it promised, and the consequent futility of 'works of the law'; of the warnings against getting circumcised; of the demonstrations that the family of Abraham is to be redefined so as to include many former outsiders and, apparently, to exclude many former insiders. All these themes need to be integrated and understood as a whole, while allowing for the constant paradox that, however many negative things Paul appears to be saying about Israel and the law, he always seems to balance his position, to refrain from lapsing into Marcionism

[32]I have argued this much more fully in my forthcoming book, *The New Testament and the People of God*.

or antinomianism. (What we are faced with here is, in fact, one particular outworking of what theologians have called the problem of nature and grace, and the two solutions mentioned above correspond to the two extreme ways of resolving that large and ancient puzzle. This, however, is the wrong end to begin in such a study as this, and is only mentioned here to underline the warning that the theological issues involved in the exegesis of Paul possess a complexity commensurate with their importance.)

These considerations suggest that the broad questions above should be broken down into subsidiary ones, which come in two sets: those concerning Israel and the church (the question of election) and those concerning Jesus and the Spirit (the question of monotheism). To take the first: in what did Paul's critique of Israel and, within that, of the Torah, consist? Is it, to use Stephen Westerholm's handy classification, good (Wilckens), bad (Bultmann), indifferent (Sanders) or what?[33] Did Paul's view here develop or change between one letter and another? What is the basis of his critique, both in the way he actually argues it and (which may not always be the same thing, as we have seen) in the way he himself arrived at his conclusion in the first place? Is Paul saying that Judaism cannot be true because Christianity is true? Or that the Torah cannot be kept properly, so some other means of justification must be found? Or that the Torah should not be kept at all? Or what? Did he begin with a 'problem' about Judaism to which he received a solution (Bultmann) or, discovering a solution in Christ, did he suddenly realize that all along he had had a problem (Sanders)? To what extent does he maintain, despite all this, a positive view of Torah? And how did Paul regard the new covenant people of God? What is its relationship to Israel according to the flesh? What are its entry requirements and boundary markers? What precisely does he mean by 'justification'? How (to put that another way) has he modified the Jewish doctrine of election? In particular, how has the Pharisaic attitude to the Gentiles—more specifically, to their place in God's purposes for the age to come—been taken up and reshaped, and why has it been done like this? And, not least in importance, how do all these questions interlock and interact, both in theory and in practice? How can they be correlated both within the particular passages where they are discussed and within Paul's overall thought? It is questions such as these which prompt the detailed exegetical investigations of chs. 7–12 in the present book.

The second set of questions concern Paul's redefinition of monotheism. What precisely does Paul say about Jesus, and how does this relate to the other central issues of his theology? Did he in any sense align, confuse, or coalesce Jesus and God, and if so did he reflect on what he was doing?

[33]See Westerholm 1988; and compare Martin 1989, Sanders 1991 ch. 9.

There has been a constant insistence in some modern writing about the New Testament that Jewish monotheism is, or at least was held to be in the first century, incompatible with what we now call a 'high' christology. The danger of anachronism, to which the cautious form of that last sentence is a response, can only be warded off by careful and detailed exegesis of key passages, and three of the following chapters (4, 5 and 6) are devoted to this task. Second, how in Paul's mind do Jesus and the Spirit stand in relation to each other and to Israel's One God? These issues are raised by, among other passages, the exceedingly complex argument of 2 Corinthians 3, which will be examined in ch. 9.

It should be clear that categories of questions such as these cannot in fact be isolated from one another. Israel and the law on the one hand, and christology and pneumatology on the other, are locked together in Paul in what often seems a very ambiguous set of relationships, and in several of the passages to be studied this ambiguity will need careful attention. (Actually, in modern scholarship this issue is seldom addressed at all, since scholars tend to discuss Israel/law/justification and christology/pneumatology in separate and isolated boxes.) Two of the cross-over points between the categories are (a) the relationship between Jesus Christ and Israel and (b) the meaning of the death of Christ. In ch. 2 I explore the first in relation to Paul's so-called 'Adam-christology', and develop the resultant incorporative meaning of Messiahship for Paul in ch.3. The second is implicit at several points, and emerges into particular focus in chs. 7, 10 and 11.

These, I suggest, are among the questions we must bear in mind as we work through exegesis of relevant Pauline texts. They include, I take it, the stock-in-trade of what Pauline Theology is all about. (Questions of rhetorical style, of social setting, of literary structure, and so forth are to be sure vital matters, but they are not exactly the same thing; I am not suggesting that one is more important than the other, merely that they are different, and that it is on the theological issues that this book is focussed.) Not all of these questions will find answers in every text, and indeed part of the discipline of exegesis is to allow the text to raise and answer its own questions in its own way. Not every text that appears to deal with God can be pressed for a fully blown theological statement of Paul's 'position', nor every text about the Torah for a final word about 'Paul and the Law'. But they provide at least an initial sense of direction.

They also do more: they indicate, or at least provide clues to, the theological 'deep structure' of Paul's thought. They show (that is to say) where Paul is to be located on the spectrum of world-views, of dualism, monism, pantheism, and so forth. Pauline Theology has not often dealt with issues such as these, because they are not themselves dealt with on the surface of the letters (and because those interested in Paul have often had what seemed to them more pressing hermeneutical concerns); but at many points (e.g. 1 Corinthians 8, Romans 14) a case could be made for seeing them as the real underlying issues, perhaps even as the 'core communication'. What I am arguing for is an approach to Pauline Theology which will neither on the one hand reduce this strange entity to a mere function of social forces or rhetorical conventions, nor on the other hand subsume it under the traditional *loci* of a different age (whether the sixteenth or any other century). The right approach will, rather, grapple with the task of understanding Paul's own thought-forms and thought-patterns, as a Pharisee and then as a Christian, and attempt to restate them coherently in such a way as to show their proper interrelation, within his total world-view, without doing them violence en route. This large task cannot be attempted in this book. The present chapters form, however, some of the necessary exegetical stepping-stones towards it, and it may be helpful, in reading them, to bear in mind their intended goal.

Part One: Studies in Paul's Christology

Chapter Two

ADAM, ISRAEL AND THE MESSIAH

(i) Introduction[1]

The question of where to begin in Pauline Theology is not necessarily as difficult, or as important, as it seems. Wherever one starts one will encounter the key issues soon enough, and the circularity of many such journeys means that we will often arrive at the end only to discover that it was, after all, the same as the beginning. However, there are certain attractions in starting where the Hebrew Bible starts, with Adam. First, questions about the use of Adam in Pauline christology bring us at once to some quite central Pauline texts. Second, these questions, and texts, introduce us to some current debates whose significance goes beyond their own immediate context. Third, this focus offers the chance of an important preliminary look at one or two aspects of the Jewish background (part (ii) below) which will have continuing significance for several of our questions. Finally, the hypothesis I shall advance about Adam offers a direct route to a theme which, again, will recur at various points, namely, Paul's retention of 'Messiahship' as a major category within his theology, and the incorporative significance which he gives to it.

The trouble that Adam causes to New Testament scholars reflects all too clearly the trouble which, according to Jewish tradition, he has caused to the human race in general. A long line of puzzled commentators and theologians bears witness to the apparently intractable nature of the problem: what part does Adam play in Paul's theology, and particularly in his christology? Scholarly opinion on the passages where Adam is explicitly mentioned (Romans 5.12–21; 1 Corinthians 15.20–49) ranges from treating them as peripheral to insisting on their absolute centrality. Some have detected covert reference to Adam in several other passages (e.g. Romans 1.18 ff., 7.7–12, Philippians 2.5–11, Colossians 1.15); others remain sceptical.

---

[1]This chapter is basically a revised version of Wright 1983. Two sections of the original paper, on Philippians 2 and Colossians 1, anticipated two more detailed studies printed in the present volume as separate chapters, and are therefore truncated here.

And if there is no agreement in sight on the question of the sources from which Paul took the idea (gnostic? Philonic? rabbinic? apocalyptic?), there is still less sign of progress in discovering what precisely he meant by it.

A full survey of the relevant secondary literature is neither possible nor necessary here. In line with most recent writers, I make the working assumption that the relevant background literature is to be found in the broad stream of Jewish writings, not in gnosticism as such.[2] This, however, focuses attention more closely on the questions: which parts of the Jewish background are relevant, what are they really saying, and what does Paul mean by his use of them? In Robin Scroggs' classic little study, the spotlight is placed on anthropology: through Adam-language 'Paul describes the reality and assurance of the restoration of man's humanity.'[3] The relevant Jewish background—the intertestamental and rabbinic writings—bear witness to an Adam-speculation which functions partly as a prediction: humanity will be restored to its state of original, or at least intended, glory. The last age will correspond to the first. More recently, S. Kim has provided a very full discussion of hypotheses on the origin of Adam-christology,[4] and, concluding that all have been to a lesser or greater extent unsatisfactory,[5] provides one of his own: Adam-christology, like wisdom-christology, is a development of image-christology, which in turn can be traced to Paul's vision of Christ on the road to Damascus.[6] This conclusion, however, is very different to that proposed by J.D.G. Dunn in his provocative *Christology in the Making*, which was in the press at the same time as Kim's book, preventing any dialogue between the two.[7] Dunn agrees with Scroggs and Kim that Adam-christology is a Jewish phenomenon, unrelated to gnostic *Urmensch* speculations, but he holds it well apart from Paul's wisdom-christology. He sees the two as distinct strands, stemming from different ideas and leading to different conclusions.[8] For him, Adam-christology is first of all a way of talking about Christ in his resurrection glory, and then, because of the christological use of Psalm 8, a way of referring to his achievement in sharing the lot of the first Adam, even unto death, in order finally to become the last Adam, that which Adam should have been but failed to be.[9] Adam-christology thus speaks, for Dunn, only of Christ's goal

---

[2]See e.g. Scroggs 1966, Kim 1981, Kee 1982 (here at 237 ff.). A survey of various views and texts can be found in Conzelmann 1975 (1969), 284–6.

[3]Scroggs, 111; see too Ziesler 1979, 104–9.

[4]Kim, 162–93.

[5]Kim, 193.

[6]Kim, 260 ff.; summary, 267 f.

[7]Though see now Dunn 1989, ch. 4.

[8]Dunn 1980, 98–128 (Adam), 163–212 (Wisdom), 258–68 (conclusions).

[9]Dunn 1980, 107 ff.

and task. It is in wisdom-christology, by contrast, that Christ is somehow identified with the pre-existent divine purposes of salvation.[10]

This lack of consensus does not mean that the debate has not been useful. Released from the stifling hypothesis of the *Urmensch* redeemer-figure, scholarship has been able to advance into new and apparently fruitful ways of reading Paul. True, not all exegetical problems have thereby been solved. Romans 5 remains very difficult: vv.15–17 prove especially intractable, and there is no agreement on how 5.12–21 as a whole fits into the flow of the letter. Nor has 1 Corinthians 15 yielded up all its secrets. The question of whether or not Adam-christology is to be detected in Philippians 2 (with Kim, Dunn, Hooker, Caird and others, though Scroggs, for one, remains sceptical) and Colossians 1 (with Kim and Caird, but against Dunn) is by no means settled, nor is it yet clear what the results would be if it were agreed that Adam is to be found there.[11] There is therefore plenty of scope for fresh investigation and new hypotheses at every level.

I suggest that the work done so far has not yet gone to the heart of the matter. Specifically, it has overlooked a central and, for Pauline exegesis, vital feature of the Jewish background. Speculation about Adam, in the intertestamental and rabbinic literature in particular (though we shall concentrate on the former) is not about 'humankind in general.' It is about Israel, the people of God. It is not, perhaps, surprising that this theme should have gone unnoticed for so long. A former generation brought to the material the questions of post-reformation dogmatics; subsequent ones have often been careful to filter off apparently unassimilable, Jewish elements in Paul. Talk about Adam was bound to be marginalized in such discussions, and ideas about the national hope of Israel likely to disappear altogether. Even now that we have heeded the warnings of Stendahl, Sanders and others[12] against such a one-sided reading of Paul, the interpretation of his Adam-theology has not noticeably improved.[13] But (as I shall argue in the first main section of this chapter) the use of 'Adam' themes in the Jewish literature which may without controversy be considered a part of the background to the New Testament—i.e. the Old Testament, the Scrolls, and the Apocrypha and Pseudepigrapha[14]—consistently makes one large and important point: God's purposes for the human race in general have devolved on to, and will be fulfilled in, Israel in particular. Israel is, or will

[10]Dunn 1980, e.g. 193–94; see too Dunn 1982, esp. 327 ff.

[11]See further chs. 4 and 5 below.

[12]See, e.g., Stendahl 1976, 133; Sanders 1977, 1–12, 33–59; Klein 1978, *passim*.

[13]There is, strangely, virtually no discussion of Adam in Sanders' massive book—a lacuna which seems the more peculiar in the light of the present chapter.

[14]The Targumim and the Rabbinic literature will, I believe, bear out my contentions about the Jewish background, though space forbids what would inevitably be a lengthy discussion of the material and of its date and relevance to the NT.

become, God's true humanity. What God intended for Adam will be given to the seed of Abraham. They will inherit the second Eden, the restored primeval glory. If there is a 'last Adam' in the relevant Jewish literature, he is not an individual, whether messianic or otherwise. He is the whole eschatological people of God. If we take 'Adam' language out of this context we do not merely distort it; we empty it of its basic content. And if we are to use this material at all for understanding Paul—as I believe we must—we cannot ignore its emphases, or imagine that Paul ignored them, but must ask what he did with them. Part (iii) of this chapter will therefore explore Paul's theology, and particularly christology, in this light.

(ii) Adam and Israel in Jewish Literature

In this section, then, I shall suggest that Adam-theology, where it occurs in the Old Testament and intertestamental writings, fulfills a specific purpose. It either advances, or develops, a claim about the place of Israel in the purposes of God. It is another way of saying that the world was made for the sake of Israel, or that Israel is, or is to become, God's intended true humanity.[15]

This view goes back at least as far as the final redaction of Genesis. In its present form, the book clearly highlights ch. 12 as its turning-point; after the curse of the fall, the flood and Babel (chs. 3, 7 and 11), God promises to bless Abram and his family. As later tradition put it, Abraham will be God's means of undoing the sin of Adam.[16] This broad theme is given significant detail by a set of recurring motifs,[17] in which the commands given to Adam in Genesis 1.28 reappear in new guise:

> 1.28: And God blessed them, and God said to them 'Be fruitful and multiply, and fill the earth and subdue it; and have dominion over the fish of the sea and over the birds of the air and over every living thing that moves upon the earth.

> 12.2 f.: I will make of you a great nation, and I will bless you, and make your name great, so that you will be a blessing. I will bless those who bless you...

> 17.2, 6, 8: I will make my covenant between me and you, and will multiply you exceedingly... I will make you exceedingly fruitful,.. and I will give you, and to your seed after you, all the land of Canaan...

[15]For a fuller statement of this, see my forthcoming projected volume, *The New Testament and the People of God*.

[16]*Genesis Rabbah* 14.6.

[17]Unaccountably ignored by all commentators I have consulted, with the sole exception of Cassuto 1961–64, 2.124 f., and Cassuto 1961, 39 f.

21

22.16 ff.: Because you have done this... I will indeed bless you, and I will multiply your descendants as the stars of heaven and as the sand which is on the seashore... and by you shall all the nations of the earth bless themselves, because you have obeyed my voice.

26.3 f.: (The Lord said to Isaac) I will be with you, and will bless you; for to you and to your seed I will give all these lands, and I will fulfill the oath which I swore to Abraham your father. I will multiply your seed as the stars of heaven, and will give to your seed all these lands: and by your seed all the nations of the earth shall bless themselves...

26.24: Fear not, for I am with you and will bless you and multiply your descendants for my servant Abraham's sake.

28.3: (Isaac blessed Jacob and said) God Almighty bless you and make you fruitful and multiply you, that you may become a company of peoples. May he give you the blessing of Abraham, to you and to your seed with you, that you may take possession of the land of your sojournings which God gave to Abraham.

35.11 f.: And God said to (Jacob) 'I am God Almighty: be fruitful and multiply; a nation and company of nations shall come from you... the land which I gave to Abraham and Isaac I will give to you, and I will give the land to your descendants after you.

47.27: Thus Israel dwelt in the land of Egypt... and they gained possessions in it, and were fruitful and multiplied exceedingly.

48.3 f.: Jacob said to Joseph, 'God Almighty appeared to me... and said to me "Behold, I will make you fruitful, and multiply you,... and I will give you this land, to your seed after you...

Thus at key moments[18]—Abraham's call, his circumcision, the offering of Isaac, the transitions from Abraham to Isaac and from Isaac to Jacob, and in the sojourn in Egypt—the narrative quietly makes the point that Abraham and his family inherit, in a measure, the role of Adam and Eve. The differences are not, however, insignificant. Except for 35.11 f., echoed in 48.3 f.,[19] the command ('be fruitful...') has turned into a promise ('I will make you fruitful...'). The word 'exceedingly' is added in ch. 17. And, most

---

[18]Cf. too 9.1, 7; 16.10.
[19]Which would seem to put Jacob on a level with Adam (1.26 ff.) and Noah (9.1–7).

importantly, possession of the land of Canaan, and supremacy over enemies, has taken the place of the dominion over nature given in 1.28. We could sum up this aspect of Genesis by saying: Abraham's children are God's true humanity, and their homeland is the new Eden.

These themes recur, in various ways, throughout the Pentateuch.[20] There are also echoes in several significant passages in the other divisions of the Hebrew Bible. The restoration of Israel after her punishment will be like a new creation, with the people once again being fruitful and multiplying in the land (Jeremiah 3.16; 23.3; Ezekiel 36.11; Zechariah 10.8). The future glory of the land itself is described in language appropriate to the paradise of Eden.[21] None of these passages allows us to say that the only significance of the allusion is the mere heaping up of grand ideas about the future of God's people. The underlying point, time after time, is that Israel, the family of Abraham, is God's true humanity. Her land is God's land. Her enemies are God's enemies, and they will be subject to her in the same way that the beasts were subject to Adam. It is within this context that we should understand those passages in the Old Testament which make similar claims about Israel's king.[22]

This whole complex of themes comes into sharp focus in the time of crisis between the exile and the start of the Christian era. Attention has been drawn often enough to the (highly polemical) restatement of Israel's role as God's true humanity in Daniel 7.[23] The righteous remnant is seen as the true Adam, given sovereignty over the 'beasts' that are oppressing God's people. It may be that here, as also in Psalm 8.4, there are royal characteristics in the picture of the 'son of man'; if so, it seems to me more likely that these have been 'democratized,' as in Isaiah 55.3 ff., than that the 'royal' meaning is primary.[24] Those plans and promises which the king had inherited are now, in the kingless state of God's people, transferred to the righteous remnant. It should be noted again that the inclusion of 'Adamic' characteristics in the whole picture is not the result of mere speculation, an attempt to construct a neat scheme in which the last time will correspond to the first. It is a strong statement of nationalist theology. The Lord of the world is the God of Israel;

[20]Ex. 1.7; 32.13; Lev. 26.9; Deut. 1.10 f.; 7.13 f.; 8.1; 28.63; 30.5, 16. Note also the theme of the 'subjugation' of the land (e.g. Num. 32.22), recalling the subjugation of the world to Adam in Gen. 1.28.

[21]E.g. Isa. 11.1 ff.; 45.8; etc.; see Scroggs 1966, 54 f.; Lincoln 1981, 48 ff.; and especially Dahl 1964, 422–43.

[22]Ps. 72.8; 110.2; Isa. 11.1 ff., etc.; compare too Ps. 8.4 f.; 68.28–30; 80.15 [see MT 80.16], 17. See Wolff 1974, 159–65; Scroggs 1965, 14 f. The connections in Jewish tradition between Abraham and David (see Clements 1967) go hand in hand with similar links between David and Adam himself (see Scroggs 1965, 14, and Schillebeeckx 1980, 172 f.).

[23]See e.g. Hooker 1967, 71 ff.; Lacocque 1979, 122 ff.

[24]See Bentzen 1955, 74–76; Emerton 1958; Moule 1977, 26.

and his righteous people will soon be in their rightful place, ruling over the nations as God's vice-gerent. The two doctrines of monotheism and election, taken together, have as their corollary the characteristic hope of apocalyptic eschatology. Israel's God will act in history to vindicate his own name by installing his people 'at his right hand', ruling over the nations of the world.

It should not be difficult to show how intertestamental Judaism continued and developed this picture—though the point may be regarded as controversial in some quarters. It is not for the sake of speculation about the future of 'man in general' that Adam is mentioned, though Scroggs (for example) often writes as though that were the case.[25] The reference is always, rather, to the claim: Israel is God's true humanity. Thus Jubilees, and the Testaments of the Twelve Patriarchs, align Israel with Adam, and the Gentiles with the beasts over whom Adam rules. 1 Enoch regards Israel as Adam's true heir.[26] The Wisdom of Solomon asserts that the righteous will be restored to God's intended place for them as lords of creation.[27] The later writings 4 Ezra and 2 Baruch witness to the same theological position: Israel will be given the rights of Adam's true heir.[28] The pre-eminence of Adam in Ben-Sira (49.16) parallels that of the great kings David, Hezekiah and Josiah earlier in the chapter. And in the well-known 'Adam' references from Qumran,[29] as well as those not so frequently cited,[30] the reference to Adam is one of the many ways in which the sect claims for itself the status of being God's true Israel, those who are to be seen as his true humanity. The passages in which the giving of the law is made parallel to the creation of humanity (e.g. Ben-Sira 17.1–4) demonstrate the same point; for the law, particularly in the troubled period between 200 B.C. and A.D. 150, was regarded not merely as a general code of ethics, but as the charter of Israel's national life.[31] As the tension between covenant promises and political reality became more and more acute, the visionaries who bequeathed Israel the apocalyptic writings used the idea of Adam and his glory to assert the

[25]E.g. 29, 55: he sees (e.g. 27, 31) the point we are making, but does not develop it as we have here. So too Ziesler 1979 regards the material as though its basic concern were with 'man-in-general.'

[26]Jub. 2.23; 3.30 f.; 15.27; 16.26; 19.23–31; 22.11–13; T Lev. 18.10; 1 En. 90.19, 30, 37 ff.

[27]Wisd. Sol. 2.23 f.; 3.8.

[28]E.g. 4 Ez. 3.4–36; 6.53–59; 9.17 ff.; 2 Bar. 14.17–19; see Hooker 1967, 49–56; Jervell 1960, 31 ff.

[29]1QS 4.23, CD 3.20, 1QH 17.15.

[30]E.g. 1Q LitPr. 2.3–6, 4Q Ps37 3.1 f.In 1Q LitPr 2.3–6 Israel takes the place of the 'seed of Man.' In the *pesher* on Ps. 37, the phrase 'the glory of Adam' is clear in the Hebrew given in *Discoveries in the Judaean Desert of Jordan*, vol. 5, 44, 171, despite Vermes' earlier placing of the phrase 'and to whom all the glory' in a bracket (Vermes 1975, 244; corrected in 3rd ed., 1987, 291).

[31]See Jervell 1960, 34 ff.

24

centrality of Israel within the divine purposes.[32] That later Rabbinic thinkers made the same connection is clear enough from the evidence compiled by Scroggs.[33] Claims, for instance, about Adam being created in the spot where the temple was to be built are not to be seen merely as speculations about the first man, but as legitimations of Israel.[34] The rabbis may well not be 'interested in making Adam into a savior figure who has a personal involvement in the acts or results of the eschatological events.'[35] They do not need such a figure. For them, Adam has become embodied already in Israel, the people of the Torah, and in her future hope.[36]

This material (as opposed to this summary of it, which has been deliberately pared down to a minimum) provides plenty of evidence for the central claims of this first section. Adam speculation is to be correlated with the many other claims about God's purposes for Israel and her Torah which the same body of literature advances. As has recently been well argued in another context, the national hope is primary. Messianic expectations, where they occur, are best understood as a function of the fervent expectations of the covenant people. Thus a Messiah, if one is envisaged, draws on to himself the hope and destiny of the people itself. He, like the nation, is called the son of God.[37] There is a fluctuation between the king and his people, seen for instance in the Davidic overtones of the Abraham stories, in the solidarity expressed in e.g. 2 Samuel 5.1–3; 19.41—20.2, and the transference of royal promises to the people at large (Isaiah 55). In subsequent writings, we find such promises again referred to the whole nation (cf. Jubilees 1.24) or to the righteous remnant (4QFlorilegium 1.18 f., 1QS 8.4–10).

If it is true that post-biblical Jewish theology applied to Israel the attributes of true humanity, another much-discussed theme finds a secure place within the same overall pattern. Whatever may have happened to the idea of 'wisdom' in later thought, the writers who, between the testaments, developed those traditions which we find embodied in the earlier chapters of Proverbs did so in a particular direction. Already in the early material 'wisdom' is seen as God's vice-gerent in creation (Proverbs 8.22–31). In

---

[32]There is no space here to enter into the details of debate about the origin, nature and aims of 'apocalyptic' in general. I am convinced, however, that until the centrality of Israel's national hope within this 'movement'—if it can be called that at all—is recognized, the material will not be in focus.

[33]E.g. 40–46; cf. Jervell 78 ff., 91 f.; Hooker 73 f.

[34]Scroggs 51.

[35]Scroggs 58.

[36]See too, in addition to the references listed by Scroggs, Jervell and Hooker, *Genesis Rabbah* 12.9, 14.6 (quoted above), and 15.4 (Adam created for the sake of Abraham).

[37]For the relation of national and messianic hopes, see Harvey 1982, 76–78. On the link of royal and national titles see Kee 1982, 237 ff.

obedience to God, wisdom is set over the created order, and thus becomes the pattern for a truly human existence, corresponding to the place intended for Adam.[38] That, indeed, is the underlying logic of Proverbs 1–9. In the Wisdom of Solomon and Ben-Sira these ideas are developed in a particular direction, already latent in the Old Testament. Since those who fear the Lord, who walk in his ways, are the children of Israel who observe Torah, wisdom becomes closely identified with Torah itself (e.g. Ben-Sira 17.11; 19.20; 24.1–34; 38.34; 39.1–11; 2 Baruch 3.9—4.4); together they form the charter for Israel's national life *precisely as* the way of life of God's true humanity. On the one hand this means that to follow Torah is to be in tune with the world. This is the aspect stressed by Hengel in his fine treatment of the subject just cited. On the other hand—and this is the important point in the context of this chapter—the identification of wisdom and Torah means, yet again, that the world is made for the sake of Israel, and that Israel is taking on the role marked out for Adam. Finally, this idealized wisdom becomes the possession, in particular, of David's heir, Solomon. By identifying him with the wisdom tradition,[39] the royal claim to be the true Israelite and hence the true Man is further enhanced.

(iii) Paul: 1 Corinthians 15.20–57

It may now be suggested that this complex of Jewish thought provides a clearer way in to Pauline christology than has hitherto been recognized. We will discover that Paul is to be understood against this background not merely at one or two isolated points but all along the line. Not that he agreed with the conclusions of Ben-Sira or 4 Ezra. He forcibly rejected them. To propose a Jewish background for his thoughts does not mean that Paul had no critique of Judaism. I suggest, however, that the reasons for his rejection of the traditional conclusions about God's purposes for Israel were not that he had acquired different categories of thought altogether, but that a new factor, arising from within the traditional matrix of Jewish ideas, had occasioned a revolution in his understanding. To put it simply: the role traditionally assigned to Israel had devolved on to Jesus Christ. Paul now regarded him, not Israel, as God's true humanity.

It will not be possible in this chapter to deal with the full range of issues raised by the presence of Adam in Paul's writings. We cannot, in particular, discuss the relation of Adam to universal sin, and hence certain key passages, i.e. Romans 1.18 ff.; 3.23; 5.12; and 7.7 ff., cannot be handled here. We may simply notice that Paul argues, there and elsewhere, that Israel too is 'in

[38]See Hengel 1974, 1.157.
[39]1 Kgs. 3.4–15; 4.29–34; Prov. 1.1, etc., and Wisd. Sol. 9 *et passim*.

Adam,' and that she cannot therefore simply be affirmed, or her national aspirations underwritten, without more ado. By shifting Israel's eschatological role on to Jesus Christ himself Paul has thus made room, we suggest, for a more radical treatment of the problem of evil than was possible for, say, the author of 4 Ezra.[40] In the present chapter, however, we will focus not on the problem of evil, but on the question of christology.

We may therefore proceed to examine the relevant passages, armed with the possibility that when Paul aligns Christ in some way with Adam the role he is thereby assigning to the former is that which, *mutatis mutandis*, his Jewish contemporaries would give to Israel, or perhaps to Israel's anointed king. In looking at passages which have been the subject of whole monographs it will, of course, be necessary to restrict the detailed argument to the minimum necessary to bring out this line of thought.

Paul's lengthy discussion of the resurrection in 1 Corinthians 15 contains two of the three passages where he explicitly places Adam and Christ in some sort of parallelism. Whoever precisely his envisaged opponents in this chapter may have been,[41] the intention of the section as a whole should be clear. Paul is explaining the nature of the future resurrection, in order to help the Corinthians to believe in it and order their lives accordingly.[42]

Within this context the first passage (15.20–28) explains that the resurrection is a two-stage process: first the Messiah, then those that belong to him. The overall point of this paragraph, within the chapter as a whole, is that the resurrection of believers is a still future event, which will complete and make sense of the present state of the church. Within this, Paul's point is that Christ is the 'first-fruits' (vv.20,23), whose resurrection as a fact of past history guarantees the future resurrection of those who belong to him. In order to make this all clear, he sets out what is fundamentally a Jewish apocalyptic scheme, though with one drastic modification: the resurrection, instead of being a single event at the end of time, has broken into history already in the single instance of Jesus Christ. This was necessary, Paul suggests, because, according to scripture, the Messiah must reign until he has put all his enemies under his feet (Psalm 110.1, quoted in v.25), so that there has to be an interval, a space of time, between his enthronement and the final completion of the task. This is the thrust of the section: the resurrection of the Messiah as a fact of history does not mean that there is no more resurrection to come, but, on the contrary, when properly understood against its apocalyptic background it actually entails the future resurrection of believers.

---

[40]See B.W. Longenecker, *Eschatology and the Covenant in 4 Ezra and Romans 1-11*, forthcoming from Sheffield Academic Press.

[41]In addition to the commentaries, see Thiselton 1978, 510–25; Lincoln 1981, 33 ff.

[42]On the many detailed points with which we cannot here deal, see now Fee 1987, 745–760.

Paul has thus set up an apocalyptic scheme, revised in the light of the gospel.[43] That is to say, he has taken the traditional Jewish framework of the apocalyptic drama and battle, in which the people of God are first surrounded by enemies and are eventually vindicated over them, and has substituted Jesus and his people for Israel, and a string of nameless enemies, culminating in Death itself, for Israel's political enemies. Within this, he has quoted or alluded to three vital passages from the Jewish scriptures, setting up a complex series of interacting echoes which need to be teased out if the full meaning of the passage is to become clear.[44]

First, there is Psalm 110.1, quoted in v.25: 'he must reign until he has put all his enemies under his feet'. This overtly royal Psalm carries clear messianic overtones, and was so read elsewhere within early Christianity.[45] The passage in question speaks of the triumph of God's appointed king over the enemies of the people of Israel, sitting at God's right hand—i.e., exercising authority—until the process of subjugation is complete. There are, of course, further echoes here of Daniel 7, in which, within the apocalyptic imagery, the human figure, standing for the people of the saints of the most high, is exalted to a position of authority at the right hand of the Ancient of Days.[46] The passage thus resonates with the victory of Yahweh's anointed, and of Israel as a whole, over their old enemies. As in the thought-patterns of much apocalyptic writing, Israel is to be Yahweh's agent in the eschatological drama. Her 'resurrection'—i.e. her return from exile, her vindication over her enemies (Ezekiel 37)—is to be the sign of his victory, the crucial defeat of his enemies. Now, in Paul's revision of the scheme, Israel's role is taken by her anointed king, and this Messiah has acted out her victory in himself, being raised from the dead in advance of his people. That which Israel had expected for herself, whether metaphorically or literally, has come true in the person of her representative, the Messiah.

Since Israel's expectation was, as we have seen, capable of taking the form that she should be God's true humanity, it is no surprise that another passage drawn into the exposition is Psalm 8, of which v.7 is quoted in v.27 of the present passage: '(God) has put all things in subjection under his feet'. The idea of subjection 'under his feet' obviously makes an explicit verbal link between Psalm 110 and Psalm 8, but it should not be imagined that Paul's mind is working solely by means of fortuitous verbal echoes; both Psalms

[43] I therefore disagree with Fee 1987, 752 f.; though the difference is, I think, mostly a matter of terminology, as can be seen in relation to Conzelmann 1975 <1969>, 269, expressing the type of 'apocalyptic' analysis against which Fee is (perhaps rightly) reacting.

[44] See Hays 1989 for the idea of 'intertextual echo'.

[45] Matt. 22.44 par., Lk. 19.27, Ac. 2.33–6, Eph. 1.20–22, Heb. 1.13, 2.5–9, Rev. 20.14, 21.4. Hays 1989, 84 suggests that, though Paul here gives the first documentation of this messianic reading of the psalm, he may well be appealing to an already established tradition.

[46] The texts are of course conjoined at Mk 14.62 par.

speak of the exaltation of God's chosen one, whether Israel, the Messiah, or the human family, and the link between all three in so much Jewish thought indicates that the verbal resonance is a mere symptom of a far deeper thematic unity. Paul then, in a manner quite unusual for him, makes Psalm 8 the basis of a detailed exposition in which the theme of subjection 'under the feet' is explored and worked out in relation to the final events culminating in the subjection of even the Messiah to the one God.

The resurrection of Jesus is thus interpreted by Paul through the widening categories of Messiahship, Israel and humanity. The Messiah represents Israel, as is seen in such verbal indications as οἱ τοῦ Χριστοῦ in v.23;[47] the true Israel is the true humanity. Thus in vv.25–28 Paul has explained his other obvious Old Testament echo, that of Genesis 1–3, which he has thrown out almost as a riddle in v.22: As in Adam all die, so in Christ shall all be made alive. God's plan, to rule his world through obedient humanity, has come true in the Messiah, Jesus.[48] That which was purposed in Genesis 1 and 2, the wise rule of creation by the obedient human beings, was lost in Genesis 3, when human rebellion jeopardised the divine intention, and the ground brought forth thorns and thistles. The Messiah, however, has now been installed as the one through whom God is doing what he intended to do, first through humanity and then through Israel. Paul's Adam-christology is basically an Israel-christology, and is predicated on the identification of Jesus as Messiah, in virtue of his resurrection.

Thus it is that Paul has addressed and answered the Corinthians' problem, at least in principle. He has argued, on the basis of Old Testament scripture, (i) that Israel's longed-for 'resurrection' had bifurcated, and was now to be seen as a two-stage process in which Jesus would rise first, solo, while his people were to follow later; (ii) that the past resurrection of Jesus *guarantees* this future resurrection of his people (v.20, which in regular Pauline style functions as a thesis statement for the following verses); and (iii) that this guarantee is given not only because Jesus is the first-fruits but also because he, now glorified, is ruling the cosmos and will eventually, in accordance with scripture, defeat all his enemies, of which the last will be death; Q.E.D.

Two questions remain, which this passage in itself does not answer. First, did Jesus then only *become* the 'last Adam' in his resurrection? This has been suggested recently, but as we shall see below the idea is based on a misunderstanding. The present passage is not concerned to offer a full statement of the parallelism (or otherwise) between Jesus and Adam. That is a construct which we have to assemble from a variety of places. The point Paul needs to make here has to do with the risen Jesus (and the consequent

[47]Compare the use of the genitive in v.20, and e.g. Rom. 8.17; 1 Cor. 1.12; 3.23; 2 Cor. 10.7 (twice); Gal. 3.29; 5.24; see Kramer 1966, 137 f., and below, ch. 3.
[48]See Hooker 1979, 40.

bifurcation of 'resurrection'), not at this stage with his death. Paul has said nothing here, one way or another, about whether Jesus was already 'last Adam' prior to his resurrection. For that we must wait.

Second, it is often held that Paul here offers a subordinationist christology, in which Jesus the Messiah is clearly put at a lower level to 'God'. It is of course true that if vv.23–8 were all we had of Paul's christology we might well draw some such conclusion. But there is a tell-tale sign that Paul is aware of the problem, and is building in to his exposition here (and we must remember that he is not here talking about the relation between Jesus and God *per se*) a hint of the fuller christology which we will see in other passages. In v.28 he speaks of the subjection of the 'son', a term introduced here for the first time into the argument.[49] This echo of another messianic psalm-theme (from Psalm 2.7) chimes in with other passages, some of which we will study in subsequent chapters, which use the motif of Jesus' 'sonship', and/or the 'fatherhood' of God, as a way of predicating a relationship which, though differentiated, allows Jesus to be seen *within*, and not outside, the Pauline picture of the One God.[50]

Having established his basic point, and reinforced it with a more personal appeal (vv.29–34), Paul turns to the question of the nature of the resurrection body itself, and this occupies him from v.35 right through to v.57, leaving only v.58 to conclude the chapter with a general exhortation. Here again it is important, in approaching the 'Adam' passage (vv.42–49), to bear in mind the clear line of thought in the section as a whole. Paul's point here, building on his previous statement of the futurity of the general resurrection, is that believers need a new *sort* of body, and that God can and will give this to them. This is clear from the analogy of the seed (vv.36–38), which is expanded into a general statement about the different sorts of bodies in the created order (vv.39–41), and the purpose of vv.42–49 in this context is therefore (not to give christological statements for their own sake, but) to apply the point specifically to the future resurrection body which believers will be given. Vv. 50–57 then sum up the argument (τοῦτο δέ φημι, v.50), again claiming that the present mortal body is not appropriate for the life of the future kingdom of God, and showing how this problem will be resolved in the final *dénouement*. Vv. 54–57 thus correspond, in the second half of the chapter, to v.28 in the first half.

The overall thrust of the passage is therefore fundamentally *anthropological*; that is, Paul is discussing the nature of humanity in its present and future conditions. This actually points the way through some of the notorious difficulties that surround vv.44–49 in particular.[51] One of the

[49]And only the second occurrence in the whole letter, the other being 1 Cor. 1.9.

[50]See below, chs. 4–6, on Phil. 2, Col. 1 and 1 Cor. 8.6.

[51]On which see Fee 1987, 786–795.

first problems we meet here is the nature of Paul's writing at this point.[52] It is customary to treat vv.42–49 as an *argument*, and then to express perplexity at how in fact this argument works. But there are good reasons for challenging this way of reading the passage. For one thing, Paul's regular logical connectives (γάρ, οὖν and ἄρα in particular) are noticeably absent from the whole passage.[53] For another, the style of vv.35–41 (in common with much of the earlier part of the chapter) is not argumentative, but simply assertive. Paul does not need to argue these points, which are quite acceptable to his hearers. As the same kind of writing continues from v.42 down to v.44a, we are thoroughly justified in treating this section in the same way. Paul is simply claiming: as in the world of plants, so in the world of human existence. (Vv.39–41 are really a parenthesis: v.42 looks back to the image of sowing in vv.36–38.) His statements are not a logical proof but an explanation. He is saying 'if you understand the matter like this, you will see what the future resurrection will be like.' This, as we will see, considerably simplifies the interpretation of vv.44–45.

Before we come to that controversial passage, though, it will be as well to look at what follows it, in order to get as many bearings on it as we can. Remembering that the whole thrust of the passage is anthropological, not christological, it is startling to realize that, without v.45, no one would ever have thought of reading v.46 as anything other than a continuation of the line of thought in vv.42–44. V. 45 appears to intrude almost as an aside. Paul's thought runs straight on:

> (44) It is sown a ψυχικός body, it is raised a πνευματικός body. If there is a ψυχικός body, there is also a πνευματικός body.
>
> (46) But it is not the πνευματικός that is first, but the ψυχικός, then the πνευματικός.

V. 46, in other words, is perhaps not discussing at all the question of two mythological 'men', and speculating on their proper chronological sequence. It is simply pointing out, in line with the passage as a whole, that the physical precedes the spiritual as the seed precedes the plant.[54] In this light it may be suggested that v.47 too should be read in the same way, with the emphasis of ἄνθρωπος falling on the type of humanity rather than the origin or nature of the particular 'man' involved: 'The first man's sort of humanity is from the

---

[52]See ch. 1 above.

[53]Indeed, they are absent from vv.35–49 entirely, with the exception of the γάρ in v.41b—which is not in fact part of the main line of thought, but merely an elucidation of part of v.41a.

[54]So Fee 1987, 788: 'Paul's concern throughout has to do with the question, "With what kind of body?"'; also 793.

earth, the second's is a gift from heaven' (picking up v.38, 'God gives it a body,' with a typical reverential substitution of 'heaven' for 'God').[55] If this understanding is correct, Adam and Christ as individuals are not the main subjects of discussion, but a buttress to the anthropological assertions of vv.42–44, 46–47. Nor, indeed, are they merely illustrations of the two types of human existence. Paul does not suppose that believers are going to become, like Christ, life-giving spirits; in that respect Christ is unique. He is, rather, the *source* of the new spiritual/bodily life promised to his people.[56] The sense in which he is the prototype for resurrection existence is not brought out until the conclusion in vv.48–49, where again the point being made is not christological but anthropological. Earthly humanity is like Adam's body, heavenly humanity like Christ's resurrection body, and believers, who presently share the one, will at the last share the other.[57]

This understanding of the passage removes from v.45 much of the weight of christological speculation which has often been heaped upon it, and which it has frequently been unable to bear. It also sets up the context within which the compressed statement about Christ can be understood, and can contribute to our overall picture of Paul's Adam-christology. There are four points which need to be made.

First, there is no need to advance complex hypotheses about gnostic or Philonic mythology in order to explain Paul's language here.[58] The passage is quite comprehensible in terms of the aim and nature of Paul's discourse as a whole: it shows the reasonableness of belief in the future resurrection, granted the nature of the created order (as in vv.36–41) and the fact of Jesus' resurrection itself. All that is being emphasized by means of the contrast of the two forms of human existence in vv.46–49 is the anthropological point.

Nor, secondly, is there any need to suppose that Paul is regarding his additions to Genesis 2.7 in v.45 as somehow themselves authoritative in the same sense that the quotation itself would be.[59] Neither the second clause ('the last Adam became a life-giving spirit'), nor the interpolations ('first' and

[55]See Lincoln 1981 45, for a similar argument. It might be objected that v.48 tells against this reading, because it speaks again of the individuals Adam and Christ over against those who are 'like' them; I think the answer to this is that v.47 does indeed refer to Adam and Christ, but does so to stress the types of humanity they represent rather than to focus on them as individuals.

[56]It is a mistake (though a common one) to see the σῶμα πνευματικόν here in totally non-physical terms: see Craig 1980.

[57]Reading, with most scholars, the indicative φορέσομεν rather than the imperative -ωμεν. The 'image' in this verse awakens, of course, a further set of scriptural echoes, of Gen. 1.26 f., and, in Paul, of such other passages as Rom. 8.29 and 2 Cor. 4.4. This is not of much further significance for the main exegesis of the passage as a whole, but it allows us to see just how clearly Paul has in mind the whole context of Gen. 1–3.

[58]See the discussions in Lincoln 1981, 44 f.; Dunn 1980 123 f.; Wedderburn 1973 and 1974.

[59]Contra e.g. Lincoln, 42; Dunn 1973, 130.

'Adam') in the first clause, are anything more than explanatory. The force of the verse is to say: 'this view of two-stage humanity, ψυχικός and πνευματικός, coheres with the statement of scripture[60] that "man became a living ψυχή": that was the first man, Adam, and his humanity was not the end of the story. There is now a new Adam, and he has become a life-giving spirit.' In other words, we are once more faced not with an argument, but with a complex *assertion*. (The same is true in v.44b, 'if there is a 'psychic' body, there is also a 'pneumatic' one.' This is not an argument ending with Q.E.D., but a claim, based on two things: (a) the analogy of the seed in vv.36–38 and (b) the fact of Christ's resurrection, to which Paul then explicitly refers in v.45).

Thirdly, there is the problem of the meaning of the implied ἐγένετο in the second half of the verse ('the last Adam *became* a life-giving spirit'). As we saw a moment ago, some have recently suggested that, according to this passage, Christ became 'last Adam' for the first time at his resurrection.[61] But this is not warranted by the passage. (a) The parallel with v.45a, in which the first Adam *becomes* a 'living ψυχή' when God breathes into his nostrils the breath of life, suggests that Christ, *already* the last Adam, *becomes* life-giving spirit at the resurrection. This parallel is made all the clearer in the light of Ezekiel 37.9–14, in which the bones first come together and form human beings, and then receive the breath, or spirit, which enables them to come alive. (b) The grammar of the verse itself suggests that, while Christ does indeed 'become' something fresh in his resurrection, the phrase 'last Adam' is not the description of what he became, but of that which he already was and continued to be. Paul does not write 'Christ became the last Adam, a life-giving spirit,' but 'the last Adam became a life-giving spirit.'[62] It is the latter phrase, not the former, that indicates the new status (if that is the right word) upon which Christ, the last Adam, has entered at his resurrection. (c) It is true that the work which the Messiah now does in his exalted state, that of ruling the world in obedience to the Father, is seen by Paul as his fulfillment of God's long purposes for humanity. Even so, his work as 'life-giving spirit' is indeed something undertaken in virtue of this sovereign, human role. But this does not mean that his role as 'last Adam' is restricted to this post-resurrection function. (d) As we will see from Romans 5 and Philippians 2, an important part of Paul's Adam-christology is precisely the

---

[60]οὕτως καὶ γέγραπται need not mean 'as is proved by...,' but simply 'whence also it follows that...'; for this meaning of οὕτως see Arndt and Gingrich, art. οὕτως, 1b. The καὶ especially supports this. It is not the case (contra e.g. Dunn 1973, 130) that the whole verse must be regarded as, for Paul, a scriptural quotation.

[61]Dunn 1973, 1980, and 1988a, 278.

[62]Dunn 1973, 140 (so too 1980, 108), equivocates by paraphrasing 'As the first Adam *came into existence (egeneto) at creation...*' (my italics). The ἐγένετο of Jn. 1.14, cited by Dunn as a parallel (1973, 139) could scarcely be taken in this way.

fact that Christ was obedient unto death. He is therefore already to be regarded as the last Adam, the true Man, in his earthly life. The possible objection to this, that until his death he was simply (so to speak) part of the first Adam,[63] will be dealt with later. It is difficult to see how, without quite different issues intruding into the discussion here, the verse could be read in any other way.[64]

Fourthly, we may enquire as to the basis upon which Paul makes this bold assertion. In his article on the verse, Dunn suggests that early charismatic experience—experience of Jesus *as* life-giving spirit within the community—formed the foundation of the idea, in two ways. First, 'the nature of the believing community's experience of Spirit enables Paul to affirm that Jesus has become πνεῦμα ζωοποιοῦν, and therefore also σῶμα πνευματικόν'—this, answering the question as to how the exalted Jesus is known to possess a spiritual body. Second, this same communal experience of Jesus as life-giving spirit 'is what enables Paul to affirm the representative significance of Jesus' resurrection and resurrection body.'[65] But there are problems with this explanation of the logic of the phrase in terms simply of charismatic experience. For a start, while experiencing the Spirit *as* Christ (in Dunn's language, p. 141) may indeed enable Paul to assert that it is Christ himself who has now become their life-giving spirit, the step from this point to Christ's σῶμα πνευματικόν is not only not stated, it would not be obvious to the opponents whom Paul is seeking to controvert. If they were, as Dunn maintains, gnostics, it would be just such a step that they would be unwilling to make. More important is the positive point, that Paul's belief in Jesus' resurrection did not depend on the experience of Jesus as Spirit, but went back to his vision on the road to Damascus (see 1 Corinthians 9.1, 15.8, etc., which are not to be reduced to inner or 'pneumatic' experiences only). Paul believed Jesus to be alive as σῶμα πνευματικόν because he had seen him with his own eyes. That is foundational to the whole chapter.

This vision, with the new awareness of Jesus' identity that resulted from it, provides a better basis for Jesus' identification with, or representation of, his people than that offered by other theories. Throughout the present chapter, and arguably elsewhere in Paul (see below), it is the notion of Jesus as *Messiah* that explains the fact that he represents his people. As in 15.20–28, where it is ἐν τῷ Χριστῷ that all shall be 'made alive,' so in 15.45: Christ is the representative of his people because, as Messiah, he stands for Israel, the

---

[63]So Dunn 1973, and 1980, 105 ff.

[64]Prof. Moule kindly points out to me that, in addition to these arguments, it is unwise to stress the (after all, only) *implied* ἐγένετο in v.45b, and that the main thrust of the passage is not on 'what Christ became' *per se*, but on the double contrast of ψυχή and πνεῦμα on the one hand and ζῶσα and ζωοποιοῦν on the other.

[65]Dunn 1973, 134, 135.

people of God, the true humanity. The Adam-christology which we discovered in 1 Corinthians 15.20–28 thus helps us to make sense of 1 Corinthians 15.45. As last Adam, the representative of the people of God in their eschatological task and role, the Messiah completes his work of obedience on the cross (see below) and, being raised up after death, enters upon a new mode of human existence, becoming in one sense the pattern and in another sense the life-giving source for the future resurrection life of those who belong to him. The best background for understanding the Adam-christology of 1 Corinthians 15 turns out to be the Jewish eschatology we sketched earlier. The last Adam is the eschatological Israel, who will be raised from the dead as the vindicated people of God. Paul's claim is that Jesus, as Messiah, is the realization of Israel's hope, the focal point and source of life for the people of God.

(iv) Romans 5.12–21

1 Corinthians 15 was not, of course, designed to give a complete picture of a hypothetical entity called 'Paul's Adam-christology'. Any such construct will have to take into account the other significant passages as well. And Romans 5.12–21, while underscoring several of the points just made, brings other important aspects into prominence.[66] In particular, the passage shows (as does Philippians 2, which we shall discuss in ch. 4 below) that Paul has not simply taken over the Jewish ideas of the eschatological humanity as they stood, but has modified them in the light of the gospel.

Perhaps the most important point about the whole section is the significance of διὰ τοῦτο at the start of 5.12. The most natural way to read this is at its face value, meaning 'for this reason,' 'so it comes about that.'[67] Paul invites his readers to stand back and see the result of the argument so far. Whether or not we admit implicit reference to Adam in 1.18 ff. and 3.23 (I would be happy with both, but my argument does not depend on this) it is beyond dispute that the argument of 1.18—4.25 as a whole has shown the plight of humanity and the salvation achieved by God in and through Jesus Christ. It is clearly this that Paul is summing up in 5.12–21, by the multiple series of 'as...so...' contrasts in 5.12, 18–21 (assuming that 5.12a contains the first half of an incomplete contrast, restated in v.18). The force of this point becomes apparent if we understand the preceding argument in the following way.[68] The gospel of Jesus Christ (1.3 f.) reveals the righteousness of God,

---

[66]For the details of exegesis, see further Wilckens 1978, 1.305–337; Dunn 1988, 269–300; Ziesler 1989, 143–153; etc.

[67]Against e.g. Scroggs 1965, 77; for recent discussion see Wilckens 1978, 1.314 f.

[68]Space forbids the detailed treatment this really requires. I have argued the position fully in Wright 1980a, ch. 2.

that is to say (in its Old Testament and intertestamental sense, *pace* Käsemann and others) his faithfulness to his covenant promises to Abraham, his impartiality, his proper dealing with sin and his helping of the helpless.[69] Ch. 4 is not simply an example of Christian faith before Christ, nor a mere proof from scripture of the abstract doctrine of justification by faith. Abraham, as in the Old Testament and intertestamental literature, is the father of the people of God. Paul's innovation in the light of the cross and resurrection is that he argues from the covenant passages themselves (Genesis 15 and 17) that this people of God must be (a) worldwide and therefore (b) characterized by Christ-shaped faith, not by race, circumcision or Torah. God's answer to the sin of humanity (of Adam, if we admit the reference in 1.18 ff. and 3.23) is the people of Abraham (here Paul simply follows Jewish tradition), and Abraham's true people are those redeemed in Christ (here he reworks it in the light of the gospel). 5.1–11 then provides an advance summary of the point which is made in various ways throughout chs. 6–8:[70] the privileges of Israel, particularly those of the fulfillment of the law and of being children of God, have been transferred to Christ and thence to those who are 'in Christ.' 5.12–21 stands in relation to 1.18—5.11 and chs. 6–8 as the link which holds the two parts together. Summing up the first, it provides the basis for the second.

The result of this for our present investigation is clearly that Paul's use of Adam, and his setting of Christ in antithesis with him, falls exactly in line with the Jewish background we have explored. The people of Abraham are the true humanity; and Paul declares that Abraham's people are to be identified as the people of the Messiah, Jesus. Unlike 1 Corinthians 15, therefore, 5.12–21 has the force of a Q.E.D. This general point is further reinforced if we allow for covert reference to Adam in 7.7 ff. and in 8.19–25. The former passage is indubitably based on 5.20 and (arguably) deals, on one level at least, with the Torah and its effects on Israel.[71] Romans 8 shows, much as in 1 Corinthians 15.20 ff., how the restoration of humanity through death and resurrection will be the occasion for the renewal of creation. God's intended order will at last be realized; obedient humanity will rule over a restored world. Christ, and his people, form the true humanity which Israel was called to be but, by the law alone, could not be.

Paul has not, however, simply substituted Christ (and his people) for the nation of Israel in current Jewish expectation. The resurrection of Jesus, bursting upon Paul's consciousness on the road to Damascus, did not merely mean that Jesus would now take the place in his thinking formerly occupied

[69]Wright 1980a, 57–65; see the brief statement in Caird 1978.
[70]See e.g. Dahl 1977, 82 ff.
[71]See below, chs. 10–12.

by Israel (and perhaps by the Messiah, though we do not need to suppose this for the hypothesis to work). The resurrection of the one who had been crucified showed Paul that the scheme of thought itself needed re-evaluation. That, I suggest, is the reason why he must add the qualifying statements of 5.15–17 before he can proceed with the unfinished sentence of v.12 (vv.13–14 are of course a parenthesis on a different topic).

Vv. 15–17, then, form a tight-packed little section. It contains two negative assertions (15a and 16a), which are then explained, if Paul's cryptic additions can be called explanations, by 15b and 16b–17 respectively. 15a denies that there is a direct balance or equivalence between Adam's trespass and God's gift in Christ: 'it is not "as the trespass, so also the free gift"'. The contrast here, judging from the explanation in 15b, seems to be between the character or nature of the two actions: a single trespass, leading merely to death, contrasts sharply with grace and a free gift which abound. A new, sovereign, creative act of unmerited grace is hardly a fitting balance for the sin which leads to death; there is an 'abundant' quality about the former, giving to those in Christ far more than mere recovery of lost ground.[72] This sets the scene for the more specific contrast of v.16a: 'it is not "as through one human sinning, the gift"', i.e. Paul is denying a direct and balancing contrast between the gift and the single act of sin. The crucial phrase in the explanation (16b, itself further explained in 17) is ἐκ πολλῶν παραπτωμάτων. Christ did not begin where Adam began. He had to begin where Adam ended, that is, by taking on to himself not merely a clean slate, not merely even the single sin of Adam, but the whole entail of that sin, working its way out in the 'many sins' of Adam's descendants, and arriving at the judgment spoken of in 1.32; 2.1–16; and 3.19–20. The task of the second Adam was not merely to replace the first Adam. It is one of Paul's chief points in Romans, especially in chs. 2, 3, 7 and 9, that Israel too is 'in Adam,' and that the law does not help her out of this plight but merely exacerbates it (2.17—3.20; 5.20; 7.7 ff.). The re-evaluation of his basic theological scheme which Paul was compelled to make meant a new understanding of the task to which the true Israel, God's true Man, was called. He had not merely to replace Adamic humanity with true humanity. He had to deal with the 'many trespasses,' and the consequent judgment, which had resulted from the sin of Adam.

Thus there comes about also in v.16 the further contrast of judgment and justification. The work of Christ does not merely inaugurate a new race of humanity, as though by starting again from scratch. It effects a favourable verdict for those who, left to themselves, would be in the dock, unable to find a defence (3.19 f.). This reversal has come about because (γάρ, v.17)

---

[72]So Dunn 1988, 280, following Barrett and others.

whereas Adam's sin allowed death to usurp the reign of man over the world, the work of Jesus Christ has restored 'those who receive the abundance of grace and of the gift of righteousness' to their proper role as truly human beings. Thus the contrasts between Adam and Christ in vv.15–17 show that the task of the last Adam was not merely to begin something new, but to deal with the problem of the old; not merely to give life, but to deal with death.[73] It is at this point that Paul, while certainly starting from the Jewish apocalyptic background in which Israel was to be God's true humanity, has given a new dimension to that picture. The cause of this re-evaluation could only be the realization that God's anointed had died on a cross, not as the result of a horrible accident but as the paradoxical and unexpected revelation of the righteousness of God (3.21–26).

One of the significant results of this for our enquiry is that the point made above in relation to 1 Corinthians 15.45 is again underlined. It is true that in the resurrection Christ became the prototype, and source of life, for the future resurrection of believers. But his task as last Adam was not confined to this. His role was that of obedience, not merely *in place of* disobedience but in order to *undo* that disobedience. That is the point made in vv.18–19, where the 'act of righteousness,' the 'obedience' of the one man Jesus Christ, undoubtedly includes a reference to his long pilgrimage to Calvary.[74] This perhaps needs spelling out in more detail. Since Paul does not call Christ 'last Adam' in Romans 5, it may be risky to build too much on the passage in answering what is at best the rather artificial question, as to when Christ *became* 'last Adam'; but since the parallel (and imbalance) between Adam and Christ is worked out in more detail here we are perhaps able to gain a more precise grasp of the theology that underlies both this passage and 1 Corinthians 15. There are two tasks, undertaken by Christ, which may be identified. The first, involving the obedience unto death, is essentially (in Paul's mind) the task by which the old Adamic humanity is redeemed, that is, the task with which Israel had been entrusted. There is a sense in which this is not 'Adamic', in that it was (clearly) not Adam's task; this is why vv.15–17 emphasize the initial imbalance between Adam and Christ. The second task, in which there is the more obvious balance, is the gift of life which follows from Christ's exaltation; this, underscored in vv.18–21, corresponds more directly to the task envisaged in 1 Corinthians 15.20–28, 45. In this latter task, Christ is the obedient human through whom the Father's will for the world is put into effect (5.21, *through* Jesus Christ). If this were all that needed to be said, there might have been something in the view that the post-resurrection task of Christ is more truly 'Adamic' than the pre-resurrection

[73]5.12–21 clearly includes within its summary scope the range of ideas expressed in 3.24–26 and 5.6–10.
[74]See below, ch. 4, on Phil. 2.

one; but this is not the whole story. The obedience because of which he is now exalted is precisely the obedience unto death. And, as will become clear when we examine Philippians 2, this obedience is in itself, however paradoxically, 'Adamic'. The weakness of the view that sees Christ as last Adam only in his resurrection is that, in sticking too closely (without, perhaps, always realizing it) to the Jewish eschatological model, it fails to provide what Paul achieves: an adequate soteriology. In reacting, not without reason, against a soteriology focused on incarnation, it has instead offered one focused on resurrection. Paul's is centered firmly on the cross.

Vv. 20–21 supply final evidence that Paul's Adam-christology in this passage is based on the Jewish view that saw Israel as the last Adam. The place 'where sin abounded' (v.20b) is undoubtedly Israel, the 'place' where 'the law came in that the trespass might abound.' Adam's trespass, active though unobserved until Sinai (vv.13–14, cf. 7.9a), found fresh opportunity in the arrival of the Torah. Again it could display its true colours as trespass, the flouting of the commands of God. And it was there that grace abounded. This point, thus far, is frequently noted.[75] What is not usually seen is the line of thought which, beginning here in Romans, runs on through 7.13–20 and 8.1–4. Here, near the end of a key christological passage, we find perhaps the most important of all Paul's beliefs about Torah, which we will explore further in chs. 7, 10 and 13 below. The Torah possesses, Paul asserts, the divinely intended function of drawing sin on to Israel, magnifying it precisely within the people of God (7.13–20), in order that it might then and thus be drawn on to Israel's representative and so dealt with on the cross (8.3). This is, as it were, the positive reason for the negative role of Torah. As a result, for our present purposes, it becomes clear that the obedient act of Jesus Christ was the act of Israel's representative, doing for Israel what she could not do for herself.[76] Adam's sin and its effects are thus undone, and God's original intention for humanity is thus restored in the Age to Come, which has already begun with the work of Jesus Christ (v.21).[77]

We may therefore draw two conclusions on the basis of 1 Corinthians 15 and Romans 5. First, the apocalyptic belief that Israel is the last Adam is the correct background against which to understand Paul's Adam-christology.[78]

---

[75]See e.g. Cranfield 1975, 293.

[76]This theme is, I believe, one of the main thrusts of Rom. 3. Israel failed to be faithful to the commission with which she had been entrusted (3.1 ff.); Jesus succeeded where she had failed (3.21 ff., reading πίστις 'Ιησοῦ Χριστοῦ in the subjective sense).

[77]I regard ζωή αἰώνιος as denoting not just indefinite continuing existence after death but the now-inaugurated 'age to come' of Jewish eschatological expectation; we might offer the tendentious translation of v.21: 'as sin reigned in death, so also grace might reign through the covenant to the life of the new age, through Jesus, the Messiah, our Lord'.

[78]Dunn 1988, 278 declares himself unconvinced by this, but does not advance reasons—which lie, perhaps, in his not seeing the full importance of the 'Israel'-theme throughout Paul.

For Paul, Jesus stands in the place of Israel. To him, and to his people, the glory of Adam now belongs in the new Age which has already dawned. But, second, the fact of the cross compelled Paul to rethink the nature of God's plan for his people. Jesus, although clearly Messiah because of the resurrection, had not driven the Romans out of Palestine. He had died a penal death at their hands. The resurrection forced Paul to regard that death as an act of grace, and hence not as a denial of Israel's role in God's purposes but as the fulfillment of that role and those purposes; which meant that God's plan, and Israel's role, had to be re-evaluated. Jesus, as last Adam, had revealed what God's saving plan for the world had really been—what Israel's vocation had really been—by enacting it, becoming obedient to death, even the death of the cross. This theme, of course, is worked out from a similar angle in Philippians 2, and we shall look at that passage presently. But before we do that we must turn aside to examine more closely the detailed implications of the hypothesis I have been advancing, that Paul made an extremely close link between Messiah and Israel, and exploited this link in calling Jesus 'Christ'. Is this really borne out by the way in which he uses the relevant words?

Chapter Three

ΧΡΙΣΤΟΣ AS 'MESSIAH' IN PAUL: PHILEMON 6

(i) Introduction

I have now argued that Paul's 'Adam'-christology is basically an 'Israel'-christology, and that there is in his thought a fluidity, corresponding to similar phenomena in other Jewish writings, between the Messiah and the people of God. This is inevitably controversial, since the majority of Pauline scholars do not read 'Christos' in Paul as a title, retaining its Jewish significance of 'Messiah', but simply as a proper name.[1] I want now to suggest that this consensus is wrong; that Χριστός in Paul should regularly be read as 'Messiah'; and that one of the chief significances which this word then carries is *incorporative*, that is, that it refers to the Messiah as the one in whom the people of God are summed up, so that they can be referred to as being 'in' him, as coming or growing 'into' him, and so forth. The best way of making this case is by means of the detailed exegesis of particular passages, showing that this account of the key phrases gives good exegetical sense in the relevant contexts. This is impossible within the scope of the present work, and we must be content with a quick summary of the case and a detailed argument about one passage (Philemon v.6) in particular.[2]

(ii) Χριστός in Paul: a preliminary hypothesis

It has been customary during much of this century to think that when Paul used the word Χριστός, he did not mean to evoke in his hearers' minds, and did not in fact evoke in his own, the meaning 'Messiah'. Paul was, after all, the apostle to the Gentile world, not the Jewish; Jewish categories, not least those that evoked Jewish nationalistic hopes, were therefore something he cannot have either wanted or needed in his work. Instead, so it is thought, he developed the category of Jesus as κύριος, Lord, which cohered better with

[1]See, e.g., Hengel 1983, ch. 4; Dahl 1974 ch. 2 (though with significant modifications); Kramer 1966, 131–50, 203–14 etc.; de Jonge 1986, 321 f.

[2]For a similar argument about the use of Χριστός in Gal. 3.16, see ch. 8 below. The more wide-ranging argument I intend to state more fully in my forthcoming book on Pauline theology.

41

the background and religious expectations of his Gentile audience.[3] As a result of this perspective, only partly challenged in the post-war reaction against the hellenistic picture of Paul, the Messiahship of Jesus has remained a matter of fairly peripheral concern in Pauline studies, and is seldom invoked to play a role of any structural or thematic importance within his thought as a whole. At most, it is thought, Paul knew the traditions about Jesus' Messiahship, and happily transcended them.

There are plenty of signs, however, that this is not the whole story, and that the time is ripe for a re-assessment of Messiahship as a major category within Pauline theology. To begin with, it is clear from other New Testament writings that the notion of Jesus' Messiahship continued to play a considerable part, not least in the gospel traditions which continued, if the form critics are to be believed, to play an influential part in the life of the church beyond A.D. 70. Matthew clearly regards Jesus as Messiah; so, arguably, does Mark; so, in his way, does Luke. John agrees. The early chapters of Acts suggest that the Messiahship of Jesus was a regular, indeed major, theme of early Christian proclamation, and the speeches put into Paul's mouth in Pisidian Antioch (Acts 13) and elsewhere have him attempting to prove from the scriptures, before a Jewish audience, that Jesus was indeed Messiah (Acts 9.22, 13.32–7, 17.3, 18.5[4]). That Jesus continued to be thought of as the Jewish Messiah, with 'royal' overtones, is clear from the odd little story in Eusebius (*Historia Ecclesiae* 3.19 f.) about the blood-relations of Jesus who were hauled before Domitian on a charge of being members of a rival royal house. The charge, and their response, indicates that, although the early Christians had abandoned the nationalistic overtones of Messiahship, the concept of Messiahship itself was so important to them that they were not prepared to go the whole way and abandon it as well.[5] At the level of history-of-religions research, it cannot be stressed too much that the appeal of Judaism itself (and of Christianity as essentially an offshoot of Judaism) to the pagan world did not consist in an abandoning of typically Jewish perspectives but precisely in the claim that Israel's God was the god of the whole world. From the Jewish (and Christian) point of view, Israel's

[3]The classical statement of this sort of position may be found in the work of Bousset 1913, Bultmann 1952. Modern repetitions of the tradition may be found in, e.g., Hengel 1979, 104–6; Kramer 1966, 219; cautiously standing out against this is Dahl 1974, 46.

[4]The reference in 17.3 is especially interesting, in that it occasions Luke's remark (17.7) that Paul and Silas were arraigned on the charge of being heralds for a king who would rival Caesar (βασιλέα ἕτερον λέγοντες εἶναι 'Ιησοῦν). This so obviously goes against Luke's normal apologetic intent that we must consider the historical value very high.

[5]Further evidence may be found in the Apostolic Fathers. Ignatius, who is usually thought to have gone further down the road to Hellenization than Paul, speaks of Jesus as the Davidic Messiah in *Eph.* 18.2 (cp. 20.2), *Trall.* 9.1, *Rom.* 7.3; and the *Didache* (9.2) and the *Letter of Barnabas* (12.10—for all the anti-Jewish polemic of the work) are likewise comfortable with the idea.

hope simply *is* the world's hope. It is when Israel is restored that the nations will be blessed.

In Paul himself, in fact, there is ample evidence, once we know what we are looking for, to support the claim that Messiahship remained a central concept. We have seen in the previous chapter how, in a key text (1 Corinthians 15), he draws on messianic psalms to make messianic points about Jesus, and that in doing so he applies to Jesus ideas which in Jewish thought belonged to Israel as a whole, in other words, that he treats Jesus precisely as Messiah, Israel's anointed representative. This, as we saw, is not surprising, since it was axiomatic for Paul ever since his conversion that what God was expected to do for Israel he had done for Jesus, raising him to life after his persecution and execution at the hands of the pagans. We may now observe, in brief, the shape at least of the evidence from the letters that points in the same direction.[6]

To begin with, there are several passages in which Paul speaks quite unambiguously about Jesus as ὁ Χριστός, the Messiah. The most obvious is Romans 9.5, but we may also note Romans 15.3, 7.[7] This use of Χριστός with the article is paralleled by such passages as 1 Corinthians 1.13, 10.4, 12.12.[8] In all of these passages, I suggest, the Messiahship of Jesus is explicitly significant for Paul.

Second, there are Paul's references to Jesus as 'Son of God'. As is well known, one of the most striking Old Testament uses of this phrase is to denote the Davidic king: Psalm 2.7 and 2 Samuel 7.14, both included in the Messianic Florilegium from Qumran Cave IV,[9] indicate that, although not frequent, this usage had at least a clear royal connotation, which correlates closely with the idea of Israel herself as God's Son (Exodus 4.22, etc.). This might be thought a mere irrelevance, or at best an odd coincidence; but there are good reasons for thinking that it had become thematic for Paul. In a passage like Galatians 3–4, for instance, the argument hinges on the promises to Abraham—promises about the family that God would give him—being fulfilled in the coming one, the Messiah (see below, chs. 7, 8). When, precisely in that context, we find references to Israel as the young son who

[6]The statistical evidence, for what such things are worth, is as follows. The concordance gives 387 uses of Χριστός in the full Pauline corpus, as compared with 270 for κύριος and 220 for 'Ἰησοῦς (the numbers are flexible because of the many variant readings at precisely these points).

[7]See, rightly, Davies 1984, 100 f., citing also Rom. 1.2–4, 1 Cor. 1.23, Gal. 3.16, 6.2. Sanders' objection to Davies' theory (1977, 495–6) is not so much to reading Χριστός as 'Messiah' but to the idea of a known Jewish belief in the messianic abolition of Torah.

[8]We may also note the interesting fact that, in 2 Cor. 6.18, Paul quotes 2 Sam. 7.14, a passage applying to the son of David, and applies it to Christians in general, much as Isa. 55.3 democratizes the Davidic covenant. This points ahead to the incorporative usage which will be studied below. I owe this point to Ellis 1957, 95.

[9]Vermes 1987, 293 f.

43

now comes to maturity, and at the same time to Jesus as the son in whom the promises are fulfilled, and to the church as the sons who now become the beneficiaries of those promises (Galatians 4.1–7), there can be little doubt that a whole train of thought is being evoked, in which Jesus, precisely as Χριστός, Messiah, represents and draws together in himself the physical family of Abraham, in order then to be the focal point of a new community, the renewed people of God.

It is precisely within this context (i.e. Galatians 3–4), and its overall argument about the redefinition of the people of Abraham, the people of God, that we find another significant Pauline usage: that of the genitive, Χριστοῦ. εἰ δὲ ὑμεῖς Χριστοῦ, ἄρα τοῦ ᾽Αβραὰμ σπέρμα ἐστέ, writes Paul at the climax of his long argument about the composition and nature of the family of Abraham. The church is 'Messiah's', the people of the Messiah. Similar uses can be found elsewhere as well.[10]

This brings us to the well–known problem of the prepositional phrases which include Χριστός. A rough count, again allowing for the presence of various alternative readings, is as follows:

ἐν Χριστῷ	26
ἐν Χριστῷ ᾽Ιησοῦ	42
ἐν Χριστῷ ᾽Ιησοῦ τῷ Κυρίῳ ἡμῶν	3
ἐν τῷ Χριστῷ	6
ἐν τῷ Χριστῷ ᾽Ιησοῦ τῷ Κυρίῳ ἡμῶν	1
εἰς Χριστόν	9
εἰς Χριστὸν ᾽Ιησοῦν	2
εἰς τὸν Χριστόν	1
σὺν Χριστῷ	4
σὺν τῷ Χριστῷ	3
διὰ Χριστόν	1
διὰ τὸν Χριστόν	1
διὰ Χριστοῦ ᾽Ιησοῦ	1
διὰ τοῦ Χριστοῦ	2

For the sake of comparison as well as of completeness, it will be as well to note the following comparative statistics:

[10]Thus: 1 Cor. 3.23, 15.23, 2 Cor. 10.7 (twice); 1 Cor. 1.12, whose parallel to e.g. Rom. 16.10 f. indicates the significance, since the people mentioned in the Romans passage are precisely the heads of households or families. The genitive in Rom. 8.17 ('fellow-heirs of Christ'), is not far off.

ἐν Ἰησοῦ	1[11]
ἐν Ἰησοῦ Χριστῷ	1
ἐν [τῷ] Κυρίῳ	47
ἐν [τῷ] Κυρίῳ Ἰησοῦ	4
ἐν τῷ Κυρίῳ Ἰησοῦ Χριστοῦ	2
διὰ Ἰησοῦ	3
διὰ Ἰησοῦ Χριστοῦ	8
διὰ Ἰησοῦ Χριστοῦ τοῦ Κυρίου	2
διὰ Ἰησοῦν	1
διὰ Ἰησοῦν Χριστόν	1
διὰ τοῦ Κυρίου Ἰησοῦ	1
διὰ τοῦ Κυρίου Ἰησοῦ Χριστοῦ	5
σὺν Ἰησοῦ	1
σὺν Κυρίῳ	1

A careful look through these statistics[12] (not to mention the contexts where the passages occur, for which see below) reveals a regular variation in phraseology. Thus, most noticeably, we see that when Paul says 'in' with a phrase denoting Jesus Christ the Lord, the word which regularly follows is either 'Christ' or 'Lord', and virtually never 'Jesus'. When, however, he says 'through', it is usually 'Jesus' or 'Lord', rather than 'Christ'. The exceptions to both generalizations actually prove the rule, as we will see presently. Most revealingly, he uses εἰς, 'into', always with 'Christ' and never with either 'Jesus' or 'Lord'. (A red herring may be disposed of at this point. It has sometimes been suggested that Paul's language about 'Christ in me/you' has more or less the same meaning as 'in Christ', etc., but this is entirely mistaken. 'Christ in you' is much closer to Paul's language about the Spirit, as is clear from Romans 8.9–11.[13])

What hypotheses are available to explain the phenomena before us? The most unlikely, it seems to me, is that which suggests that it is all a matter of euphony or mere unconscious variation.[14] Less improbable, but still not very

[11]Plus one alternative reading in Gal. 3.14.

[12]Which do not show the uses of 'in him', 'in whom', etc., which would add to the numbers without altering the relative frequencies.

[13]See too 2 Cor. 13.5, Gal. 2.20, 4.19, Eph. 3.17, Phil. 1.20, Col. 1.24, 27.

[14]E.g. Kramer 1966, 84 ff., 133–50, etc. Kramer's ability to see what is going on in Paul's theology is seriously hampered (a) by his treatment of many of the relevant phrases as pre-Pauline tradition taken over with little thought by the apostle, (b) by his analysis of the phrases according to where they come within sentences without reference to the actual arguments of

likely, are the theories which explain (for instance) the ἐν Χριστῷ formula on the analogy of 'in Adam' or 'in Abraham', and then extrapolate from these into the other apparently 'incorporative' phrases.[15]

I suggest, instead, that by far the most likely and satisfactory explanation of the phenomenon is as follows. (a) The usage of Χριστός is incorporative, that is, Paul regularly uses the word to connote, and sometimes even to *de*note, the whole people of whom the Messiah is the representative. (b) The best explanation for this incorporative sense is that Χριστός still bears, for Paul, the titular sense of 'Messiah', and that it is precisely on the basis of that meaning that he is able to coin (possibly to re-use; but there is actually very little evidence to suggest that this is what took place) the various prepositional formulae in which this incorporative idea is summed up. (c) The distinction between Χριστός and Ἰησοῦς in these various phrases, and indeed where they occur by themselves in Paul, is quite straightforward. Though both words *denote* the same human being, Paul uses Ἰησοῦς to refer to that man as Jesus, the man from Nazareth, who died on the cross and rose again as a human being, and through whose human work, Paul believed, Israel's God had achieved his long purposes; and he uses Χριστός to refer to that same man, but this time precisely as Israel's Messiah in whom the true people of God are summed up and find their identity.[16]

But why should 'Messiah' bear such an incorporative sense? Clearly, because it is endemic in the understanding of kingship, in many societies and certainly in ancient Israel, that the king and the people are bound together in such a way that what is true of the one is true in principle of the other.[17] In two very striking Davidic passages we find actual incorporative language being used in such a way as to make this quite clear. In 2 Samuel 19.40–43, following the defeat of Absalom's rebellion, the men of Israel dispute the right of the men of Judah to have a prior claim on the king's attention, by claiming: 'We have ten shares in the king, and in David we have more than you':

עשר־ידות לי במלך וגם־בדוד אני ממך :MT

---

the passages in question, and (c) by his discussion (e.g. 86) of which cases the phrases occur in without reference to the prepositions employed.

[15]See e.g. Wedderburn 1971, 86 ff., with the discussion in Moule 1977, 87. Wedderburn has somewhat revised his position in 1985, 91.

[16]We cannot pursue this latter point here. But it makes sense (a) of the various phrases that speak of God achieving something 'through Jesus' and (b) of the otherwise bewildering variety of usage in a passage like Rom. 8.9–11.

[17]See the well-known theme of 'corporate personality', which, though it must now be used carefully (see Wedderburn 1985, 97 n. 52, and other refs. there) is certainly not to be abandoned altogether.

(LXX: δέκα χεῖρές μοι ἐν τῷ βασιλεῖ, καὶ πρωτότοκος ἐγὼ ἢ σύ, καί γε ἐν τῷ Δαυιδ εἰμὶ ὑπὲρ σέ).

Their membership in David's people is expressed graphically by this incorporative idiom. Immediately after this incident Sheba, the son of Bichri, announces his rebellion with words later echoed by Jeroboam the son of Nebat: We have no portion in David, nor an inheritance in the son of Jesse (2 Samuel 20.1, cf. 1 Kings 12.16). While these texts are not sufficient in and of themselves to suggest that such language was familiar in the first century, it does at least suggest a matrix of ideas out of which a fresh incorporative usage could grow, namely, that of the king representing the people.

Returning to Paul's language, I suggest that there are several occurrences of the phrase 'in Christ', etc., which are clearly incorporative, and where the sense of 'Messiah' for Χριστός arguably gives good sense. Perhaps the most obvious are those in Romans 6–8 and Galatians 3. In Romans 6.11 the result of being baptized 'into Christ' (see below) is that one is now 'in Christ', so that what is true of him is true of the one baptized—here, death and resurrection. This occurs within the overall context of the Adam-Christ argument of ch. 5, with its two family solidarities; the Christian has now left the old solidarity (Romans 6.6) and entered the new one. 6.23 may be read by analogy with 6.11; those who are 'in Christ' receive the gift of the life of the new age, which is already Christ's in virtue of his resurrection—that is, which belongs to Israel's representative, the Messiah, in virtue of his having drawn Israel's climactic destiny on to himself. Similarly, in Romans 8.1, 2 the point of the expression 'in Christ' is that what is true of Christ is true of his people: Christ has come through the judgment of death and out into the new life which death can no longer touch (8.3–4, 8.10–11), and this is now predicated of those who are 'in him'. In Galatians 3.26 the ex-pagan Christians are told that they are all sons of God (a regular term for Israel, as we saw) in Christ, through faith.[18] It is because of who the Messiah is—the true seed of Abraham, and so on—that Christians are this too, since they are 'in' him. Thus in v.27, explaining this point, Paul speaks of being baptized 'into' Christ and so 'putting on Christ', with the result that (3.28) πάντες γὰρ ὑμεῖς εἷς ἐστε ἐν Χριστῷ 'Ιησοῦ. It is this firm conclusion, with all its overtones of membership in the true people of God, the real people of Abraham, that is then expressed concisely in 3.29 with the genitive: εἰ δὲ ὑμεῖς Χριστοῦ... When we consider Galatians 3 as a whole, with its essentially *historical* argument from Abraham through Moses to the fulfillment of God's promises in the coming of Christ, a strong presupposition is surely created in favour both of reading Χριστός as 'Messiah', Israel's

---

[18]Not 'through faith in Christ': διὰ πίστεως and ἐν Χριστῷ 'Ιησοῦ modify υἱοὶ θεοῦ in independent parallelism. See Eph. 3.17.

representative, and of understanding the incorporative phrases at the end of the chapter as gaining their meaning from this sense.[19] Because Jesus is the Messiah, he sums up his people in himself, so that what is true of him is true of them.

In the light of these passages there are several others that can arguably be read as expressing substantially the same point. Romans 12.5, for instance, with its emphasis on unity: we, the many, are one body in Christ. Or Philippians 3.9, whose context is precisely Paul's discovery that to belong to the people of God, to Israel, he had to share the death and resurrection of Israel's representative: 'that I may share his sufferings, becoming like him in his death, that if possible I may attain to the resurrection from the dead (3.10 f.)—all of this follows from, and explains, what he means in v.9 by 'that I may be found *in him*'. Or 2 Corinthians 5.11–21, whose whole argument draws out the meaning from the exposition of the ministry of the new covenant in ch. 3 (below, ch. 9), and whose constant thrust, summed up in the incorporative phrases in vv.17, 21 is that what is true of Christ is true of his people. Even a throwaway remark like Romans 16.7, describing Andronicus and Junias as being 'in Christ before me', bears witness to the sense the phrase has of membership in a community: these two men were part of the family, presumably by baptism, before Paul, and were thus, from the perspective of the mid-50s, already Christians of two decades' standing. In particular, the whole letter of 1 Corinthians, with its constant emphasis on the unity of the church, offers several examples of the incorporative usage. The transfer of attributes—what is true of the Messiah is true of his people—is explicitly stated in 1.30: ἐξ αὐτοῦ δὲ ὑμεῖς ἐστε ἐν Χριστῷ Ἰησοῦ, ὃς ἐγενήθη σοφία ἡμῖν ἀπὸ θεοῦ, δικαιοσύνη τε καὶ ἁγιασμὸς καὶ ἀπολύτρωσις. When we consider the way in which this passage picks up the theme of Wisdom of Solomon 6–9, that the Davidic king is the truly wise man, through whose rule Israel becomes the truly wise people, the theme gains cultural and historical reinforcement as well as depth.

Many other passages could be adduced in favour of this reading, but my concern here is not to make an exhaustive case so much as a workable hypothesis. We may just glance, though, at the use of εἰς Χριστόν, which in various ways provides interesting support, and then examine one use of it in particular. Romans 6.3 clearly refers to entry, through baptism, into the people of God; here Χριστός is basically shorthand for 'the people of the Messiah'. 2 Corinthians 1.21 is striking: ὁ δὲ βεβαιῶν ἡμᾶς σὺν ὑμῖν εἰς Χριστὸν καὶ χρίσας ἡμας θεός. If we were to bring out the force of the verbal echo between Χριστός and χρίσας we would have to paraphrase: 'the one who strengthens us with you into the anointed one and anointed us is

[19]See further below, chs. 7–8.

God'. There could hardly be a better indication of Paul's intention to mean 'the anointed one', i.e. 'the Messiah', when he says Χριστός, or of the incorporative significance that the word then carries. We must note, in particular, that despite frequent mistranslation[20] εἰς Χριστόν does *not* mean the same as ἐν Χριστῷ. Paul is precise and careful about his prepositions. The baptismal overtones of the passage link it with Romans 6, although the sense of 'into Christ' here seems to be not merely the entry *de novo* into the Messiah's people, but of the growth together of Paul and the Corinthian church *into* what Ephesians 4.13 calls 'the measure of the stature of the fullness of Christ'. And with that we are ready for the verse which in some ways serves as a test case for my argument, both for the precision of Paul's prepositional usage and for the incorporative sense according to which the word Χριστός refers, in itself and without addition, not merely to the Messiah as an individual but to the people of the Messiah, precisely as the united new humanity. Although I think this sense is clear in Galatians 3 (ch. 8 below), and although a good case can be made for it in 1 Corinthians 1.13 (μεμέρισται ὁ Χριστός;) and 12.12 (οὕτως καὶ ὁ Χριστός), not discussed here, in each of those passages exegetes have had, and no doubt will have, contrary opinions. In the case of Philemon verse 6, however, I am not aware that there is any reading other than the one I shall now propose which comes close to doing justice to the fine-tuning of Paul's language and theology.

(iii) Philemon 6

We come, then, to Philemon v.6, which has been a thorn in the exegetes' flesh for a long time. Paul prays for Philemon, having heard of his love and faith,

ὅπως ἡ κοινωνία τῆς πίστεώς σου ἐνεργὴς γένηται ἐν ἐπιγνώσει παντὸς ἀγαθοῦ τοῦ ἐν ἡμῖν εἰς Χριστόν.[21]

This has caused headaches, too, for the translators. The King James Version has:

That the communication of thy faith may become effectual by the acknowledging of every good thing which is in you in Christ Jesus.

[20]Arndt and Gingrich (s.v. βεβαιόω), incidentally, are culpably loose in translating the phrase 'he who strengthens us in Christ' instead of 'into Christ': they cite Dinkler 1962 as arguing, convincingly, that the phrase belongs to 'baptismal terminology'.

[21]The variant readings are not particularly significant. Some MSS have ὑμῖν for ἡμῖν. Some add Ἰησοῦν at the end.

The Revised Version of 1884 reads:

> That the fellowship of thy faith may become effectual, in the knowledge of every good thing which is in you, unto Christ.

The RSV reads:

> that the sharing of your faith may promote the knowledge of all the good that is ours in Christ.

The New RSV exchanges this for a more active sense of εἰς Χριστόν:

> that the sharing of your faith may become effective when you perceive all the good that we may do for Christ.

The NEB offers two options:

> that your fellowship with us in our common faith may deepen the understanding of all the blessings that our union with Christ brings us. [Footnote: *Or* that bring us to Christ.]

The NIV boldly paraphrases:

> that you may be active in sharing your faith, so that you will have a full understanding of every good thing we have in Christ.

The Jerusalem Bible, like the NRSV, attempts to retain the εἰς Χριστόν:

> that this faith will give rise to a sense of fellowship that will show you all the good things that we are able to do for Christ.

The Revised English Bible carries the sense of κοινωνία forward into the second half of the verse:

> that the faith you hold in common with us may deepen your understanding of all the blessings which belong to us as we are brought closer in Christ.

The verse gives, clearly, the content of Paul's prayer for Philemon (as opposed to further reasons for thanksgiving, to which Paul appears to return in v.7). But this is almost the only thing about the verse that scholars and translators have been able to agree on. Each part of the verse presents its own puzzles, though it may well seem that the εἰς Χριστόν at the end has caused the greatest problem of all. I shall suggest that reading Χριστός in an incorporative sense will seal a reading of the verse that commends itself on all sides.

The full range of problems may be detailed as follows.

(a) Does ἡ κοινωνία τῆς πίστεώς σου ἐνεργὴς γένηται refer to a deepening of Christian fellowship (as NEB), an activity, perhaps evangelism (as NIV, and perhaps RSV)? Could κοινωνία here have some such sense as 'liberality' or 'generosity'?[22] Does σοῦ go with κοινωνία or with πιστίς?

(b) Does ἐν ἐπιγνώσει refer to Philemon's growth in knowledge, or to that of the whole Colossian church? What is the significance of the ἐν?

(c) Does παντὸς ἀγαθοῦ refer to final salvation, to present blessings of Christian living, or what?

(d) How are we to understand the final pair of phrases, ἐν ἡμῖν εἰς Χριστόν? Literally they mean 'in us unto Christ'; but most translators, as we have seen, give up the attempt to maintain Paul's exact wording. It seems impossible to catch the exact nuance of the phraseology, as is witnessed by the NEB margin, which, keeping εἰς Χριστόν intact, makes ἐν ἡμῖν inexplicable.

(e) What does the sentence as a whole *mean*? What precisely is it that Paul is praying *for*? If we take the first phrase to mean Philemon's sharing of his faith with others, the natural way of reading the second part of the verse is that these others will grow in understanding; but what has this to do with the rest of the letter, to which, as regularly with Paul's introductory prayers, the passage seems closely related? If, however, we take the first phrase to mean the Christian fellowship proper to Philemon's faith, how can we translate ἐνεργὴς γένηται ἐν ἐπιγνώσει? NEB, making this choice, opts for 'may deepen the understanding'; this is comprehensible in itself, but is not actually a translation of what Paul wrote.

I suggest that the interrelation of the prayer and the letter as a whole provide a more satisfactory solution than any adopted by the commentators and translators known to me. Paul's whole argument in the letter is based on the idea of 'interchange', that mutuality of Christian living which, arising from a common participation in the body of Christ, extends beyond mere common concern into actual exchange.[23] In the present context, Paul urges Philemon to welcome Onesimus as if he were Paul, and to debit Paul's bill as if he, Paul, were Onesimus (vv.17–19). If we were searching for a Greek

[22]So O'Brien 280; he lists other possibilities on 279 f. See further below.

[23]Compare 2 Cor. 1.6–7, 4.10–15, Col. 1.24, etc. For the theme of the letter see Wright 1986c, 164–71 and the commentary. I have not been persuaded to abandon my (comparatively traditional) reading of the letter by the recent work of such writers as Winter (1987) and Petersen (1985), however important the latter work may be at the level of method.

word that reflects this state of affairs, it would of course be κοινωνία, as is clear from such passages as Philippians 2.1–5, 3.10 and 2 Corinthians 1.7.[24]

But what precisely does κοινωνία mean?[25] 'Fellowship' is often reduced to the idea of the mutual enjoyment of Christian company; 'sharing' implies mutual giving and receiving of material things, or, in the special case of 'sharing faith', the notion of personal evangelism; 'interchange' itself, through useful in some ways, seems too mechanical to cover the full required range of meaning.[26] The idea we need to grasp, which is in fact the dominant idea of the whole letter, is that, in Christ, Christians not only belong to one another but actually become mutually identified, truly rejoicing with the happy and genuinely weeping with the sad.[27] This is the more fundamental meaning of κοινωνία, and it explains and undergirds the other uses, particularly that of 'generosity' or 'almsgiving' (Romans 15.26, 2 Corinthians 8.4): Christians give to one another because they belong to one another. The other suggested meanings are considerably weaker and far harder to integrate into the letter; in particular, the idea of 'sharing one's faith' (NIV), in its contemporary colloquial usage, is simply not what the letter is about. Nor can κοινωνία mean 'sharing' in the sense of dividing something up or parcelling it out.

Rather, the key idea is *mutual participation in Christ*, that feature of Christian living which forms the basis of Paul's whole appeal to Philemon.[28] The genitive πιστεώς modifies this, so that the phrase as a whole will mean 'the mutual participation which is proper to your faith'. (The faith is referred to as Philemon's, not because it is different to anybody else's, but because it

---

[24] This idea has some parallels with the idea of *societas*, 'partnership', in the Roman world: see Sampley, 1980. Sampley notes Philemon 17 as an expression of this *societas*, but does not see the way in which it is here based on the deeper idea of κοινωνία itself.

[25] See, in addition to the dictionary articles, the still important works of Seesemann 1933 and Campbell 1965 (1932), 1–28. The argument of Campbell and Seesemann, that the root word refers to 'participation' *in something* rather than 'fellowship' *with someone*, has still not been taken sufficiently seriously.

[26] Campbell 1965 (1932), 18 f., suggests that 'participation' here gives the sense of other Christians sharing Philemon's faith; but, as he sees, this turns the sentence into a prayer about the church rather than about Philemon. Campbell does not seem to see the possibility that Paul may here be beginning that play on the κοινωνία root which he exploits in v.17, where it means 'business partner' (Campbell 10). Seesemann 1933, 79 ff. rejects Campbell's suggestion as 'sprachlich unmöglich' (82 n.1), and suggests 'Anteilhaben am Glauben'. This too, I think, misses the possibility that within the general sense of κοινωνία argued for by these two writers Philemon 6 might have the sense of that partnership between Philemon and Paul which then becomes the focus of the argument in the climax of the letter.

[27] Rom. 12.15, cf. 1 Cor. 12.26, 2 Cor. 11.28 f. Hooker, who has popularized the term 'interchange', is well aware of its potential shortcomings, and offers further suggestive reflections on it in her new collection of essays (1990, 4 f., 8 f.).

[28] See Collange 1987, 49. This actually strengthens the overall case of Campbell (see above) as to the root meaning of the word, while challenging his reading of it in this particular instance.

is he to whom the appeal is made; part of the point is that the faith is precisely something he has in common with all other Christians.[29])

The rest of the sentence will then begin to fall into place. Paul prays that the fact of this 'mutual participation' will 'work powerfully' within Philemon so that he will come to realize fully 'every good thing...' It is Philemon himself who is to grow in knowledge as a result of the process, as the parallel passages make clear.[30] The 'knowledge' in question is not mere theoretical understanding, but an integrated and operational grasp of 'every good thing'. The word 'realization' carries the right set of overtones here: understanding and practical outworking. 'Every good thing' is a large and unwieldy idea, but the context suggests that it be related to 'good' in v.14: 'something which is *done* or *performed*..., rather than a *possession* or the *object of knowledge*'.[31] Philemon, in other words, is to work towards a realization in practice of the sum-total of what God is doing in Christ and by the Spirit for his people, more specifically of κοινωνία in its full effect. He must allow this principle, which is itself part of his faith in Christ, powerfully to inform his thinking and living. If he does so he cannot but accede to the request that Paul intends to make.

This understanding of the first half of the verse clears the way for a satisfactory solution to the problems posed by the last four words. One of the keys here is the idea of God 'working', as expressed by the root ἐνεργής in the first half of the verse. It seems likely that we should allow this idea to continue affecting the second half: it is God who is 'accomplishing' or 'performing' these things in his people. We may compare 1 Corinthians 12.6: the same God *works* all these things in all people; 2 Corinthians 4.12: life is *at work* in you; Galatians 3.5: God *works* miracles in your midst; Philippians 2.13: it is God who *works* in you to will and to work for his good pleasure; and so on.[32] This at once provides a proper sense for ἐν ἡμῖν: God is at work *in* his people to produce the conduct which will delight him. We should, in effect, understand ἐνεργουμένου in between τοῦ and ἐν ἡμῖν: 'every good thing which *is being worked* in us. Such omissions of words or phrases, especially when cognate forms have occurred earlier, is of course common in Paul.[33]

This leaves us, at last, with the apparently troublesome εἰς Χριστόν. One might be inclined at first blush to think that the NIV had expressed better what Paul really meant, and that he should have written εἰς ἡμᾶς ἐν Χριστῷ, 'which are [given] to us in Christ', that is, the spiritual riches which are found

[29]Cf. Rom. 12.3; and also 'my gospel' in Rom. 2.16.
[30]See the parallels to this idea in Eph. 1.17, Phil. 1.9, Col. 1.9, 10.
[31]Moule 1957, 143: italics original.
[32]See also Eph. 3.20, Col. 1.29, 1 Thess. 2.13.
[33]See Blass-Debrunner-Funk, paras. 479–83.

in Christ and imparted to those 'in' Christ because they belong to him. But Paul is not here talking about 'spiritual' riches in that narrow sense, but about things that Philemon must *do*. Alternative suggestions have included the idea of the second coming of Christ, or that the phrase means 'for the glory of Christ', or (NRSV, JB) of things that are to be done for the sake of Christ; but none of these really fits.[34] It seems to me, rather, that 'unto Christ' can be taken perfectly well here in the sense expressed in Ephesians 4.12 f.: 'so that the body of Christ may be built up until we all reach unity in the faith and in the knowledge (ἐπιγνώσις) of the Son of God and become mature, *attaining to the whole measure of the fullness of Christ'*. We might also compare Ephesians 1.23.[35]

I suggest, in other words, that Paul uses 'Christ' here as a shorthand way of referring to that unity and completeness, and mutual participation, which belongs to the church that is found 'in Christ', that is, in fact, the people of the Messiah. This does not mean, as many still suggest, that the phrases ἐν Χριστῷ and εἰς Χριστόν are synonymous.[36] Being already 'in Christ', the church is to grow more fully 'into him', that is, it is to explore and realize more completely what true corporate Christian maturity means in practice. This use of 'Christ', though often unrecognized, has in fact close parallels elsewhere in Paul, of which the clearest—when that verse in turn is properly understood—is Galatians 3.16.[37] Paul's desire is that the fact of mutual participation, enjoyed by Philemon and his fellow Christians, will result in the full blessing of being 'in Christ', i.e. the full unity of the body of Christ; and he refers specifically in this case to the intention that the slave and the master, finding (as in Galatians 3.28) that in 'Christ', in the one Christian family, there is no meaningful distinction between them, will treat each other as the brothers that they really are. In fact, all the cases where Χριστός most clearly carries this sense refer in some way or other to the breaking down of traditional barriers, whether Jew/Gentile, slave/free or simply the cultural barriers between, for instance, Paul and the Corinthian church, and to the establishing instead of a truly human community in which such things have ceased to function as dividing walls. In the case of Philemon and Onesimus, moreover, Paul clearly intends his own role to be crucial; there will be a complex triple 'interchange' between Philemon, Paul and Onesimus, resulting in reconciliation and growth into the full stature of 'Christ', i.e. of the Christian family.

[34]See O'Brien 1982, 281 for these and other suggestions; and Collange 1987, 50 f.

[35]The REB captures the sense of this while still translating the last phrase as 'in Christ': 'as we are brought closer in Christ'.

[36]Against e.g. O'Brien 281.

[37]See ch. 8 below.

The verse as a whole, then, could be paraphrased as follows: 'I am praying that the mutual participation which is proper to the Christian faith you hold may have its full effect in your realization of every good thing that God is accomplishing in us, to lead us into the fullness of Christian fellowship, that is, of Christ'. To read the verse in this way does justice to the apparent peculiarities of what Paul has actually written, imports no ideas extraneous to the epistle, and prepares the way exactly and thoroughly for the appeal that is to come.

(iv) Conclusion

It would be foolish to imagine that by providing a quick overview of a hypothesis (section ii above), and a detailed exegesis of one neglected and misunderstood verse, one had solved all the problems of Paul's notorious incorporative christological language. But a start has been made, and the later chapter on Galatians 3.15–20 will provide further confirmation. With this, however, we must turn away from the ecclesiological side of Paul's christology and look more closely at the theological—not that the two can ultimately be separated: it is one of the many fascinating features of his thought that, with his picture of Jesus, ideas about the people of God and ideas about God himself seem to meet. There are three passages in particular in which Paul seems to treat Jesus as ranking alongside Israel's God. We must look at each in turn.

Chapter Four

JESUS CHRIST IS LORD: PHILIPPIANS 2.5–11

(i) Introduction

Philippians 2.5–11 is, by any showing, one of the most remarkable passages in all of the New Testament. Since its quasi-poetic structure is not immediately apparent in all printings, whether Greek or English, we may set it out as follows:[1]

(5)   Τοῦτο φρονεῖτε ἐν ὑμῖν
           ὃ καὶ ἐν Χριστῷ Ἰησοῦ,

(6) ὃς ἐν μορφῇ θεοῦ ὑπάρχων
           οὐχ ἁρπαγμὸν ἡγήσατο
           τὸ εἶναι ἴσα θεῷ,

(7)   ἀλλὰ ἑαυτὸν ἐκένωσεν
           μορφὴν δούλου λαβών,
           ἐν ὁμοιώματι ἀνθρώπων γενόμενος·
   καὶ σχήματι εὑρεθεὶς ὡς ἄνθρωπος

(8)   ἐταπείνωσεν ἑαυτὸν
           γενόμενος ὑπήκοος μέχρι θανάτου,
           θανάτου δὲ σταυροῦ.

(9)   διὸ καὶ ὁ θεὸς αὐτὸν ὑπερύψωσεν
           καὶ ἐχαρίσατο αὐτῷ τὸ ὄνομα
           τὸ ὑπὲρ πᾶν ὄνομα,

(10) ἵνα ἐν τῷ ὀνόματι Ἰησοῦ
           πᾶν γόνυ κάμψῃ
           ἐπουρανίων καὶ ἐπιγείων καὶ καταχθονίων

(11) καὶ πᾶσα γλῶσσα ἐξομολογήσεται ὅτι
           κύριος Ἰησοῦς Χριστὸς
           εἰς δόξαν θεοῦ πατρός.

[1]There are of course many possible ways of addressing this task, discussed adequately in the commentaries; and see Hooker 1990, 6. I follow the line-divisions of the Nestle-Aland 26th edition, grouping them according to the connecting words (compare Col. 1.15–20, discussed in ch. 5).

Philippians 2.5–11 has been the subject of innumerable articles and studies, several monographs, and of course much discussion in commentaries. It has several aspects which, though they are important, cannot be examined here.[2] The features I propose to look at are the occurrence of 'Adam-christology' in the passage, and its implications (section (ii) below), and the meaning of the troublesome word ἁρπαγμός in v.6 (iii). This will clear the way for some specific considerations of the underlying christology of the passage (iv), and some more general conclusions (v).[3]

To begin with, it must be stressed that my concern here is with the christology of Paul, not that of his hypothetical predecessors. They are no doubt of considerable interest for our (equally hypothetical) reconstruction of that shadowy phenomenon called pre-Pauline Christianity; but I am not nearly as certain as some of my colleagues in the field that we are in a position to say very much that is useful about them.[4] The close links, both in language and thought, between 2.5–11 and the context in which it now stands[5] show that, whether or not the poem had a pre-history (and there has always been a significant number of scholars who have questioned this) it now says what Paul wanted it to.[6] This will have certain implications as we proceed.

(ii) Adam in Philippians 2

Romans 5.12–21 and Philippians 2.5–11 contain one obvious parallel: the common theme of Christ's obedience unto death. This provides sufficient initial justification for postulating a close link in thought between the two passages. There are, however, several other good reasons for asserting that

[2] I shall discuss these in my forthcoming commentary on Philippians, in the I.C.C. series.

[3] The first and fourth parts of this chapter originally formed part (pp. 373–84) of the 1983 article on Adam-christology (= Wright 1983). It was while writing that article that I became dissatisfied with the current state of discussion on v.6, and from that there grew the 1986 *JTS* article (Wright 1986a) which is here printed, with a certain amount of revision to take account of subsequent debate, as part (iii) of the present chapter.

[4] I am thus starting out in a very different way from many writers on this passage, particularly Murphy-O'Connor 1976, 26 and Schenk 1984, 185–213 (185: 2.6–11 is 'Ein Zeugnis philippischer Christologie und Frömmigkeit'). The indispensable work on this passage is still Martin 1983 <1967>, hereafter cited by author's name only; see too Hofius 1976. Among recent commentaries we may note that of Hawthorne (1983) in the Word series.

[5] See the evidence presented by Hooker 1975, 152 f.; and see further below. The whole question is extremely important, but we cannot go into it in detail within the scope of this present chapter.

[6] See Hooker, loc. cit.; Kim 1981, 147; Johnston 1957, 30; Caird 1976, 100–104, and 1968, 66. The once-usual deletion of θανάτου δὲ σταυροῦ as a Pauline addition is now widely questioned: see Stuhlmacher 1986 <1981>, 172. It has even been questioned whether the passage is a poem at all (G.D. Fee, in an unpublished paper, 1990).

the Philippians passage is a further example of Paul's Adam-christology. Although most scholars are now happy to read it in this way, doubts are still sometimes expressed on the subject, and there is certainly no agreement among those who do see Adam here as to what conclusions should be drawn from this supposition.

To begin with, we may establish the virtual certainty of a reference to Adam. In addition to the obvious link, already noted, with Romans 5.12–21, there is also a link with 1 Corinthians 15.20–28 in the statement of Christ's exaltation (Philippians 2.10 f.), especially as the themes of those verses are echoed in Philippians 3.20 f., where—as in 1 Corinthians 15.27—reference is made to the exalted position of humanity in Psalm 8.7. Again, the theme of exaltation and lordship (2.9 f.), with its overtones of Genesis 1.27 f., confirms a reference to the creation story, or at least to ideas which developed from it. What we have here, in fact, is another example of the phenomenon of multiple 'intertextual echo'. A reader alert for such echoes will find, without difficulty, Psalm 8, Genesis 1, and especially—since it is quoted directly in vv.10 f.—Isaiah 45.23. We might suggest, in addition, that the theme of a humiliated and then exalted figure who is given great authority and power alongside the one God of Jewish monotheism reminds us irresistibly of Daniel 7. These passages no doubt have several ramifications which would be worth pursuing further. For our present purposes I simply note that they all point towards the nexus of thought which we have seen in ch. 2 above: the obedience of Israel, the obedience of Adam, the exaltation of the human figure and/or the Israel-figure to a position of pre-eminence in virtue of that obedience. This is precisely that Adam-christology, and that Israel-christology, for which I argued earlier.

A more subtle, but no less persuasive, argument was advanced by G. B. Caird. He suggested (a) that each possible meaning of Philippians 2.6 is open to the objection that the idea could have been expressed more simply, (b) that the complexity is probably due to an implied contrast between Christ and someone else, and (c) that of the possible candidates for the contrasting figure only Adam will do, and he does very well.[7] When we add to this the close apparent contrast with Adam made at point after point in the poem (see Martin 163 f.), a good *prima facie* case can once again be made for seeing Adam implicit in the hymn as a whole.

Nor are the possible objections to this view as strong as they are sometimes supposed to be. For a start, the fact that the passage may be pre-Pauline does not mean that it cannot be aligned with Romans 5 and 1 Corinthians 15. Even if there were agreement about the origin of these verses, there can be no doubt that they are well anchored in their present

[7]Caird 1976, 120 f.

context in Philippians, and that this context—particularly 3.2–21—contains many passages which show that the author of the letter had the material and language of 2.5–11 in his bloodstream.[8] Nor is it the case that finding Adam-christology in Philippians 2 depends on accepting the *res rapienda* view of ἁρπαγμός in 2.6 (see below).[9] Dunn has briefly but adequately answered the objection of Vincent and Glasson, that there is no real parallel between the sin of Adam in Genesis 3 and the grasping at equality with God implied in Philippians 2;[10] and the final possible objection, that the contrast would seem to make the true man *become* man, and that it is difficult to see what this might mean, is partly answered by Hooker,[11] and will be further resolved below. We may therefore proceed on the assumption that Philippians 2.5–11 is another example of Adam-christology, and hence of Israel-christology.

Since, however, this is already quite widely agreed, the real question is: so what? Three conclusions have at different times and in different ways been held to follow from the presence of Adam-christology here: a lack of reference to the Isaianic Servant of the Lord, the *res rapienda* view of ἁρπαγμός, and the absence of incarnational theology. I suggest, however, that none of these conclusions is necessary, and that Adam-christology in fact (a) provides a context within which a reference to the Servant of the Lord is quite possible, and may even be held to be likely, (b) strengthens a quite different view of ἁρπαγμός, and (c) actually entails, rather than ruling out, incarnational christology. The first of these can be dealt with comparatively quickly, and the second and third will form parts (ii) and (iv) of this paper.

First, then, the question of Adam and the Servant. The nature of Christ's obedience—in particular, the explanation of *why* the shameful death on the cross was in fact the perfect expression of the love of God—is opened up in a new way if we set the hymn's Adam-christology, i.e. its complex parallel and contrast between Adam and Christ, against the Jewish background we outlined earlier and its outworking in 1 Corinthians 15 and Romans 5. I suggested in ch. 2 that, for Paul, Christ as last Adam takes on the role of Israel in the purposes of God, and moreover that the cross, shown by the resurrection to be the crucifixion of the Messiah, forced Paul to re-evaluate the way in which that role should be understood. If Paul's Jewish background contained the idea that Abraham's family was to be the means of solving the problem posed by Adam's sin, the resurrection showed Paul that this purpose had now been accomplished not by the nation as a whole but by

---

[8]Contra e.g. Scroggs 1966; see, for instance, the links with 3.2 ff. as noted by Bultmann, and by Käsemann 1967, 1.51–95. See also Hooker 1971, 356 f. (= 1990, 20 f.); and further, below, p.88.

[9]Contra Scroggs, *loc. cit.*

[10]Dunn 1980, 311 n. 73, against Glasson 1974; see too Dunn 1989.

[11]1971, 162 f.

one person (since, as is clear from 1 Corinthians 15, the resurrection of Jesus is to be seen as the beginning of the Age to Come). In this light, the cross indicated to Paul that God's purpose had been accomplished not in the way one might have expected but by the shameful and penal crucifixion of the Messiah. It is within this context, not that of a hunt for miscellaneous proof-texts or mere verbal allusions, that we may suggest that Paul's description of Jesus' self-humiliation and death in vv.7–8 owes more than a little to the picture of *Israel*, the obedient Servant of the Lord, in Isaiah 40–55.[12]

The strength of this suggestion is twofold. First, the echoes of Isaiah 40–55 are clear in the passage, as we have already seen. When we find in a passage with such echoes a figure whose obedience undoes the disobedience of Adam, and who is then exalted to glory and honour, we are looking straight at the pattern of Israel's humiliation and exaltation in Isaiah 40–55, a pattern focussed on and worked out in the strange figure of the Servant, not only in Isaiah 53 but in the whole 'servant'-theme as it is worked out both in the 'songs' commonly recognized and in ancillary passages. Second, finding a clear allusion to the 'servant' theme here provides a strong theological structure, which coheres completely with the one we located in Romans 5 and 1 Corinthians 15. That Jesus, as last Adam, should take on a role apparently marked out for Israel in the Old Testament fits excellently with the overall understanding we have seen elsewhere. It is well known that Jewish exegesis of Isaiah 53 is hard to pin down when it comes to the precise identity of the Servant of Yahweh.[13] It seems very unlikely (here I differ from, say, Jeremias) that there was a well-known pre-Christian Jewish belief, based on Isaiah 53, in a coming redeemer who would die for the sins of Israel and/or the world, such that Paul could simply slot Jesus into a ready-made framework. On the contrary, it seems to me far more likely that it was the cross itself, which Paul's Damascus Road vision compelled him to recognize as the paradoxical climax of God's saving plan, that forced him to rethink the *nature* of that plan. And when, in the book of Isaiah which he knew so well,[14] he found a description of Israel which nevertheless fitted remarkably well with the events of Jesus' cross, and which lent to those events a significance in the realm of soteriology, we should not be surprised if he made use, albeit allusively, of this description. Within that context the verbal echoes make

[12]See the debate in Martin, 211–13; Hofius 1976, 70 ff.; and Feuillet 1972, 92–100.

[13]See e.g. Driver and Neubauer 1876–7; Zimmerli and Jeremias 1968. It seems likely that some Jewish interpreters at least, prior to the rise of Christianity, understood the passage in relation to the Messiah, but that this reference was, understandably, rejected in later times. It is, incidentally, misleading to say, as is frequently done, that all 'servant' passages in the LXX use παῖς, not δοῦλος, to translate עֶבֶד; compare Isa. 42.19; 48.20; and 49.3,5.

[14]See Hickling 1980, Hays 1989.

their own point (as they do in the parallel passage of Romans 5.12–21).[15] The theological structure I have proposed shows that Servant-christology and Adam-christology belong well together, and cannot be played off against each other. Both, in the last analysis, are *Israel*-christologies.

Objections have, of course, been raised to the 'discovery' of references to Isaiah 53 in Philippians 2.5-11. Of these, most are in fact objections not to the view we have suggested, but to the idea that 'the Servant' was a well-known title in contemporary Judaism, now applied to Jesus.[16] This view is, however, not only not necessary for my case but actually made less likely by it. The meaning of the cross was not, according to Paul, something for which Judaism was well prepared; quite the contrary.[17] Professor Hooker—herself no enthusiast, to say the least, for discovering references to Isaiah 53 in the New Testament—states my position well:

> ...the proper question to ask in this case is whether Jesus is understood to be exercising the role which is described in Isaiah 53—not whether he is 'identified' with some imaginary figure.[18]

I suggest that the answer to this question is an emphatic affirmative. What Hooker herself says two pages earlier, with reference to Jesus', and Israel's *sonship*, applies equally well if not better here: 'Israel should have been obedient to God; this obedience has now been fulfilled, so Paul argues, in the person of Jesus Christ.'

This understanding of the nature of Christ's obedience shows, again, that the argument from the order of clauses is not compelling, i.e. that the mention of μορφὴ δούλου *before* the mention of Christ's becoming 'in the form of men' does not rule out a reference to the task of the servant, Israel, as described in Isaiah 40–55.[19] It is not the case that Christ first became human and then adopted the role of the servant. His fundamental mission—the reason for his coming into the world—was to accomplish the task which was marked out for Israel, namely, to undo the sin of Adam. In order to achieve this goal, he became human. It is quite true that in

[15]See too Rom. 4.24 f., etc. On this theme in Paul see now Hays 1989, 62 f., and also his 37, 215 n.92, 225 f. n.48; and other passages in Hays' index s.v. 'Isaiah'. Hays' careful reading seems to me not only to help establish beyond doubt a frequent and deliberate Pauline reference to Isa. 40–55 but also to demonstrate the multi-layered theological intention of this reference.

[16]As expounded by Jeremias (e.g. 1968).

[17]Cf. 1 Cor. 1.23 ff., etc. The real scandal is not simply the death of the Messiah but the shameful and penal mode of that death, particularly in relation to the corporate significance of the Messiah.

[18]Hooker 1979, 68 n.

[19]Against Caird 1976, 121, and with (e.g.) Furness 1967–8.

becoming human he became subject to the powers that govern human existence in general, and in particular to death itself. It is also important not to miss the point that crucifixion was the form of penal death reserved particularly for δοῦλοι—and this could be one reason why Paul has chosen this word rather than παῖς, which, though one regular LXX rendering of עֶבֶד, could carry also quite different connotations to do with Jesus' sonship. If this is correct, the weight of Paul's soteriology here lies neither on incarnation nor on exaltation per se, but on the cross, understood as the climax and completion of the divine plan of salvation. The task marked out for Israel has been accomplished by her representative.

It is clear, however, that the poem does a great deal more than simply speak of one who undertakes the task and role of the servant of Yahweh in order to undo the sin of Adam. But what precisely this extra meaning is has been the subject of long and tortuous debate. The problem has focussed particularly on the meaning of v.6, and by looking at that verse in considerable detail we will be able to gain a perspective both on the problems and on their potential solution.

(iii) ἁρπαγμός and the meaning of Philippians 2.5–11

The troublesome word ἁρπαγμός continues to play an obviously crucial, but often baffling, role in the second half of v.6:

ὅς ἐν μορφῇ θεοῦ ὑπάρχων, **οὐχ ἁρπαγμὸν ἡγήσατο** τὸ εἶναι ἴσα θεῷ.

The word is troublesome for more than one reason. Occurring only here in the New Testament, never in the LXX, and only rarely in extra-biblical Greek (with most of the instances being Patristic quotations of, or allusions to, Philippians 2.6 itself), it has proved a sore trial to philologists and lexicographers, and to those who rely on their work.[20] It has been credited with a wide range of meanings and nuances, each of which has given a subtly different twist not only to the clause, but also to the whole passage in which the word stands. These shades of meaning have become so complex, and the shorthand ways of referring to them so involved, that even the task of describing the different senses on offer has become problematic.

It is with this last headache that we must begin, if we are to introduce some order, perhaps even some peace, into the scholarly battlefield. In the first part of this section, therefore, I shall suggest that two of the classical descriptions of the problem—those of J.B. Lightfoot in the last century and

---

[20]One possibility, that of textual emendation, is rightly ruled out altogether by the great majority of scholars, e.g. Martin 153.

R.P. Martin in this—have been in certain respects quite seriously misleading. This will clear the ground for the second part, in which I shall attempt to line up the problem in a less unsatisfactory way, and to criticize some of the various senses that thus appear. Finally, in the third part, I shall state my own case, building on the work of R.W. Hoover (one of the problems with recent accounts of the state of the question has been that his work, though often cited, has not so often been understood or taken seriously), and showing that, while his arguments tell against the central philological argument advanced by C.F.D. Moule, several of Moule's ancillary points, particularly the theological emphasis he gives to the hymn as a whole, can and should be salvaged, and that the arguments which have been advanced against his theological position can be satisfactorily met.[21]

(a) Lightfoot and Martin

J.B. Lightfoot set out two, and only two, major options for the interpretation of ἀρπαγμός, ascribing the first to the Latin Fathers and the second—which he himself espoused—to the Greek.[22] The first, followed in the Authorized Version (Christ 'thought it not robbery to be equal with God'), takes ἀρπαγμός in the abstract sense of 'an act of aggression'.[23] The result of this meaning for the sentence as a whole is that Christ, knowing himself to be equal with God, knew also that this equality did not constitute—or, perhaps, was not the result of—an act of aggression; i.e. he knew that it was his by right. This has immediate implications for the force of v.7: even though he knew that equality with God was his by right, he nevertheless emptied himself... In other words, Christ was under no necessity to relinquish his place of divine splendour (v.6b), but nevertheless did so voluntarily (v.7a).

Lightfoot argues against this position, and prefers his second category, that of the Greek Fathers. Noting that ἀρπαγμόν τι ἡγεῖσθαι conforms to a standard Hellenistic idiom (of ἀρπαγμός and similar words used in a double accusative phrase with a verb of thinking, reckoning, etc.), he suggested the meaning of 'a treasure *to be greedily clutched and ostentatiously displayed*' (132, my italics). This alters the flow of thought from v.6 through to v.7. On the Latin view, Christ's being in the form of God and his unchallengeable right to equality with God are two ways of saying the same, or almost the same, thing, and it is in the ἀλλά-clause that the new idea ('nevertheless...') is introduced. For the Greeks—according to Lightfoot—the contrast begins

---

[21]See Hoover 1971; Moule 1970, both of which are cited hereafter by author's name only.

[22]Lightfoot 1868 (hereafter cited by author's name only), 109 ff., 131–5 (the pagination is only slightly different in the other editions sometimes cited).

[23]See Moule 271 n. 1.

already with οὐχ ἁρπαγμὸν ἡγήσατο, which is seen as in itself 'a statement of his (i.e. Christ's) condescension' (p. 133). This condescension is expressed, according to this view, in the negative form in v.6b and in the positive in v.7a. Christ did not do *x*, but he did *y*, its apparent opposite, instead.[24] Lightfoot then understands this in the sense that Christ did not regard the rank and privilege of his equality with God as something to be clung on to greedily, but instead gave them up;[25] and this, he argues, is the correct way to read the verse. Both meanings, he points out, take for granted the divinity of Christ. It is no credit not to cling on to something that does not belong to you. Lightfoot dismisses briefly two other interpretations, those of Chrysostom among the Fathers and Meyer and Alford among his own contemporaries.[26] To these other options we shall return.

If we try to categorize the two senses discussed by Lightfoot, it comes as a shock to realize that, perhaps despite his intention, both of them fall within the meaning that subsequent debates have attached to the Latin tag *res rapta*. In recent times, as we shall be seeing presently, that phrase has come to designate the view in which Christ possessed equality with God antecedent to the action described in v.6. But, when the Latin Fathers advocated *res rapta*, Paul was understood to be denying that Christ regarded his equality with God as something he had obtained by snatching; if we are to give *res rapta* its proper force ('a thing having-been-snatched'), this must be it. Confusion easily arises here, however, because it is the second meaning, that of the Greek Fathers, which is usually today referred to as *res rapta*. In fact, as Moule has pointed out, it should really be *res retinenda*:[27] the point being made is not so much that equality with God had (or had not) been *obtained* by snatching, but that it was (or was not) *clung on to* in a grasping fashion. This meaning, as both Moule and Hoover have pointed out, is simply a philological impossibility. Part of the trouble, as we shall see, is that the phrase *res rapta* has itself become an idiomatic phrase in scholarly jargon. Leaving behind its proper sense of 'something obtained by snatching', it has come to be used, in the debate as to whether or not (in this passage) Christ is said to have possessed equality with God before his human birth, as a shorthand way of indicating the answer that he did. This, as we shall see, has led to further confusions in the modern debate. To summarize, therefore: Lightfoot distinguished two senses of the key clause, that of the Latin Fathers (properly called *res rapta*, in which Christ is said not to have regarded his divine equality as something obtained by snatching, i.e. to have regarded it as

[24]See Lightfoot 134.
[25]Lightfoot distinguishes carefully between ἴσος θεῷ and ἴσα θεῷ: 'the former refers rather to the *person*, the latter to the *attributes* (110, Lightfoot's italics).
[26]Lightfoot, 134-6.
[27]Moule 267.

being his by eternal right) and that of the Greek Fathers (properly, though not usually, called *res retinenda*, in which Christ is said not to have regarded his divine equality, already possessed, as something greedily to cling on to). Finding the emphasis of the passage to rule out the former, he opted for the latter as the only viable alternative.

R.P. Martin's account of the clause, written nearly a century after Lightfoot's, groups the rival theories under four headings. He begins with (what he calls) the active sense, which he indicates by the translation 'an act of robbery or usurpation'. His three other senses are variations on the passive meaning. The first two he labels, respectively, *res rapta*[28] and *res rapienda*. The latter view, which grew up chiefly in the post-Lightfoot era, holds that ἁρπαγμός must refer to something *not* already possessed, an equality with God which Christ could have grasped but did not. This view has often been linked with the supposition of an implicit contrast with Adam.[29] Martin claims that his final view—the third of the passive senses—combines the *res rapta* and *res rapienda* positions into one.[30] Christ existed eternally in the form of God, but refused to snatch at the further honour of world sovereignty ('being equal with God'), choosing instead to receive it as the result of obedient suffering and death. Martin's classification, then, is as follows:

(a) active sense, i.e. *raptus* ('an act of robbery');
(b) passive sense (i), i.e. *res retinenda* ('something to be clung on to', misleadingly classified as *res rapta* because the *res* in question is already possessed);
(c) passive sense (ii), i.e. *res rapienda* ('something to be grasped *de novo*, something, that is, not already possessed');
(d) passive sense (iii), i.e. Martin's supposed blend of *res rapta* and *res rapienda*.

There are, however, several signs of confusion in this analysis. We may begin with (a). Martin has placed together in this first category, the 'active' sense, at least three quite different solutions, namely those of Ross and Hooke, of Feuillet, and of the Latin Fathers, and has used criticisms proper only to the last as though they applied equally to all three. As we have seen, the active sense of the Latin Fathers is (theologically) identical with *res rapta* properly understood; even though their sense, strictly, is passive, it makes the same theological point, i.e. a comment on the nature of Christ's divine

[28]By which he really means *res retinenda*: on 138 he describes *res rapta* as 'a shorthand expression for the sense of ἁρπαγμός as a prize which, already in the possession of the owner, is held on to'.
[29]See Martin 139–43.
[30]148–53. He describes this as the 'more popular sense' (144).

equality.[31] It is against this Latin view, rather than that of Ross, that the criticisms of Lightfoot which Martin echoes make a strong point (see below).[32] Ross's interpretation looks at the *implications which Christ might have drawn* (but did not) from his equality with God: the Latins, at *the means by which Christ might have obtained* that equality. The difference between the two is particularly apparent in the relation of the clause to its neighbours on either side.[33]

Martin's description of the 'passive' meanings is equally confused. Thus:

Under (b), we have noted that by *res rapta* he really means *res retinenda*. He is right to cite Lightfoot as a leading representative of this view, but it is odd that he does not mention Lightfoot's reasons for taking this position, namely, the (supposed) meaning of the idiomatic phrase ἁρπαγμόν τι ἡγεῖσθαι (which Martin associates rather with his final view, the one he himself champions) and the impossibility of the classic Latin position which Lightfoot regarded as the only serious alternative.[34]

Under (c), his account of the *res rapienda* view is similarly problematic. J. A. Beet, whom he cites here, did indeed attack Lightfoot, but did so in order to put forward a view very close to that of Ross in 1910 or Moule in 1970.[35] Some others cited here by Martin belong properly in his third category (e.g. E. Stauffer).[36] For definite examples of *res rapienda* we must look elsewhere.[37]

Under (d): Martin's 'third possibility' (pp. 143 ff.) fares no better at this initial level, i.e. in the analysis of differing views. He has again collected several quite distinct positions as though they were more or less identical. Starting from the idiom mentioned above, and failing to see that Lightfoot and his followers have used this to support *their* sense, he draws in Bonnard, Käsemann, Cerfaux, and Lohmeyer as 'representatives' of this option. But,

[31]It is in this category, not that of Ross and Hooke, that we should place the comment of Barclay 1958, here at 42 (cited by Martin 136 n.1).

[32]Though the other criticism urged by Martin 136, citing Lightfoot and Gifford (1911), is odd: in what way is this position 'incompatible with the validity of the Lord's claim to be on an equality with God'? No objection like this appears in Lightfoot or Gifford. Martin does not mention Lightfoot's first, and major, objection, which concerns the *non sequitur* between the Latin view and the exhortation to humility.

[33]So already Furness 1957–8, 93 f.; Griffiths 1957–8, 237–9. For Feuillet's view see below (Moule 271 already saw that Feuillet did not belong with the others in Martin's first category); Martin has, perhaps, been misled by Feuillet's note (1942, 62) that he is treating ἁρπαγμός as 'substantif actif'.

[34]This confusion was pointed out by Glasson 1974–5, 135 ff.

[35]See J. A. Beet, in *Expositor* (3rd series, vol. 5, 1887), pp. 115–25, *Expository Times* iii (1891–2), 307–8, and *Exp.T.* vi (1894), 526–8. Beet was followed by F.G. Cholmondeley, *Exp.T.* vii (1895–6), 47–8.

[36]See Stauffer 1955, 117 ff., 283 f.

[37]See, for instance, Kennedy 1912, 436 f.; Bengel 1862, 723; Badham 1907–8; Scott 1935, 192; Beare 1959, 79–81.

while Bonnard does, broadly speaking, follow Lohmeyer by taking the phrase to mean that Christ, possessing divine equality, refused to exploit the privileges of this position,[38] Käsemann (followed by Bornkamm) understands it to mean that Christ actually gave them up altogether (Bornkamm goes so far as to refer to Christ's 'giving up of his divinity' or of his 'divine mode of existence').[39] Käsemann's article is in fact a sustained critique of Lohmeyer, whose view is the real basis for Martin's solution (oddly, since Martin agrees with Käsemann in rejecting Lohmeyer's ethicizing interpretation of the hymn as a whole).[40] Cerfaux and Henry, lumped together as taking 'a somewhat similar line' to Käsemann,[41] in fact neither agree with each other nor come anywhere close to Käsemann. Henry[42] ends up supporting Lightfoot's position, using the phrase *res retinenda*. He too sees the possibility of Lohmeyer's line of thought, but rejects it. It is in Lightfoot's sense, not Cerfaux's, that he writes that equality with God 'est le bien, possédé, que le Christ rénonce à exploiter': i.e. he means by this that Christ *did not cling on to* this status, not that he retained it but did not use it for his own advantage. We have to do with 'une chose possédé à laquelle il ne s'accroche pas'. Cerfaux, for his part,[43] understands the verse to refer to a prize already possessed, *not* given up, but not to be used 'orgeuilleusement et comme par bravade', referring to Christ's conduct of his earthly life. In fact, the only link between Cerfaux's view and Martin's is that both claim (Cerfaux in fact with more justice than Martin) to avoid the dichotomy between *res rapta* and *res rapienda*. All that Martin means by this is that there is (a) a sense in which Christ already possesses 'equality with God' (this is not in fact, as we have seen, the true meaning of *res rapta*) and (b) a sense in which he does not snatch at this equality: see below.

None of these writers, then, is making the point to which Martin is leading up, for which Lohmeyer is the real source: that 'the motif of the hymn is the determination of the path Christ chose as the way to his lordship'.[44] His view is that Christ was always in the form of God, but that he did not yet possess equality with God. Refusing to snatch at this higher state, he attained it instead by the path of humble suffering and death. This view, which has found other supporters since Martin wrote,[45] is in fact a new version of the

[38]Bonnard 1950, 43.

[39]Bornkamm 1969, 113, 114.

[40]Käsemann 1968. The reason why Martin draws Käsemann into this category is simply that he wants to use his 'functional', as opposed to 'ontological', reading of τὸ εἶναι ἴσα θεῷ (151 f.).

[41]Martin 146.

[42]Henry 1950, here at col. 27.

[43]Cerfaux 1951, 290.

[44]Martin, 147.

[45]E.g. Houlden 1970, 74 f.; Gibbs 1971, 83.

res rapienda meaning of ἁρπαγμός.[46] Martin, however, suggests that it includes *res rapta* as well: 'His installation as Kyrios betokens that "equality with God" which He refused to aspire to in His own right. Yet it properly belonged to Him; hence *res rapta* is true equally with *res rapienda*.'[47]

There are, then, several confusions of analysis present here:

First while it is true that Lohmeyer's meaning does indeed take ἁρπαγμός as *res rapienda*, it cannot be said to mean *res rapta* either in the sense intended by the Latin Fathers (whose question concerned how Christ *came by* his status of equality with God in the past) or in the sense Martin himself uses, which we have characterized as *res retinenda*. Martin's use of *res rapta* as a shorthand expression referring to Christ's pre-existence leads him into further confusion, for instance on p. 152, where he refers to μορφὴ θεοῦ, rather than τὸ εἶναι ἴσα θεῷ, as *res rapta*. This is misleading, to say the least, since μορφὴ θεοῦ is certainly not the object of οὐχ ἁρπαγμὸν ἡγήσατο.[48]

Secondly, Martin seems to take the idea of 'equality with God' in two different senses, first a bad one and then a good one. Christ did not try to acquire a cosmic sovereignty independent of God, but attained at last to a *valid* 'equality' after his suffering and death. It is at this point, rather than in his category of *res rapta*, that Martin introduces the tag *res retinenda*,[49] but by it he means: 'He had the equality with God as His Image, but refused to exploit it to His personal gain.'[50] But this appears to say that Christ was after

[46]So, rightly, Hoover 1971, 101. Hoover accuses Martin of 'philological obfuscation' on the grounds (*inter alia*) that he makes the word carry both active and passive senses at the same time. But this may not be strictly the case. By *res rapta* Martin does not really mean to refer to the active sense (even if, strictly speaking, he should). What he is advocating is actually a combination of *res retinenda* and *res rapienda*.

[47]The final example of a combination of *res rapta* and *res rapienda* is that of Barrett 1962, 69 ff. (see Martin 149 n.3). Barrett is the only writer, in fact, who actually achieves this combination without collapsing *res rapta* into *res rapienda*: but he does so at the cost of an extremely split christology, in which, as Man, Christ did not possess the equality with God which he *did* possess as God's eternal Son. Barrett may well be right in seeing that some of the confusion in the passage is caused by Paul's squeezing a contrast between Christ and Adam into the argument: but (a) describing how he does this as combining *res rapta* and *res rapienda*, though ingenious, may not be the most helpful analysis (see below); and (b) Barrett is not at all making the same point as Lohmeyer or Martin.

[48]That this is indeed Martin's view is confirmed by the preface to the new edition, where he says (xxiii) that the 'soteriological drama moves forward from the station the pre-existent one held as ἐν μορφῇ θεοῦ ὑπάρχων to His decision not to use such a platform as a means of snatching a prize (τὸ εἶναι ἴσα θεῷ), but chose rather to divest Himself of that advantage and take the μορφὴ δούλου as an act of voluntary humiliation. This (a) makes the mistake noted, of regarding 'being in the form of God' as the object of the verb, and (b) thus misuses Hoover's analysis of the key term, with which he professes to agree—although Hoover in fact pointed out the impossibility of the position Martin still advocates. See too Martin 1959, 98 f. A similar confusion appears in Schillebeeckx 1980, 170.

[49]Leading Marshall 1968, 109 to think that this was Martin's own preferred label for his view.

[50]Martin, 149.

all equal with God, which cuts against Martin's subsequent exposition of τὸ εἶναι ἴσα θεῷ,[51] and to refuse to exploit something is not the same thing as not to retain it; in fact, it may be held to entail retaining it, since that which one has given up one is no longer in a position to exploit.

Finally, Martin tries to hold his (and Lohmeyer's) view together with the proverbial sense of ἁρπαγμὸν ἡγεῖσθαι. But the proverbial sense, properly understood, points (as we shall see) in a quite different direction.

There have, of course, been many other analyses of the different possible meanings, within this passage, of ἁρπαγμός.[52] I have concentrated thus far on Lightfoot and Martin because they have been taken by so many others as standard reference- and starting-points for future work. That work has, however, moved in a wide variety of different directions, and it is necessary to take some account of other interpretations before offering my own conclusions.

(b) Other Analyses

The clearest method of describing the different options for the interpretation of Philippians 2.6b would seem to be to look at the wider unit of meaning as a whole. Strict concentration on grammar can, as we have seen, lead one to hold together things dissimilar, or to put asunder things that should be joined. The key points to ascertain, in order to differentiate between distinct opinions, are therefore not merely the analysis of ἁρπαγμός itself, but also (a) the rough meaning assigned to ὅς ἐν μορφῇ θεοῦ ὑπάρχων; (b) the meaning of τὸ εἶναι ἴσα θεῷ; and (c) the result of the action referred to by οὐχ... ἡγήσατο, in terms of its effect on its grammatical object, τὸ εἶναι ἴσα θεῷ. Using these together, we can distinguish at least ten significantly different analyses.[53] In exposition of these points of view, we will allot most space proportionately to those of Moule and Hoover, since they form the basis of the proposal to be advanced in the concluding section. At the same time, it is important to realize that, though Hoover's philological argument is vital to the whole case, the other views are not ruled out because of that alone. Most of them contain internal weaknesses of their own, and it will be helpful to point out some of these as we go along, lest it be thought that the argument hangs by a single thread.

1. Lightfoot, as we saw, began with the observation of the idiomatic phrase ἁρπαγμόν τι ἡγεῖσθαι, aligned it with other similar phrases employing words like εὕρημα, discovered that the Greek Fathers, using this phrase, seemed to regard οὐχ ἁρπαγμὸν ἡγήσατο as a statement not of

[51]Martin 1983, 151 f.; see Martin 1959, 96 f.
[52]See, e.g., Feuillet 1972, 113 ff.; Caird 1976, 120 f.
[53]For ease of reference, these are set out in tabular form on p.81 below.

Christ's proper majesty but of his condescension, and concluded that it referred to that abandonment of the privileges of equality with God which took place at the incarnation. Lightfoot was careful to point out that this view in no way undermined a belief in Christ's divinity. On the contrary, it presupposed it, discovering it in the phrase ἐν μορφῇ θεοῦ ὑπάρχων, and suggesting that ἴσα θεῷ, as opposed to ἴσος θεῷ,[54] meant not divinity itself but the privileges of divinity. This view is undeniably attractive, particularly in its smooth transition from v.6 to v.7, and can claim considerable support.[55] It is the one Martin calls *res rapta*, though as we have seen it is really *res retinenda*.

2. Despite Lightfoot's carefully nuanced orthodox reading of the clause, the kenotic understanding of Philippians 2 comes very close to his, needing only to make an adjustment in its view of τὸ εἶναι ἴσα θεῷ. Once make that phrase mean, more or less, 'divinity', the apparent meaning of vv.6–7 is that the pre-existent, divine Christ abandoned that divinity in becoming human (to receive it back again, presumably, in his exaltation (vv.9–11)). The former popularity of this view, and the arguments which have led most scholars to avoid it, are well known,[56] though the idea recurs in almost casual phrases from time to time.[57]

3(a). The solution offered by such German writers as Käsemann and Bornkamm is more or less a variant on the kenotic version of the *res retinenda* view.[58] Understanding Christ's pre-existent state to be that of an equality with God held in virtue of his identity as the divine *Urmensch*, they see this status as being abandoned.[59] This line of thought avoids kenoticism proper at the cost of importing into the hymn the quite alien idea of gnostic speculation.[60]

[54]See n. 25 above.

[55]E.g. Henry 1950; Prat 1926, 1.319; Caird 1976, 120 f.; Beasley-Murray 1962, 986 f.; Hofius 1976, 103 (his translation of the hymn); and perhaps Vincent 1897, 57ff.; though Vincent is not entirely clear on the matter. L. Bouyer (1951–2, 281–8) takes a similar view, emphasizing the parallel with Adam. Recently Demarest (1980) has supported Lightfoot's position with the claim that it is 'dynamic and ontological' whereas Moule's scheme is 'purely static or ethical' (141 n.54).

[56]See Martin 1983, 169; Henry 1950; Prat 1926–7, 1.319 f.; Barth *Church Dogmatics* 4.1.182 f.; Fairweather 1959.

[57]E.g. Bornkamm 1969, 113 f.; Martin 1983, 138f n. 4. Gibbs (1970, 1971) attempts to revive the kenotic view. But the strong point of his argument (the 'dynamic movement of God in Christ', 1970, 279) does not, in fact, support 'kenosis' proper, but can be seen equally well in several other solutions, including our own (see below).

[58]Though Gnilka 1980b <1968> 117 classifies it as *res rapta*.

[59]So too Jervell 1960, 229 f.; Gnilka 1980b (1968), 116 f.

[60]So, rightly, Georgi 1964, 263–93; Hurtado 1984, 116 ff.; and others listed in Martin 1983, xix f.

3(b). The position of Oscar Cullmann is really a variant on 3(a), though the similarity is obscured because he labels it (rightly) *res rapienda*.[61] He too believes that Paul refers to a heavenly *Urmensch* who becomes man, but instead of seeing his heavenly existence as equality with God (as Käsemann and Bornkamm), he regards that equality as a further stage at which the *Urmensch* refused to grasp, choosing instead to become man.

4. The next solution is the most complicated in its subdivisions. Classifying ἁρπαγμός as *res rapienda*, this view has to address the question: what is it that Christ did not already possess, and at which he refused to snatch? The answers on offer are (a) divinity (the classic *res rapienda*);[62] (b) the status of 'cosmocrator' (Lohmeyer, Martin: see below); (c) divine honours to be enjoyed during the time of incarnation (Feuillet).[63] This is not too different in *meaning* from Lightfoot's sense, but is clearly reached by a different route. Feuillet has, however, drawn back from this position in his most recent writing on the subject,[64] and offers it only as an alternative to Cerfaux's view, which, as he rightly sees, is supported by Hoover's argument (see his summary, pp. 130–2).

A fourth variation (d) on *res rapienda* is offered by M. D. Hooker, though she does not label it thus. Emphasizing the implicit contrast between Christ and Adam, she suggests that Christ did not need to snatch (like Adam) at divine equality *because he already possessed it*.[65] There are problems with this view at the level of classification. Hooker follows Carmignac's central point (see below) that the negative οὐχ apparently modifies ἁρπαγμόν rather than ἡγήσατο (though this does not seem to affect her translation of the passage). And, whereas for Carmignac Christ considered his divine equality a non-usurpation in the sense that he enjoyed divine honour during his earthly life, for Hooker Christ did not regard his divine equality as something he now needed to grasp, because he already possessed it. Carmignac has Christ looking back at an honour he did not grasp in the past; Hooker has him looking forward, realizing he does not need to grasp it in the future. Thus, while this view is classified as *res rapta* by Martin,[66] it is more properly, as we have seen, *res rapienda*. Hooker's view thus straddles different categories.

---

[61]Cullmann 1963, 177 f.

[62]See Martin 1983, 139 ff.; Hawthorne 1983, 84, and above n. 35. Prat 1926–7, 1.317 f. regards this view as Arian and therefore impossible. See further the revival of this position—almost as if it were a new thing!—by Harvey 1964–5, 337 ff. Harvey is answered by Hudson 1965–6, 29. See now also Wanamaker 1987, 188 f.

[63]Feuillet 1965, 366 f.

[64]Feuillet 1972, 112–32.

[65]Hooker 1975, 151–64 (= 1990, 88–100, here at 97 f.).

[66]1983, 138 n. 2: he gives no examples of scholars who hold it.

This of itself is, of course, not an objection. One might say, so much the worse for the categories. But at the part of her argument crucial for our discussion (her analysis of the poem, and her defence of its subtle and rich paraenetic thrust in its present context, are extremely valuable) the argument becomes awkward. To begin with, it is not the case that only with some sort of *res rapienda* view can the contrast between Christ and Adam be maintained, as she suggests (p. 160); Caird, for instance, fits it nicely into his revival of Lightfoot's position. More importantly, I am not convinced by her suggestion that τὸ εἶναι ἴσα θεῷ can be read as a direct reference to Genesis 1.26 (pp. 160 f.): the asserted equivalence of μορφή and εἰκών in the LXX, upon which this suggestion partly rests, seems to me illusory.[67] Nor do I think it necessary for her main points of interpretation to be sustained (that Paul is deliberately contrasting Christ and Adam, and that 'his very action in becoming what we are is a demonstration of what he eternally is' (p. 164)) that one should rely, as she seems to on p. 161, on the Rabbinic tradition that saw Adam as already possessing the thing at which, in Genesis 3.5, 22, he grasped. This is scarcely the most natural way to read the combination of Genesis 1.26 and 3.5 ff. Finally, although Hooker's point (pp. 162 f.) about the irony of ὁμοίωμα and σχῆμα is well taken, it seems odd to describe the pre-incarnate Christ as 'the true Man' (p. 163), 'the one who is truly what Man is meant to be', unless one wishes, as Hooker does not, to join Käsemann and Cullmann. Hooker's main points, as I shall show, may be retained in a scheme which eliminates these problems.

Since Martin's own view has gained considerable currency,[68] it is important to point out its inherent weaknesses, in addition to those of its categorization which we noted earlier. First, it cannot (as Martin thinks) claim support from the idiom as analysed by Hoover.[69] Secondly, it drives a sharp wedge between ὅς ἐν μορφῇ θεοῦ ὑπάρχων and τὸ εἶναι ἴσα θεῷ, which does violence both to the regular usage of the articular infinitive (see below) and to the sense of the passage, as is apparent from Martin's confusion as to whether the μορφὴ θεοῦ is given up or not. Thirdly, the idea of Christ's equality with God meaning the status of 'cosmocrator' is

[67]Hooker 160 n. 14. Only once, in Dan (LXX) 3.19, does μορφή translate צֶלֶם , which the LXX translates with εἰκών in Gen. 1.26 and in several other instances.

[68]See Houlden 1970, Gibbs 1971; and cf. Grelot 1973, 41 f. Glasson 1974–5, noting Martin's appeal to the idiomatic sense, wrongly assumes that he is thereby following Lightfoot. See too Coppens 1967, 199. Compare Coppens's earlier article (1965) against the kenotic theory. See too Gewiess 1963; Gewiess's view is summarized, and criticized on the basis of the idiomatic sense, by Gnilka 1980b (1968), 115 ff.

[69]See above. If μορφὴ θεοῦ really were the object of οὐχ ἁρπαγμὸν ἡγήσατο, as Martin seems to think, a new sort of kenoticism would result, and it is clear that Martin does not want that either. The ambiguity still remains in Martin 1976, 98: 'what he might have seized, he relinquished.' That which one might seize, one does not already possess: that which one does not possess, one cannot relinquish. See Marshall 1968, 126.

inherently unclear. (a) What does this status consist in if it is so different from his being in the form of God (in the fully divine sense Martin intends)? (b) Why should τὸ εἶναι ἴσα θεῷ mean 'cosmocrator' in this different sense? (c) Why should world lordship be a thing to which Christ should not aspire? and (d) Why is he then entitled to it because of suffering and death? Fourthly, in what way is this view 'soteriological' rather than 'ontological'? Martin, claiming this, nevertheless indicates that the point of the status ἴσα θεῷ would be that it *was* in a particular relation—specifically, independence—to God the Father (p. 152). Fifthly, the parallel between Adam and Christ is obscured: at no point is the contrast clear between what Adam did and what Christ refused to do.[70] Finally, the emphasis of the hymn is thrown in what, as we will argue, is quite the wrong direction. (a) It fits (as Martin recognizes) very badly in the paraenetic context; (b) the second member of the contrast (οὐχ ἁρπαγμὸν ἡγήσατο... being the first) is delayed for an intolerably long time, only appearing in v.8. It is much more natural to see the second member in ἀλλὰ ἑαυτὸν ἐκένωσεν.

5. The next view is that of the Latin Fathers.[71] They (with exceptions, of course) understood our clause as a statement not of condescension, but of majesty: Christ did not regard his equality with God as a usurpation. Though this view is quite clear in itself, its categorization (is the sense active or passive?) is not: some have seen it as giving ἁρπαγμός an active and abstract sense ('an act of aggression'), but others have taken it as *res rapta* (passive and concrete: Christ did not regard his equality with God as *having been obtained by* usurpation).[72] This view falls, either way, by its own weight: Lightfoot's critique remains very damaging. The natural phrase to follow v.6, if taken in the Latin sense, is ἀλλὰ φύσει (he considered his equality with God to be not a matter of usurpation but something he had by nature).[73] If Paul had wanted to say that Christ's divine equality was his by right, there would surely have been simpler ways of doing so than our present sentence.

A variation on the Latin view is provided by J. Carmignac, who argues that the position of the negative (with the noun, not the verb) indicates that the sentence refers to the *earthly* Christ regarding his divine glory as being his by right.[74] This, however, places an impossible strain on the rest of the

[70]*Pace* Houlden 1970, 75. Was Adam grasping at world sovereignty?

[71]See the very full details in Henry 1950. Other examples of this view are Barclay 1958 and Schumacher 1914–1921.

[72]So Moule 1970, 271 n.1. Moule suggests *res rapienda*, something 'requiring to be snatched', as another possibility; but this view (listed above as no. 4 (d)) is surely not that of the Latin Fathers.

[73]See the *sed natura* of Augustine and Anselm of Canterbury, noted in Carmignac 1971–2, 146, 147, etc.

[74]Carmignac 1971–2. Carmignac's view was anticipated in its essentials by Chamberlain 1892–3, who, beginning from J.A. Beet's articles, argued, without apparently realizing that this is what he was doing, for this variant on the Latin view. Carmignac has been subjected to damaging criticism from Grelot 1973 and Feuillet 1972.

sentence, which then has to read: 'who, during his earthly life, regarded equality with God as being his by right; nevertheless, he *had* emptied himself, and *had* taken on the form of a servant, and *had* been born in the likeness of men....' (Then back to the ordinary aorist again) 'and he humbled himself...'. Carmignac's interesting point, that the negative appears to modify the noun (ἀρπαγμόν) rather than the verb (ἡγήσατο), as one might have expected on grammatical grounds, is fully taken into account once we recognise that the whole phrase is a composite idiom, and that the negative must therefore modify it as a whole, coming before its first word (see below, solution 10).

6. The account of our passage given by K. Barth in the *Church Dogmatics* cannot be fitted into any other category.[75] In one sense it looks like the *res rapta* of the Latin Fathers, in another like Lightfoot's *res retinenda*. Even if it combined those two, that would make it a new variant; but in each part it is subtly different. The crucial passage reads:

> The *kenosis* consists in a renunciation of His being in the form of God alone... He did not treat His form in the likeness of God... as a robber does his booty. He was not bound by it like someone bound by his possessions... He did not treat it as His one and only and exclusive possibility... It was not to him an inalienable necessity to exist only in that form of God... only to be the eternal Word and not flesh...

Strictly speaking, this treats ἀρπαγμός as *res rapta*, something that has been seized, emphasizing (unlike the Latin Fathers' version of *res rapta)* the *attitude towards* one's booty rather than the question of whether or not it actually is booty at all, i.e. whether it is something that has been *obtained by* snatching. Christ, according to Barth, does not regard his equality with God in the manner of a robber gloating greedily over his hoard. Then, whereas the Latin Fathers took the clause as a second assertion (after ὅς ἐν μορφῇ θεοῦ ὑπάρχων) of Christ's divine status, Barth interprets the *res rapta* idea in the sense of *res retinenda*, with the help of the word 'only': Christ's existence *only* in the form of God was 'given up' in favour of the new state of being *both* in the form of God *and* in the form of a servant. But, while Barth's insistence on the continuing divinity of the man Christ Jesus is (I believe) healthy, his ingenious interpretation seems over-subtle; and it hardly does justice to ἐκένωσεν to see it as not so much (within the image being used) as Christ emptying himself of anything but rather as adding to himself something new.

7(a). Several scholars have attempted to read v.6 as a reference not to Christ's pre-existence but to his (perfect) human life. Thus, for instance,

---

[75]*Church Dogmatics* 4.1.180: see too Barth 1947, 59 f. (English translation, 60 ff.).

J. Murphy-O'Connor sees τὸ εἶναι ἴσα θεῷ not as the possession of divine nature, but as the 'right to be *treated* as if he were god', and says that the force of this clause is that Christ did not regard this right 'as something to be used to his own advantage'.[76] It was a right 'of which he was free to dispose'. He had this right not because he actually was God but because he was a sinless human being (an idea also invoked by Dunn at this point in the argument).[77] This kind of view has become popular recently, and it is therefore necessary to point out some of its inherent weaknesses.[78] Murphy-O'Connor seems unclear as to just what the phrase in question means: he leans towards Hoover in the idea of 'using something to one's own advantage', but asserts—in the teeth of Hoover's conclusions—that 'linguistic evidence unclouded by presuppositions weighs the balance of probability decisively in favour of *res retienda*' [*sic*] (pp. 38 f.). The idea that Christ, as a mere man, could ever have had the 'right to be treated as if he were god' is hardly a notion which a Jew could grasp without asking at once whether, in that case, this man had in some sense *always* been God.[79] Again, this interpretation reads a great deal into the phrase τὸ εἶναι ἴσα θεῷ: it has to mean not only 'being treated as if he were God' but also *the right to be* treated thus; and it is never clear whether this right is simply not made use of, or whether it is not claimed at all, or whether it is possessed originally and then given up. Finally, Murphy-O'Connor's view in effect omits v.7, the stage of Christ's becoming human. His own summary of his position (p. 40) jumps, revealingly, straight from v.6 to v.8.[80]

Two other variations on this theme may be noted more briefly.

7(b). J.A.T. Robinson attempted to use Moule's arguments (see below) to support the idea that τὸ εἶναι ἴσα θεῷ referred to the exalted state of the truly human man, given up when Jesus embraced the vocation of suffering and death. This appears to combine the grammatical analysis of ἁρπαγμός as *raptus* (active and abstract, meaning 'self-assertion') with the theological understanding of the clause as *res retinenda*, a thing to be retained.[81]

7(c). P. Trudinger and D.W.B. Robinson both attempted to use the arguments of L.L. Hammerich (see below) to suggest the meaning that Jesus

[76]Murphy-O'Connor 1976, 39 (his italics).

[77]Murphy-O'Connor 40; Dunn 1980, 120 f.

[78]See, for example, the criticisms of Howard 1978, 371 f., Hurst 1986, and Wanamaker 1987. Dunn's reply (1989, xxxiv ff.) does not seem to me to have grasped the point that the Adamic reference does not preclude the presence of a pre-existence theology such as the one I am advocating.

[79]See, on this point, Bauckham 1980–1, 333 ff., and France 1982.

[80]His exposition of vv.7–8 (pp. 42–5) is very unsatisfactory, leaning heavily on the hypothesis (criticized by Howard) of a derivation from wisdom speculation. Howard's own position, however (1976, 377), fares little better: like Murphy-O'Connor he quotes Hoover approvingly while in fact tacitly disagreeing with one of his main conclusions.

[81]Robinson 1973, 162 ff.

refused to use his equality with God as a way of escape from his vocation to suffering.[82] None of these views has received subsequent support. There are, it appears, several different ways of making the subject of ἡγήσατο the human Jesus, some of which imply his pre-existent divinity[83] and some of which do not; but all raise more problems than they solve. The late G.B. Caird, in commenting on a draft of the article underlying the present chapter, wrote that the real difficulty with any 'human Jesus' view of the phrase 'is that it abandons any attempt to take the clauses in chronological, or even logical, order'. This is similar to my point made above in relation to Carmignac.

8. A quite different twist was given to the modern debate when C.F.D. Moule published his article in the first F.F. Bruce *Festschrift*.[84] He argued strongly that ἁρπαγμός is not to be confused with ἅρπαγμα: the -μος ending signifies the action of the verb, the -μα ending its results.[85] This forces him to set on one side the solution of Lightfoot and (since he apparently accepts Lightfoot's understanding of them) the Greek Fathers also, and to support the active, abstract sense of 'snatching', 'grasping': 'he did not regard equality with God as *consisting in* snatching' (266, Moule's italics).

There are more writers on Moule's side than one might realize at first sight. At the beginning of the century not only J. Ross, but also J. A. Beet and, following Ross, W. Warren[86] took this position, for substantially similar reasons to Moule. They had been preceded by the great commentators Meyer and Alford, and have been followed recently not only by Moule but also by J. M. Furness, S. H. Hooke and G.F. Hawthorne.[87] It is harder to assess the position of B. Reicke,[88] since he seems to combine three separate and perhaps ultimately incompatible views. His main emphasis is close to Moule's:

[82]Trudinger 1967–8, 279; D.W.B. Robinson 1968–9, 253 ff. These senses thus take ἁρπαγμός as *raptus*, abstract and passive: 'a being snatched away'. The word *raptus* is of course ambiguous, admitting of both active (=*rapina*) and passive senses.

[83]E.g. Carmignac, Feuillet (at least in his earlier view). As Howard points out (1978, 378 n. 29), Feuillet took this position in order to avoid apparent kenoticism.

[84]Moule 1970.

[85]But what would the 'result' be in this case? See Vokes 1964, 673.

[86]Ross 1909; Beet 1887, 1891–2, 1894; Warren 1911.

[87]Meyer 1885, 68 ff.; Alford 1865, 3.166 f.; Furness 1957–8 (simply a restatement of the position of Ross and Warren); Hooke 1961; Hawthorne 1983, 84 f. See too the theological position of Hooker 1975, 164, though she does not analyse the phrase grammatically in the same way as these writers. Griffiths (1957–8), writing after Furness, misunderstands the position, and aligns it with the *res rapienda* view of Kennedy, Michael 1928, 88 f., and Hunter 1961, 45–51. Hudson 1965–6, referring (presumably) to Furness's article, also adopts the same view as Moule, in opposition to the *res rapienda* view of Harvey 1964–5.

[88]Reicke 1962.

Jésus-Christ,...ne considerait pas son égalité avec Dieu comme une occasion de commettre rapine, de tirer des choses à soi avec violence. (209)

But he then[89] regards this as a description of the *human* Christ, and proceeds (p. 210) to move towards a position somewhat like Lohmeyer's. Finally, F.E. Vokes[90] argues strongly, like Moule, for the strictly abstract meaning of ἁρπαγμός. He acknowledges (672) that, according to the grammarians, the word can, in fact, 'take on a concrete sense', but still follows Ross (and F.C. Baur) in understanding the passage to mean that 'Jesus did not make his being on an equality with God a means for self-aggrandisement, for seizing wealth or booty for himself'.[91]

Some recent writers have referred approvingly to Moule's argument without seeming to know what to do with it, leaving it in the end on one side.[92] Others have argued against it, but few of the arguments are cogent; I shall reply to the major ones when expounding my own position shortly, since several of Moule's points are contained within my own.

9. The Danish philologist L.L. Hammerich proposed a distinct sense which has frequently been confused with Moule's.[93] He agreed with Moule that the word is abstract ('raptus'), referring to the action of the verb, but then took it in a passive sense, meaning 'rapture' in the sense of being caught up to heaven, as in a vision. For an ordinary mortal, experiencing such a thing *would* be a 'rapture', but for the pre-existent Christ it was not; it was his normal state. This gives the meaning that, for Jesus (who was in the form of God), 'the being equal with God was no *rapture*, no ἁρπαγμός; it was his by nature'. Hammerich then says that, in the incarnation, Christ voluntarily 'gave up his nature, his being with God, and debased himself'. He is thus close theologically to the Latin Fathers, while at the same time seeming almost kenotic: Christ gave up his nature. This view has not commended itself to subsequent scholars.

10. Like Lightfoot and Jaeger, R.W. Hoover begins from a study of the Greek idiom which appears to be employed in our clause.[94] Unlike them, he

---

[89]Like Chamberlain 1892–3.

[90]Vokes 1964.

[91]Moule 1970, 275 objects that Vokes then slips back into regarding ἁρπαγμός as a concrete noun (a 'means of self-aggrandisement', Vokes 674 f. (not 624 as in Moule)); but this is surely a linguistic optical illusion. There is hardly any distinction in meaning between 'he did not think that his status *meant* "snatching"' and 'he did not regard his status *as an occasion for* "snatching"'. The parallel phrases offered by Reicke 1962, 209 (eg. Jas. 1.2), show that his sort of meaning is quite possible.

[92]E.g. Dunn 1980, 116, 313 n. 93; Caird 1976, *ad loc* .

[93]Hammerich 1966. Hammerich's views are summarized in English (and his name misspelt) in *Expository Times* lxxviii (1967), 193–4.

[94]Hoover 1971. See the seminal article of Jaeger 1915; and Foerster 1964 (1933); and cf. Gnilka 1980b (1968) 116.

argues not for the sense of 'regard something as a prize (sc. to be clutched on to)', i.e. *res retinenda*, but for the sense of 'regard something as a thing to be taken advantage of'. Though the idiom is parallel in *form* to that which employs ἕρμαιον and εὕρημα, it is not identical in *meaning*. Whereas ἕρμαιον/εὕρημα ἡγεῖσθαί τι means 'to prize something as an unexpected windfall', ἁρπαγμὸν ἡγεῖσθαί τι means 'to regard as something to be taken advantage of' or 'to regard as something to be used for one's own advantage'.[95] However, ἁρπαγμός and ἅρπαγμα do both appear in virtually interchangeable contexts *within this idiom*, both taking on a special sense not identical to their usual one.[96] Despite the impression given by many scholars who have referred to his work, Hoover argues specifically that, *within the context of this idiom*, ἁρπαγμός cannot mean either *res rapienda* or *res retinenda*: the former is ruled out because the object under consideration is always something already possessed, the latter because that meaning would make no sense in the non-biblical examples Hoover has collected. *Res rapta* is likewise ruled out by the idiomatic sense; and, though Hoover does not refer to the line of thought now represented by Moule, an insistence on the abstract (and, for Moule, active) sense of ἁρπαγμός is not warranted. The idiom refers, Hoover argues, not to the act of acquiring something (whether before the time envisaged, i.e. *res rapta*, or after, i.e. *res rapienda*), nor to the act of clinging on to it in a grasping way. It refers to *the attitude one will take towards something which one already has and holds and will continue to have and hold*, specifically, to the question of whether that attitude will or will not consist in taking advantage of this possessed object.

If Hoover is right (and, though his conclusions have often been misunderstood, he has not been conclusively challenged on philological grounds[97]), the views of all the other scholars we have reviewed for the sake of clarity in the current debate are undercut at a stroke. This apparently sweeping judgment may be reinforced by two considerations. First, most of the theories discussed already possess, as we have seen, serious internal weaknesses of their own, which prompt us in any case to look elsewhere. Secondly, Hoover's theory is capable of making excellent theological sense, as we will presently show, and of including within itself many of the strong points of the other theories.

Although Hoover's analysis of the idiom clashes at a formal and philological level with Moule's, the overall sense achieved by both is similar. For both, the action or attitude envisaged is not the grasping of, or clinging

[95]Hoover 102–6, including a discussion of an apparent exception in Isodore of Pelusium, *Ep.* iv.22. Hoover's evidence runs counter to Lightfoot's interpretation of the same passages (Hoover 108 f. n. 20), and to Arndt and Gingrich col. 108.

[96]Details in Hoover 102 ff.

[97]The sole challenge has come from O'Neill 1988: see below, 85 f.

on to, equality with God, but the attitude—of advantage-taking, of 'getting', of behaving like an oriental despot—*based on* that equality. For both, ultimately, the word is abstract and active with a *future* connotation (what one will, or might, do on the basis of something), as opposed to the Latin Fathers' *rapina*, which was abstract and active with a *past* connotation (what one might be supposed to have done). The Latin understanding could, as we saw, equally well be presented as concrete (*res rapta*) and passive, since the thing one might be supposed to have grasped was the τι in question, in this case τὸ εἶναι ἴσα θεῷ. But for Moule and Hoover the 'grasping' or 'advantage-taking' does not *aim at* τὸ εἶναι ἴσα θεῷ: it *begins from* it. Nevertheless, in English at least it is just as easy, and not damaging to the meaning, to turn the phrase around and express the same idea in concrete and passive terms: 'he did not regard his equality with God *as something to be used for his own advantage*'.[98] If Hoover is right, a native speaker of Hellenistic Greek, faced with that English sentence, would very likely, and quite correctly, render it into idiomatic Greek in the very words of Philippians 2.6. And because of this closeness of actual significance, it is not difficult to see how in fact ἁρπαγμός and ἅρπαγμα could, *precisely within this idiom*, be so nearly interchangeable in meaning.[99] The word, within the same sentence, could, depending on how one might look at it, be *either* abstract *or* concrete without a change in the actual meaning of the total sense-unit. And that meaning, combining Moule's theology and Hoover's philology, is 'Christ did not consider his equality with God as something to take advantage of...'.

This theory has a further incidental advantage. The proposal of J. Carmignac, discussed earlier, hinged on the fact that in Greek the negative adverb οὐ/οὐχ normally comes immediately before the verb it modifies, so that for it to precede a noun instead, as here, suggests that it is the noun *rather than the verb* which is negated. But if, as Hoover has so strongly argued, the phrase ἁρπαγμὸν ἡγεῖσθαί τι *as a whole* forms a recognizable idiom, then the natural place for the οὐ(χ) to come is before the phrase as a whole: which is exactly what we find. It is as though, in English, the phrase were hyphenated: 'he did not consider-it-something-to-take-advantage-of'.

It is probably in this category that W. Foerster should be placed.[100] The proverbial meaning—a contrast between what one might expect someone to do and what Christ actually did—is in fact quite close to Hoover's sense:

---

[98]See the comment of Vokes 1964, 672, referring to some similar abstract nouns which take on a concrete sense.

[99]For other similar pairs which come to be more or less interchangeable, see e.g. Lightfoot 1868, 109, etc.

[100]Foerster 1964 <1933> (= *Theological Dictionary of the New Testament*, ed. G. Kittel, i.472 ff.); see also the discussion in Gnilka 1980b <1968>, 116. Foerster is not to be dismissed, as he is by Martin 153, as though he were 'taking the phrase as a complete proverb which has no Christological value, except perhaps an incidental one'.

'Jesus did not regard equality with God as a gain to be utilized.'[101] Foerster is, however, quite vague in his exposition of this idea and its alternatives, only giving three possible senses and dismissing the active sense[102] with the objection, noted already, about the lack of an object.

Hoover has also been supported by L. Cerfaux and, in his most recent comments, A. Feuillet. The latter leaves his previous view and Hoover's as alternatives: 'Le Christ...n'avait pas régardé comme un bien précieux à saisir d'être traité sur la terre à l'égal de Dieu' (i.e. *res rapienda*), 'ou encore comme un avantage à exploiter d'être par nature égal à Dieu.'[103] Despite the formal differences occasioned by Cerfaux's reading of ἁρπαγμός in a passive sense ('Le butin...c'est plutot un objet possédé'), his overall understanding corresponds closely to Hoover's. Christ did not regard his equality with God as something to be exploited for his own gain.[104]

This position has considerable strength, more than its proponents have usually realized. Before proceeding to demonstrate this, it may be helpful to display the ten senses now outlined.[105] The columns show, respectively, the meaning assigned to μορφή,[106] to τὸ εἶναι ἴσα θεῷ, the result of the action of ἡγήσατο, and the grammatical description, and sense, of ἁρπαγμός itself. The final column lists representative holders of the view in question, or a label by which it is well known.

[101]Foerster 474.

[102]For which he cites (474 n. 7) Ewald, Schmidt, and G. Kittel.

[103]Feuillet 1972, 132. This latter idea, as he rightly sees, is not far from that of Cerfaux (1951, 290), who (after only a brief review of the debate, and with no reference to others who take this view) writes that Christ's equality with God is 'un objet possédé sans doute justement mais dont il ne faut pas user orgeuilleusement et comme par bravade'.

[104]Collange 1973, 90, comes close to this without seeing that it is substantially the same theological position as that of Furness and Vokes, which he had earlier rejected. Ridderbos 1975, 74 f., expounds a position apparently similar to Hoover's: 'Christ did not regard this equality, in which he already shared, as a privilege that had come to him for his own advantage, on the ground of which he could have refused the way of self-emptying and humiliation.' But Ridderbos misleadingly classifies this view as *res rapta*. See too Gnilka 1980b <1968>, 116 f. Schenk 1984, 212 translates: '... hielt er diese Würdegleichheit wirklich nicht für einen auszunutzenden Vorteil...'; but he reaches this on very different grounds to those I have used. See too Ernst 1974, 67 ('nicht egoistisch für sich ausnützen'), though he seems to think there is no difficulty in arriving at this meaning, and offers no argument for it except the good sense it makes of the passage—with which, of course, I agree.

[105]I have not attempted to show on this table the further position of O'Neill 1988, who proposes to substitute μή for τό: οὐχ ἁρπαγμὸν ἡγήσατο μὴ εἶναι ἴσα θεῷ, invoking an old friend of textual critics, the pious scribe, as the culprit who gave a more apparently 'orthodox' reading of a text which originally described the humility of Christ, who 'thought it not robbery not to be equal with God'. If texts can have negatives inserted at will, they can be made to mean literally anything. O'Neill's description of his proposal as 'modest' is a fine example of Swiftean irony.

[106]There is no space here to go into the details of debate about this word. For our purposes it is sufficient to note (a) whether or not it is taken as in some sense a preindication of divinity and (b) whether or not it is more or less parallel in meaning to τὸ εἶναι ἴσα θεῷ.

Jesus Christ is Lord: Philippians 2.5–11

μορφή	τὸ εἶναι ἴσα θεῷ	Meaning of οὐχ...ἡγήσατο	Analysis of ἁρπαγμός	Representative or label
1. divine	divine prerogatives	abandoned	idiom: understood as 'prize', i.e. *res retinenda*	Lightfoot
2. divine	divinity itself	abandoned	passive and concrete: *res retinenda*, though often called *res rapta*	Kenotic
3. pre-existent Urmensch	(a) divine state already possessed	abandoned	passive and concrete: *res retinenda*, often called *res rapta*	Käsemann
	(b) divine state *not* already possessed	not snatched at	passive, concrete: *res rapienda*	Cullmann
4.(a) not yet divine	divine equality	not snatched at	passive, concrete: *res rapienda*	Kennedy
(b) divine, but not yet cosmocrator	cosmocrator, independent of the Father	not snatched at	passive, concrete: *res rapienda* (wrongly described as idiomatic and as combining *res rapta* and *res rapienda*)	Lohmeyer, Martin
(c) divine	divine honours enjoyed during incarnation	not snatched at	passive, concrete: *res rapienda*	Feuillet
(d) divine	divine likeness (like Adam's)	not needing to be snatched at (because already possessed)	passive, concrete: *res rapienda*	Hooker
5. divine	divine equality	(a) not obtained by snatching	passive, concrete: *res rapta*	Latin Fathers
		(b) not equivalent to robbery	active, abstract: *raptus*	Latin Fathers, understood differently
	(c) divine equality *during incarnation*	regarded as not being an act of usurpation	active, abstract: *raptus/rapina*	Carmignac
6. divine	divine equality (and that alone)	not regarded as having been stolen and therefore as something to cling on to	passive, concrete: *res rapta/res rapienda*	Barth
7. human	(a) the right to be treated as divine	not claimed/clung to	passive, concrete: *res retinenda*, but some hints of *rapienda* too	Murphy-O'Connor
	(b) divine equality *qua* truly human being	not meaning self-assertion	active, abstract: *raptus*, but hints of *retinenda* too	J.A.T. Robinson
	(c) divine equality	not regarded as entitling Jesus to Ascension/last-minute deliverance	passive, abstract: *raptus*	Trudinger, D.W.B. Robinson
8. divine	divine equality	not regarded as meaning 'snatching'	active, abstract: *raptus*	Moule
9. divine	divine equality	not regarded as a heavenly 'rapture', i.e. it was his by right (yet given up)	passive, abstract: *raptus* with hints of *retinenda* too	Hammerich
10. divine	divine equality, already possessed	not regarded as something to be taken advantage of	idiomatic usage, with sense determined by whole phrase	Hoover

It is interesting to note at this point the way in which the modern English translations have tried to come to terms with the problem. Most opt for ambiguity between *res retinenda* and *res rapienda*: thus RSV 'did not count equality with God a thing to be grasped', and similarly NASV, NIV. The Authorized Version adopted the Latin view ('thought it not robbery to be equal with God'), and the Good News Bible, equally clearly, opted for Martin's, confusions and all ('did not think that by force he should try to become equal with God. Instead, of his own free will he gave it all up'). The NEB and JB retain ambiguity with the help of marginal alternatives. Thus NEB text has *res rapienda* ('did not think to snatch at equality with God'), while the margin suggests *res retinenda* ('did not prize his equality with God'). The Jerusalem Bible glosses its text ('did not cling to his equality with God'—clearly *res retinenda*) with a note explaining that Christ did not regard this equality (further explained as divine honours and prerogatives) as something to grasp (*rapienda*?) or hold on to. Until 1990 none, so far as I have seen, had attempted to express either Moule's or Hoover's understanding; now, however, we have the new RSV: Christ 'did not regard equality with God as something to be exploited'. This may not be perfect, but comes a lot closer than the others. The last part of this section of the chapter will suggest some reasons why this line of thought is emphatically to be preferred.

(c) On Not Taking Advantage

We may begin with Hoover's strongest point. The idiom here used clearly assumes that the object in question—in this case equality with God—is already possessed. One cannot decide to take advantage of something one does not already have. If, therefore, there is to be any ultimate distinction of meaning between Christ's being in the form of God and Christ possessing τὸ εἶναι ἴσα θεῷ, such a distinction does not, at least, involve seeing either phrase as referring to something less than divinity and/or the honours pertaining to that state. Both expressions mark out Christ Jesus, in his pre-existent state, as one who is indeed, and fully, *capax humanitatis*, but at the same time different from all other human beings in his nature and origin.[107]

---

[107]Hoover's study does not of itself rule out the possibility that τὸ εἶναι ἴσα θεῷ (and, *a fortiori*, ἐν μορφῇ θεοῦ ὑπάρχων) could be taken in a strictly humanitarian sense; it only affirms that this equality is already possessed. But we have already argued, on other grounds, against the humanitarian interpretation. The true humanity of Christ, in its differences—precisely in being the genuine, uncorrupted article!—from all other examples of humanity, is perhaps the point of the irony (noted by Hooker 1975, 163 f.) in the words ὁμοίωμα and σχῆμα.

A further reason, not usually noticed, for taking τὸ εἶναι ἴσα θεῷ in close connection with ὅς ἐν μορφῇ θεοῦ ὑπάρχων is the regular usage of the articular infinitive (here, τὸ εἶναι) to refer 'to something previously mentioned or otherwise well known'.[108] Among over a dozen possible examples are Romans 7.18 (τὸ γὰρ θέλειν παράκειταί μοι, τὸ δὲ κατεργάζεσθαι τὸ καλὸν οὔ, where both infinitives refer to the immediately preceding discussion) and 2 Corinthians 7.11 (τὸ κατὰ θεὸν λυπηθῆναι, 'this (just mentioned) godly grief'). We should therefore expect that τὸ εἶναι κτλ. in our present passage would refer back, epexegetically, to ὅς ἐν μορφῇ θεοῦ ὑπάρχων, and might even suggest the stronger translation 'this divine equality'. Among other corollaries, this clearly indicates the impossibility of any *res rapienda* view which begins from the assumption that Christ, although in the form of God, did not yet possess divine equality.[109]

The sense of οὐχ ἁρπαγμὸν ἡγήσατο will then be that Christ, in contrast to what one might have expected (this is the force of Foerster's point), refused to take advantage of his position. This is not (as, for instance, in Feuillet's view) a matter of not adopting, in his incarnate existence, a life-style of divine splendour, whatever that might mean in practice. The emphasis of v.7 shows that the refusal described by the phrase was a refusal to use for his own advantage the glory which he had from the beginning. The all-important difference in meaning between this view and the standard *retinenda* approaches is that *nothing described by either* ἐν μορφῇ θεοῦ ὑπάρχων *or by* τὸ εἶναι ἴσα θεῷ *is given up*; rather, it is reinterpreted, understood in a manner in striking contrast to what one might have expected. Over against the standard picture of oriental despots, who understood their position as something to be used for their own advantage, Jesus understood his position to *mean* self-negation, the vocation described in vv.7–8. In Moule's phrase, divine equality does not mean 'getting' but 'giving'. It is properly expressed in self-giving love. We could then translate v.6 f.: 'who, being in the form of God, did not regard this divine equality as something to be used for his own advantage, but rather emptied himself...'[110]

If we apply this understanding of vv.6 f. to the passage as a whole, a new coherence results. The pre-existent son regarded equality with God not as

---

[108]Blass-Debrunner-Funk 1973, 205; rightly seen by Hawthorne 1983, 84.

[109]E.g. Wanamaker 1987, 188 f.

[110]Professor Moule points out to me that ὑπάρχων can then be understood not as concessive but as causative—'precisely because he was... he recognized what it meant'. This potential ambiguity is not without parallel in Paul: see, e.g., Rom. 9.22 (θέλων). If my whole argument is correct, the causative sense is clearly the one required. G.B. Caird, commenting on a draft of this part of this chapter, suggested the following: 'he was in the form of God, and did not regard his equality with God... but rather...' Some biblical and historical examples of the sort of behaviour contrasted here, by implication, with that of Jesus are suggested by Cholmondeley 1895–6, 47–8. Perhaps the most suggestive passage would be 1 Kgs. 3.4–15, 28 (not mentioned by Cholmondeley).

excusing him from the task of (redemptive) suffering and death, but actually as uniquely qualifying him for that vocation. It is here, not in the views of Käsemann or Martin, that the real underlying soteriology of the 'hymn' is to be found.[111] As in Romans 5.6 ff., the death of Jesus is understood as the appropriate revelation, in action, of the love of God himself (compare too 2 Corinthians 5.19). ἐκένωσεν does not refer to the loss of divine attributes, but—in good Pauline fashion[112]—to making something powerless, emptying it of apparent significance. The real humiliation of the incarnation and the cross is that one who was himself God, and who never during the whole process stopped being God, could embrace such a vocation. The real theological emphasis of the hymn, therefore, is not simply a new view of Jesus. It is a new understanding of God. Against the age-old attempts of human beings to make God in their own (arrogant, self-glorifying) image, Calvary reveals the truth about what it meant to be God. Underneath this is the conclusion, all-important in present christological debate: incarnation and even crucifixion are to be seen as *appropriate* vehicles for the dynamic self-revelation of God.

This view is strengthened by five considerations. First, it makes sense of the relevant extra-biblical Greek evidence. Though the majority of the Patristic references to Philippians 2 do not help very much in elucidating our phrase, there are one or two passages which, it may be claimed, fit very well into the case for which I have argued. Most of the Latin Fathers, as we saw, and among the Greeks Chrysostom in particular, were so concerned to combat Arianism that they read the clause not as a statement of condescension but as an affirmation of rightful divinity.[113] To this extent Lightfoot's analysis is correct: the earlier, and linguistically closer, Patristic evidence is in favour of reading the clause as (part of) a statement of Christ's humility. But beyond that most of the references pose the same problem as our text itself. Lightfoot is right in what he denies—that the Greek Fathers supported the Latin view—but wrong in what he affirms (the *retinenda* view). This does not mean, as Moule suggests (p. 268), that the Greek Fathers have led us up the garden path; merely that we have read them wrongly, which is all too easy to do since, with most of the references being themselves allusions to our passage, we have no external standard from which to get our bearings.

There are, however, just a few passages which lend support to my argument. In Eusebius' *Historia Ecclesiae* 5.2.2 the writer quotes from the

[111]See the valid criticism of Martin by Marshall 1968, 124 f., and the warning of Hurtado 1984, 123 f. against trying to force soteriology on to a passage which is about something else.

[112]See Hooker 1975, citing, e.g. Rom. 4.14; 1 Cor. 1.17; 9.15; 2 Cor. 9.3.

[113]See the surveys, already noted, by Henry 1950; Feuillet 1972, 113 ff.; Grelot 1971, 897–922, 1009–26; Gewiess 1963, 75–81. Compare also Lightfoot's account (134 f.) of Chrysostom's position.

letter circulated by the churches in Lyons and Vienne, and describes how the martyrs, despite their sufferings, would neither proclaim themselves as martyrs nor allow others to address them as such. This, says the document, is evidence of their imitation of Christ, with a reference to Philippians 2.6. It is easy to see how Hoover's sense will work here: the martyrs did not regard their sufferings as something to take advantage of. Eusebius clearly regards them as martyrs anyway; there is no question of their refusing to grasp at a glory they did not possess, or of actually giving up one they did. They continued to be Christlike martyrs, and *as evidence of that* (in Eusebius' eyes) they did not use the fact as something to take advantage of.[114] In a subsequent passage (8.12.1 f.), in which Philippians 2.6 is not quoted but may well be in mind, Eusebius describes the martyrs of Antioch who, to avoid torture, committed suicide, τὸν θάνατον ἅρπαγμα θέμενοι τῆς τῶν δυσσεβῶν μοχθηρίας. This *could* be read as *res rapienda*. O'Neill tries to get from the text a sense which, he claims, is different to Hoover's: 'this death was regarded as an actual piece of good fortune, stolen from cruel men...'[115] But Hoover's understanding seems to me more probable.[116] The martyrs knew that they were going to die anyway. But, instead of regarding that death as something to be feared or shunned, they regarded it as something to be taken advantage of, to the extent that they were prepared to anticipate their execution by committing suicide, thus using the death they were going to die anyway as an opportunity for stealing a march on their persecutors. The other relevant texts from Eusebius are adequately discussed by Hoover. The disputed passage from Cyril of Alexandria's comment on the angel's visit to Lot also supports his view,[117] and actually makes Moule's philological position very difficult. In the vital passage οὐχ ἁρπαγμὸν τὴν παραίτησιν ὡς ἐξ ἀδρανοῦς καὶ ὑδαρεστέρας ἐποιεῖτο φρενός, the meaning cannot be—as it would have to be if Moule were correct—that Lot did not regard the angels' refusal[118] as *meaning* advantage-taking, as though it (i.e. the refusal) had come from a feeble and vacillating mind. The sense must be that Lot renewed his invitation because, unlike someone with a feeble and vacillating mind, he did not regard their refusal as something to take advantage of.[119]

---

[114]So Foerster 1930; Hoover 1971, 108 f.; Martin 1983, 146; Feuillet 1972, 130.

[115]O'Neill 1988, 446.

[116]Hoover, 109: 'There can be no suggestion of robbery or of violent self-assertion in this remark, nor can a self-inflicted death under such circumstances be considered an unanticipated windfall. [This last is the point which tells against O'Neill.] What is said is that, given the alternative, death seemed an advantage to be seized.' I find this altogether clearer than O'Neill's alternative.

[117]*De Ador*. 1. 25 (*PG* 68.172c); see Hoover 110 f.

[118]Martin 144 understands παραίτησις here as 'demand'; this seems clearly wrong.

[119]O'Neill 1988, 446 f., has objected to Hoover's reading here. He takes παραίτησις as 'entreaty', and suggests 'revocable' as a translation for ἁρπαγμόν: 'Lot considered his entreaty as not to be revoked'. This seems to me very strained, both in general and in its treatment of

Second, this view explains the relation of vv.9–11 and vv.6–8 in a much more satisfying way than the other views. The logic which underlies the διό in v.9—the turning-point in the hymn—is best understood as follows:[120] 'and *that* is why...'. The exaltation of the crucified one is not to a nature or rank which only then became appropriate for him. The honor given to Christ in vv.9–11 includes the title κύριος, and the adoration which, according to Isaiah 45.23 (quoted in Philippians 2.10), belongs to the one God and to him alone. But this is not a mere apotheosis of a hero as a reward for a difficult job well done. Nor is it the climax merely of a passage *per ardua ad astra*. It is organically related to what has gone before. It is the affirmation, by God the Father, that the incarnation and death of Jesus really was the revelation of the divine love in action.[121] In giving to Jesus the title κύριος,[122] and in granting him to share that glory which, according to Isaiah, no one other than Israel's God is allowed to share, God the Father is as it were endorsing that interpretation of divine equality which, according to v.6, the Son adopted. Christ's exaltation and divine honor are the public recognition that what was accomplished in his obedience and death was the outworking of the very character of God, the revelation of *divine* love. There is then no sense of an arbitrary reward in v.9, nor of an exaltation to a divine rank or nature not already possessed (both before and during his human life). The connection between the two parts of the hymn works better, it may be claimed, on this

---

ἁρπαγμόν in particular. Sensing its weakness, perhaps, O'Neill says that even if we take παραίτησις as 'refusal' we must read the line as 'Lot did not consider the angels' refusal as an occasion for reaping an advantage'—which, although it differs technically in grammar from Hoover's understanding, makes in fact exactly the same point. O'Neill's objection, that Hoover has to add 'his invitation' as the object of the main verb, is not telling: the positioning of ἐποιεῖτο in the sentence makes it clear that the ὡς-phrase goes with the idiomatic clause. The meaning must be, in other words, that Lot did not regard the angels' refusal as something to take advantage of, as he would have had he been faint-hearted. This is, incidentally, supported by the Latin translation of Cyril given in *PG* 68.171: *neque tanquam frigide parvumque ex animo illos invitaret, illorum excusationem pro occasione rapuit*. O'Neill's objection to Hoover's reading of another Eusebius text, from the commentary on Luke (*PG* 24.537c: see Hoover 109, O'Neill 446), seems to me to amount to no more than a rewording of the same reading (Hoover: 'crucifixion was not an honour to be shunned, but an advantage to be seized'; O'Neill, 'he thought of it as... the act of reaping an advantage'). The difference between seizing and reaping an advantage does not seem to me great enough to warrant O'Neill's claim to have successfully challenged Hoover's reading of the idiom.

[120]See, on this point, Caird 1976, 123, and Moule 1972a, 97. My argument in this section includes by implication a critique of other proponents of a non-incarnational reading of Phil. 2, e.g. J.A.T. Robinson 1973, 162 ff.

[121]See Hurtado 1984, 124 f.

[122]Against e.g. Moule 1970, 270.

view than on any other.[123]

Third, the whole hymn as I have interpreted it, and not merely vv.6–8, fits very well into the paraenetic context both of vv.1–5 and (though this is not so often discussed) of vv.12 ff. Käsemann may have been right to reject Lohmeyer's comparatively shallow ethicizing of the passage. But this should not prevent a very thorough integration of the hymn into its context in Philippians. The verbal links (e.g. ταπεινοφροσύνη, ἡγούμενοι in v.3: ὑπηκούσατε, v.12: see too μέχρι θανάτου, v.30) are undergirded by a common *theme*. 'If you are really in Christ, indwelt by the Spirit, inspired by the divine love, prove it by acting this way, the way of divine self-abnegation' (vv.1–4); 'be obedient, don't grumble—God is at work in you, so behave as his children in the world' (vv.12–16). If we read the hymn as I have suggested the paraenetic significance does not stop with v.8, as Martin suggests,[124] but continues all through. God himself recognizes and endorses self-abnegation as the proper expression of divine character. This removes any doubt in the Philippians' mind as to the nature of the behaviour to which they are urged in vv.1–5. It is not merely the imitation of Christ: it is the outworking of the life of the Spirit of God. Though the word ἀγάπη is not used in the hymn itself (as it is in vv.1–2), vv.6–8 might almost serve as a definition of what it means in practice—and vv.9–11 would then affirm that this love is none other than the love of God himself, at work supremely in Christ and now also, by his Spirit, in his people. The implication is clear: as God endorsed Jesus' interpretation of what equality with God meant in practice, so he will recognize self-giving love in his people as the true mark of the life of the Spirit. Christ's own example is held up for the church to imitate; not that his incarnation, death and exaltation are *merely* exemplary, but they are *at least* that.[125]

This point, too, meshes with the underlying Adam-christology of the poem. As Caird pointed out, for the passage to work in its paraenetic context (2.3–5,

[123]There is certainly no need to split the hymn up as does Jervell (1960). My view of the passage does not necessarily require that the prefix ὑπερ- in the verb ὑπερύψωσεν (v.9) should be taken to indicate Jesus' exaltation to a higher glory than that which he possessed at the beginning, and it is quite likely that the prefix should not, in fact, be pressed in this way. Nevertheless, this view does make available a possible sense of further exaltation, which is not the same as that suggested by Martin (1983, 240 ff.) and others. In his exaltation Christ does not merely return to a state of glory corresponding to that of his pre-existence, but is now exalted as *man*, God's intended ruler of the world. Here again the *appropriateness* of the incarnation is underlined. See ch. 2 above, in relation to 1 Cor. 15.

[124]See Marshall's criticisms (1968, 117 ff.), and similarly Stanton 1974, 101 f.; Larsson 1962, 230 ff. Larsson (234) rightly compares Rom. 15.1–7; see also Hoover 1971, 118.

[125]The objections of Käsemann 1968 to an ethical interpretation of the hymn are really objections, on quite non-exegetical grounds, to a soteriology that focuses exclusively on *Imitatio Christi*—which I am certainly not advocating. Käsemann is adequately answered at this point by e.g. Hooker 1975.

87

12 ff.), the point being made must be that, in contrast to Adam's grasping at a status to which he had no right, Christ voluntarily renounced a status to which he had every right.[126] In fact, this is supported not only by the immediate paraenetic context, but also by the further application of the same point in 3.4 ff., where Paul describes the glories of his position as a Jew and tells how, for the sake of gaining Christ, he had turned his back on them. The christological pattern worked out in the doctrine of justification is one of privilege renounced, leading to death and to new life the other side of death (3.7–11; see below). In other words, the undoubted presence of Adam-christology here does not mean that Adam and Christ *must* be parallel in *every way*, that Christ must have 'faced the same archetypal choice that confronted Adam.'[127] On the contrary, we have already seen that in fact the task of the second Adam was more than merely succeeding where the first Adam failed, and we can now see that the logic of Philippians 2 and 3 requires that Christ and Adam should *not* be set in exact parallel.

Fourth, the frequently observed parallel between 2.6 ff. and 3.4 ff.[128] works very well on this understanding. Moule (247 f.) is anxious that the parallel would only hold if, as Paul had flung away what formerly seemed precious to him, receiving in exchange something else, so Christ had 'deemed equality with God sheer loss' and had abandoned it. I suggest, however, that in 3.4 ff. Paul is first outlining the privileged status he enjoyed (and continued, in some senses to enjoy) as a member of Israel, the people of God, and then showing that, because of Christ, this membership had to be regarded as something not to be taken advantage of. He did not give up his membership; he understood it in a new way, avoiding all possibility of taking advantage of it for self-aggrandisement. This clearly fits into the context of 3.2–3, in which Paul transfers attributes of Israel to the church in Christ. Belonging to God's people did not, he now realized, mean a privileged status, outward symbols of superiority, an elevated moral stature in the world. It meant dying and rising with the Messiah. In hoping for vindication at the resurrection (3.11) Paul is claiming that the thing which, for him as an erstwhile Pharisee, had always been the hope of God's people, was now to be his because, and only because, he was 'in Christ'. So, in 2.5–11, Christ, as himself the true Jew, had led the way for this reinterpretation of what it meant to be the people of God.

Various elements in the position I am advocating have been subject to criticisms, and these must now be answered by way of conclusion. Lightfoot regarded the view of Meyer and Alford, which is similar to that of Moule, as

---

[126]Caird 1976, 121. The link with the paraenetic context is clearly made by the repetition of the verb ἡγεῖσθαι; see Hooker 1975, 152 f.

[127]Dunn 1980, 117.

[128]See Hooker 1990, 7 f.; and above, n.8.

'somewhat strained', but this subjective judgment was really part of his overall view of the meaning of the idiomatic phrase—which, as we have seen, has to be modified in the light of Hoover's arguments. Foerster and Martin[129] argue that Moule's meaning is impossible on the grounds that, if the word has an active sense, it should have an object. But, as Moule replies, this simply misses the point. An abstract noun like 'snatching', 'grasping', or 'getting' does not need an object; it refers, intransitively, to a particular way of life, namely, that which characterized pagan rulers, and indeed pagan gods and goddesses such as the Philippians might have worshipped in their pre-Christian days.[130] Martin's more recent objection[131] confirms the impression that he has not understood Moule's point, but is merely treating his view as if it were (a) dependent on that of Hammerich and (b) subject to the weaknesses of the old Latin view (with which he confused Ross's position in *Carmen Christi*: see above). Moule's interpretation—and, *mutatis mutandis*, mine—does not lose the mutual tension between vv.6 and 7, as Martin claims. V.6 says that Christ did not regard his status in one way; v.7 says that he took the opposite way instead. It is of course true that to say 'he did not regard *x* as *y*' could be stated in the form 'he regarded *x* as *not-y*', and *not-y* would then become an anticipation, albeit in negative terms, of the next clause, which states how he acted on that basis. But this is a mere verbal trick, which does not alter the tension or the sequential progress of the hymn. The fact that v.6 states a *thought*, and v.7 an *action*, is itself evidence of this. Martin's restatement of his own position ('v.6b...states what Christ might have done, i.e. seized equality with God; only in v.7 does it say what he chose to do, i.e. give himself') is in fact an overstatement. V.6b does not simply 'state what Christ might have done': it says that he did not do it. Allowing for this, Martin's way of formulating the passage to demonstrate its tension and movement could very easily be reworded into Moule's view, or mine, with the tension perfectly well maintained: Christ might have regarded his equality with God as meaning snatching (or, as something to take advantage of), but on the contrary he chose (to regard it as meaning) the way of self-giving, and, further, to act on that understanding.[132]

Moule disarmingly suggests some potential weaknesses in his view, but they are not in fact as damaging as they might seem. We have already seen that the Greek Fathers' use may not be as far from his as it would appear from Lightfoot's reading of them. Nor, as we have seen, is the parallel between 2.5–11 and 3.2–11 lost (Moule, 274); it is in fact enhanced. Finally,

---

[129]Following Kennedy 1912, 436 f. For Foerster see above, pp. 79 f.

[130]See an alternative counter-argument in Beet 1887, 122.

[131]In his New Century Commentary (1976), pp. 96 f., and his new introduction to *Carmen Christi* (1983), xxii f.

[132]See Moule's parody, 1970, 269.

Moule feels as a weakness the fact that vv.7–8 appear now to indicate not a descent from 'equality with God', but the true expression of that equality—which looks odd in that it destroys the apparent pattern of 'descent and ascent' (273).[133] Moule's own answer to this is that we are in the presence of irony: *'essentially,* that humiliation *was* itself exaltation' (274, Moule's italics). But this is surely unnecessary. To read ἁρπαγμός as he has done does not *identify* the humiliation of Bethlehem and Calvary with the exaltation either of the pre-existent glory or the post-Easter triumph. There is still a real 'humiliation' followed by a real 'exaltation', and to use the latter word to describe the former event, while obliquely making an important theological point, may in fact obscure the real issue. Better, perhaps, to say that the *via crucis* of 2.6–8, consisting as it does in a real change of state, a real humiliation, for the pre-existent one, is—admittedly only to the hindsight of faith—the full revelation of what it meant, in practice, to be equal with God. The one who was eternally 'equal with God' expressed that equality precisely in the sequence of events referred to in vv.6–8.[134]

(iv) Adam and the Incarnate Lord

But perhaps the strongest argument for the solution I have proposed is that it is able to integrate three elements within the poem which are sometimes held to be mutually exclusive. Christ as Adam, Christ as Servant, and Christ the pre-existent one—these are not usually combined, and are in fact sometimes played off against each other. I have already argued that, since both Adam-christology and Servant-christology are really Israel-christologies, they belong well together, here and elsewhere. It is now possible and necessary to show, against the run of much current discussion, that Adam-christology coheres extremely well with the incarnational theology I am proposing for the poem as a whole. The parallel between Christ and Adam in the poem has often been thought to necessitate the *res rapienda* view, in which Christ does not yet possess equality with God; Dunn uses it as the basis of his particular interpretation, in which the hymn simply refers to Jesus as a human being; so that opponents of either of these ideas have often felt compelled to deny the presence of Adam-imagery here.[135] But this is

---

[133]This point is seized on by Nagata 1981, quoted by Martin 1983, loc.cit., who contrasts the 'static' nature of Moule's scheme with the 'sequential' progress of the hymn. But this, as we have seen, is to misunderstand the real nature of Moule's view.

[134]Martin 1983, xxiii, follows Nagata in claiming that the οὐχ... ἀλλά... sequence 'militates against seeing two sides to Christ's being equal with God as if they were complementary'. But this is nothing like what Moule is saying.

[135]See e.g. Wanamaker 1987. Wanamaker has demonstrated, I think, the probability of 'Son of God' imagery here as well, but this should not be taken to exclude the (to me quite clear) Adamic reference.

unnecessary.[136] The contrast between Adam and Christ works perfectly within my view: Adam, in arrogance, thought to become like God; Christ, in humility, became human.

Adam-christology has been used, in particular, as the basis of an argument against seeing any reference to Christ's pre-existence in the poem. Until recently it was an automatic assumption that in this passage above all others Paul attributed to the one whom he now knew as Jesus of Nazareth, the Lord Christ, an existence prior to his human birth. Moreover, during this existence this figure made a conscious choice, described in the two verbs οὐχ ἡγήσατο...ἀλλὰ ἐκένωσεν. This traditional view has found it easy to read v.6 as the Pauline equivalent of, say, John 1.1–14, and to align it with such other passages as 2 Corinthians 8.9, in which a similar choice appears to be attributed to the pre-existent Christ, and with passages like 1 Corinthians 8.6; Colossians 1.15–20, which have usually been taken to refer to the activity of this same figure in mediating the creation of the world. The majority of scholars this century have agreed that this view of Jesus stems from pre-Christian speculation about a heavenly redeemer figure, though the precise origin of such speculation has remained a matter of considerable debate. This view has, however, come under strong attack in the last few years, notably from Professor J.D.G. Dunn, who may be regarded as the leading proponent of the view that, since the poem likens Christ to Adam, no reference to 'incarnation' can be intended.

It will be clear that I agree with Dunn in his assertion that Adam-christology is central to the passage, and, more particularly, in his seeing Philippians 2.6–8 as setting up a contrast between Christ's obedience and Adam's sin, and 2.9–11 as placing Christ in the role designed for man, namely Lord of the world (in obedience to God). I also find completely convincing his arguments against a gnostic background for the hymn and in favor of a Jewish one, and agree totally when he rejects the idea of a pre-existent *man* as the controlling concept in 2.6 ff.[137] Dunn's underlying polemic against the incarnational soteriology that he sees as a corollary of the 'pre-existence' view of 2.6 f. is likewise in order up to a point. It is quite true that an over-emphasis on incarnation, i.e. to the exclusion or at least the downplaying of the cross and resurrection, pulls Paul's theology badly out of shape. But his central contention is subject to certain very damaging objections.

(a) The hymn, both in outline and in detail, makes much more sense if we see Christ and Adam as contrasted but not in strict parallelism—exactly, of course, as we saw in Romans 5.12–21.[138] Christ's obedience is not simply the

---

[136] See above, pp.57–62; and Martin 1983, xxi.

[137] Against Cullmann 1963, 174 ff.

[138] Above, ch. 2. Cf. Hooker 1990, 98 f.

replacement of Adam's disobedience. It does not involve merely the substitution of one sort of humanity for another, but the solution of the problem now inherent in the first sort, namely, sin. The temptation of Christ was not to snatch at a forbidden equality with God, but to cling to his rights and thereby opt out of the task allotted to him, that he should undo the results of Adam's snatching.[139] As Lohmeyer pointed out, only of a divine being can it be said that he was *obedient* unto death, since for all other human beings since Adam's death comes as a mere necessity. (Murphy-O'Connor's objection to this causes more problems than it solves, since it postulates the sudden appearance of a sinless human being, whose sinlessness was a known fact that became the basis of a good deal of theological speculation, without anyone raising the question as to *how* such total obedience was possible, or what it implied about the person concerned.)[140] And, as Marshall has argued, vv.6–7 are very odd if the person referred to had never been anything other than a human being.[141] The contrast between Christ and Adam, which Dunn is correct to claim as the context within which the terms of the hymn must have their sense determined,[142] is thus made most effectively if Christ is understood to have renounced the rank and privileges to which he had—and continued to have—every right. The presence of Adam-christology, then, says nothing of itself against pre-existence. It may actually require it, and when we set such a christology alongside the meaning of v.6 for which we have argued it coheres with it very well indeed.[143]

[139]Cf. above, ch. 2, on Rom. 5.15 ff.

[140]Lohmeyer 1961, 41; see Murphy-O'Connor 1976, 42.

[141]See Marshall 1982, 6; also Wanamaker 1987, 182 f.

[142]Dunn 1980, 119.

[143]It is, therefore, not to the point to demonstrate that Adam was not thought of as pre-existent (Dunn 1980, 119). It is not surprising that Dunn has considerable difficulty in showing *how* in some sense Christ faced the same choice as Adam; the parallel he draws with Rom. 7.7 ff. proves, if anything, my point, not his, and he never explains why Christ's freely embracing, within his ministry, the fallen lot of humankind should constitute the archetypal choice by which Adam's sin is undone—nor why, if this choice is the all-important moment in the drama of salvation, Paul does not say so more clearly (120 f.). Rom. 7.7 ff., arguably, picks up the thought of 5.13–14, 20, that the arrival of the Torah effects a new stage in Israel's position. Dunn's paragraph from pp. 120–21 is full of problems. He can hardly claim that 'to press this question' (i.e. the question of when or in what sense the earthly Jesus faced the same sort of choice as Adam) 'is probably...to misunderstand what the hymn is trying to do' when he has been arguing very strongly that Adam-christology is *the* context of meaning within which individual words and ideas must be understood. His alternative ('Quite possibly the author assumed Christ's sinlessness and was in effect trading on its corollary—viz. that he who did not sin need not have died'...Christ's 'whole life constituted his willing acceptance of the sinner's lot'...'every stage of Christ's life and ministry had the character of a fallen lot freely embraced') raises the questions (among others): how could Paul have accounted for Jesus' astonishing sinlessness, and why, if this was so important as the foundation of the train of thought, is it mentioned so rarely? What soteriological value is there in the 'free embracing of a fallen lot' per se—and what precisely does that phrase mean? And, again, *in what way* were these

(b) Turning to the second half of the poem, Dunn is again right to see Adam-christology here, but wrong, I think, in the conclusions he draws from this. Jesus is indeed exalted to the place designed for humanity, according to Psalm 8 (and for the Messiah, according to Psalm 110: see the discussion of 1 Corinthians 15 above). But[144] Paul expresses this in language drawn directly and obviously from Isaiah 45.23, which is not merely taken from a passage whose basic theme is monotheism (see the repeated affirmations of Isaiah 45.5, 6, 14, 18, 21, 22) but is actually the climax of that passage, the fullest statement of the belief that Israel's God, Yahweh, is the only God of all the earth:

> (22) Turn to me and be saved, all the ends of the earth! For I am God, and there is no other. (23) By myself I have sworn, from my mouth has gone forth in righteousness a word that shall not return: 'To me every knee shall bow, every tongue shall swear.' (24) Only in the Lord, it shall be said of me, are righteousness and strength; to him shall come and be ashamed, all who were incensed against him. (25) In the Lord all the offspring of Israel shall triumph and glory.[145]

Whatever value is to be given to κύριος in v.11—whether, that is, it would be recognized as the equivalent of the Tetragrammaton[146]—this use of Isaiah 45 does incomparably more than merely 'add a new dimension to the christological claim.'[147] If we are indeed to 'attune our twentieth-century ears to the concepts and overtones of the 50's and 60's of the first century A.D. in the eastern Mediterranean,' to 'read these texts with a sympathetic sensitivity to the presuppositions of the first readers' (Dunn, 125)—as surely we must—then we can hardly allow ourselves not to notice what would have been glaringly obvious to any even moderately educated Jew, let alone a

---

choices of the human Christ antithetical to Adam's—as they must be for Dunn's whole argument to work?

[144]Moule, in his review of Dunn (*Journal of Theologial Studies* 33 (1982) 259 f.), questions whether 2.9–11 can be 'squeezed into a purely Adamic pattern'. My argument suggests that, while part of the point of 2.9–11 is that this is the place of the true Man, those verses in fact go beyond anything that could be said of any man other than Jesus.

[145]The question of which text Paul intended to refer to here is vexed. The LXX departs in various ways from the Hebrew of Isa. 45, not least at the end of v.23 and the start of v.24. The Hebrew, which unlike the LXX has 'the Lord' at the start of v.24, may have given Paul the clue for his use of the previous verse (the LXX has 'every tongue shall confess to God' at the end of v.23); but the LXX, which puts κύριος and θεός side by side in v.25, could be read by Paul as anticipating the distinction which he makes here and in 1 Cor. 8.6 (see ch. 6 below). Manns 1977 points out that the text corresponds to that in the Targum of Ps-Jonathan.

[146]See Hengel 1976, 77–83; the straightforward equivalence is questioned by e.g. Howard 1977.

[147]Dunn 1980, 118; see too Murphy-O'Connor 1976, 47.

Pharisee of the Pharisees. In Philippians 2.10 f. Paul credits Jesus with a rank and honour which is not only in one sense appropriate for the true Man, the Lord of the world, but is also the rank and honor explicitly reserved, according to scripture, for Israel's God and him alone.

But, if this is so, we can scarcely suppose that Paul did not reflect—indeed, had not already reflected before committing such an enormous claim to writing—on the implications of this identification. And when, within the same passage (specifically, in v.6) we find what, *prima facie*, appears to be precisely the result of such reflection (Christ's 'equality with God'), we are justified in concluding that he had indeed done so. For consider: if the God who will not share his glory with another has now shared it with Jesus (the position asserted in 2.9 ff.), then there are only three possible conclusions that can be drawn. It might be the case that there are now two Gods. Or Jesus—who up until then had been a man and nothing but a man—might now have been totally absorbed into the one God, without (so to speak) remainder. Or there might be a sense—requiring fuller investigation, exploration and clarification, no doubt—in which Jesus, in being exalted to the rank described in 2.9 ff., is receiving no more than that which was always, from before the beginning of time, his by right. As Moule says in his review:

> A polytheist can accommodate the apotheosis of a Heracles. Can a monotheist rank Jesus in a transcendent category (very different from that of a translated Moses or Elijah) and still manage not to perceive that this must imply eternal existence?[148]

It should be clear that Paul remained a monotheist, and never sold out this position to any sort of hellenistic ditheism or polytheism.[149] It is also clear from dozens of passages that he regarded Jesus Christ as still Jesus Christ, not simply absorbed into God the Father. There is obviously the closest of unions between Son and Father, as the last phrase of the hymn indicates: honour to Jesus glorifies the Father. But if Jesus is not one-for-one identical with the Father, and if Paul is still a monotheist, then the assertions of 2.9–11 must mean that Jesus—or, more accurately, the one who *became* Jesus—must have been from all eternity 'equal with God' in the sense of being himself fully divine. When, therefore, we find in this same passage a statement which both appears to assert this on other grounds (see above) and *must* mean this if the logic of the passage is to work, we have every reason to conclude that the statement in question—Philippians 2.6–7—refers to the choice made by the pre-existent one (whom we now know by his human

[148]Moule's review of Dunn (above, n. 144) 262.
[149]Against e.g. Schoeps 1961, 160 ff. See chs. 5, 6 below.

name, Jesus) to be obedient to the saving purposes of the Father by becoming human and dying on a cross.[150]

At the same time, the whole context of Adam-christology enables Paul to hint that this incarnation of a pre-existent divine being, and the subsequent glorification to divine splendour of a crucified man, are not in fact incongruous, but on the contrary appropriate. The task of the man who would represent Israel and so save the world is a task which, in Old Testament language, is (however paradoxically) reserved for God himself. The final position of the obedient man—set in glorious authority over the world, in fulfillment of Genesis 1.26 ff., Psalm 8.4 ff., and Daniel 7.14—is one which (according to Isaiah 45) is thoroughly appropriate for God himself. And, to look at the question from the other side, the nature of a human being, that is, the fact that humans are made in the image of God, means that becoming human is thoroughly appropriate for one who from the beginning was ἐν μορφῇ θεοῦ. It may be that, after all, μορφή here is Paul's way of describing the pre-existent Christ as being, so to speak, a *potential* man. Εἰκών might have implied (as it has, probably rightly, been taken to imply in Colossians 1.15; see below, ch. 5) that the one so described was already a man; the same might be true of ὁμοίωμα. Μορφή does not need to carry these implications, and is thus able to indicate the appropriateness of the becoming human of the pre-existent one without implying that this incarnation has already happened.[151]

From this argument it follows, in relation to the whole debate about incarnational theology in this passage, that much of the usual view of 'pre-existence' is not in line with Paul's conception.

(a) It is not a hellenistic idea, pulling early christology away from its Jewish roots; it has no necessary connection with any gnostic, or Philonic, speculations about an *Urmensch* or Primal Man. Dunn's speculation that the development of christology moved from a non-incarnational Philippians 2 to a gnostic view of the passage (and/or other passages), and thence to the 'orthodox' view of pre-existence, is not nearly so likely as the following alternative: that an incarnational Philippians 2 was taken up (i) by a Greek

---

[150]See ch. 2 above on 1 Cor. 15, and 'son' there. From this perspective it is straightforward to understand 2 Cor 8.9, with almost all scholars, as referring to the choice of the pre-existent one (against Dunn, 121 ff.). It is scarcely 'manichaean' (Dunn, 122) to contrast the glory of his pre-existence with the whole story of his human life and death; the contrast being made is not between divinity and humanity per se (though such a contrast surely still exists!) but between Christ's pre-existent state and the humble humanity, and its consequence, that he actually took.

[151]See the discussion in Kim 1981, 195–200. The objections of Talbert 1967 can be quite easily overcome: to his summary (141 n.2) it may be answered (a) that kenosis is, as we have seen, not required, (b) that 2 Cor. 8.9 provides a good parallel, and (c) that several options are still open to the exegete without his begin forced to say that the pre-existent one abandoned his divinity.

theology which, being unwilling to posit apparent 'changes' in God, understood that pre-existence as the pre-existence of a *man* and (ii) by gnostic speculations.

(b) This position is not to be conceived as a departure from Jewish monotheism. Paul, at least, intends to keep it firmly within this framework (see chs. 5 and 6 below).

(c) It does not involve the abandonment of Paul's eschatological perspective;[152] on the contrary, it depends on it and indeed fills it out (we might compare Galatians 4.4, 'when the time had fully come, God sent forth his Son,' though of course the precise meaning of the formula-like second clause is itself disputed).

(d) It has nothing to do with the idea of a pre-existent *man* (hence, a *fortiori*, it does not refer either to a pre-existent *Messiah*). One of the weaknesses of Dunn's account is that he tends to assume that 'pre-existence' must mean the pre-existence of a human being. But the γενόμενος of Philippians 2.7, which of course (taken in this sense) is not far from the cognate verb's meaning in John 1.14, positively rules this out. This naturally raises the question as to what language it is possible for us to use in referring to this pre-existent being. To call him either 'Jesus' or 'Christ' appears anachronistic. Perhaps Dunn's own illustration in a different context, where it may after all not belong,[153] will work here: when we say 'the Prime Minister studied economics at Oxford' (or perhaps, *mutatis mutandis*, 'the President acted in cowboy movies'), we are not saying that Mrs. Thatcher was Prime Minister while at Oxford, or that Mr. Reagan was President while riding bareback into the sunset.[154] We are using an easily comprehensible shorthand in order to say '*the person who became* Prime Minister, or President, and to whom we can most easily refer by that title, did these things in her, or his, earlier days.'[155] The best parallel to this sort of shorthand in Paul's writings is clearly 2 Corinthians 8.9: '...our Lord Jesus Christ, who though he was rich, yet for your sake he became poor.' Paul's use of the words 'Jesus Christ' cannot be taken to indicate that only his human existence is in view, since there would still then be the anachronism of the word κύριος. The fact that this phrase ('our Lord Jesus Christ') is the easiest

[152]As Dunn suggests (1980, 124).

[153]1980, 334 n.121; see Moule's sharp criticism in *JTS* 33, p. 260.

[154]It is remarkable how quickly times can change. At the time of going to press (March 1991) these examples already feel astonishingly dated.

[155]A parallel from Paul's own century may be provided in Josephus' references to Titus as Καῖσαρ at the time of the Jerusalem siege (*War* 5.63, 94, 97, etc.). Though the title could be used for the heir apparent, Vespasian himself had at that stage only just been hailed as Emperor, and it seems to me more likely (not least because the passage in question is so flattering to Titus) that Josephus was writing or at least revising during Titus' brief principate (79-81). See Hengel 1989 <1961> 11; and, on the date of the *Jewish War*, Attridge 1984, 192 f.

way for Paul, or for us, to refer to *the person who became* Jesus Christ should alert us to the fact that it was in this sense, rather than in that of a pre-existent humanity, that he was speaking.

(e) The fact that the nearest antecedents to this christology are apparently *personifications* (of, e.g., Wisdom or the Torah) in the relevant Jewish literature does not mean that Paul's talk about Jesus' pre-existence is equally to be taken as a mere figure of speech. As Caird points out, Philippians 2.6 f. and 2 Corinthians 8.9 attribute a conscious choice—a choice which can be used, in each case, as an ethical example—to this pre-existent one. No mere personification, then, but a person, a conscious individual entity, is envisaged.[156] Equally, the line of thought explored above (in relation to the corollaries of Paul's ascription of Isaiah 45.23 to Jesus) shows that the one thus exalted is to be identified as an individual entity existing, equal to God the Father, prior to his human birth. We shall follow this up more fully in the next two chapters.

(v) Conclusion

These considerations strengthen further the already impressive argument for the underlying theological emphasis of Moule's view of Philippians 2.5–11. When that view has undergone the adjustments necessitated by the arguments of Hoover, these strengths remain in the view I have advocated. The thrust of the passage in itself is that the one who, before becoming human, possessed divine equality did not regard that status as something to take advantage of, something to exploit, but instead interpreted it as a vocation to obedient humiliation and death; and that God the Father acknowledged the truth of this interpretation by exalting him to share his own divine glory. In its wider context, this means that the passage is well able to fulfil the role which, *prima facie*, it has in Paul's developing argument, namely, that of the example which Christians are to imitate.[157] God acknowledged Christ's self-emptying as the true expression of divine equality; he will acknowledge Christian self-abnegation (2.1–4, 12–18) in the same way (3.2 ff., especially 3.11, 21).

I have said little about the much discussed question of the hypothetical pre-Pauline context in which this poem came to birth. But if, finally, there is a conclusion to be drawn from this study in the realm of the linguistic background of the hymn, it is that whoever wrote v.6 was using a precisely

---

[156]We cannot here go into the complexities of the word 'person' except to express the wish that a word with less potential for creating theological and philosophical red herrings were available for the task.

[157]See Hurtado 1984.

nuanced idiom in a characteristically Hellenistic way. This does not *prove* that the passage was originally composed in Greek, but it makes it very easy to imagine that it was.[158] In addition, the passage fits its present context so well that it is very hard to see it in any way as a detached, or even detachable, hymn about Christ.[159] It belongs exactly where it is. It is of course possible that Paul, realizing that it was going to be appropriate to quote the hymn (assuming that there was one) worded 2.1–5 accordingly, and then continued to echo the same themes later on in the letter. But if someone were to take it upon themselves to argue, on the basis of my conclusions, that the 'hymn' was originally written by Paul himself precisely in order to give christological and above all theological underpinning to the rest of Philippians, especially chs. 2 and 3, I for one should find it hard to produce convincing counter-arguments.[160]

[158]See Deichgräber 1967, 129. Of course, a hymn's being composed in Greek does not necessarily indicate that it expresses a 'Hellenistic' theology—whatever that might mean—as opposed to any other sort.

[159]It is not, despite the common assumption to the contrary, a hymn *to* Christ (see, e.g. Martin 1983, 1 ff.: so, rightly, Deichgräber 1967, 118 f.).

[160]Among many writers who have stood against the tide on this question see Furness 1959–60 and 1967–8; Caird 1968, 66 f.

Chapter Five

POETRY AND THEOLOGY IN COLOSSIANS 1.15–20

We now proceed from one giant of a passage to another. There are many things that could be said about Colossians 1.15–20, but in this chapter I want to argue simply for three points. (i) Colossians 1.15–20 exhibits, without the deletion of any of its parts, a clear structure which can, in some meaningful senses, be called 'poetic'. (ii) The passage, *read as a poem* in the way I shall suggest, fits very well against the background of Jewish wisdom-traditions. (iii) The passage, understood in this way, exhibits a characteristically Pauline form of what we may call christological monotheism, not dissimilar to that which we have found in Philippians 2. This will point on to some further suggestions regarding the place of the passage within Colossians as a whole.[1]

(i) The Poem

Suggesting that Colossians 1.15–20 exhibits a poetic structure is, of course, nothing new. Several recent writers have offered competing analyses of the passage, and in view of the abundance of secondary literature there is no need to traverse this part of the ground again.[2] Two features of these regular treatments, however, suggest that it is worthwhile to reconsider the problem from new angles. First, there is no agreement as to the actual structure of the supposed poem. Second, and related to this, there is an abundance of theories as to possible 'insertions' by the author of Colossians into the poem, which is presumed to predate the writing of the letter.[3] Further ways of approaching this nest of problems seem called for.

---

[1]This chapter (substantially the same as the article which first appeared in *New Testament Studies* 36, 1990, 444–468, with a few small alterations largely occasioned by the kind comments of Prof. C.F.D. Moule, Fr. Benedict Green, and the Revd. Michael F. Lloyd), thus provides groundwork for the treatment of the passage in my commentary (Wright 1986c), to which reference may be made for some of the details of exegesis. I am grateful to the editor of *NTS* for permission to reprint the substance of the article.

[2]For recent treatments, see Gabathuler 1965; Kehl 1967; Schweizer 1970, 1982; Lohse 1971; Benoit 1975; Gnilka 1980a; Aletti 1981; O'Brien 1982; Bruce 1984; Balchin 1985; Baugh 1985. Full bibliography and listing of options can be found in Balchin, Schweizer 1982, 55 n.1, Bruce 55 n.73, Benoit 260–3, Lohse 41 n. 64, and Aletti *passim*.

[3]I have argued in my commentary for Pauline authorship of the letter. Nothing in the present chapter necessarily presupposes this, although some of my arguments may help to strengthen the case. Those who take an alternative view may substitute 'the author' for 'Paul'

There are other difficulties with the usual views, as has been noted in several recent methodological comments.[4] For instance, the notion of Schweizer that the Colossian community, recognizing the opening words of the poem, or perhaps the passage immediately preceding it (i.e. 1.13–14), would thereupon join in and sing or recite it together as it was being read, comes badly unstuck when coupled with Schweizer's own theory of interpolations. Nothing would be more calculated to puzzle a congregation than tampering with a hymn they are in the act of singing.[5] Again, hypothetical additions to an original poem are one thing, problematic in themselves but not totally impossible.[6] But if someone has taken the trouble to add extra text, there is nothing to say that they would not also have omitted portions: and once that possibility is held open, as logically it must be (not least in view of the fact that the poem as it now stands begins with a relative pronoun, demanding that we understand an invisible antecedent), all reasonable hope of reconstructing it in its hypothetical original form must be abandoned.[7] Finally, there is no agreement as to the status of the passage immediately preceding (1.13–14). It too might be claimed to exhibit some kind of poetic structure, but as it, too, consists grammatically of relative clauses it cannot as it stands provide any sort of completeness to 1.15–20. The suggestion[8] that 'the beloved son' in v.13 is taken from the first (now suppressed) line of the actual hymn is simply unproveable speculation. It merely demonstrates the point that, if insertions are to be allowed, omissions should be as well, making the task of reconstruction virtually impossible.

These considerations suggest that the best way to proceed is to treat the passage, in the first instance, as it stands, and to see if it will yield satisfactory sense. This is in any case correct methodologically in terms of the exegesis of Colossians as a whole: despite the efforts of (e.g.) Schweizer to read between the lines and provide different interpretations for the original poem and the one we now have, the first task of the exegete—arguably in this case the only possible one—is to deal with the text that we possess.[9]

---

throughout.

[4]E.g. Vawter 1971; Caird 1976, 174 f.; Frankowski 1983; Balchin 1985.

[5]Schweizer 55 n.1, 298–300: see Caird loc. cit.

[6]Though cf. Beasley-Murray 1980, 170.

[7]See Pollard 1981, here at 572 f.

[8]Schweizer 1967, 5 n.3.

[9]See Vawter, esp. 80 f.: Caird 174 f. Schweizer's answer to Caird (1982, 55 n.1, 299) is that doctrine and worship use different languages. The sense in which this is (almost self-evidently) true does not, however, undermine the fact that Col. 1.15–20 contains many statements which (a) could not but be doctrinally significant in early Christianity, not least in its task of self-definition over against both Judaism and paganism and (b) are actually used in this doctrinal sense in the later sections of the letter.

The obvious starting point in the analysis of the passage is the parallelism between words and phrases in the different sections.[10] The sentence structure is quite unlike that employed by Paul when mounting a theological argument, for which purpose he uses connecting words such as γάρ, οὖν, διό, etc. Here the connectives are relative and personal pronouns. Of these the most obvious, which has given rise to the usual bipartite division, is the parallel between ὅς ἐστιν εἰκών... πρωτότοκος... in 15 and ὅς ἐστιν ἀρχή... πρωτότοκος... in 18c–d (for the subdivision of verses by letter see below). But once we start making parallels out of the relative pronouns, and using them to indicate the structure of the whole, it becomes clear that there are a great many more, which suggest a more subtle, though equally comprehensible, division:

ὅς ἐστιν (15a)
    ὅτι ἐν αὐτῷ (16a)
        δι᾽ αὐτου καὶ εἰς αὐτόν (16f)

καὶ αὐτός (17a)
καὶ αὐτός (18a)

ὅς ἐστιν (18c)
    ὅτι ἐν αὐτῷ (19)
        δι᾽ αὐτοῦ... εἰς αὐτόν (20a)

This quite impressive parallelism is clearly further strengthened both by the repeated πρωτότοκος of 15c and 18d but by the parallels between 16 and 20:

τὰ πάντα
    ἐν τοῖς οὐρανοῖς καὶ ἐπὶ τῆς γῆς (16a–b)

τὰ πάντα...
    εἴτε τὰ ἐπὶ τῆς γῆς εἴτε τὰ ἐν τοῖς οὐρανοῖς (20a, c).

The pattern which all this suggests is clearly that of a parallel between two halves of a poem or quasi-poem, and it is for this reason, obviously, that the suggestion has frequently been made that we have to do here with an essentially bipartite structure.[11] The problems begin to arise just here, however: what about the bits that do not fit? O'Neill (1979, 88), for example,

[10] See the classic analyses of Robinson, Bammel, etc., and now Aletti and others as in n.2 above.
[11] See Robinson, Ellingworth 1962, etc., and the surveys noted above.

has argued that the structure is 'wrecked' by vv.17–18a, and the proliferation of interpolation- and dislocation-hypotheses indicates that all is not well at this point. It is unfortunate, in particular, that the notorious τῆς ἐκκλησίας of 18b (my numbering: see below) has embroiled the debate in much wider questions of history-of-religions analysis and consequent theological questions, which have to do more with the attempt to place an earlier text of the poem into a hypothetical life-setting than with the understanding of the text as it now stands.[12] Aletti's suggestion (1981, 32 ff.) that 17 is in parallel with the end of 16 has something to commend it, but even though he retains τῆς ἐκκλησίας he does not show how the material fits into a coherent pattern on its own. Balchin's argument (1985, 67 f., 80) that the parallelism is not as impressive as it appears, since (a) the two apparent halves use the relevant words in different senses, and (b) the 'redemption theme' begins too early, is I think answered by the analysis, both theological and structural, which I shall offer below.

I suggest that the troublesome lines make excellent sense if they are taken as a pair of couplets, forming the centre-point of a chiasmus in the form ABBA:

> A   15–16
> B 17
> B 18ab
> A   18c–20

Thus the crucial middle pair would look like this:

(17)   καὶ αὐτός ἐστιν πρὸ πάντων
         καὶ τὰ πάντα ἐν αὐτῷ συνέστηκεν

(18)   καὶ αὐτός ἐστιν ἡ κεφαλὴ
         τοῦ σώματος τῆς ἐκκλησίας

This keeps the parallelism between 15–16 and 18c–20, requires no additions or emendations, and makes (as we shall see) very good sense of the poem as a whole. This suggestion is close to some other recent chiastic schemes,[13] and has (I think) the merit of overall simplicity: it does not depend on the convoluted schemes that sometimes disfigure analysis. If a reason is required as to why the parallelism of 17 and 18ab has hitherto gone unnoticed, my guess would be that most writers have come with the

[12]See particularly Käsemann 1964, and others listed in Aletti 25, etc.
[13]E.g. Baugh 1985, McCown 1979; see Balchin 1985, 84 ff. I only read McCown's article after formulating for myself the solution here proposed.

assumption that τῆς ἐκκλησίας is a gloss on a text which originally spoke of Christ as the head of the body, i.e. the *world*,[14] and have then naturally not seen the close similarity of line-length—perhaps helped in this by the large difference between the syllable-length in English or German on the one hand and Greek on the other. The syllable count in the four lines is in fact very close: eight in the first, eleven in the second, and nine each in the third and fourth.[15] It would be easy to read the lines rhythmically, with three stresses to each, although our comparative ignorance of Hellenistic-Greek poetry, or even pronunciation, forbids any attempt at precise metrical analysis.[16] The important point is that we have a credible and indeed probable ABBA structure, which not only rehabilitates 18b as part of the original poem[17] but also rescues the analysis from the need to make v.17 parallel to something in the second 'A' section (18c–20),[18] a task which has, not surprisingly, proved difficult.[19]

This analysis thus highlights the *poetic structure* of Colossians 1.15–20. Avoiding precise conclusions as to whether or not the passage is or reflects an early Christian *hymn* as such,[20] the structure indicates that we have here something more elevated and carefully thought-out than straightforward prose. It is some kind of poem. What kind, precisely, remains to be seen.

Further support for this analysis comes from the work of C.F. Burney, whose theory, never disproved but only dismissed, can in fact be further strengthened.[21] The poem as I have analysed it highlights, structurally, the main features of his analysis.

We may therefore set out the complete poem in Greek and English as follows:

[14]E.g. Schweizer 1982, 58 f., and many others before (though not so many since).

[15]So Aletti 40 f., though without drawing the same conclusions as this. Balchin's dismissal of arguments from syllable-counting (1985, 83 f.) is aimed simply at those who use them as evidence of textual alteration.

[16]See Houlden 1970, 157: 'In neither case is it a question of obvious Greek poetic form; the rhythm and pattern come, as in the Psalms... from verbal repetition and the reiteration of ideas in regular order.'

[17]Thus making 17 parallel to 18ab, so answering the objection of Balchin (1985, 82) that this 'intermediate verse' is not parallel to anything elsewhere.

[18]Or, with Aletti, in the first 'A' section.

[19]Since this chapter was first published in article form, Fr. Benedict Green has kindly pointed out to me that the two halves of the poem as I have analysed it have an identical number of words, 55 in each case. (This assumes that δι' αὐτοῦ in 20b is an addition.) Similar phenomena have also, he points out, been observed in Matthew, e.g. in the Beatitudes.

[20]This has been challenged recently: see Berger 1984, 345, suggesting a more Hellenistic rhetorical analysis; Riesenfeld 1979; Frankowski 1983; Balchin 1985. Riesenfeld and Frankowski rightly emphasize strict criteria for 'hymns'; but this does not rule out this passage's being a *poem*.

[21]Burney 1925; see below.

A	15a	ὅς ἐστιν εἰκων
	15b	τοῦ θεοῦ τοῦ ἀοράτου
	15c	**πρωτότοκος** πάσης κτίσεως
	16a	**ὅτι ἐν αὐτῷ** ἐκτίσθη **τὰ πάντα**
	16b	<u>ἐν τοῖς οὐρανοῖς καὶ ἐπὶ τῆς γῆς</u>
	16c	τὰ ὁρατὰ καὶ τὰ ἀόρατα
	16d	εἴτε θρόνοι εἴτε κυριότητες
	16e	εἴτε ἀρχαὶ εἴτε ἐξουσίαι
	16f	τὰ πάντα **δι᾽ αὐτοῦ καὶ εἰς αὐτὸν** ἔκτισται
B	17a	<u>καὶ αὐτός</u> ἐστιν πρὸ πάντων
	17b	καὶ τὰ πάντα ἐν αὐτῷ συνέστηκεν
B	18a	<u>καὶ αὐτός</u> ἐστιν ἡ κεφαλὴ
	18b	τοῦ σώματος τῆς ἐκκλησίας
A	18c	**ὅς ἐστιν** ἀρχή
	18d	**πρωτότοκος** ἐκ τῶν νεκρῶν
	18e	ἵνα γένηται ἐν πᾶσιν αὐτὸς πρωτεύων
	19a	**ὅτι ἐν αὐτῷ** εὐδόκησεν
	19b	πᾶν τὸ πλήρωμα κατοικῆσαι
	20a	καὶ **δι᾽ αὐτοῦ** ἀποκαταλλάξαι **τὰ πάντα εἰς αὐτόν**
	20b	εἰρηνοποιήσας διὰ τοῦ αἵματος τοῦ σταυροῦ αὐτοῦ [δι᾽ αὐτοῦ][22]
	20c	<u>εἴτε τὰ ἐπὶ τῆς γῆς εἴτε τὰ ἐν τοῖς οὐρανοῖς.</u>

A	15a	**who is** the image
	15b	of God, the invisible
	15c	**firstborn** of every creature
	16a	**because in him** were created all things
	16b	<u>in the heaven and in the earth</u>
	16c	the seen things and the unseen
	16d	whether thrones or lordships
	16e	whether rulers or authorities
	16f	all things **through him and to him** were created
B	17a	<u>and he</u> is before all things
	17b	and all things hold together in him
B	18a	<u>and he</u> is the head
	18b	of the body, the church.
A	18c	**who is** the beginning
	18d	**firstborn** from the dead ones
	18e	so that he might become in all things himself pre-eminent
	19a	**because in him** was pleased
	19b	all the fulness to dwell
	20a	and **through him** to reconcile **all things to him**
	20b	making peace by the blood of his cross [through him]
	20c	<u>whether things on the earth or things in heaven.</u>

[22]See Metzger 1971, 621.

Two further comments are necessary at this point:

(a) I have, as I explained, allowed the connecting words and the basic pronouns to dictate the basic form of the poem. This is normal and regular, and allows the other obvious parallels to stand out: πρωτότοκος, of course, in 15c/18d, and the mention of heaven and earth (in the opposite order) in 16b/20c. The two 'A' sections are thematically parallel, each beginning with a statement about Christ, amplifying it with the title 'firstborn', and then explaining it (ὅτι, 16a/19a) in relation to Christ's position vis-à-vis the created order. This much is scarcely controversial.

(b) It is also clear, however, that the parallelism between the two 'A' sections is not exact. εἰκών is qualified by a phrase interposing between it and πρωτότοκος, whereas ἀρχή is not: on the other hand, there is no parallel at the end of v.15 to the ἵνα-clause in 18e. In v.16 there are three lines which amplify ἐν τοῖς οὐρανοῖς καὶ ἐπὶ τῆς γῆς, but there is no such qualification in v.20. Nor is there any parallel, in the first 'A' section, to 20b. These should not be taken as weaknesses in the hypothesis, which never envisaged an exact symmetry. Demands of content may just as easily have influenced the original writer to soften the exact lines of a parallel structure. Thus (a) the second clause of v.15 (τοῦ θεοῦ τοῦ ἀοράτου) is a necessary explanation of εἰκών , while the ἵνα-clause of 18e, though not an explanation of 18c–d, sums up the effect of those two lines. The result is in each case a three-line introduction (in each case, lines of five and eight syllables respectively, followed by a longer third line) followed by a clause beginning with ὅτι ἐν αὐτῷ... . (b) 16d–e, with the repeated εἴτε, is not without links in the second 'A' section (i.e. 20c, which is parallel in content with 16b). (c) 20b, which intrudes into the second 'A' section at nearly the same point as 16c–e does in the first, does not (as is often suggested[23]) alter the theology of the poem. It simply explains how the reconciliation spoken of in 20a was effected. (d) 16b and 20c, and 16f and 20a, are parallel in content, but not in their placing within their respective sections. This again reflects the demands of content, as follows. 16b qualifies 16a, and 16f sums up the total effect (note the perfect tense in place of the preceding aorist[24]). 20a, however, introduces a different idea to v.19, and 20c, following the further clarification in 20b, rounds off the poem by emphasizing once more the universal scope of Christ's saving rule.

[23]E.g. Lohse 60.

[24]Beasley-Murray's reconstruction (1980, 170) of a hypothetical original seems to me very weak at this point, since 16f seems almost tautological if it comes after 16a; something like the expansion in 16b–e is necessary if 16f is to have is apparent force of summing up, not just repeating what has already been said.

It is easier to perceive a quasi-rhythmical structure in the first 'A' and the two 'B' sections than it is in the second 'A', especially after the end of v.18.[25] One possible hypothesis to explain this is that the second 'A', while composed in deliberate parallelism with the first, was allowed by its author to grow into a fuller statement than strict balance would have required.[26] There is certainly no need to postulate a shorter original. Most of the lines would not, in fact, admit of shortening without doing violence to the balance that their content displays with their equivalents in the first 'A': thus, for instance, 20a remains close to 16f, and 20c picks up 16b.

The question raised by all these comments on the structure is: so what? We have no particular reason for expecting exact parallelism throughout every feature of the poem, no comparable poems from other similar sources to serve as a standard or model. It is precarious, to say the least, to attempt to go beyond the conclusion that we have here an original piece of free-form poetry, whose clear main structure allows for minor variation.[27] In addition, as we will shortly see, the balance of the whole poem suggests strongly that it was conceived, at least in outline, *as* a whole. If there are parts which appear to us as irregularities within a closely worked basic structure, that may be evidence more for our false expectations than for different stages of composition.

The close parallelism between the two 'A' sections, and the tightly fitting 'B' sections in the middle, all contribute to the conclusion that, whether or not we deem this section a 'hymn', it is certainly poetical in form.[28] Without prejudice as to what a Greek speaker (or, for that matter, a reader of Hebrew) in the first century would have classified under a word such as 'poem', we can safely read the passage as a carefully constructed artistic whole. This propels us forward to ask some fundamental questions about its background within the history of religions and about its meaning.

---

[25]The question, what sort of rhythm one might have a right to expect, is not usually investigated by commentators, though it properly should be. No-one, so far as I know, has suggested that anything like classical metre or oratorical prose-rhythm is to be found in the Colossians poem, and the earliest traces of Greek accentual clausula, according to the *Oxford Classical Dictionary*, are found in the C3 A.D. orator Menander. The revival of interest in rhetorical criticism at the present time might perhaps contribute something to the present enterprise, but this unfortunately would take us too far afield at this point.

[26]See, e.g., Benoit 1975, 229.

[27]This conclusion thus cuts through the tangled speculations discussed by Schweizer 1982, 55–63, Martin 1974, 61–4, and Gnilka 1980a, 51–9. The word-count (above, n.19) may also tell in favour of my reading.

[28]See Balchin 1985 for a recent argument against reading the passage as a 'hymn' *per se*.

(ii) The Background of the Poem

There have been two main proposals for the background against which, within the history of religions, Colossians 1.15–20 is to be understood. In the light of the analysis just offered, I suggest that the first can be rejected outright, and the second set in a different, and clarifying, context.

The first option is, of course, the now largely abandoned Gnostic redeemer-myth, which used to be held by several scholars to have provided the earliest version of the poem now in our text.[29] If the poem has anything like the structural parallel we have observed, it is making, by its very form, the point which gnosticism essentially sought to deny: that creation and redemption are to be traced to the same beneficent divine origin. Gnosticism saw the created order as inherently wicked, and understood redemption as rescue *from*, not renewal *of*, creation. Even if it should be argued that vv.15–16 (and perhaps v.17) were the only original parts of the poem, and that 18–20, or some parts thereof, were added later; even if the suggestion should be made that vv.15–17 are, or embody, a pre-Christian 'wisdom' poem: that would not produce any connection with either Gnosticism proper or a looser 'gnosis', since this hypothetical earlier form of the poem would still be a celebration of the goodness of the created order.[30]

The second history-of-religions context regularly suggested, with variations, is that of Jewish 'wisdom'-thought.[31] Here, I suggest, the problem is that the cart has been put before the horse: verbal and conceptual parallels between details of the poem and (e.g.) Sirach and the Wisdom of Solomon have been explored at length, before the poem *as a whole* has been allowed to make the impact within which these detailed (hypothetical) allusions can be understood. When we get things the right way round, reading the poem as a whole first and the allusions afterwards, we may be able to unpick the significance of such material with more success.

The fact is that the poem as it stands presents a pattern well known within the context of mainline Judaism. The parallelism between its two halves, nuanced in the ways we have explored, invites the reader or listener to draw the conclusion that the creator is also the redeemer, and *vice versa*. In other words, the poem at its most basic structural level exhibits the standard pattern of *Jewish monotheistic confessions*, known not only from many Psalms[32] but also from the pattern and shape of the Torah itself. We may

[29]See particularly Käsemann 1964, and several others cited in the literature (above, n.2: see particularly Lohse 45, 60 n.205).

[30]As is clear from Pöhlmann's article (1973), the parallels with various Greek fragments can only be achieved by heavy-handed and arbitrary omissions from the text.

[31]See the very full discussion in Aletti 1981: and see below for Burney and subsequent debates.

[32]E.g. Pss. 96.5, 146.5–6; compare Isa. 40.12–31, etc.

take as a particular instance the book of Genesis, whose (final) whole structure (1–11, 12–50) seems designed to say that Israel's God is to be identified as the creator of the whole world, and *vice versa*. Israel's monotheism and her awareness of election are two sides of the same coin, and the joining of the two is a matter of celebration, a stimulus to prayer, a reason to hope, within the whole Hebrew Bible and on into the intertestamental literature as a whole. This, arguably, should even include apocalyptic, despite the frequent assertion that it is dualistic; in fact, its fundamental insistence, expressed in highly charged symbol and metaphor, was that the Lord of all the earth was the God who was committed to rescuing Israel and establishing his kingdom. This extremely basic Jewish self-understanding[33] is reflected in many of the hymns and prayers recently suggested as the proper background for understanding similar material in the New Testament.[34]

The poem, then, asks to be read in the light not merely of one particular branch of Jewish tradition (i.e. 'Wisdom'), but of the entire Jewish worldview of which the wisdom-tradition was simply one of many facets. And this worldview has as its most obvious characteristic the particularly Jewish form of monotheism, which we may call creational and covenantal monotheism as opposed to the pantheistic variety known in Stoicism and elsewhere. For this worldview, there is one God; he made the world, and is neither identified with it (as in pantheism and its various pagan cousins) nor detached from it (as in dualism); he is in covenant with Israel; and he will, in fulfilling that covenant, reclaim and redeem his whole creation from that which at present corrupts and threatens it. Poems like the one before us arise naturally within the context of this worldview, whether in tragedy (as urgent petition) or triumph (as celebration). From this point of view, the important thing about the analysis of the poem is not how long its lines are, but the fact that, although written in Greek and with some possible verbal echoes of ideas current in other worldviews, its overall emphasis belongs within the broad and rich tradition of Jewish psalmody.[35]

[33]On the fundamental nature, within Judaism, of monotheism and election, see Schechter 1961; Urbach 1987; etc.

[34]See Charlesworth 1982. We may, for instance, compare the collection of psalms in 11QPs(a) (Vermes 1987, 208–14); the great poem of 1QS 10–11 (Vermes 76–80); the Song of the Three Young Men (in which the Creator is praised as the one who will deliver those who have been faithful to Israel's covenant); Jud. 16.1–17; etc. Charlesworth does not suggest in the article the possibility of reading Col. 1.15–20 in the light of this basic *theological* feature of the Jewish prayers he cites. We may note the same pattern elsewhere in the NT, most obviously in Rev. 4–5.

[35]Cf. Aletti 127 ff., suggesting parallels with OT hymnic passages, but again without observing the theological *structure*: e.g. he cites (129) Pss. 100.3, 95.7 as parallels to the mention of the church in Col. 1.18, but only sees the theme of God's care for Israel (and, in Col., his creation of the church) as a particular example of his general beneficence.

That this broad Jewish (and, specifically, monotheistic) religious tradition is the proper context for understanding Colossians 1.15–20 is reinforced by the echoes of Jewish redemption-ideas in vv.12–14, which evoke in particular the imagery of the Exodus, the time when Israel's God showed himself to be God of the whole world by defeating both the Egyptians and the mighty waters of the sea. The Exodus was an act of new creation, bringing the chosen race to new birth out of the chaos of slavery. The same impression is given by the verses (21–3) which follow the poem, in which the God of all the earth (v.23) has become responsible for the reconciliation of the Colossians and their grafting in to his true people (22). Whatever conclusion is drawn about the hypothetical pre-history of these short passages, and their relation to vv.15–20, they awaken—as they stand, and in any credible reconstruction of their earlier form—the same overall echoes of religious traditions. To a Jew of the first century, of course, a reference to the Exodus would not simply be of antiquarian interest. It would speak of the redemption still to be accomplished, the greater 'return from exile' in which Israel would finally be redeemed from her bondage. The Colossians poem, understood in this way, is asserting, astonishingly from the Jewish perspective, that this final redemption, with all that it signified, has already taken place in Jesus Christ.

In other words, the thought of vv.12–23 as a whole moves from redemption to creation and back again, in order better to understand the cosmic significance of that redemption through its organic connection with creation itself. This is the standard emphasis within regular Jewish monotheistic statements, and is regularly made the basis of a fresh understanding of the redemption which is envisaged. In Isaiah 40–55, for instance, which provides both in outline and in detail many good examples of the same kind of pattern, the overall emphasis of the writer is to remind Israel that her God is none other than the creator himself (and, conversely, that the creator of the world is none other than the covenant God), and thereby to evoke faith and hope. In the monotheism of Paul's day this was again the classic shape of the doctrine, as we see in the apocalyptic writings. Faced with national disaster, the apocalyptists affirmed, in their own characteristic fashion, that Israel's God was not merely one national deity among many but rather the sovereign lord of the whole world, who had both the right and (because of the covenant) the duty to step in at last and rescue his people from their oppressors. (The questions, why the world arrived in its present condition, and why its creator did not act sooner and swifter to put it to rights, are raised in some Jewish (4 Ezra) and early Christian (Romans) writings, but are often left unraised, as in Colossians.)

This shows that the wisdom-traditions so often explored in the quest to understand the poem can be set within precisely that broader understanding of Jewish theology within which they properly belonged in any case. As has been increasingly realised in recent years, Jewish wisdom-ideas belonged firmly within this same monotheistic home base, and were indeed a way of maintaining a monotheistic position over against the tendencies towards either pantheism or dualism.[36] To speak of God's Wisdom as active within the world, as making her home in Israel, as enabling humans to be what the creator intended, was an effective way of warding off any incipient ontological dualism: that is to say, it was a way of affirming that the transcendent creator was also the immanent, ever-present enabling God. It was at the same time a bar to any moral dualism: in being endowed with the divine Wisdom, humans became more human, not less, as the whole tradition of Proverbs makes clear. The created order was ennobled, not obliterated or ignored, when Wisdom made her home there. But at the same time the wisdom-motif forbade any casual identification between the creator and his world. The whole theme was not merely a bit of idle metaphysical speculation, but a powerful tool, at the level of religious language, for continuing to affirm Israel's basic theological convictions and thus to uphold her distinctiveness vis-à-vis her pagan neighbours.[37] All of these themes are seen to good effect in passages such as Ecclesiasticus 24.3–12, built on the foundation in 1.1–10; the specific application to Israel and Torah is made in 1.10 ('To all mankind he has given her in some measure, but in plenty to those who love him'), 24.8 ('my Creator decreed where I should dwell. He said, "Make your home in Jacob; find your heritage in Israel."'), 23 ('All this [sc. the wisdom-teaching just given] is the covenant-book of God Most High, the law which Moses enacted to be the heritage of the assemblies of Jacob.'), etc.[38] Israel's God is the Creator; Israel is his true humanity.[39] His Wisdom dwells in her midst as his εἰκών: 'She is the reflection of everlasting light, the flawless mirror of the active power of God, and the image of his goodness' (Wisdom 7.26).

It is within this context that the theory of C.F. Burney must be recalled. Burney has been attacked, and sometimes ignored, but without good reasons: once we consider the poem in the way I have suggested, his theory is given an excellent context, though some modifications in it may be called for. He is not vulnerable to the criticism of Schweizer, who seems to think that he was suggesting a rabbinic background as opposed to a Hellenistic-Jewish one for the poem;[40] Burney makes it quite clear that he is talking about Hellenistic-Jewish ideas, though it is true that his theory is then used by W.D. Davies

---

[36]See, for instance, Dunn 1982.

[37]On the whole theological understanding evidenced in the wisdom-traditions, see now Gilbert 1984, Schürer 1973–87, 3.198–215.

[38]The translations are those of the NEB apocrypha.

[39]For this last theme, see ch. 3 above, section 1.

[40]Schweizer 1982, 65 f. n.25.

(perhaps the real target of Schweizer's attack?) as part of his case for finding 'rabbinic' material in Paul.[41] In fact, though there is plenty of rabbinic support for the theory that the poem reflects midrashic expositions of Genesis 1.1, *via* the notion of Wisdom,[42] such exposition is equally at home in much older Jewish wisdom-traditions.[43]

Burney's theory is basically an *explanation* of how such a poem could come to birth. It is, he suggested, an exploration of the different possible meanings of בראשית in Genesis 1.1, made possible by the identification of ראשית with Wisdom implied in Proverbs 8.22. He suggested that 15c (πρωτότοκος πάσης κτίσεως) is a direct allusion to Proverbs 8.22,[44] and that the ב of בראשית is expounded in its three possible forms by ἐν αὐτῷ, δι' αὐτοῦ and εἰς αὐτόν (16a, 16f, repeated in 19a, 20a) and the ראשית by πρό παντῶν, τά πάντα συνέστηκε [*sic*], κεφαλή and πρωτότοκος (17a, 17b, 18a, 18d). Thus we have beginning, sum-total, head and firstfruits, leading to Paul's conclusion, which according to Burney is found in 18e: 'Christ fulfils every meaning which may be extracted from ראשית—ἵνα γένηται ἐν πᾶσιν αὐτὸς πρωτεύων.

I want now to suggest that, if we set Burney's explanatory theory within the broader context of Jewish monotheism I have outlined, its basic argument will appear sound, its residual oddities may be ironed out, and it may aid us in the task of interpretation that lies beyond mere explanation.

First, the oddities. (a) It is indeed strange that Burney did not highlight ἀρχή itself (18c), which might be thought the most obvious translation of ראשית. He instead merely subsumes it under πρωτότοκος. (b) In all his references to Genesis 1 and its links with Wisdom, Burney never drew attention to εἰκών itself, despite its obvious place in Genesis 1.26, Wisdom 7.26, and Colossians 1.15a.[45]

These may be dealt with as follows. (a) We may suggest a modification of his scheme, in which the poem would read as follows, with the intended overtones and echoes in parentheses:

1. (15a) He is the image [like Wisdom herself, and evoking Genesis 1.26]
2. (15c) He is the firstborn [like Wisdom herself: the first meaning of ראשית]

[41]Davies 1980 <1948>, 150–2.

[42]See Hengel 1974, 1.170 f., 2.111 f.; citing e.g. Gen.R. 1.1, Targ. Jer. I on Gen. 1.1. See also Manns 1979, citing Sifre Deut. 11.10 as well, and suggesting a *Sitz im Leben* for the poem in the context of Passover celebrations.

[43]As is emphasized by Feuillet 1965a, stressing Job 28.23 ff. and Wisd. 7.22 f., and Glasson 1967, highlighting Ecclus. 24.

[44]Burney 1925, 173 f., pointing out that a weaker form of the same suggestion was made by Epiphanius.

[45]On p. 175 he begins his running paraphrase of the poem with 'Christ is *the First-begotten of all creation*' (italics original).

3. (17ab) He is supreme (πρὸ πάντων) and the consummation of all things (τὰ πάντα συνέστηκεν) [the second meaning of ראשית, including Burney's second and third]
4. (18a) He is the head [the third meaning of ראשית]
5. (18c) He is the beginning [the fourth, and climactic, meaning of ראשית]
6. (18d) He is the firstborn—this time from the dead [like Wisdom again, but now firmly as a human being]

The attractiveness of this scheme is the more apparent when we put it together with the chiastic structure suggested in part i above: for the four basic meanings of ראשית thus correspond to the four sections (ABBA) of the poem, with 15a (ὅς ἐστιν εἰκών) standing as the introduction to the whole:

A   He is the image—the *firstborn*
B   He is *supreme*
B   He is the *head*
A   He is the *beginning*

This has a further implication which should not be missed. The weight of the whole falls on the final word in the series—ἀρχή itself, which of course stands in the LXX for ראשית in Genesis 1.1 and Proverbs 8.22 f.[46] An alert listener, picking up the implied sequence (and we must remember that such things were the staple diet of some Jewish exegesis, as they still are in places), would be waiting for the final term, much as an alert listener to a symphony waits for the full re-statement of the developed theme. This reinforces the conclusion already drawn from the analysis in part (i) above, that 18c and what follows are not an addition to an original shorter poem, but are the intended climax of the whole. Just as in a Jewish monotheistic poem, or an extended work such as Ecclesiasticus or (particularly) the Wisdom of Solomon, the divine activity in creation is celebrated for its own sake, but reaches its climax in the divine activity by which Israel is called into being (and/or delivered from bondage) as his chosen people, so in Colossians 1.15–20 the celebration of creation reaches its peak in the creation of a new people by means of the resurrection of Jesus from the dead.

So much for the first oddity in Burney's theory: I suggest that we keep his overall structure, but see the fourfold sequence in the words highlighted above. As for his second (b), the apparent ignoring of εἰκών: the climax of Genesis 1 is clearly the creation of man and woman in the image of God in v.26, and the importance of Wisdom in Proverbs, Ecclesiasticus and the

---

[46]Compare Ecclus. 24.9. In Prov. 8.23 ἐν ἀρχῇ is missing in A.

Wisdom of Solomon is not least that Wisdom is what is required if humans are to *be* truly human, taking that place over creation which, outlined in Genesis 2.15–20, is then spelt out in more detail throughout Proverbs. Humans are to be the vice-gerents over God's creation, and are therefore to take the place within the divine economy that in Proverbs 8.22 ff. is given to Wisdom herself.[47] Israel is (as we saw) to be the particular place where this Wisdom dwells, establishing her as the creator's true humanity; and, where we find messianic expectation cherished in Judaism, we find it as the focal point of the aspiration of the nation as a whole. Solomon, David's son, is at the same time the model of the coming great king and the model of the truly wise man.[48] The categories fit neatly together: Israel's vocation to be the true humanity, indwelt by the divine Wisdom, is focussed on one man, her representative king, who in Psalm 89.27 is described as Yahweh's 'firstborn'.[49]

I suggest, therefore, that Burney's basic insight was indeed sound, and that, when these modifications are made to his detailed theory, it both lends support to my analysis and is in turn confirmed by it. Together they point, at the level of explanation, to the following results: (a) that the poem of Colossians 1.15–20 was conceived as a whole, within the framework of Jewish monotheistic celebration of creation and election, (b) that it was intended to evoke a well-established tradition in which Genesis 1.1 and Proverbs 8.22 were read as mutually explanatory, (c) that it was therefore intended to evoke the figure of 'Wisdom' as the means of creation and as the key to the election of God's people, and (d) that it was intended to apply all that might be said about Wisdom and hence about ראשׁית to Jesus himself, no mere hypothetical hypostasis but a human figure, an 'image of God' of recent memory. Wisdom-theology is a characteristic Jewish way of asserting creational and covenantal monotheism; so is the writing of poems, and longer works too, in which celebration of creation is balanced by celebration of election and redemption. In Colossians 1.15–20 these two strands of Jewish tradition (specifically, but not exclusively, Hellenistic-Jewish tradition) are brought together under the impact of Jesus and the resurrection. This enables us, in conclusion, to move from explanation to interpretation. What is the poem thus saying about the one to whom it refers in this remarkable fashion?

---

[47]See Caird 1976, 177.
[48]Wisd. 9.1–13, and the whole tradition that associated Wisdom with Solomon in particular.
[49]The term is elsewhere used, of course, for Israel: Cf. Ex. 4.22, Jer. 38.9 LXX, Ps. Sol. 18.4.

(iii) Poetry and Theology

There was considerable debate among the early Fathers as to whether 1.15 referred to the pre-incarnate Word of God or to the man Jesus, now exalted.[50] This debate has re-emerged in the present day, with something of a feeling of *plus ça change*.[51] On the one hand it has been argued (e.g. by Lightfoot) that the referent of ὅς in 1.15, and of the other pronouns thereafter, is the pre-existent Christ, who, like the λόγος in Philo, is the Father's agent in creation, and who, unlike Philo's λόγος but like John's in his prologue, becomes incarnate. Objections to this position have been raised both in ancient and modern times on the grounds of (i) the present tense in v.15 (ὅς ἐστιν appears to refer to Jesus, the Lord, as he is in the present), (ii) the essentially *human* meaning of εἰκών (cf. 3.10, and of course Genesis 1.26), and (iii) the emphasis, picked up from the Old Testament (Psalm 8.7) in Ephesians 1.22 and 1 Corinthians 15.27, as well as in Hebrews 2.5–9, on God's intention to sum up all things under his chosen *man*.[52]

If the latter points are pressed, two options appear to be open for the interpretation of vv.16–17. Either these verses refer not to the original creation but to the new creation, the remaking of the world in redemption. Or they may refer to the original creation, but instead of claiming that Christ was active in mediating this creation at the beginning they may be suggesting simply that it was always God's intention, in creating the world, that it should find its fulfillment in him. But there are problems with each of these solutions. To the first it must be replied that the language of v.16, and its background in Proverbs 8 and Genesis 1, simply does not leave this option open, and that part of the whole point of the hymn in its context in Colossians is to show the close integral relationship between creation and new creation, precisely in order to mount a classic statement of Jewish monotheism. To the second it may be said that it reduces ἐν αὐτῷ and δι' αὐτοῦ to terms simply of εἰς αὐτόν in a way which would scarcely be comprehensible to any first century reader acquainted with the Jewish background of Paul's thought.

What then is the alternative? I suggest that we should read the poem as an expression of what I shall call *christological monotheism*, intending by that term the phenomenon, of which this passage is not the only example in the New Testament, of an explicitly monotheistic statement, of the Jewish variety (i.e. creational/covenantal monotheism, as opposed to pantheism or Deism), in which we find Christ set within the monotheistic statement itself. The best example of this is 1 Corinthians 8.6, which I shall discuss in the next chapter,

[50]See the summaries in Lightfoot 1876, 143–50, Gnilka 1980a, 77–81.
[51]See Caird 1976, 175–8: Dunn 1980, 187–94: Gnilka, *loc. cit.*
[52]See particularly Caird, op. cit., 175–8, cp. 47–9.

and in which the *Shema* is actually expanded so as to contain Jesus within it. The parallel is instructive: like Colossians 1.15 ff., 1 Corinthians 8.6 contains a clear wisdom-christology expressed in terms of Christ as the mediator of creation.[53] Within an argument whose force is 'we are Jewish monotheists, not pagan polytheists', Paul has modified Jewish monotheism so as to place Jesus Christ within the description, almost the definition, of the one God. And in this radical redefinition of monotheism there is also contained the radical redefinition of election, whereby the people of God are now to be understood as the people of Jesus Christ.[54] Similar points could be made about other passages as well, not least Philippians 2.6–11, discussed in the last chapter. When Paul speaks of new creation in Christ (2 Corinthians 5.17, Galatians 6.15), he indicates that the same agent was responsible for both creations. There is no dualism at the heart of his cosmology or soteriology.

Colossians 1.15–20 may therefore be seen as a clear and sharp expression of an early Christian phenomenon evidenced elsewhere. One implication of this phenomenon is that the boundaries of history-of-religion analysis are being burst: Jewish parallels cannot by themselves explain this new departure, however much those who initiated it were claiming to remain within, and to re-interpret from within, the central Jewish tradition of creational and covenantal monotheism.[55] It will therefore not do simply to analyse partially parallel Jewish motifs and deduce from them the shape of the new doctrine being articulated. They provide the (historically) original theme, not its new variation. In particular, to refer to the christology of the poem as 'wisdom-christology' cannot be taken as an indication that the problem of interpretation is in principle solved, with the details simply to be worked out in terms of Jewish wisdom-ideas.

What then is here being said about the one to whom the poem refers? I suggest that the structure and language of the poem enables its writer and/or editor to hold together two things which subsequent theology found very difficult: the complete humanness of Jesus, and his complete identification with a being who, though not to be thought of over against the one God of Jewish monotheism, can be spoken of in ways which imply that within the full description of this one God there must be room for (at least) bipolarity. Thus, on the one hand, it is indeed the case that the poem envisaged God's purpose in creation as being to sum up all things in the man Jesus. It is, further, extremely likely that by writing ὅς ἐστιν εἰκὼν τοῦ θεοῦ τοῦ ἀοράτου the author intended to refer to the human (and now exalted) Jesus. But these points need not force us to abandon any reference in vv.15–17 to

[53]*Pace* Dunn *loc. cit.*, Murphy-O'Connor 1978.
[54]See Meeks 1983, 165–70.
[55]*Contra* O'Neill 1979, who claims that the entire christology of Colossians is derived from Jewish ideas simply put together by the Christian writer.

one who, though not yet a human being (the idea of *human* pre-existence is completely foreign to this world of thought), was God's agent in the creation of the world, and thus perfectly fitted to *become* human and so to take the leading role in the unfolding drama of God's purposes for recreating the world. In becoming, under God, the predestined human lord of the world, he has taken his rightful place, since from the beginning he was the Father's agent, as the true Wisdom of God, in the work of creation. The word εἰκών, though almost certainly referring primarily to Christ as being now the perfect human being, carries with it (particularly when viewed against its background in Hellenistic Judaism) the idea of the *appropriateness* of the position he now enjoys. He has, in that sense, become what he always was. The pre-existent lord of the world has become the human lord of the world, and in so doing has reflected fully, for the eyes of the world to see, the God whose human image he has now come to bear. This explains once more, as we saw in the last chapter, the nature of the language often used to describe this figure: as in 2 Corinthians 8.9, the pre-existent one, who (strictly speaking) had not yet 'become' Jesus of Nazareth, can be referred to by that name in advance, much as we might say 'the Queen was born in 1925'.[56]

This means, I think, that the recent questions raised about the idea of pre-existence in this passage can be quite satisfactorily answered. (It is one of the oddities of recent scholarship that most writers have assumed that pre-existence is here spoken of, without stopping to enquire what precisely it might mean in the first century; only a few have argued against the idea, so that in recent literature at least the battle has not really been joined.) First, it is true that the figure of Wisdom in Hellenistic-Jewish literature does not become a divine being apart from or other than the one God of Jewish monotheism; but, as we have seen, this does not settle the question, (a) because *Religionsgeschichte* cannot take us all the way into what is essentially a new and radical development and (b) because the whole point of 'christological monotheism' is that, however we understand it, it never intends to assert that Christ is divine in a sense apart from or over against the one true God.[57] Second, the idea in v.18d of Christ's *becoming* pre-eminent cannot be taken to indicate that he was not pre-eminent already:[58] the poem presupposes that between creation and redemption there has taken place the great rebellion whereby the world, created through and for Christ, comes to stand in need also of reconciliation through him. The poem is not simply about a two-stage scheme in which Christ takes the throne which was already

---

[56]See above, p. 96 f.

[57]*Contra* Murphy-O'Connor 1977, 48: Pollard 1981, 574: Caird 1976, 177. Aletti 1981, 141–82 distinguishes 'wisdom-influence' from 'wisdom-christology', finding the first but not the second here; I think my view differs from his more in form than in substance.

[58]Against Caird 179 f.; see Dunn 1980, 332 n. 99.

his: it envisages his *becoming*, in the resurrection, what by right of creation he already was, and what he had apparently lost through the usurpation of evil. The apparent tension of 18e and 16–17 is thus resolved. Third, while it is no doubt true that a first-century Jew would understand God to have had various purposes in mind from the beginning, and that a first-century Christian Jew would have understood the life, death and resurrection of Jesus to have been among those purposes, this of itself does not mean that the apparent references here to the pre-existent Christ can be reduced simply to terms of a 'divine intent'.[59] Nor will it do simply to say that 'Christ is divine in no other sense than as God immanent, God himself acting to redeem as he did to create':[60] this still leaves open the question of how Christ is to be spoken of alongside God the Father—as Paul, and the author of Colossians if other than Paul, regularly do speak. We are forced to say that if the language employed here means anything, it means that Christ is *both* to be identified as the divine Wisdom, i.e. none other than the one creator God active in creation and now in redemption, *and* to be distinguished from the Father, not as in a dualism whereby two gods are opposed, nor as in a paganism where two gods are distinguished and given different (and in principle parallel) tasks, but within the framework of Jewish creational monotheism itself. It is, happily, being realized increasingly within New Testament studies that such a phenomenon is to be reckoned with in several parts of the New Testament.[61] It is now, I believe, necessary to assert that, although the writers of the New Testament did not themselves formulate the doctrine of the Trinity, they bequeathed to their successors a manner of speaking and writing about God which made it, or something very like it, almost inevitable.[62]

This poem, therefore, read as a poem in the way I set out in part (i), and as a new and creative expression of wisdom-theology as explored in part (ii), gives voice to a view of Jesus in which two Jewish theological themes are joined together, each of which speaks of the transcendent creator God as savingly active within his world. Within that context, of course, the poem has a good deal besides to add: we might note the allusion to Temple- and Shekinah-theology in 19a/b (cf. 2.9, and Ecclesiasticus 24.3–12), where the 'fulness' of God is 'pleased to dwell' in Christ, as in Psalm 67.17 (LXX) God had been pleased to dwell on Mount Zion.[63] But the main point is made: we have here a belief which, though expressed in language borrowed from the wisdom-tradition, goes beyond *religionsgeschichtliche* parallels and articulates

[59]As is suggested, e.g., by Pollard 574; cf. Caird 177 f.
[60]Dunn 1982, 330. See too the very imprecise and elusive formulations in Dunn 1980, 195 f.
[61]See Hurtado 1988, Kreitzer 1987, etc.
[62]See Young and Ford 1987, 255–60.
[63]See Schweizer 77, Beasley-Murray 177.

a form of Jewish monotheism not before envisaged, in which the Messiah himself is the dwelling-place of the divine wisdom, the immanent presence of the transcendent God, the visible image of the invisible God.

(iv) Conclusion

What role does the poem, thus interpreted, play in the developing thought of the letter as a whole? There is no space here to expound that view of Colossians which I believe to be correct—that the writer is not opposing an actual heresy in the church, but is writing to warn a young church against the blandishments of the synagogue which had proved so devastating to the young church in Galatia.[64] But further support for this position may be found in the actual emphases of the poem as I have explored it.[65]

The poem clearly transfers to Christ language and predicates which had, in some form or other, belonged in Judaism to Wisdom and Torah. This, coupled with the observations about the form of the poem in part (i), indicates that a claim is being made for Christ (and his people) which has a double cutting edge.[66] First, it tells against Judaism itself. All that Judaism had hoped to gain by belief in the one God, whose Wisdom was given to them in the form of Torah, was now to be gained through Christ. For him, and not for Israel, all things were created.[67] Having Christ, God's true Wisdom, the Colossian church possesses all that it needs (cf. 1 Corinthians 3.22 f.). Second, therefore, it tells against paganism, in just the same way, *mutatis mutandis*, that Jewish polemic had done: there is one creator/redeemer God, and both dualism and polytheism are shown up as metaphysically incorrect (and, for that matter, morally bankrupt). The poem thus has an implicit ecclesiological and perhaps even sociological function, behind the issues of form, background and theology: a community that believed these things would be distinct from neighbours both Jewish and pagan.

This, alas, would only help us with the vexed question of authorship (both of 1.15–20 and of Colossians as a whole) if there were more certainty about Paul's own attitudes on such matters. But the theology of the poem as a whole seems to me thoroughly consonant with what we know of Paul from

[64]See Wright 1986c, 23–30 and *passim*.

[65]In what follows some similarities will be found to the article of Hooker 1973. I believe that my analysis enables her position to be both securely established and further developed.

[66]In what follows, compare Meeks 1983, 164–70, locating such polemic within the social world of the Pauline churches.

[67]For the idea that the world was made for the sake of Israel, see e.g. 2 Esdr. 6.54–9, 7.11, 2 Bar. 14.18 f., 15.7, 21.24, *Pirke Aboth* 6.11–12 (a passage with several parallels to our present subject-matter), Ps. Sol. 18.4.

elsewhere. And, after all, if the letter were deutero-Pauline, and the poem were written earlier than the letter, why should not the shadowy poet be Paul himself? This suggestion, though perfectly logical, is not often made, perhaps because the real reason for refusing to attribute Colossians to Paul is because its overall theology, including that of 1.15–20, is held to be different from his. Another reason could be that it would give the game away, since it might appear that (a) Colossians 1.15–20 fits very well where it stands in the letter,[68] and that (b) in form, background and theology it belongs closely with the essential hallmarks of that worldview which, arguably, underlies all of Paul's thought: monotheism and election, redefined by means of christology.[69]

[68]See Getty 1985.
[69]See chs. 1 and 14 of the present volume.

Chapter Six

MONOTHEISM, CHRISTOLOGY AND ETHICS: 1 CORINTHIANS 8[1]

(i) Introduction

There are several issues at stake in the study of 1 Corinthians 8.[2] (1) What is the problem Paul is addressing, and what is his solution to it? What is the social setting within which this all occurs? Is his audience basically pagan with a Christian overlay, basically Jewish in their thinking, or what? (2) What is Paul's basic solution to the problem? Does this solution make sense, or is there a *non sequitur*, as is often thought, between vv.1–3 and 4–6? How do vv.1–3 relate, in other words, to the question with which he begins, and which he subsequently addresses, concerning idol-meat? At the larger level, how does ch. 8 relate to chs. 9–10? Does the argument of the entire section actually work? (3) Against what background in the history of first-century religion is the problem, and Paul's advice in particular, best understood? Is Paul simply picking up themes from the gentile world and playing variations on them? Is he, on the other hand, simply requiring of his converts that they follow basic Jewish practice? Does the debate have any relation to the so-called Apostolic Decree of Acts 15? If so, what? If not, why not? Does Paul's position owe anything to Jesus? Is it perhaps a completely fresh formulation, with only tangential relation to some or all of the above? (4) How, using this passage as something of a test case, are (what we call) theology and ethics related in Paul? Is the tie between them simply pragmatic, with Paul trying out different ethical guidelines according to different situations, and inventing theological rationalizations for them as he goes along, or is there a deeper coherence than that? One instance of this problem would be the question already raised: does he employ different, and perhaps contradictory, arguments in chs. 9 and 10 to that which he sets out in ch. 8? Or has he, as is sometimes suggested, offered a comparatively 'lax' view in ch. 8, and in 10.23—11.1, but a 'stricter' one in 10.1–22? (5) What on

---

[1]Earlier versions of this chapter were given to the Pauline Studies section of the Society of Biblical Literature in Anaheim, California in November 1989, and to the New Testament Seminar in Oxford in May 1990. I am grateful to members of both groups for their comments.

[2]This list expands somewhat those in Conzelmann 1975 <1969>, 137–8 and Fee 1987, 358. See too, in addition to the other obvious commentaries, Barrett 1964–5; Fee 1980; Murphy-O'Connor 1978a, 1978b; Horsley 1978a, 1980; Willis 1985; Tomson 1990, chs. 4 and 5.

earth—or anywhere else, for that matter—does v.6 mean, with its apparently extraordinarily 'high' christology? What did Paul intend by using this formulation? Where did it come from, and why? It is this last question that ties the present discussion to the topic of the first half of this book, though we cannot fully appreciate what Paul says about Jesus here without seeing the whole chapter as its context.[3]

The basic argument I shall advance here cannot deal, of course, with all these problems as fully as they might deserve. I shall suggest that Paul, in addressing a very specific situation and problem, argues from basic, and thoroughly theological, principles to a view which is, in terms of the history of religions, specifically and uniquely Christian, and that in the middle of his argument v.6 functions as a Christian redefinition of the Jewish confession of faith, the *Shema*.

I begin with some general observations. The first concerns the problem that we face in discussing (what we call) 'ethics' in the post-Kantian world. The word 'ethics' now functions within modern Western discourse in relation, I suggest, to a specifically Kantian scheme, which has traditionally opposed *ought* to *is*, imperative to indicative, and so forth. Within this tradition, it is commonly assumed that all human beings in all societies thought this way. At this stage I simply want to register this as a problem, and to suggest that we must consciously think our way out of anachronisms if we are to hope to understand Paul (or for that matter anyone else in the first century).

The second observation is that we live not only in a post-Kantian world but also, in the Western church at least, in a post-Lutheran world. Seen through the haze of the Romantic movement, this produces in Western minds a strict antithesis between a religion that depends on, or largely consists in, 'rules', and one that has done away with them in the interests of grace and/or spiritual freedom. This perspective has sometimes encouraged interpreters to play off (for instance) Galatians against 1 Corinthians, since Paul seems to be against rules and regulations in the first and in favour of them in the second. Paul is, by turns, a libertine and a legalist. It seems to me, however, that this is another false dichotomy. There is no need to postulate that Paul had a change of mind or heart between the writing of these two letters. Nor has the situation taken Paul by surprise, as though he had imagined that his Corinthian church was perfect and then, discovering that they had problems like everybody else, panicked and shot from the hip with whatever pragmatic solutions came to mind. He does not, as we shall see, alter his basic theological stance in order to address the issue at hand. He did not need to.

---

[3]My whole argument will show why I regard as misguided such statements as that of W.L. Knox (1939, 124), who sees the reference here to Jesus as the Wisdom of God as completely irrelevant to the question of the unity of God and the eating of εἰδωλόθυτα.

This leads to my third observation: that in modern theology and exegesis we are encouraged to play off the merely situational from the fundamental and foundational. I have already looked at this in ch. 1 above. The fact that someone has a reason for saying something, or actually an agenda which is influencing the way they present a case, does not mean *ipso facto* that the case is flawed or badly argued, full of rationalizations, deserving instant dismissal by those who can come without bias. The latter ideal is, of course, illusory. Let him without an agenda cast the first stone.

My fourth and final observation leads into the consideration of the chapter itself. It seems to me that in the categories we habitually use to understand Paul, borrowed as they are very largely from the sixteenth, eighteenth and nineteenth centuries, we have actually ignored certain quite different categories of thought that we know perfectly well, for good reasons within the history of first-century religion and theology, were of enormous importance to anyone within the Jewish, and nascent Christian, world. The major issues at stake there were monotheism, idolatry, election, holiness and how these interacted. And if that list sounds abstract, removed from the actual life-setting of actual churches, it is because we have forgotten, or have not yet learned (e.g. from the work of Meeks) that precisely these 'theological' issues functioned as shorthand ways of articulating the points of pressure, tension and conflict between different actual communities, specifically, Jews and pagans. It is therefore scarcely surprising if one part of the early church, on which a bright spotlight happens to be shed by Paul's correspondence, should demonstrate tension in just these areas; nor is it surprising if we find that categories like these, instead of those bequeathed to us by either the Enlightenment, the Reformation or any other more recent movements, should turn out to be more helpful than later ones in working out the inner logic of Paul's argument.

(ii) The Setting within First-Century Religious History

We may begin by looking at the background to the whole debate within the history of first-century religion. At this point we run, of course, into the celebrated problems that have dominated so much study of 1 Corinthians; indeed, it is the puzzles generated by the chapters we are looking at that have caused several scholars to abandon the integrity of the letter and settle for some form of partition-theory.[4] This being the case, it is as well to look at the religious background first; decisions taken here will affect the shape of the subsequent argument.

[4]See the discussions of Barrett 1971, 11–17; Fee 1980, 172 ff., 1987, 15–16; Brunt 1985, 122 n.2.

There are two suggestions which can be safely set aside from the beginning. The first is that there was, in the ancient world in general at this time and in Corinth not least, a fully-blown Gnosticism of the sort we find in the (much later) Nag Hammadi texts. Paul, on this view, is combating Gnosticism but at the same time sailing quite close to its prevailing wind in his own theology. This view still finds support from time to time, but it has now been massively undermined, as we see in the work (for instance) of Hengel. The second is that Paul was faced in Corinth with the so-called 'Judaizing' movement that faced him in Galatia. Although (as we will see) there is considerable evidence of Jewish influence on the church to whom he is writing, this strong view of the Jewishness of the Corinthian problem fails completely to explain why it is that Paul never uses in this letter the sort of arguments, or even the tone of voice, that we find in Galatia. Clearly he is able to differentiate between one sort of problem and another, even though both may well contain elements of Jewish thinking.

Another suggestion that must be taken far more seriously has recently been made by R.A. Horsley.[5] He has argued that we can find the background to Paul's argument—and to the implicit argument of those he is opposing—in the sort of Hellenistic Judaism represented by the works of Philo, and by the book known as the Wisdom of Solomon. Leaving aside the question, which he does not address, as to whether the latter work really belongs in the same category as Philo, we may note first the shape of Horsley's suggestion: that there was in the first century a well-established Hellenistic-Jewish mission in Gentile territory, which attempted to persuade Gentiles to believe in the one true God of Judaism, who had made the world by his Wisdom, his σοφία. Knowledge of this one true God was the true γνῶσις, and this gave to the knower a wisdom, a σοφία, which was identical in fact to the Wisdom by which the world was made in the first place. This enabled the knower, the wise person, to dismiss all paganism as simply spurious nonsense: idols were non-existent, and could be treated with the contempt they deserved. The passages in Wisdom and Philo which Horsley adduces to support this hypothesis speak of Wisdom, or of the λόγος, as the one 'by whom/through whom all things were made'.[6]

Horsley's suggestion, then, is that among the Corinthian Christians, perhaps among the leaders of the church, were some who had drunk deeply

---

[5]Horsley 1978a, 1980. On the same theme see also the much earlier article of Feuillet 1962–3, quoting e.g. Marcus Aurelius 4.23. Feuillet, however, draws back from deriving Paul's thought here from the parallel Hellenistic material.

[6]Thus, e.g.: Wisd. 9.1–2, ὁ ποιήσας τὰ πάντα ἐν λόγῳ σου καὶ τῇ σοφίᾳ σου κατασκευάσας ἄνθρωπον...; Philo *Quod Deterius* 54, where the reader is exhorted to honour the creator as a father, and to honour Wisdom as a mother, through whom the totality was completed: μητέρα δὲ τὴν σοφίαν, δι' ἧς ἀπετελέσθη τὸ πᾶν...; cf. too Philo, *De Cherub.*, 127, etc., and other references in Horsley 1978a, 132 f.

at this well, and who were teaching the church in accordance with this style of Hellenistic Judaism. They were not gnostics of the usual pagan kind, denying the goodness of the created order; they were Jewish-style gnostics, whose γνῶσις enabled them to affirm creation. (Horsley does not make it clear whether he thinks that these people were in fact pagans who had themselves been won over by the Hellenistic-Jewish mission before or after becoming Christians, or rather simply Hellenistic Jews who had become Christians; this might be a significant distinction in the circumstances.) In particular, they were teaching three things which Paul is concerned about: we all have γνῶσις, idols have no real existence, and we are therefore free to eat what we like. They are, in other words, the 'strong' Christians in Corinth, backing up their liberated attitude to idol-meat with a Hellenistic-Jewish theology. Horsley then suggests that Paul, in reply, insists on love of the community as the primary obligation, substitutes Christ for σοφία in their theological scheme (as he had done already in 1.24, 30, etc.), and then argues for the alternative Jewish theological analysis of idolatry, namely, that worship of idols is really worship of demons.[7] On this basis Paul attempts, according to Horsley, to undermine the ethic of the 'strong' without really coming to head-on disagreement with them.

There are several strengths to this analysis. It has clearly highlighted an important feature of the Jewish background, and makes good sense of some parts of the text.[8] It explains, for instance, the apparently 'gnostic' references without adding the nonsense of supposing that Paul's opponents are gnostics of the Nag Hammadi (or other later pagan) type. But there are certain problems with it as well. For a start, I am not convinced that there were two types of Jewish attitude to idols, easily separable and distinguished, the one Hellenistic (idols are non-existent) and the other Palestinian and 'apocalyptic' (idols are demons in disguise).[9] This seems to me to over-simplify the evidence quite considerably, as well as perpetuating the dichotomy, now repeatedly shown to be far too simplistic, between Greek and Palestinian Judaism (and for that matter between apocalyptic and non-apocalyptic thought). In particular, Horsley's scheme does not explain why Paul emphasizes the love of *God* in v.3;[10] it does not explain the extremely interesting usage of θεός and κύριος in v.6; and it leaves the argument as a whole loose and untidy, with the suggestion of *non sequiturs* still in the air. I

---

[7]See Horsley 1980, 50.

[8]Fee 1987, 370 f. n.7, does not seem to me to have done justice to this when he describes Horsley's analysis as 'nearly irrelevant'. He is right to stress that Paul's opponents had become Christians, and that this must have relativized their background beliefs; but this does not prevent us from seeing Hellenistic Judaism as the religious milieu which had informed their belief-structures before and might well do so still.

[9]See the more nuanced discussion in Tomson 1990, 155–7.

[10]Horsley 1980, 49.

want, therefore, to make a suggestion which, though broadly compatible with Horsley's analysis, goes beyond it and locates the centre of Paul's argument in a Judaism which is more fundamental than any distinction between Greek and Palestinian, gnostic or apocalyptic. Paul, I suggest, goes back to the foundation of all Jewish spirituality: he argues for a Christian understanding of the *Shema*.[11]

(iii) Monotheism as the Foundation of Paul's Argument.

One of the most basic features of Paul's argument in ch. 8 has been surprisingly ignored or downplayed in most of the literature, and it is this, I suggest, that has resulted in the charge of *non sequiturs*, or the comment that Paul's argument is full of holes. He is facing the issue of how Christianity is to function, sociologically and culturally, within pagan society, and his basic rule of thumb for addressing this question is, as one might have predicted from a Jewish background, the reassertion of Jewish-style monotheism. Failure to highlight this central aspect of the chapter results in problems, which are not alleviated by the various things regularly done with the passage, such as isolating the remarks of Paul's opponents and attempting various mirror-reading exercises.[12]

What precisely is this monotheism, and how does it work out at the initial level? Jewish monotheism at this period was not a matter of theoretical belief, of speculative investigation of the being of God for its own sake. It was the fighting doctrine which engaged in battle on two fronts: against dualism, the rejection of the goodness of the created order, and against paganism, the deification of the created order or parts of it, or of forces within it. The second of these (paganism) seems to have been more important in the period we are considering. The belief that Israel's God was the God of all the earth committed Judaism to a radical anti-pagan stance, as we see precisely in the wisdom literature; and, conversely, the oppression and frequent invasion suffered by Judaism at the hands of pagans in the same period reinforced the Jew's belief that her one God, as the rightful sovereign of all the earth, would eventually take his rightful power, vindicate his people, and put her oppressors in their place. Monotheism was therefore exactly the doctrine to which one would appeal in going back to first principles when faced with the question as to how a group that asserted its

---

[11]I thus agree with Dunn 1980, 179 and nn., in saying that the formula, though containing echoes of a good deal in the Hellenistic background, itself represents something of an innovation.

[12]It is remarkable that so careful and valuable a study as that of Tomson 1990, ch. 5 does not bring Paul's revised monotheism into the argument at all.

continuity with the (Jewish) people of God (cf. 1 Corinthians 10.1, etc.) might behave when faced with living in a pagan society.

Equally, it is clear that Paul, like many Jews of the period, was just as alert to the dangers of lapsing into a metaphysical or ontological dualism. This, the natural temptation for someone recoiling in horror from pagan excess, would lead to a rejection of the goodness of the created order; and against this, too, Jewish-style monotheism set its face. If there was one God, the creator of the world and the God of Israel, the world and everything in it was basically good, however much corrupted by pagan idolatry and its consequences. This lies at the heart of some of his argument in the previous chapter: marriage and sex are basically good, even though circumstances may call for abstinence in particular times and cases.[13]

This two-pronged battle, I suggest, helps to explain the delicate nature of Paul's argument throughout 1 Corinthians 8. He is determined to maintain the balance of genuine creational monotheism, warding off the dangers (as he would see it) of dualism on the one hand and of paganism on the other. Dualism of a serious kind is probably not an option in the present argument: as we saw, the kind of γνῶσις hypothetically embraced by his opponents did not involve a rejection of the material order; yet it remained as a theoretical possibility within the ancient world, pointing towards an asceticism that would have simply told the Corinthians that they had better stop worrying about food altogether, give up whatever they could do without, and cultivate a pure non-material spirituality. Paul never takes that course. Equally, he refuses to move in the other direction. For the church to embrace the hypothetical 'strong' position would be, from his point of view, to remove the taboos against eating meat offered to idols (i.e. virtually all meat in the average pagan city),[14] and thus to lose its basic critique, again typically Jewish, of its pagan environment.[15] The church must retain the true dimensions of monotheism, standing firm against dualism and paganism alike.

Paul's argument, starting from this position, may be understood as follows. He is reaffirming the basic Jewish tradition about paganism—that it is idolatry, and that genuine monotheists must not flirt with it. But he then argues (a) that the 'strong' position of his opponents (whether they were one party within the church or, as Fee thinks, the church as a whole) might, after

[13]See 1 Cor. 7; and compare 3.22 f.

[14]Barrett, following Erhardt 1964, suggests that non-sacrificial meat was available, and that in any case many people did not eat meat regularly (see too Tomson 1990, 189). But it remains likely that the bulk of meat available had been offered in idol-worship (see Lane Fox 1987, 70), and that (Erhardt, 279) in a city like Corinth pagan temples served as the equivalent of modern restaurants.

[15]See, e.g., Rom. 1.18–32, 1 Thess. 1.9, both with multiple echoes of the regular Jewish critiques of paganism.

all, lead them into an accidental paganism (this comes out most strongly in 10.1–22, on which see below), and (b) that true monotheism is found, not in a Hellenistic-Jewish γνῶσις and its accompanying σοφία, but in Jesus Christ.[16] In other words, he both analyses and criticizes his opponents' position on the basis of the *Shema.*

The first result of this suggestion is that it explains at a stroke the reason for vv.1–3 in the argument as a whole. Paul responds to the claim to γνῶσις by insisting on the primacy of (not love in general, but) the Jewish-style allegiance to the one God: Hear, O Israel, the Lord our God, the Lord is one. Thus:

> Concerning idol-meat, we know that 'we all have γνῶσις'. Γνῶσις puffs you up,[17] but love builds you up. If someone imagines that he 'knows' something, he does not yet 'know' as he ought to 'know';[18] but if someone 'loves God', he is 'known' by him.

Paul is about to quote the *Shema* explicitly in v.4, but it should be clear from this that he already has it firmly in mind, so that the quotation in v.4 merely reveals what was under the argument all along. The question, it seems, is not simply about a matter of behaviour. It is about the definition of the people of God; and, for Paul, that definition can be stated, in Deuteronomic terms, by means of the *Shema.* The real *Gnosis*, Paul is saying, is not your *Gnosis* of God but God's *Gnosis* of you, and the sign of that being present is that one keeps the *Shema*: you shall love the Lord your God with all your heart. Paul's references to humans loving God, as opposed to vice versa, are few and far between, and in this case at least, and arguably in some of the others, the reason for the reference is that he wishes to allude to, or echo, the Jewish confession of monotheistic faith.[19]This brings Paul to the clear statement of monotheism itself:

[16]It is possible that here we may see some parallels with the underlying argument in Col. 1.15–20, studied in the previous chapter, and this might increase the likelihood that in 1 Cor., too, there is a veiled polemic against Jewish Torah-speculations; but this would take us too far out of the way in the present argument.

[17]Note how thoroughly this theme belongs within 1 Cor. as a whole: of the seven occurrences of φυσιόω in the Pauline corpus, six are in this letter (4.6, 4.18, 4.19, 5.2, 8.1, 13.4), and the seventh, Col. 2.18, is from a context whose polemic is arguably quite similar.

[18]The inverted commas are designed to indicate that Paul, perhaps contemptuously, is tossing around the root which is cognate with γνῶσις itself.

[19]See Rom. 5.5 (debatable, of course, but a case can be made); 8.28; 1 Cor. 2.9. Compare Ecclus. 1.10. It is remarkable that so few have noticed the reference to the *Shema* in v.3. For Conzelmann (1975, 141) it is simply a matter of 'the individual's immediate relationship to God' being logically prior to 'love of the brethren'. In Horsley's case, it seems to have something to do with his determination to read as much of Paul as he can on the basis of Greek philosophy rather than the Hebrew Bible: see, for instance, Horsley 1980, 35. In Fee's case, his insistence that Paul's theology grows out of his Christian belief, while true, has led him to the strange position whereby the relevant parts of Deut. do not figure at all in his entire discussion of 8.1–6 (Fee 1987, 357–376).

(4) Concerning meat offered to idols, then, we know that 'there is no idol in the world' and that 'there is no god but one'.

Paul is agreeing in principle with his opponents. Monotheism is what matters, and one must not think of the cosmos as being peopled with multiple deities of whom the god of Abraham, Isaac and Jacob is but one. There are, however, problems (he insists) with a simplistic understanding of this; and in his initial analysis of these problems (vv.5–6) we can find contained in a nutshell the entire subsequent discussion, with all its subtlety.

(5) Well, though, there may be many so-called gods, whether in heaven or on earth—just as there are many 'gods' and many 'lords'—...

The pagan pantheon cannot simply be dismissed as metaphysically nonexistent and therefore morally irrelevant. It signals an actual phenomenon within the surrounding culture that must be faced and dealt with, not simply sidestepped.[20] For this reason—which Paul will deal with in more detail in ch. 10—the allegiance of local paganism to this or that 'god' and 'lord' must be met with nothing short of the Christian version of Jewish-style, *Shema*-style, monotheism. It is this that Paul now states. Whatever its links with the Hellenistic-Jewish world of Philo and others, v.6 resonates thoroughly with echoes of the far more ancient and widespread formula from Deuteronomy 6.4.[21] In the Hebrew the confession of faith begins with the words:

[20]We cannot address in detail here the question of Paul's beliefs about idols and demons, important though it is for a full understanding of chs. 8–10 as a whole. Barrett 1964–5, 148, cites Billerbeck's phenomenology of Jewish attitudes to idols (Strack-Billerbeck 3.48–60), which gives already five categories as opposed to the two oversimplified ones offered by Horsley 1980; the two which correspond to Horsley's (idols are demons in disguise; idols are non-existent) are supported with texts which show that his classification of the former as Palestinian and apocalyptic and the latter as Hellenistic will not do, since, to look no further, Jub. is found as a witness on both sides (22.17 for the 'demonic' view, 12.1 ff. for the 'non-existent' view). Chrysostom, *Hom. on 1 Cor.* 20.2 (*PG* 61.163), cited by Conzelmann 143 n. 33 and Lietzmann 1969, 37, shows that Horsley's two views can easily be combined: idols exist, but are powerless; they are not gods, ἀλλὰ λίθοι καὶ δαίμονες. See further Elmslie 1911, 42 f., citing the 'demonic' view not only Bar. 4.7 and the proem to Sib. Or., but also Athenagoras Πρεσβεῖα 26 (*PG* 6.950–2). Elmslie's conclusion is that the 'demonic' view is rare, and probably belongs within Judaism among the uneducated and those influenced by Hellenistic ideas. However overstated this may be, it shows how difficult it is to maintain that this view is *the* 'Palestinian' or 'apocalyptic' view over against the Hellenistic one, as Horsley tries to do. See further below, and n. 39.

[21]It is extraordinary that Nestle-Aland have no marginal reference to Deut. 6.4 beside v.6, but only with v.4. Even so detailed a study as Willis 1985 does not mention the *Shema*. Dunn 1980, 179 f. and n. 67, sees the same phenomenon as I do here, but draws different conclusions. See, similarly, Grässer 1981, 199 f.

שמע ישראל יהוה אלהנו יהוה אחד

In the Septuagint this reads:

ἄκουε Ἰσραηλ· κύριος ὁ θεὸς ἡμῶν κύριος εἷς ἐστιν.

What Paul seems to have done is as follows. He has expanded the formula, in a way quite unprecedented in any other texts known to us, so as to include a gloss on θεός and another on κύριος:[22]

> ἀλλ' ἡμῖν
> εἷς θεὸς ὁ πατήρ,
>> ἐξ οὗ τὰ πάντα καὶ ἡμεῖς εἰς αὐτόν,
> καὶ εἷς κύριος Ἰησοῦς Χριστός,
>> δι' οὗ τὰ πάντα καὶ ἡμεῖς δι' αὐτοῦ.

Paul, in other words, has glossed 'God' with 'the Father', and 'Lord' with 'Jesus Christ', adding in each case an explanatory phrase: 'God' is the Father, 'from whom are all things and we to him', and the 'Lord' is Jesus the Messiah, 'through whom are all things and we through him'. There can be no mistake: just as in Philippians 2 and Colossians 1, Paul has placed Jesus *within* an explicit statement, drawn from the Old Testament's quarry of emphatically monotheistic texts, of the doctrine that Israel's God is the one and only God, the creator of the world. The *Shema* was already, at this stage of Judaism, in widespread use as *the* Jewish daily prayer.[23] Paul has redefined it christologically, producing what we can only call a sort of christological monotheism.[24]

This fact is becoming more widely recognized in recent scholarship, though its omission from some of the older literature remains remarkable.[25]

---

[22]See Hurtado 1988, 97 f., Wright 1986b, 208. Héring 1962, 69 notes that εἷς θεός in v.6 'reminds us of the famous "Shema Israel"', but does not pursue the significance of the parallel—though he does note the closeness of this christology to that of Col. 1.

[23]Cf. mBer. 1 ff., etc.

[24]The question, whether he is also redefining old pantheistic formulae, lies, I think, further off, despite Conzelmann 1975, 144. Conzelmann's description of a casual change of the meaning of formulae, from Stoic pantheism to Jewish-style creational monotheism leaves one rather breathless: such a total change in worldview is not accomplished with a stroke of the pen. If Paul has inherited formulae and adapted them, they were, I think, already creational, not pantheistic, in their content.

[25]See Rainbow 1987, Hurtado 1988, etc.

What we do with it at the level of a further analysis of Paul's christology, however, is as yet uncertain. We may begin with some comments about the immediate effect of this astonishing statement in terms of the Corinthian worldview, as (for instance) reconstructed by Horsley. Jesus, in this newly coined formula (newly coined, that is, either by Paul or by someone not long before)[26] takes the place of κύριος within the *Shema*, and also takes the place of σοφία within the hypothetical Hellenistic Judaism. In a manner very similar to that of the Colossians poem, Paul has indicated that everything one might hope to gain through possessing σοφία can be gained rather by possessing Christ.

This explains at a stroke the thing which neither Horsley, Conzelmann, nor others writing in similar vein, can explain: why, in addition to referring the phrases δι' οὗ τὰ πάντα καὶ ἡμεῖς δι' αὐτοῦ to Jesus, rather than to σοφία, has Paul produced a formula in which there is an implicit distinction between θεός and κύριος? The answer should now be clear. He is not simply answering Hellenistic Judaism in its own terms, though he is also doing that as it were *en route*. He is going back to the foundations, and laying the claim that the people defined by *this* formula of belief form a new family with a new code of family behaviour.

Before exploring this aspect of the passage, though, we must be sure to draw out the full christological implications of the formula now before us. As in some other passages we have already studied, Paul refers to the creator God as 'Father', so that, though he does not in this passage call Jesus 'son', the idea is certainly present by implication, just as in Philippians 2.11.[27] This is the mirror-image of 1 Corinthians 15.28, where the distinction is between the son and 'God' or 'the one who subjected all things to him'. Paul seems to be aware that he is at the edge of normal language at this point—hardly surprising, considering the enormity of the theological move implied in v.6—but nevertheless seems happy with the following basic position: that when he wants to express the unprecedented bifurcation within monotheism that he believes must be expressed, the language for which he reaches is father/son language, or (if you like) God/Israel or God/Messiah language. This language, by its new *context*, is thereby given new *content*, which does not cancel out the content it used to have within the Hebrew Bible and subsequent Jewish writing, but rather actually emphasizes it. The Jesus of whom these astonishing things are said is none other than the Jesus who is recognized as Messiah, the Jesus who has done what Israel was called to do.

[26]As elsewhere, I do not find speculation on the pre-Pauline provenance of v.6 profitable. However, those interested in such things may like to note that the word-count of the formula, discounting the initial connecting ἀλλ', is, line by line, 5/8/5/8, and the syllable-count is 8/11/9/11. See the remarks on the Col. 1 poem, ch. 5 above.

[27]So, rightly, Langkammer 1970–71, 194; on the other side, Conzelmann 1975, 144, suggesting that 'father' here means simply 'creator'.

Nor is the wisdom-context thereby relativized. The role undertaken by Jesus within the formula, that of being the creator's obedient agent, ruling wisely over the world, is one that can now devolve appropriately onto humans, made as they are in the creator's image. Thus, for instance, Wisdom 9.2: Solomon, acknowledging that the divine σοφία is that by which the world was made, asks specifically for σοφία so that he can rule God's people wisely. This indicates a point of enormous importance which lies right at the heart of this newly-coined Pauline christology. The becoming human of the one by whose agency the world was made was not a category mistake, a forcing of square pegs into round holes, but was the appropriate climax of a theme already well known. Paul denotes, with the human name 'Jesus', and the human title 'Messiah', the one who would become human, and be given that name and that title, and who would be obedient to their implication by doing within the human sphere that which, prior to becoming human, had already been his task and role. He would be the creator's mediating agent in his work in the world, as in making, so now in remaking. Conversely, if—as Paul clearly believes—Jesus is the one through whom his people are reconciled to the creator, through whom therefore is being brought about the dawn of the new creation, then it must follow that he is indeed the σοφία θεοῦ, the one through whom the creator himself is operating to remake that which, already made, had been spoilt through sin and corruption.[28]

It will not do, therefore, to say either that the whole formula is concerned simply with redemption, and not with creation,[29] or that 'Paul is not making a statement about the act of creation in the *past*, but rather about creation as believers see it *now*'.[30] Dunn's own arguments against Murphy-O'Connor tell as well against his own position: the point of what Paul is saying concerns the Christian attitude to creation itself; and in any case the background to the phrase in the complexities of religious history tells strongly in favour of a statement, here as in Colossians 1.15–16, of the pre-existent activity, mediating the creation, of the one who then became human as Jesus of Nazareth. To say that Christ's Lordship 'is the continuation and fullest expression of God's own creative power'[31] is to affirm Paul's continuing monotheism at the cost of unclarity in christology; and to spell this out by saying that 'Christ is being identified here not with a pre-existent being but with the creative power and action of God' simply begs the question, especially in the light of our exegesis of Philippians 2 and Colossians 1.[32]

---

[28]On the wisdom-christology, there is a list of relevant older German works, and a useful collection of primary references, in Conzelmann 1975, 145 n. 49.

[29]So Murphy-O'Connor 1978a, rightly criticized by Dunn 1980, 329, n.69.

[30]Dunn 1980, 181 (italics original), citing also Thüsing and Wainwright.

[31]Dunn 1980, 182; the whole clause is in italics.

[32]Ibid.; again all in italics. Dunn claims (183) that it is only when we remove the phrase from its present context that it becomes 'a vehicle for a christology of pre-existence'; my present argument suggests that it is this precisely as it stands, in its exegetical setting, its

This christology therefore stands firmly beside that which we have found in Philippians 2 and Colossians 1. Here, as there, we find a statement of the highest possible christology—that is, of Jesus placed within the very monotheistic confession itself—set within an argument which is itself precisely and profoundly monotheistic. One of the strange things, in fact, about the history of the exegesis of this passage is that no-one so far as I know has commented on this fact, which one might have thought would have been the most interesting feature of the entire chapter. But if the argument of 1 Corinthians 8 thus provides a showcase to set off the high, and characteristically Pauline, christology, the reverse is also true. We can understand the argument of the chapter (and the whole section) better, now that we have seen its central theological underpinning.

(iv) Monotheism, Christology and the New Community

This analysis of the central christological confession, then, reveals the coherence of the train of thought in the chapter as a whole. It is not a string of *non sequiturs*. Nor does the formula reach 'far beyond the context',[33] except in the obvious sense that all major christological statements have far-reaching implications: the Christianized *Shema* is exactly what Paul needs at exactly this point in his argument, when he is reasserting monotheism on the one hand and arguing on the other for the primacy of love. The love of God—the fulfilled *Shema*—is the central characteristic of the true people of God, over against a spurious γνῶσις which simply leaves them inflated with their own self-importance. This love of God is focussed more precisely in the christological monotheism expressed in the confession of v.6, in which, just as in Colossians 1, the true God stands over against all the created orders, heavenly and earthly. It is therefore this confession which marks out the people of God against their neighbours, both Jewish and pagan, much as in the tripartite division of 10.32 ('Jews, Greeks and the church of God').[34] The confession of 'one God, one Lord' marked the community out sociologically as well as theologically.

Such a redefined monotheism could never remain, either, a mere replacement for the Jewish confession. The redefinition effected by putting

---

history-of-religions context, and its theological meaning. Dunn, not perhaps for the first time, appears to be working with a limited view of what 'pre-existence' might mean, and assuming, against what seems to me the tenor of Paul's thought, that it is incompatible with that robust Jewish monotheism which Paul continues to affirm.

[33]Conzelmann 1975, 144.

[34]See Meeks 1983, especially 164–170.

Jesus at the heart of the Jewish belief-system was bound to affect the way the belief worked itself out in practice, and that is precisely the point of 1 Corinthians 8. If Jesus himself, the crucified and risen one, is the one through whom the creator has been at work to remake his creation, then the recognition of the cross at the heart of the creator must lead to an answering love for those who, like oneself, belong to the family that is being recreated. This family is none other, in incorporative language, than the Χριστός, the Messiah-and-his-people (see chs. 2 and 3 above), and love for the God who is revealed as Father/Creator and Messiah/Lord must therefore include, as a first priority, love for those who along with oneself belong to the family. This is essentially the point of vv.7–13, whose focus is vv.11–12:

> (11) The weak person is destroyed by your 'knowledge', the brother for whom Christ died. (12) Thus, sinning against the brothers and wounding their weakened conscience, you sin against Χριστός.

It is worth noting that in v.11 Paul has picked up, in order to expound, exactly those categories he has explored in vv.1–6. The opponents, with their 'strong' theology of a γνῶσις which enables them to eat what they like, secure in the non-existence of idols, fail to realize that at the heart of Christian monotheism stands a call to love all those who share the same faith, and to put their interests ahead of one's own permitted liberties. We are here, of course, in very much the same world as Philippians 2.1–5 and 6–11. What Paul has done in this chapter, addressing as it does an issue often regarded as theologically marginal and hermeneutically irrelevant, is to redefine *both* the central Jewish doctrines, monotheism and election, and to do so by means of the crucified and risen Jesus. God and the people of God are both redefined through Jesus the Messiah.

The result of this is that Paul's so-called ethic in this chapter, and in chs. 8–10 as a whole, can be seen not as a bit of *ad hoc* legislation, in which the apostle casts around in his mind for different (and incompatible) ways of persuading his congregation to do what he intends that they should do, but as the presentation of a new worldview, within which certain forms of behaviour are seen to be appropriate and certain forms inappropriate.[35] It is not, after all, a matter of simply dividing Christians into 'strong' and 'weak', and giving appropriate instructions to each group.[36] And the worldview which Paul articulates is easily recognizable. It is that of Colossians 1.15–20 and other passages, and it looks like this.

[35]Against Sanders 1983, 104, etc.

[36]My view is thus not dependent on any particular reconstruction of groups within Corinth, though I am inclined to agree with Fee that the 'weak' are Paul's hypothetical invention, faced with a church that is basically 'strong'.

There is one God, the creator. He has no rivals: there are no alternative 'gods', but merely those power-structures, the principalities and powers of heaven and earth, which were created 'through him and for him' (Colossians 1.16, cf. 1 Corinthians 8.5). This means that Paul can make two affirmations which have often been held to be in mutual tension. On the one hand, idols do not possess the same level of existence as the true God. This leaves Paul free to permit the eating of meat offered to them; the true God made all things, and all belongs to him (10.26, quoting Psalm 24.1[37]). On the other hand, Paul can designate the worship of these non-gods, these lesser beings, these essentially created power-structures, as the worship of demons: when humans worship that which is not God, they give to it a power over themselves, and perhaps over others, which by rights it does not have.[38] Here is the paradox of evil in Paul's thought, which is not understood by simplistic divisions between Hellenistic and Palestinian Judaism and the claim that Paul oscillates between the two.[39] This allows Paul, quite consistently, to ban the eating of meat in an idol-shrine itself. In the marketplace, all is permitted: once off the idol's turf, the food reverts to the sphere of the God who made it. But to enter an idol's temple, and eat there alongside those who are actually intending to share fellowship with this non-god, this hand-made pseudo-god—this is to invite created powers to have an authority over one which they do not possess, a power which belongs only to the creator-God revealed in and through Jesus the Messiah.[40]

We therefore arrive at the following analysis of Paul's argument, and at the conclusion that it is not muddled or self-contradictory. To the question, whether to eat meat offered to idols, Paul replies that if you mean going to an idol's temple, the answer is 'no': you may be observed by recent converts who would be tempted to revert to paganism (8.10), and you are in danger of

---

[37]Barrett 1964–5, 149 f., suggests that this reference is intended to evoke the Rabbinic justification (Tos. Ber. 4.1) of uttering benedictions over food, and to point to the good creation and the inaugurated new creation as the fundamental reasons for Paul's affirmation. This accords well with my whole argument.

[38]So Conzelmann 1975, 145: 'the gods *become* gods by being believed in, and faith in the *one* God and the *one* Lord creates freedom no longer to recognize these powers' (italics original).

[39]See above, n. 20. I thus incline to a tighter analysis of the way in which Paul holds together the belief that idols are non-existent and the belief that those who worship idols are worshipping demons than that of, e.g., Barrett 1971, 191: 'Paul himself undoubtedly believed in the real existence of demonic beings, and that these beings made use of idolatrous rites; the fact that they had been defeated, and were ultimately to be completely put down, by Christ, did not remove their threat to Christians, nor did the fact that the object of worship was in itself no more than a piece of wood or stone.' Compare Barrett 1964–5, 149 f.; and see too Robertson and Plummer 167. A good recent analysis is that of Wink 1986, 112 f. and notes.

[40]Tomson 1990, 207 argues against this solution, in the interests (I think) of maintaining slightly more continuity between Paul and his hypothetical Rabbinic background than is strictly warranted.

actually participating in demonic idolatry (10.1–22).[41] If, however, meat in the marketplace is all that is meant, then in principle the answer is 'yes' (8.8, 10.23–11.1): to say anything else would be to lapse into a dualism, to imagine that the creator has had to rule some areas of his creation permanently off limits (not least since, because most if not all meat available in a city like Corinth had been offered in sacrifice, to abstain would mean vegetarianism). If, however, purchasing meat in the marketplace elicits a comment from a puzzled recent convert, at risk in the way before described, then, quite consistently with the overall principle of love, abstention is the (temporary) rule (8.9, to which 8.10 appears to be a specific and more detailed case, and 10.28–9). Underlying it all is the same principle which Paul articulated in Philippians 2.1–5, and for which he drew up the 'lordly example' of Christ in Philippians 2.5–11: one must gladly give up one's rights for the sake of the unity of the body of Christ. This helps to explain the otherwise intrusive ch. 9. This chapter demonstrates the many rights which Paul has as an apostle but of which, for the sake of the church, he fails to avail himself; in addition, it is quite possible, perhaps even likely, that Paul is here asserting the independence and full validity of his own apostleship over against any suggestion that he is inferior to the Jerusalem apostles, and over against any suggestion that his pagan converts should be bound by the so-called Apostolic Decree.[42] Paul has perhaps been accused of inconsistent behaviour, and answers these charges in 9.19–23, referring back to the point in 10.29–30.[43] The overall effect of ch. 9 is summed up, together with the argument of the whole section, in 10.31–11.1:

> (31) Whether, then, you eat or drink, or whatever you do, do all to the glory of God. (32) Be blameless before Jews, and Greeks, and the church of God, (33) just as I aim to please everyone in every way, not seeking my own advantage but that of the many, that they may be saved. (11.1) Be imitators of me, as I am of Christ.

(v) Conclusion

We have now, I think, addressed and basically solved the range of questions set out at the start of this chapter. In relation to the history of religion, I have argued that Paul is taking up, and is conscious of taking up, a new position, like that of Judaism in that it opposes paganism with creational

[41] I am inclined to agree with Fee (1980) that 8.1–13, as well as 10.1–22, is about eating in idol-temples, not just eating of sacrificial meat; but my argument would, I think, stand without this.

[42] So Barrett 1964–5, 149 f.

[43] So Fee 1980, 194 ff.

monotheism, but unlike Judaism in that at the heart of that monotheism, redefining election also, there stands the crucified and risen Messiah, Jesus. A quite new entity, sociologically as well as theologically, is thereby called into existence, and this is apparent in Paul's own language at 10.32. In relation to theology, too, we see the emergence of a strikingly new phenomenon: christological monotheism. Though this is now the third passage we have looked at in the present book in which this phenomenon clearly occurs, it is probably the first chronologically, and must thus rank as one of the greatest pioneering moments in the entire history of christology. Within what is commonly called 'ethics' we have a new position, consistent with the redefined monotheism and election, carrying at its heart not the rights and freedoms and/or spiritual advancement of the individual, but the giving up of these rights and freedoms in obedience to the command of love. I have forsworn hermeneutical reflections in most of the present work, but at this point at least a passage in Paul often thought irrelevant to the contemporary church and world possesses, to my mind at any rate, all kinds of possibilities worth exploring.[44]

One of the most significant by-products of these conclusions is the fact that, though the solution Paul has arrived at is in some ways very Jewish, he has precisely *not* reached for Jewish categories, especially for Torah, in a kind of knee-jerk reaction to a situation in which he felt at a loss. He has clearly thought through the entire issue on the basis of his Christian worldview. Continuity with Judaism of course remains: it was, after all, 'our fathers' who experienced the Exodus (10.1). But the Jewish worldview by itself stands in need of redefinition, a redefinition provided in the gospel. That is to say, the worldview whose boundary-marker was Torah has been challenged, even though Torah itself, in which the *Shema* formed the basic confession of faith, is reaffirmed. This passage thus propels us forward into the second main section of the book.

---

[44]Against Murphy-O'Connor 1978b, 543.

Part Two: Paul and the Law

Chapter Seven

CURSE AND COVENANT: GALATIANS 3.10–14[1]

There are (at least) two ways of dealing with the vexed question of Paul's attitude to the law. One is to approach the task by means of a theological debate: Luther thought Paul was against the law, Calvin thought he was in favour of it, Schweitzer thought the question was wrongly put, and the twentieth century has been writing footnotes to all three.[2] A very different approach is to work through the key passages which must feature in any serious discussion, set them in their exegetical context, and see what sense can be made of them as they stand, leaving the 'systematic' questions until later (insofar as that is really possible: see ch. 1 above). The task of the present section of this book falls squarely within the second of these models. I shall look at four of the best-known passages in which Paul discusses the Jewish law (three if we count the first two as one, which we really should), adding as it were two extended footnotes to the last one (chs.11 and 12, on two detailed aspects of Romans 7.1—8.11), and allow them, as best I can, to speak for themselves, leaving the wider theological questions somewhat to one side for the moment.

(i) Galatians 3: Introduction

There are several passages of which one might say, not least when addressing a student audience, that 'this is one of the most complicated and controverted passages in Paul'. But Galatians 3.10–14 must surely be well up the list in the battle for any such accolade. It is here, on the one hand, that many battles have been fought over the theological meaning of Paul's words: what sort of an atonement-theology is he offering? Here too, on the other hand, has been found a rich source of supposed Pauline inconsistencies,

---

[1]Earlier versions of this chapter were given as papers at the NT seminar in Oxford and at the 1988 Society of Biblical Literature Annual Meeting in Chicago. I am grateful to colleagues for their responses and comments.

[2]See Moo 1987 and Westerholm 1988 for excellent summaries of recent debate. Compare also Martin 1989.

proof-texts wrenched from contexts, and so forth, giving evidence, it is thought, of his flailing around wildly trying to argue for a position reached on other grounds.[3] What I have to offer here, in debate with various points of view, is not a total exegesis, but some lines of thought which seem to me both hitherto unexplored and potentially profitable. They have to do in particular with the covenant theology which I believe to be implicit in the whole chapter, and which, I suggest, is at work particularly in Paul's use of Deuteronomy here.

Galatians 3.10–14 is the beginning of the long central section of Galatians 3, which runs on to v.22. Paul here faces the question of what happens when promise and Torah meet. Exegesis of this passage is complicated by a number of factors. One is the apparently bewildering use of the first person plural in vv.13–14, which some take to refer to Jewish Christians only, others to all Christians, and others to a confusion in Paul's mind. Another is the use of various Old Testament passages here: Paul seems at first sight to be reading them in a particular and idiosyncratic fashion, which differs moreover from his treatment of some of them in Romans. A third, indeed, is the frequent parallels that can be observed between these verses and several passages in the longer epistle. Looming up behind all these issues is the double problem: what exactly is Paul saying about the death of Jesus and its significance? and what exactly is he saying about the Torah? And how does what he says here on these two topics cohere, if it does, with what he says about them elsewhere? In this passage, therefore, and for that matter in its sequel, to be discussed below, we find our twin themes, Christ and the Law, tied closely together. What precisely, then, is he arguing in this passage? What has occasioned this tight and tortuous argument, and what are its inner connections? There are various solutions on offer, and I am uneasy about most of them.[4]

One traditional reading of the passage treated it simply as a *locus classicus* of Paul's atonement-theology, a statement of the general problem of sin and the general divine solution, namely, redemption through the death of Christ. But this (as I think most would now agree) distorts the passage, and prevents the precise contours of Paul's argument from showing through, thus disguising the train of thought that runs on from the previous section, through the present one, into that which follows. As with all Paul's references to the death of Jesus, without exception, the language here is designed for a particular task within a particular argument, not for an abstract systematized statement.[5]

---

[3]See e.g. Sanders 1991, 56-60.

[4]Though there is not space to discuss this here, I am in considerable agreement with Hays 1983, who offers in his ch. 3 a narrative analysis of this and other passages in Galatians.

[5]This is not to say that some exegetes do not still treat the passage in effect in this way: e.g. Kertelge 1984, 388; Stuhlmacher 1986, 176 f. Wilckens 1981, 169 tries, it seems to me, to read

More recently, some have seen in this passage the clue to Paul's conversion and its link to justification by faith: the law cursed Jesus, but the resurrection proved the law wrong. Paul, on this theory, had in his pre-Christian days regarded Deuteronomy 27.26 as a key anti-Christian proof-text. A crucified Messiah is cursed by God, therefore is not Messiah. The resurrection of Jesus, however, or more precisely Paul's belief in that resurrection, convinced him that Jesus was after all Messiah, and therefore that the law, which had seemed to curse him, must have been wrong: Christ, therefore, is the end of the law, in the sense of bringing the Torah and all that it stood for to a full stop, declared redundant in the new revelation of God's plan.[6] This view, I shall suggest, is seriously if quite interestingly misguided.

There are those, more recently again, who have seen the passage as another example of Paul's sheer muddle-headedness. He is rationalizing, stringing together a bunch of irrelevant prooftexts,[7] arguing backwards from his conclusion (that the law is now abolished) to a variety of different, and mutually incompatible, premises.[8] Again, I shall show that this solution does not get near the heart of the passage.

Finally, there is the suggestion of Donaldson and Dunn: the cursing of Jesus and his subsequent vindication means that Gentiles, formerly cursed, are now welcome into the people of God.[9] This is much closer to the truth than many other views, but still, I think, fails to catch all the precise nuances of Paul's argument.[10]

---

far too much of a wide general character into this very particular and specific argument: 'von Gal. 3. 13 her ist die gesamte Rechtfertigungslehre des Galaterbriefe zu verstehen: Es geht um iustificatio peccatorum...' (all in italics in original). Gundry 1985, 25, imports into the passage the quite extraneous idea of 'eternal life'.

[6]So Harvey 1970, 608: 'Thus, by Christ, the law was discredited'. See too Stuhlmacher 1978, 29, and 1986, 13, 177; Hooker 1982, 55; Bruce 1982, 166; Kim 1981, 46 f., 270–4, etc. See the discussion, and other references, in Räisänen 1986a, 249–51, and Sanders 1983, 25.

[7]E.g. Sanders 1977, 483, and especially 1983, 20–24, 53 n.25: 'Paul's argument proves the case to those who are convinced by proof-texts'; 1991, 56: '[Paul] was not concerned with the meaning of biblical passages in their own ancient context.' Similarly, Betz 1979, 137.

[8]Sanders 1983, 21–27 (27 'a sometimes bewildering series of arguments, quotations, and appeals'); Räisänen 1986a, 59–61, 96, etc.

[9]Donaldson 1986, quoting Howard and Gaston in recent support; Dunn 1990, 5, 230. There are various differences between the positions of these two scholars (see e.g. Dunn 236), but the thrust at this point is the same.

[10]It is perhaps important to say that, while I disagree with Dunn's exegesis of this particular passage, I am in substantial agreement with his general thesis about 'works of law' in Paul, and indeed I think that my reading of this text supports this position better than his does. As his note indicates (1990, 205, n.36, cf. Moo 1987, 293 f.), I had already articulated my basic reading of Paul and the Law in work written in the late 1970s (e.g. Wright 1978), and the work of Sanders, and later Dunn, has served in some ways as confirmation of the general line I had taken, despite my frequent disagreements with both scholars.

The basic thesis I wish to argue here hinges on Paul's use of the covenantal theme, and can be seen particularly in his exposition of Deuteronomy and Genesis. His use of these books is not arbitrary, I suggest, and has nothing of the mere prooftexting mentality about it; that is, he does not snatch texts out of context because of mere convenient verbal associations. First, the chapter as a whole should be seen as an extended discussion of Genesis 15. This is one of the great covenantal chapters in the Jewish scriptures, and describes how Israel's God came to make the initial and fundamental covenant with Abraham and his family, his 'seed'. Paul is well aware of this overall context, and is working within it from beginning to end. His use of the Abraham story is fundamental to his theology, not brought in merely for polemical purposes or because Genesis 15 happens to contain, juxtaposed, the ideas of righteousness and faith. Second, Paul's use of the 'curse' terminology here belongs exactly within this overall covenantal exposition, since it comes from one of the other great covenantal sections, Deuteronomy 27–8.[11] We are here faced, once again, with echoes of scripture which exegesis will show to be intentional on Paul's part.[12]

In order to understand the significance of this covenantal context for Paul's use of Deuteronomy we must look a little more closely at the context of the passage from which he quotes twice (Deuteronomy 27).[13] It describes, and indeed appears to enact, the making of the covenant in Moab, the covenant which holds out blessing and curse. The blessing and curse are not merely 'take-it-or-leave-it' options: Deuteronomy declares that Israel will in fact eventually make the wrong choice, and, as a result, suffer the curse of all curses, that is, exile (Deuteronomy 28.15—29.29). But that will not be the end of the story, or of the covenant. Deuteronomy 30 then holds out hope the other side of covenant failure, a hope of covenant renewal, of the regathering of the people after exile, of the circumcision of the heart, of the word being 'near you, on your lips and in your heart' (30.1–14). In other words, Deuteronomy 27–30 is all about exile and restoration, *understood as* covenant judgment and covenant renewal.[14]

---

[11]Thus, when we reach διαθήκη in v.15, we should not be surprised, nor should we reduce it to 'will'. This is a far tighter connection than suggested by, e.g., Sanders (1983, 25), according to whom the argument simply jumps from 'blessing' to its opposite, 'curse'. The covenantal context indicates that no jump is required: see below.

[12]On the use of Deuteronomy here and its possible parallels in Judaism see Eskanazi 1982, referring particularly (121 f.) to 1QS 2.11 ff. Eskanazi is wrong, however, to draw a contrast between Paul and Qumran on the grounds that the former believed all humanity to be under the curse: see below.

[13]On this see now Thielman 1989, 65–72. The considerable convergence between Thielman's views of Galatians 3 and my own became clear at the 1988 SBL Annual Meeting, where we both presented papers on this passage.

[14]This should make it clear that, while there are some similarities between my view and that of Noth 1966, 118–131, my main emphasis is quite different. Noth thinks that Paul saw his situation as *parallel to* that of Deuteronomy; I am suggesting that he saw the condition of

This, I suggest, is the basic context in which we can understand Galatians 3.10–14 in itself and in its relation to the rest of the chapter. In particular, 3.13 is not an isolated explanation of the cross, or a prooftext for justification by faith, or anything so atomistic. It is the sharp expression of a theme which occupies Paul throughout the chapter: the fact that in the cross of Jesus, the Messiah, the curse of exile itself reached its height, and was dealt with once and for all, so that the blessing of covenant renewal might flow out the other side, as God always intended. In order to see the force of this we must recognize, as has been argued by Knibb and others in relation to Qumran, that at least some Jews in this period understood the exile to be still continuing, since the return from Babylon had not brought that independence and prosperity which the prophets foretold.[15] Roman occupation and overlordship was simply the mode that Israel's continuing exile had now taken. Granted the high-flown nature of the prophecies of restoration the other side of exile (in, for instance, Isaiah or Ezekiel), it is inconceivable that any Jew living in the first century could seriously claim that these prophecies of return from exile had yet been fulfilled. As long as Herod and Pilate were in control of Palestine, Israel was still under the curse of Deuteronomy 29. This was not a matter of private theological judgment or insight, not a matter about which one needed to conduct theological debate. Paul's opponents could not have objected to it, as though it were a tendentious or rationalizing theological judgment. It was publicly observable fact. That Paul himself thought in this way is clear from e.g. Galatians 1.4, where he speaks in regular Jewish language of 'the present evil age'.

(ii) The Starting Point

With this, we come to the details of the passage. We must begin with the flow of thought between vv.10–14 and the paragraph immediately preceding it, vv.6–9. The γάρ at the start of v.10 indicates a connection with v.9, but at first sight it is hard to see the precise link. On the one hand, Paul may be adducing an extra reason for the conclusion of v.9: having demonstrated that

---

Israel in his own day as *that predicted in* Deuteronomy—and that many of his contemporaries would have agreed. Noth does not give due emphasis to the fact that Paul was working from the same perspective as those, several centuries before, for whom the fact of the curse was something indisputable, written into Israel's history; nor does he see the way in which, in Deut. 30, the curse is to be overcome by the return from exile—which, in Rom. 10.6 ff., Paul implies has now happened in the gospel events. See the discussion in Betz 1979, 145; Räisänen 1986a, 124–7; and Thielman 1989, 68 f.

[15]See, e.g., Knibb 1987, 20, expounding CD 1.5–8; but the point could be made from many sources.

the family of Abraham consists of those characterized by faith, he now says 'and this is further proved by the fact that there is no way into this family by works of Torah'. But, on the other hand, it seems better to take the connection as being made through the theme of the covenant, and particularly through the covenantal words 'blessing' and 'curse'. To any Jew schooled in Torah these words, occurring together, would at once most likely evoke the great covenant document Deuteronomy, in particular chs. 27–30, with its listing of Israel's obligations to God and its detailing of the blessings which would follow obedience and the curses which would follow disobedience. In case there is any doubt that Paul is thinking of this passage, he quotes in 10b the concluding verse of the list of curses (Deuteronomy 27.26): 'cursed is everyone who does not continue in all that is written in the book of the law, to do it'. This means that the connection with v.9 is not merely 'this is further proved by the fact that works of Torah cannot provide entry to the family', but 'this is further proved by the fact that works of Torah, so far from providing blessing, hold out curse instead.'[16] Moses' somewhat acid comments in Deuteronomy, to the effect that Israel is bound to go the wrong way, as she has always done so far, set the appropriate context. This is not a matter of counting up individual transgressions, or proving that each individual Israelite is in fact guilty of sin. It is a matter of the life of the nation as a whole.

The thought which drives Paul into this paragraph, then, has to do with the question of what happens to the promises to Abraham, granted the plight of the Jews which is brought about by the Torah. This is more than simply the plight of the sinner convicted by a holy law; more, too, than the plight of Israel caught in the trap of nationalism.[17] The thought is as follows: God promised Abraham a worldwide family, characterized by faith. The promises were entrusted to Israel, the people whose life was lived ὑπὸ νόμου. The Torah, however, held out over this people, the agents of promise, the curse which had in fact come true, and was still being proved true, in the events of the exile and its strange continuance right up to Paul's day and beyond. How could the promises, the blessings promised to Abraham, now reach their intended destination?[18] The Torah looks as though it might render the promise to Abraham, and to his worldwide family, null and void. Paul is here

---

[16]See Hays 1989, 109: 'the blessing-curse opposition in that subtext [i.e. Gen. 12.3] subliminally smoothes the otherwise abrupt transition'.

[17]Against Dunn 1990, 226 f.

[18]This is close to the reading of Duncan 1934 and Lagrange 1942 <1918>: see Räisänen 1986a, 19 f., who does not seem to me to have given this idea proper consideration when he asks, rhetorically, 'how could the redemption of the Jews from the curse of the law bring the blessing to the Gentiles?' Paul's counter-question might be: how could the blessing intended for the Gentiles ever reach them if Israel, the chosen messenger, were unfaithful? Here is the problem articulated in Rom. 3.1–2, and answered in 3.21 ff. and then further in 9–11.

concerned to show that this conclusion does not in fact follow, without at the same time saying that the Torah is somehow in itself evil. This gives to the whole passage its particular flavour, and incidentally means that any attempt to understand Galatians 3 without recognition that its central theme is the family of Abraham must be doomed to failure—which is not to say that any solution that *does* emphasize this theme must automatically be correct.

It is this balance between the relativization and reaffirmation of Torah, as much as anything else in all his writings, which has caused commentators to accuse Paul of self-contradiction and a host of other wicked things. It is worth noting, however, what Paul does not say. He does not deny the premises of the argument: Abraham's promises of blessing remain the vital thing, and the Torah really does place a valid interdict on those promises.[19] He shows that the problem has been dealt with. The covenant has reached its climax in the death of the Messiah.

This, then, tallies completely with the emphasis which emerges at the close of the paragraph: the death of Christ means that now the blessing of Abraham can come upon the Gentiles, and that 'we' may receive the promise of the Spirit through faith. To this extent, Donaldson and Dunn are correct in their emphasis on the inclusion of the Gentiles as a major theme here. But precisely at this point there comes a major diversion between my view and that of Dunn, who here is in company with Räisänen, Sanders and others.[20] I take 'we' here to mean 'Jewish Christians', just as I take 'us' in v.13 to be Jews.[21] This is, I submit, the most natural and straightforward reading. It is Jews who are under Torah; Gentiles are only in that state by a peculiar sort of extension, which is only seen (in my judgment) in Colossians 2.14 f., which is itself not such an easy passage as to provide a basis for the exegesis of Galatians or Romans. (When Paul aligns the plights of Jews and of Gentiles in 4.1–11, he does not say that Gentiles were under the Torah, but that Jews were under the στοιχεῖα. This has implications for his view of Torah, to be sure, but it cannot mean that the Gentiles were 'under' a law they never possessed.)[22] Somehow, Paul's argument runs as follows: God

[19]Contrast Harvey 1970, 606, who (like Dodd 1959, 184 ff.) writes as though Paul should have denied all this and was restrained from such Marcionism only by his vestigial (and illogical) Jewishness.

[20]Dunn 1990, 225–230; Sanders 1983, 82 (citing others); Räisänen 1986a, 19; Hahn 1976, 55 n.80; Westerholm 1988, 195; Kim 1981, 309. Hill 1982, 198 hedges his bets, including gentile Christians in 'us' only insofar as they 'confirm their state of bondage by accepting circumcision and thereby lapsing into the domain of the law'.

[21]This preserves the careful balance of v.14, which otherwise can easily be read in the sense that 'the heirs must be the gentiles' (Hill 1982, 198, cf. Betz 1979, 152). An interesting parallel to the double emphasis that v.14 thus acquires is found in Rom.15.8–9, in an important though often neglected section of the longer letter.

[22]So, rightly, Donaldson 1986, 94, citing several others; Gordon 1987, 40 f. My view, I think, strengthens Donaldson's position against the criticism of Martin 1989, 101 f. Martin's own exegesis of 3.13 (112 f.) is very generalized, and misses the specific thrust of Paul's

promised to Abraham a blessing intended for the whole world; the Torah looked like preventing that blessing getting to its destination; the death of Christ has broken through this problem, and now the blessing can reach its destination securely. (The meaning of 3.14b will be considered below.)

One further note on the place of vv.10 ff. may be in order. It is often said that this section provides part of the 'proof from scripture' of the point that Paul is arguing.[23] There is clearly some sense in this: the chapter is a sustained exposition of various parts of the Jewish scriptures, and Paul obviously intends them to have the force of authority (compare v.22 especially). But it would be a complete mistake to think that Paul's actual *point* is a general or abstract one, a truth about salvation or justification which could be expressed in principle without reference to the story of Israel, the family of Abraham, and so forth, and which therefore simply needed a 'proof from scripture' in the same way as the writers of the Westminster Confession added scriptural footnotes to 'prove' their supposed general or timeless truths. The whole question at issue between Paul and his opponents is clearly: to whom do the promises really belong? Who are the children of Abraham? Paul argues this point from scripture not because he is appealing to an authority which stands outside the argument but because scripture is where the promises, the foundations of the covenant whose terms are the point at issue, are to be found.

(iii) The Curse: 3.10

Verse 10 may, however, still be read in various different senses, which naturally have an effect on the total understanding of Paul's view of the Torah.[24] One quite usual way would be to see it as forming a syllogism with a suppressed minor premise:

> *a.* All who fail to do the whole Torah are cursed;
> *b.* (suppressed) No individual in fact does the whole Torah;
> *c.* Therefore all who are ἐξ ἔργων νόμου are cursed.[25]

---

argument. An earlier exponent of a view similar to that of Donaldson was Duncan 1934, 99. Betz 1979, 148, 152 seems initially to support this point, but then draws back from it.

[23]E.g. Betz 1979, 137 f.; Hill 1982, 197.

[24]For reasons that will become apparent, I cannot agree with Watson 1986, 71 that v.10 in itself constitutes a *non sequitur*.

[25]This is the regular view, taken by (e.g.) Westerholm 1988, part 2; Hill 1982, 197 f.; Gundry 1985, 24; others listed in Stanley 1990, 482.

It is possible, however, to read it in a slightly different sense, without the suppressed minor:

> *a.* All who fail to do the whole Torah are subject to a curse;
>
> *c.* Therefore all who are ἐξ ἔργων νόμου are *under the threat of* this curse.[26]

A different sort of suggestion comes from those who see the problem of 'nomism' looming larger in Paul's mind than the problem of sin:[27]

> *a.* Living ἐξ ἔργων νόμου means being committed to earning one's own salvation;
>
> *b.* Such a process is an arrogant attempt to establish a claim upon God;
>
> *c.* Therefore all who are ἐξ ἔργων νόμου are under a curse.

None of these, I believe, is correct. The problem here—which is a problem for either view—has usually been seen to be: how does Paul know that no-one does the whole Torah? Did he not himself say that he was blameless as to righteousness under the Torah (Philippians 3)? And, if he did incur blame, was there not a remedy at hand within the law itself, that is, the remedy of repentance on the one hand and the whole sacrificial system on the other? No Jew who failed to keep Torah, and knew that he or she was failing to keep Torah, needed to languish for long under the awful threat of either exclusion from the covenant people or, for that matter, eternal damnation. Remedies were close at hand, prescribed by God's grace within the Torah itself. How then can Paul imply that anyone who fails to keep Torah has this curse suspended for ever over his or her head?[28] This problem crops up also, of course, in passages like Galatians 2.16c and Romans 3.20: what does Paul mean when he says 'by works of the Torah shall no flesh be justified'? It is at this point in particular that many have recently accused Paul of slinging abuse at the Torah without really having a basis for what he says. Is it possible to see an underlying logic here?[29]

The covenant theology of the passage, and in particular the Deuteronomy passage Paul refers to here, provides an answer which seems to me eminently

[26]So Stanley 1990, who helpfully exploits the possibilities of the argument syllogistically, but who never sees the significance of the underlying *narrative*. This has the effect of reducing the force of the 'curse' theme (see his summary, 495). His many other interesting points are, I think, consistent with my overall understanding.

[27]For the discussion, see e.g. Westerholm 1988, *passim*, and e.g. Hübner 1984, 37 f.

[28]G. F. Moore believed that Paul's argument in Galatians so ignored the regular Jewish teaching on repentance that it would have been unintelligible to a Jewish audience: see Moore 1927–30, 3.150–51. I owe this reference to Dr. F. Thielman.

[29]See the discussions in Sanders 1983, 21–7 and Räisänen 1986a, 94–96, etc.; also Wilckens 1974, 77–109 and, very helpfully, Moo 1987, 292–8. The idea of Gager (1983, 222) that the dilemma of v.10 is peculiar to Gentiles, not Jews, is in my view utterly groundless.

145

satisfactory. In Deuteronomy 27–30 Israel is warned about the blessing and the curse, and is warned moreover that she is likely to incur the curse, through her hard-heartedness and wilful disobedience.[30] The remedy for this *held out in this passage in Deuteronomy itself* is *not* the usual Rabbinic scheme of repentance, sacrifice and atonement; it is the scheme, which so many books of the Old Testament see worked out in Israel's history, of exile and restoration, of judgment followed by mercy.[31] And the pattern of judgment and mercy ends (Deuteronomy 30) with the renewal of the covenant by God's circumcising of the hearts of his people so that they love him and keep his Torah from the heart. What is envisaged, in other words, is not so much the question of what happens *when this or that individual sins*, but the question of what happens when *the nation as a whole fails* to keep *the Torah as a whole*. That Paul is familiar with this train of thought, and exploits it at just this moment in his theology, is clear from Romans 2.17–29 and 9.30—10.13, which there is clearly not space to consider here.[32] We are therefore justified in appealing to this background in attempting to understand the present passage.[33] The result is the Pauline version of the new covenant theology characteristic of some groups within second-temple Judaism. For Paul, the death of Jesus, precisely on a Roman cross which symbolized so clearly the continuing subjugation of the people of God, brought the exile to a climax. The King of the Jews took the brunt of the exile on himself. Once again we are face to face, in Paul, with a *messianic* christology.

The normal objection to Paul at this point is therefore quite irrelevant. It is true that the Torah does not envisage that all Jews will be perfect all the time, and it therefore makes provision for sin, through repentance and sacrifice, so that atonement may be made and Israel not come under continuing divine displeasure. But, if Paul really is invoking the train of thought of the last chapters of Deuteronomy, his point is not that individual Jews have all in fact sinned, but that Israel as a whole has failed to keep the perfect Torah (see Romans 3.1 ff.), and, as a result, that Torah cannot therefore be the means through which she either retains her membership in the covenant of blessing *or* becomes—and this is the point of vv.10–14—the means of blessing the world in accordance with the promises to Abraham. From that point of view the emphasis of v.10 is not so much on the fact of individual sins (the suppressed minor premise in the first reading, above),

[30]The curse, it should be noted, is here highly Israel-specific, and has nothing directly to do with 'wrath' in general (against Gaston 1987, 10).

[31]Cf. e.g. Dan. 9.11, Jer. 29.18. This is the point missed, I think, by Noth: see above.

[32]Though it is worth noting that a similar line of thought can provide a better way through Rom. 2.17–25 than is offered by the regular commentaries or, e.g., by Sanders 1983, 123–35.

[33]This argument is further strengthened by Thielman's consideration of the covenantal context of Lev.18, on which see below.

though no doubt Paul, like all other Jews, would have had no problem in agreeing that everyone did in fact sin in some way or another.[34] Nor is it a matter merely of a threat which hangs over those who are ἐξ ἔργων νόμου. Nor, again, does it have to do simply with the meta-sin of 'nomism', or again of nationalism. The emphasis, rather, lies on the inability of the Torah to give the blessing which had been promised. I therefore suggest that the substantial argument may be analysed as follows:

    a. All who embrace Torah are thereby embracing Israel's national way of life;
    b. Israel as a nation has suffered, historically, the curse which the Torah held out for her if she did not keep it;
    c. Therefore all who embrace Torah now are under this curse.

This in turn rests on the prior assumption that:

    a. Israel as a whole is under the curse if she fails to keep Torah;
    b. Israel as a whole failed to keep Torah;
    c. Therefore Israel is under the curse.

If it is replied that some of this seems a bit obvious, the answer is, yes, precisely; and that is presumably why Paul did not see the need, which has only arisen because he has been misunderstood, to spell it out at such boring length.[35]

This way of reading the passage has the additional advantage that no Jew would have disagreed with Paul's premise. As long as we persist in reading v.10 as a statement of the sin of all individuals, it is easy to suggest that there might in principle be exceptions, especially if one were to read Romans 2.14 ff. in that sort of way. And it has likewise been easy for Sanders, Räisänen and others to suggest that this blanket denunciation of all humans, or all Jews, as sinners, is simply the reflex of Paul's conviction that salvation is to be found in Christ and nowhere else.[36] One must paint the world black, artificially and against the evidence if necessary, so that the light of Christ

---

[34]Thus the emphasis of Westerholm 1988, part 2, on the contrast of 'deeds' and 'faith' is, in my view, misplaced as an analysis of the heart of the argument of this passage.

[35]My solution thus has some analogies to that of Dunn, but with important differences: see below.

[36]See particularly Räisänen 1986a, 109: 'No "normal" Jew would have subscribed to such an "overstrained definition" of the claim of the law; there are indications that at bottom Paul agreed with them' (quoting Moore 1927–30, 3.150). See also Räisänen 1986b, 14 f.; Sanders 1977, 137, 138 n.61, where the debate between Sanders and Hübner is rendered unnecessary by the reading I propose. Similarly, the idea of Gaston 1987, 75 (followed now by Stanley 1990, 498 f.) that 'those who are of Torah' does not include Jews, but only Gentiles who embrace Torah, is shown to be completely misleading and unnecessary.

may shine the stronger. But if Paul is thinking of Israel as a whole, and of the curse of Deuteronomy not in terms of the future *post mortem* damnation which hangs over the heads of sinners, but in Deuteronomy's own terms as Israel's exile, her subjugation at the hands of pagans, then no Jew of Paul's day would dream of denying that the exile had indeed happened, and few would deny that the real return from exile—the glorious future predicted in Isaiah or Ezekiel, for instance—was yet to be realized. When might it come about that the Gentiles would change from being the agents of Israel's curse, the oppressors through whom the darker side of the covenant was being fulfilled, and become the objects of the blessing of Abraham? Paul, starting from the agreed premise that Israel had suffered the curse and was still waiting for the blessing that should follow, has simply drawn the whole train of thought on to Jesus and the Spirit. But this is to run ahead of the argument.[37]

(iv) Habakkuk and Leviticus: 3.11–12

This interpretation is, I suggest, confirmed by v.11, with its quotation from Habakkuk 2.4, a passage of considerable importance in current Jewish apocalyptic thought.[38] Paul's exegesis, like that of some of his contemporaries in content though not in style (i.e. he does not employ the *pesher* method of Qumran, etc.), focusses on that which had been central for Habakkuk too, re-applying this to his own day. Habakkuk, faced with the imminent destruction of Israel, had seen the covenant community being redefined in terms of faith: the δίκαιος will now be the one who believes, and will be vindicated in the eschatological deliverance.[39] Paul thus ties in Habakkuk's redefinition of the covenant community with the original promise to Abraham, and thereby argues that (11a) 'no-one is reckoned within the covenant community on the basis of Torah'.[40] (I am assuming here a controversial point, that the δικαι- language is best rendered in terms of 'membership within the covenant'.) This use of Habakkuk, it then appears, is neither as odd nor as arbitrary as it is sometimes made out to be. Of course in one sense the verse is used as a prooftext, but its wider context is the same as that which Paul—and Deuteronomy 27–30—envisages: the

[37]It is also to suggest that the reform initiated in Pauline studies by Sanders in particular has not gone far enough, even in Sanders' own work. Even those who attack the Reformation reading of Paul continue to misread him—in precisely a 'Reformation' way.

[38]Cf Strobel 1961.

[39]Once again there is convergence between my view and that of Thielman: see Thielman 1989, 70.

[40]We might question the precise significance of ἐν here: does it mean 'on the basis of'? 'in'? 'by means of'?

redefinition of the covenant community by means of divine judgment. Paul's point, in using Habakkuk in this way, is that *when* that redefinition comes about, the demarcating characteristic of the covenant people is to be precisely their *faith*, their belief in Israel's God; and this, obviously, enables him to align Habakkuk, in his redefinition of the covenant people, with the promise to Abraham, and its initial definition of that people as 'those of faith' (3.6–9).[41] The covenantal overtones are emphasized again by the word 'live': 'life' is the chief blessing of the covenant, as death is its chief curse (Deuteronomy 30.15). This is, I suggest, the real theological link between δικαιοσύνη and ζωή, a link often observed but usually smudged by an exegesis that ignores covenantal categories.[42]

Verse 12 then provides negative confirmation of the same point, that the Torah cannot be the place where the covenantal blessing is found. Granted Genesis 15 and Habakkuk 2, which together make the point that God's intended covenant membership is demarcated by faith, the Torah, which offers its covenantal 'life' on the basis of 'doing' what it says, cannot be in itself the means of faith and hence of life. Here we run into a further problem. Leviticus 18.5 occurs in Romans 10.5 as well. There it seems, I believe, that the 'doing' of the law is expounded (in Romans 10.6 ff.) in terms of faith itself. Here Paul seems, on the contrary, to be setting it over against faith. Is Paul playing fast and loose even with his own prooftexts? The answer which suggests itself, to me at least, is as follows. In Romans 10 Paul is showing that, in the *new* covenant, even that 'doing' which the law required is taken up and paradoxically fulfilled in faith (compare Romans 8.1–11, on which see ch. 10 below). Here, however, within the scheme of the Torah itself, Habakkuk is saying that covenant membership is not demarcated by Torah, because that would set up the 'doing of the law' as the covenant boundary marker, which would then mean ultimately that the covenant was determined by race. Therefore Leviticus, historically considered as part of the Mosaic dispensation, is relativized by Habakkuk,[43] even though, in Romans, Paul can go on to show that this relativization is in the ultimate service of a larger overall unity.

---

[41]We cannot here go into the debate about ἐκ πίστεως, specifically, the question of whether it goes with δίκαιος or ζήσεται when Paul quotes the verse in Rom. 1.17. Here it seems to me fairly clearly to belong with ζήσεται. See Cranfield on Rom. 1.17, etc., and particularly now Cavallin 1978; on the other side, Sanders 1983, 53..

[42]At the time of going to press it has been suggested to me by my student Christopher Palmer that an alternative way of reading v.11 would be to place the comma before δῆλον, instead of after, so that 11a becomes the support for 11b instead of *vice versa*. This has the grammatical advantage that the phrase δῆλον ὅτι is, as the dictionaries show, more common than ὅτι... δῆλον, separated by a whole clause (cf. e.g. 1 Cor. 15.27, 1 Tim. 6.7 v.l., Ign. *Eph.* 6.1). The theological and exegetical ramifications of the proposal are too wide, and interesting, to go into here.

[43]Notice how the ἐκ πίστεως is repeated.

This argument can in fact be supplemented further, as follows.[44] The context of Leviticus 18, from which Paul quotes v.5, is the warning that, unless Israel keeps the covenant charter properly, the land itself will eject those who are thereby polluting it. This is emphasized in 20.22–5, 26.14–43. Leviticus is thus pointing to the same threat held out in the covenantal passage in Deuteronomy. Failure to keep the covenant will result in the curse of exile.

This is not, then, to say that the Torah is bad; merely that, in the face of divine covenantal judgment on Israel, one cannot say that the Torah, and the attempt to keep it, provide the way to life. Nor therefore is this to deny, what Paul will later argue in both Galatians and Romans, that there is a true fulfillment of the law—actually, that there are various true fulfillments of the law—which come about through faith. This passage simply asserts that the Torah *as it stands* is not the means of faith, since it speaks of 'doing', which is best taken in the sense of 'doing the things that mark Israel out',[45] and hence cannot be as it stands the boundary-marker of the covenant family promised to Abraham and spoken of by Habakkuk, i.e. the family that is a single worldwide family, the family that is created the other side of judgment, the family characterized by πίστις. Paul is not here speaking of those problems with which existentialist theologians have wrestled—'achievement', 'accomplishment' and the like; nor yet with those traditional in Protestantism, 'legalism' (or 'nomism'), 'self-righteousness', and so forth.[46] Nor is he offering an abstract account of 'how one gets saved'. His argument, in outline and in detail, makes little sense if read in this way, and it has been his fate, particularly at the hands of writers like Schoeps and Räisänen, to be scolded for this nonsense as if he were the perpetrator of it. He is not. He is expounding covenantal theology, from Abraham, through Deuteronomy and Leviticus, through Habakkuk, to Jesus the Messiah, and is showing, albeit paradoxically, that the Torah *per se* rules itself out from positive participation in this sequence. For Paul, then, the covenant is not detached from the realities of space and time, of the this-worldly orientation which was characteristic of Israel's covenant. Rather, the covenant was precisely working its way out through exile and restoration. The climax of the exile had been reached, as we shall see in a moment, in a great event of recent memory, and now the true restoration was beginning, a restoration in which Gentiles were, quite properly, being invited to share. As the great prophets

[44]I here follow Thielman 1988, 1989 70 f.

[45]To this extent, clearly, I agree with Dunn's reading of the passage. See too, in an interesting anticipation of Sanders, Dunn and myself, Tyson 1973, 428 ff. I do not think, however, that my view is subject to the criticisms of Dunn made by Stanley 1990, 485 n.20.

[46]Against e.g. Betz 1979, 147, etc.

believed, when Israel is restored, then the Gentiles will share in the blessing.[47]

Of the many questions raised by this conclusion, Paul will tackle two or three later on in this chapter. First, though, he has to show how the immediate problem is resolved.

(v) The Cross: 3.13

The immediate problem was: granted the covenant promises to Abraham, what will happen to those promises in the light of Torah? There are many reasons why Torah would come between the promises and their fulfillment: Paul will later speak of its being given to one nation only, whereas God envisaged a worldwide family (see below), but here he concentrates simply on the fact that the law brings curse, not blessing (compare Rom. 4.15: the law brings wrath). It cannot of itself produce the faith which, according to Genesis and Habakkuk, is the true demarcation of the covenant people, Abraham's family. How then is the blessing of Abraham to come on either Jew (enclosed and threatened by Torah) or gentile (whose promised blessing will thus never reach him)?

The solution is found, very precisely, in the death of the Messiah. Here is a further outworking of that theology of the cross found in 2.19–20. The clue to it all is Paul's corporate christology which, as I have already argued, characterizes his theology in so many key passages, and which indeed comes to some of its clearest expressions in Galatians 3. Because the Messiah represents Israel, he is able to take on himself Israel's curse and exhaust it. Jesus dies as the King of the Jews, at the hands of the Romans whose oppression of Israel is the present, and climactic, form of the curse of exile itself. The crucifixion of the Messiah is, one might say, the *quintessence of* the curse of exile, and its climactic act. The context thus demands the first person plural for which Paul has been criticized by some and misunderstood by others: he is not here producing a general statement of atonement theology applicable equally, and in the same way, to Jew and gentile alike. Christ, as the representative Messiah, has achieved a specific task, that of taking on himself the curse which hung over Israel and which on the one hand prevented her from enjoying full membership in Abraham's family and thereby on the other hand prevented the blessing of Abraham from flowing out to the Gentiles. The Messiah has come where Israel is, under the Torah's curse (see 4.4), in order to be not only Israel's representative but Israel's *redeeming* representative. That which, in the scheme of

[47]This is the main point of Donaldson's paper (1986), and it is hereby set, I think, on a firmer footing.

Deuteronomy, Israel needed if she incurred the curse of the law, is provided in Christ: the pattern of exile and restoration is acted out in his death and resurrection. He *is* Israel, going down to death under the curse of the law, and going through that curse to the new covenant life beyond.[48]

Before pursuing this conclusion any further, it is worth noting the way in which this line of thought dramatically anticipates that which runs from Romans 5.20, through 7.13–20, to 8.3 f. and on into chs. 9–11 (see chs. 10, 13 below). The Torah has the effect of, as it were, piling up the sin of the world in one particular place, that is, in Israel. This highly negative assessment of the Torah's purpose is then, however, shown to have an underlying positive aim, in that the Messiah, as Israel's representative, allows the full weight of it to fall on himself. What is in Romans said of 'sin' is here said of the 'curse', but the effect is not very different—except that, unlike sin, the curse is Israel-specific. The result in each case, however, remains the same. Torah draws sin/curse on to Israel in order that it may then be dealt with in the death of the Messiah.

From this perspective, we can see that one very common view of the origin of Paul's view of Torah, noted already, is simply mistaken. It is important to note, once more, what he does *not* say. He does not say 'the law cursed Jesus, but the resurrection showed the law to be in the wrong'. His argument actually *depends on the validity of the law's curse*, and on the propriety of Jesus, as Messiah, bearing it on Israel's behalf. It is therefore impossible to argue from the present passage, as is often done, that Paul rejected Torah because he saw it had been shown to be in the wrong.[49] According to this passage, the Torah was correct to pronounce the curse. It merely did not have the last word. Exactly as foreseen in Deuteronomy 30, there was blessing the other side of the curse, restoration the other side of exile. And this means that we must call into question those views of Paul's conversion which have given Galatians 3.13 a central role. No doubt the implicit curse on the crucified Jesus may have been one element in the fanatical rejection of the Christian message by Saul of Tarsus. But we may not simplistically imagine that it was the only or the central element, nor that it was removed by his imagining that the Torah had been proved wrong in the resurrection.[50]

[48]Paul does not here specifically mention the resurrection, but it is clearly presupposed: so rightly Hooker 1971, 351 f.

[49]Note the significant distinction drawn by Hays 1989, 203 f., between κατάρα νόμου as a possessive and as an epexegetical genitive, that is, between the curse which the law pronounces (which can be done away without doing away with the law) and the law itself seen as a curse (cautiously advocated by Betz 1979, 149).

[50]So, rightly, Räisänen 1986b, ch. 3; 1986a, 249 f. It is ironic to note the flagrant contradiction between this latter passage and that on 1986a, 59 where he speaks of Paul as having argued, in this paragraph, for the abolition of the law—and where he accuses Paul of yet one more illogicality in doing so! As very frequently, one gets the impression that the real target of Räisänen's anger—it is not too strong a word—is not the Paul of history but the Paul of certain churchly traditions. As in the case of Schoeps, it is easy to criticize such a Paul; but

Nor is the train of thought postulated by Dunn either necessary or likely. It is true that Christ's bearing of the curse results in the blessing for the Gentiles, but the steps by which Paul, according to Dunn, reached this conclusion, are tortuous and improbable.[51]

The death of Jesus is thus understood in covenant-renewing terms. Those with ears to hear might well hear other covenantal and/or sacrificial overtones: references to the scapegoat, for instance,[52] or to the Aqedah.[53] But the fundamental note is that of the covenantal curse, Israel's curse, being taken by Israel's anointed representative in an act which itself symbolized very precisely all that the curse of exile stood for. The death of the king, hanged on a tree in the midst of his own land, thereby polluting that land—this is not an arbitrary piece of theology, a convenient abstract mechanism whereby a 'curse' which theoretically hung over the head of 'sinners' in general should be transferred to someone else who happened, like a great many other young Jews in the first century, to be executed by a means which itself conveyed a 'curse'. If we are to press this passage for a way in, at least, to Paul's theology of the cross, that way must be *via* the themes of God's covenant with Israel and the climax of that covenant in the death of Israel's anointed representative.[54]

(vi) The Result: Blessing and Spirit (3.14)

From this point Paul's argument, and our own, can move swiftly to their proper conclusion. Paul does not abandon the precision which has characterized him throughout.[55] On the one hand, the fundamental problem addressed in vv.10–11 (how will the blessing get to the Gentiles) has been dealt with. On the other hand, there is a subsidiary problem. What happens to Jews in and through all of this? Are they simply left out of account while

---

exegesis will not sustain Räisänen's implicit portrait, any more than it will Schoeps'.

[51]Dunn's line of thought (1990, 230) runs: Christ was placed outside the covenant, therefore in the place of the Gentiles; therefore God is on the side of the Gentiles, and therefore the law as boundary marker is abolished. This is going in the right direction, but as it were by a bumpy back road: none of the steps in the argument as Dunn reconstructs it corresponds with what Paul actually says.

[52]See Schwartz 1983.

[53]See Wilcox 1977, and the discussion of his view and those of others in Bruce 1982, 167 f.

[54]To this extent I agree with the positive emphasis of Sanders 1977, 466 (3.16 in his text should read 3.13), while suspecting that the negative he infers does not follow. 'Participation' does not of itself exclude 'substitution', however frequently that spurious 'either-or' is asserted.

[55]Against Davies 1984, 127, suggesting that Paul has not explained how the cross has opened the promise up to the Gentiles.

the promises go on their way from Abraham, through the Messiah, to the Gentiles? In a sense, then, this verse looks on to the far larger exposition of Romans 9–11 (on which see ch. 12 below). Here it remains a miniature statement, but exact for all that.

The first result of Paul's argument, obviously, is that the Gentiles can after all inherit the blessing they were promised in Genesis 12, 15 and 18. Christ, as the true seed of Abraham, is the means of doing what Abraham's seed had otherwise failed to do, namely, being a light to the nations. And, in keeping with the theme which gradually takes over the chapter, reaching its climax in 3.23–29, the means by which Gentiles thus enter Abraham's family is clarified: 'in Christ Jesus'.[56]

The second result, again as in Deuteronomy 30, is that the new covenant is inaugurated: 'in order that we might receive the promise of the Spirit through faith'. The Spirit is here, as I believe elsewhere in Paul, first and foremost seen as the blessing of the renewed covenant; part of the evidence for this is precisely within this chapter, in 3.1–5, and the link of that section with the present argument has perhaps been underestimated.[57]. Mention of the Spirit is thus not simply an allusion to a new dimension of religious experience, but more precisely an indication that the covenant has been renewed, the return from exile inaugurated. Although Paul's celebration of this fact focusses on the miraculous fact that Gentiles are at last being admitted into the family of Israel's God, this cannot be to the exclusion of Jews; all those who believe are assured of their membership in the eschatological people. This time, it may be granted, the 'we' could quite well be inclusive––'all we Christians'—in which case it echoes just this passage, 3.2, 5. But it seems to me far more likely that it remains exclusive, 'we Christian Jews'. The dual problem caused by the clash of Torah and Abrahamic promise is given a dual solution: blessing for the Gentiles, which they had looked like being denied, and new covenant for Israel, which she had looked like failing to attain. (This would not, of course, be to deny that gentile Christians too belong to the new covenant, but would simply be the narrow answer to the narrow problem which these verses have been tackling.) And the emphasis would fall, rightly, on the last phrase, διὰ τῆς πίστεως: Christian Jews enter the renewed Abrahamic covenant not by works of Torah, but by faith, just as Christian Gentiles do (3.2, 5: this corresponds exactly to Romans 11.5–6, and,

[56]If the variant 'in Jesus Christ' is read (with ℵ, B and the Peshitta), this will indicate the chronological sequence postulated by much of the rest of the chapter: it is with the coming of Jesus, the Messiah, that the blessing reaches the Gentiles at last. But the text as it stands (P46, A, C, D and the majority) is probably to be preferred, introducing as it does that corporate christology (on which, see ch. 3 above) which is to be such a major feature of the rest of Gal. 3.

[57]See now Stanley 1990, 492–5. It has also been pointed out to me (by Sylvia Keesmaat) that the theme of the Spirit returns in 4.6 f. in such a way as to make a circle: 3.1–5 and 4.1–7, flanking the self-contained argument of 3.6–29, one of whose central and pivotal points is 3.14.

mutatis mutandis, to Romans 3.28–30, especially 30b.). At this point the categories of 'getting in' and 'staying in', made popular by E.P. Sanders, seem to need more nuances: 'getting *back in*', for instance, or 'staying in when it looked as though one had been ejected'.[58] Israel's peculiar plight is that, through the exile, she has been, in one sense, still inside the covenant and, in another, outside it. Gentiles simply come in, from nowhere; Jews have their membership renewed, brought back to life, by sharing the death and resurrection of their Messiah.

(vii) Conclusion

The result of this paragraph, in terms of the wider issues of the section as a whole, and of Paul's theology in Galatians as well as elsewhere, may be summarized as follows. The Torah brings the curse for Israel, because Israel has not kept it. I do not mean by this that individual Jews do not keep it fully; that is not what is here at issue, and in any case that would not be sufficient for Israel as a race, from Paul's point of view, to be affirmed as they stood as God's people. Rather, Israel as a whole has failed in her task of being the light to the nations, of being the seed of Abraham through whom the varied families of the world would be blessed. This is the central affirmation, I think, of 2.16 f.: this is why 'by works of the Torah shall no flesh be justified'. Paul is not saying, in any form, that 'achieving' is a bad thing, as though what was wrong with the Torah was that it entices one to think that 'keeping' or 'achieving' is a good thing: this is the existentialist misinterpretation which Wilckens and others have rightly attacked, and which also makes no sense in the proper historical and covenantal context of Paul's theology. The consequence of the curse was that the blessing bequeathed to Abraham, to be enacted through his seed, looked as though it would never reach its destination. In addition, Paul argues that from the perspective of the Old Testament itself the Torah could not be thought of as accomplishing its apparent task of demarcating the covenant family. Genesis and Habakkuk, when read alongside Leviticus and Deuteronomy, indicate that God all along envisaged a different demarcation line, namely faith. Thus it is that the death of Jesus, precisely as the Messiah who draws Israel's destiny on to himself, is, historically, the climactic point of the curse of Deuteronomy 27–8, and thus functions *theologically* as the fulfillment, not of a few prooftexts merely, but of the whole paradoxical history of Israel.[59] This

---

[58]Sanders 1977, frequently. See the unpublished doctoral dissertation of G. Harper (1988) of McGill University.

[59]It is this paradox that makes sense of the shallow 'contradiction' imagined by Räisänen (1986b, 9): the law was a temporary addition, yet a dramatic act was needed to liberate men from its curse.

theme will be dealt with again in chs. 10 and 13 below. More specifically, here, the death of Jesus finally exhausts the curse which stood over the covenant people, so that the blessing of Abraham might after all come upon the Gentiles. And the demarcating mark of this new covenant family, of Gentiles and Jews together, is of course precisely faith: the faith which was Abraham's faith at the beginning, the faith which Habakkuk points to as the defining mark of the people of God at the time of judgment and restoration.

There is one final note, of considerable significance for the whole understanding of Paul's theology. Although I have not had space here to argue the point fully, I believe that my original assumption, that Galatians 3 should be treated as 'covenant theology', has been fully vindicated.[60] I do not think it is possible to get very far, in the basic discussions of Paul, the law, justification, Judaism and the Gentiles—in other words, in most of the major debates that rightly concern Pauline scholars—unless we take this fully into account. Covenant theology is characteristic not only of Jewish thinking in this period, but also of Paul's whole worldview. But Paul is not simply offering another form of 'covenantal nomism'. The covenant is now the renewed covenant; and the badge of membership is faith.[61]

---

[60]Against, e.g. Gaston 1987, 114, 224 n.59. Gaston's agenda—that Paul should avoid saying anything which implies that the position of non-Christian Jews is in any way called into question by the gospel—has led him, it seems to me, into serious misreading of the relevant texts. See, for the contrary view and its documentation, Davies 1984, 344 n.24.

[61]On the categories of 'covenantal nomism', etc., see Hooker 1982. A question was raised at the 1988 SBL seminar, after a version of this chapter was given as a paper, by Prof. R. Jewett: what about 1 Thess. 2? My answer is as follows: the Jewish context itself suggests strongly that when the new covenant is brought into being there will be some Jews who will miss out. This seems presupposed by all Jewish eschatology. There is then a bifurcation within the destiny of Jews, as seen from a Pauline standpoint: either they must come the way of the cross, finding the new covenant, the Spirit and faith, or they will head down the road whose τέλος is A.D. 70. 1 Thess. 2.15 f. then shows that Israel *as a whole* is heading on this latter course, rejecting the call of God to the new covenant. But the 'we/us' in Gal. 3.10–14 is not thereby abandoned. The Israel of 1 Thess. is the 'Israel in principle', which does not mean that individual Jews are as it were *automatically*, still less irrevocably, destined this way or that. The problem then awaits its full resolution in Rom. 9–11.

Chapter Eight

THE SEED AND THE MEDIATOR: GALATIANS 3.15–20[1]

(i) Introduction

I want now to propose a new interpretation of two paragraphs, Galatians 3.15–18 and 3.19–22, generally reckoned among the most difficult in Paul. In Galatians 3:16 he writes

τῷ δὲ 'Αβραὰμ ἐρρέθησαν αἱ ἐπαγγελίαι καὶ τῷ σπέρματι αὐτοῦ. οὐ λέγει· καὶ τοῖς σπέρμασιν, ὡς ἐπὶ πολλῶν ἀλλ᾽ ὡς ἐφ᾽ ἑνός· καὶ τῷ σπέρματί σου, ὅς ἐστιν Χριστός.[2]

The regular translations show well enough how the verse is usually read. The RSV reads: 'Now the promises were made to Abraham and to his offspring. It does not say "And to offsprings," referring to many; but, referring to one, "And to your offspring," which is Christ'. The NIV has: 'The promises were spoken to Abraham and to his seed. The scripture does not say "and to seeds", meaning many people, but "and to your seed", meaning one person, who is Christ.'

Three verses later (3:19 f.), as if bent on outdoing even this cryptic statement in obscurity, he writes of the law that it was

(19b) διαταγεὶς δι᾽ ἀγγέλων ἐν χειρὶ μεσίτου.

He then adds:

(20) ὁ δὲ μεσίτης ἑνὸς οὐκ ἔστιν, ὁ δὲ θεὸς εἷς ἐστιν.

Here, perhaps understandably, the translators diverge further. We may itemize some of the main ones:

AV/RV: Now a mediator is not a mediator of one, but God is one.
RSV: Now an intermediary implies more than one; but God is one.

[1]This chapter was originally given as a paper at the 1984 SBL Annual Meeting in Chicago, and at the 1986 British SNTS Meeting in London. I am grateful to colleagues in both groups for their comments, questions and criticisms.
[2] Instead of ὅς, D, 81, 2495 read ὅ: FG οὖ. These are clearly secondary.

NRSV: Now a mediator involves more than one party, but God is one.

Phillips: The very fact that there was an intermediary is enough to show that this was not the fulfilling of the promise. For the promise of God needs neither angelic witness nor human intermediary but depends on him alone.

NEB: but an intermediary is not needed for one party acting alone, and God is one.

NIV: A mediator, however, does not represent just one party; but God is one.

TEV: But a go-between is not needed when there is only one person; and God is one.

JB: Now there can only be an intermediary between two parties, yet God is one.

It is scarcely surprising that writers on Paul in general, and commentators on Galatians in particular, have arrived at no consensus about these verses, save that they are very difficult and obscure. It is often suggested that they reflect simply a Rabbinic type of argument[3] which, however useful *ad hominem* in Galatians, is something of an embarrassment to modern scholars struggling to think Paul's thoughts after him,[4] and is simply a product of wild secondary rationalization.[5]

The problems appear to lie as follows:[6]

(a) In v.16 Paul appears to be arguing, on the basis of the singular form of σπέρμα, that the promises made to Abraham and his seed point exclusively to Christ, not to the patriarch's many other physical descendants. This seems to leave Paul on the very shaky ground of a purely semantic trick, since in the LXX σπέρμα in the singular, when referring to human offspring, is in fact almost always collective rather than singular.[7] And, if v.16 is as weak as this, the argument of the whole passage is weakened also: Paul's line of thought appears to run 'the promises are made to Abraham's seed; Christ is Abraham's seed (v.16); you belong to Christ (vv.26–9a); therefore you are heir to the promises (v.29b), and therefore do not need to submit to the Torah (vv.17–18, 19–22, 25, etc.).

It is true that Rabbinic parallels have been found to arguments of this

[3]E.g. Rohde 1989, 149 f.: Barclay 1988, 89.
[4]E.g. Hübner 1984, 53: 'a piece of bold and arbitrary exegesis'.
[5]See Räisänen 1986a, 62.
[6]From the many discussions in commentaries (cited subsequently by author's name only), see particularly Betz 1979, 156–7, 161–173 (171 n.78 gives older bibliography on 3:20); Bligh 1970, 287–9, 308–9; Burton 1921, 181–2, 190–2, 505–10, citing older literature; Mussner 1974, 237–40, 248–50; Ridderbos 1953, 132–4, 139–40. Among other secondary literature note particularly Bring 1966, 1969 ch. 3; Callan 1976, 1980; Giblin 1975; Lacan 1963, 1. 113–125; Mauser 1967; Stolle 1973; Vanhoye 1978; Newman 1984.
[7]So e.g. Guthrie 1974, 102. Hays 1989, 85 attempts to show that this is not as arbitrary as it might appear, since there is a suppressed reference to 2 Sam. 7.12–14. This is ingenious, but I think unnecessary, and is actually corrected in principle by what Hays says on 106: 'the message preproclaimed to Abraham is a gospel about God's people rather than about a Messiah'.

158

sort.[8] But there are four serious problems with this. (i) It still seems to be asking a lot for Paul to jump from collective to singular and then (v.29) back to collective again; (ii) if this really is his argument, it seems to imply that the promises meant nothing at all until the coming of Christ; (iii) the point seems to depend on v.29 for its completion, and is therefore not fully comprehensible as it stands; (iv) in the apparent parallels between this passage and Romans 4 and 9 (see below) σπέρμα, though important for the argument, is never used thus. If an alternative solution were available which avoided these problems, it would deserve serious consideration.

(b) In v.20 Paul is usually understood to be offering a partial definition of a 'mediator' (namely, that the existence of such a figure implies a duality of parties) as part of an argument for the inferiority of the Torah to the Abrahamic promises. If this is indeed what Paul is doing (for different opinions, see below), his argument looks very peculiar. Literally hundreds of different solutions have been proposed to this problem without agreement being reached.[9] The problem concerns the inner logic of v.20, in particular the relation of 20b (ὁ δὲ θεὸς εἷς ἐστιν) to 20a (ὁ δὲ μεσίτης ἑνὸς οὐκ ἔστιν). Most scholars offer some variant on the theme that mediation implies a plurality of parties, which in turn implies inferiority.[10] This, however, fits badly with 20b, since the covenant between God and Abraham, not to mention the fulfillment of that covenant in Christ, can only be seen as *not* involving plurality[11] if one engages in a theological balancing act, claiming that God in fact acts on both sides of the covenant, or that Paul is here making an implicit claim for the divinity of Christ, or some similar suggestion. Many writers on Paul now simply skirt round the problem without addressing it head on.[12] Some even suggest that v.20 adds nothing of real value to the argument.[13]

Attempts have been made to evade this problem by suggesting that Paul's point is that a mediator implies a plurality of parties on one or both sides of the agreement: the agreement is between God and all the Israelites, or

---

[8]See Dahl 1977, 175: 'in no other place is [Paul's] style of argumentation more similar to that of the rabbis than in Galatians 3'. We might compare mSanh. 4.5: 'it says not "the blood of thy brother", but "the bloods of thy brother"—his blood and the blood of his posterity.' See too Davies 1984, 177, noting that a serious weakness of Betz's commentary is its failure to take seriously the Jewish exegetical background of Galatians. Dahl notes rightly, however, that the actual *thrust* of the argument is totally non-Rabbinic.

[9] Older solutions are listed in Oepke 1971, *ad loc.*; and see Callan 1976, ch. 1; Mauser 1967, 258–263; Hübner 1984, 27; Gaston 1987, ch. 2; Martin 1989, 35–7. On Moses and mediators in Jewish literature see the survey in Goldin 1968.

[10] So e.g. Guthrie 105: 'secondary revelation'.

[11]As is attempted by e.g. Ridderbos 1953, 138–40: compare his 1975, 216.

[12]E.g. Westerholm 1988, 177 ff.; Thielman 1989, 76; even more, Hahn 1976, 55 f., Dunn 1990, 248–51.

[13]So Duncan 1934, 115.

between the many angels and Israel,[14] or between several angels and all the Israelites,[15] or between one angel representing all the others and Moses representing the children of Israel.[16] No doubt there are more possibilities yet to be explored down this line. It would, in fact, be useful at this point to have a mediator to present all the different scholarly points of view. But any solution like this is open to serious problems. In terms of the text, it is still not clear how 20b provides not only a contrast but actually a counter-argument demonstrating the inferiority of this mediated Torah. In terms of the whole argument, it is not clear that Paul's Christian position, in which many Christians are in covenant with God, is not open to the same problem.

The older solution, that there is an oblique reference to Christ as the true mediator, is likewise open to serious objections.[17] (i) It fits very awkwardly into the argument: why should ἑνός be in the genitive? How does a statement of incarnational christology belong in the logic of what Paul is saying? (ii) It assumes that Paul's readers would be so familiar with the idea of Christ as mediator (as in e.g. 1 Timothy 2.5) that they would at once make the jump from Moses, who is indisputably the mediator referred to in v.19, to Christ. But this is both an unwarranted assumption and an unnecessary complication to the argument. Within this part of Galatians 3 Christ is, if anything, the seed, not the mediator.

Is Paul, then, mounting an oblique attack against a gnostic or proto-gnostic theology of mediation, suggesting that the angels through whom[18] the law was given were evil, and warning the Galatians to have nothing to do with the Torah as a result?[19] Though there is not space here to discuss this

[14] See e.g. Lacan 1963; Giblin 1975, 541; Mussner 1974, 248–50; Lührmann 1978, 63.

[15] Schweitzer 1968 <1931>, 70; Wilckens 1981, 172.

[16] E.g. Vanhoye 1978, now followed by Bruce 1982, 179. For criticism of this view see Fernandez 1983, Fung 1988 ad loc.

[17] See, following Jerome and Chrysostom, Gabris 1968. Compare Giblin 1975, 543, who speaks of Christ as 'the *im*mediator' (his italics). Compare too Bligh 1970, 308; and see Tremenheere 1931, 35, and Fernandez 1983.

[18] Or even, in the extreme form of this view, *by* whom: see the discussion of this possibility in Danieli 1955; Schoeps 1959, 182 f.; Räisänen 1986a, 129; Hübner 1984, 26 f. (German original, which is necessary because of an unfortunate misprint in the Eng. trans., 27 f.). Hübner tries to argue backwards for this conclusion from the view of v.20 according to which the 'plurality' in question is that of the angels, which as we shall see is not the best way to take that verse. Sanders 1983, 66–8, (and 1977, 550) seems to me unconvincing: he accepts without demur the Bultmannian assumption that 3.19 is a denial of the law's god-givenness, and this makes his (otherwise justified) rejection of Hübner's position quite weak. Martin 1989, 35 offers a truer perspective.

[19] See the discussions in Westerholm 1988, 176–9 and Gaston 1987, 43. The view is that of Bultmann 1952, 1.174, 268, followed—and criticized as if this were Paul's view—by Schoeps 1961, 183. The 'gnostic' view was championed by Schlier in the earlier editions of his commentary, but in the later ones (1965, 161–3) he changed his mind and suggested that the idea derived from Qumran. See too Reicke 1951; Räisänen 1986a, 130–3; Beker 1980, 53. Bultmann is criticized by e.g. van Dülmen 1968, 43–5. Barclay 1988, 91, 210 says that here Paul 'almost denies the divine origin of the law'; Davies 1984, 7, 87, 239 assumes that the

matter in full detail, such a solution seems to me both unlikely and (as it will appear) unnecessary. Paul never says in Galatians that the Torah itself is a bad thing. It came, albeit indirectly, from God: προσετέθη and διαταγείς (v.19) are clearly circumlocutions for divine action,[20] and the clause ἄχρις οὗ ἔλθη τὸ σπέρμα ᾧ ἐπήγγελται[21] which links those two words explains the divine intention in giving the law (compare v.22). One need hardly add that there is nothing in pre-Pauline Jewish or pagan literature to prepare us for the idea of the Torah being given by demonic beings, though there are clear signs that some at least associated it with (good) angels.[22] Paul, in other words, manages to downplay the role of the Torah in fulfilling God's promises without lapsing into what we think of as Marcionism. There is no suggestion in the passage that the angels are evil angels, nor is there a necessary link between them and the στοιχεῖα of 4.4, 9;[23] even if there were, it is the existence of a mediator, not that of angels, that is the basis of the argument of v.20. And, as we will see, the mediator is much more likely to be Moses than an angel.[24]

A quite different position in the debate was taken by R. Bring.[25] He argued that ὁ δὲ μεσίτης referred, not to mediators in general, but to the mediator mentioned in v.19, i.e. Moses.[26] According to Bring, Paul is

---

reference is derogatory, and says this is a Christian innovation. So it is; but, in my view, a modern one.

[20]Against Räisänen 1986a, 130, and with Mussner 247.

[21]Reading οὗ with P46, ℵ, A, C, D, etc., rather than the ἄν of B, 33, etc.

[22]Despite Gaston 1987, ch. 2, I think that texts like Acts 7.53 (which has verbal links with Gal. 3.19) and Hebr. 2.2 indicate that many early Christians held this view, and it seems odd that they should have made it up. Some at least of the Jewish texts often cited in this connection are therefore likely to have had the meaning normally assigned to them, and now disputed by Gaston; see Davies 1984, ch. 5 for discussion of Josephus *Ant.* 15.134–137, where Davies' conclusion (that the referent of δι' ἀγγέλων '*may* be to prophets'—italics original) is extremely cautious (87). Gaston may well be right, however, to suggest that the idea of angelic mediation of Torah is less frequent than is normally assumed. His arguments, though, would not in any case affect my reading of v.20, since there Paul discusses the mediator, not the angels.

[23]Rightly, Räisänen 1986a, 131 f.

[24]Grässer 1981, 204 n.95, thinks that Paul is arguing in 3.20 that, because of the unity of God, the Torah is not given by God but by a mediator. This can scarcely be right: see below.

[25] See Bring 1966, and his commentary (1968). Bring was anticipated in some respects by Rendall 1912, 172. His position is seriously misrepresented by Callan 1976, 25–6, who imagines Bring to be advocating the quite different view of Gennadius, that, whereas in v.19 the mediator is Moses, in v.20 the Mediator is Christ, who is not (as, on this view, Moses is) the mediator of one nation only.

[26] For other writers who have taken this point of view, without thereby agreeing with the rest of Bring's scheme, see e.g. Gaston 1982 (= Gaston 1987, 35–44); Giblin 1975, 540–541; Isaacs 1923–4, offering the ingenious solution that Moses, who appears as an *historical* mediator between Abraham and the Christian church, is not (according to Paul) needed in that role.

asserting (a) that Moses is not the mediator of one race only, and (b) that because God is one he desires a universal family. Just as the promise was universal, so was the Torah: it was not for Israel only, but for the whole world. This position is ingenious, but is nevertheless open to serious linguistic and theological objections.[27] The δέ at the start of v.20b would be irrelevant if Bring were correct, since both halves of the verse would be making the same point, 20b undergirding 20a rather than undermining it.[28] It is significant that Bring has to try to make δέ mean 'and' here, but even this would not fit his case: if he were right, it should be γάρ, which is hardly interchangeable with δέ. Further, if v.20, especially its final phrase, were a vindication of the law, Paul would scarcely go on to ask 'is the law then against God's promises?' (v.21). The whole argument of Galatians 3, in short, suggests that the Torah is not, as Bring supposes, designed to be a universal revelation for Gentiles as well as Jews, but is specific to ethnic Israel. Bring has, nevertheless, put his finger on an important point in drawing attention to the specificity of ὁ δὲ μεσίτης. This must be taken seriously in any eventual solution.

We proceed, then, to look at the two interrelated problems one by one.

(ii) The Single Seed: 3.15–18

Without in any way denying that there are difficulties and obscurities in these two passages, I suggest that a single line of thought can be observed, as one strand in the chapter as a whole, which makes good sense both of the details of these verses and of their wider context. Though this solution does not depend on evidence from outside Galatians, it is strongly supported by two passages from Romans which, though set of course within a very different overall argument, draw nevertheless upon closely parallel ideas.

[27] See e.g. Räisänen 1986a, 130; Romanuik 1981; Stolle 1973. Stolle is right to point out that Bring's point looks strange in a passage which is manifestly arguing *against* the law. His own solution (that Moses himself does not partake of the quality of 'oneness', taking ἑνός as a qualitative genitive) has been picked up by Callan 1980, 566–567, who tries to improve on it, without (in my view) attaining plausibility. Stolle's idea of reading the genitive ἑνός as a genitive of quality is picked up by Gaston 1987, 43 and given a new twist: the mediator in question is not one of a kind, since there were seventy mediators, i.e. the angels of the nations. This (like a lot of Gaston's reconstructions) seems to me ingenious but implausible. Cranfield's attempt (1979, 857–60) to avoid reading Paul as saying anything derogatory about the Torah is, to this extent, parallel to Bring's concern; though he is (I believe) correct to defend Paul against Marcionism of all sorts, and does not deserve all Räisänen's criticisms (to which he replies in Cranfield 1990), he has not got to the bottom of our present passage.

[28] So, rightly, Martin 1989, 37.

The clue lies in the idea of *unity*. This is a common factor to vv.16 and 20. Indeed, it contributes substantially to the problems we encounter in both verses. In v.16 the 'seed' is said to be one, not many: in v.20 'the "mediator" is not of one, but God is one'. But these are not the only places in the chapter where the idea of unity is important. In precisely that passage where Paul is summing up his whole argument, not least that of vv.15–18, he writes 'for you are *all one* in Christ Jesus: and, if you are Christ's, you are Abraham's seed, heirs according to promise' (v.28b–9). In the context of vv.21–9, the particular force of this is quite clear. The law consigned all things under sin, so that the promise should be for those who have faith in Jesus Christ (vv.21–2). *All* those who believe in Jesus Christ and are baptized into him (vv.26–7) form one single family, so that there are not, in Christ, *different* families composed of Jews on the one hand and Gentiles, or Gentile Christians, on the other, as there would be if the traditional Jewish distinctions between Jews and Gentiles (or for that matter men and women, slaves and free) were maintained (v.28).[29] This is what, according to Paul's whole argument, the Galatian church needs to hear: having become Christians from a pagan background, they must be reassured that they do not need to 'judaize' in order to belong to the true people of God. Paul does not respond to his shadowy opponents, whoever they were, by denying that Christianity has anything to do with Abraham or Israel. He attempts to demonstrate that the promises to Abraham, which do indeed form the ground plan of salvation, are inherited not through the Mosaic Torah but in Christ. The Galatians are not second-class citizens in the people of God if they remain outside the realm of Torah.

If, as would accord with good exegetical practice, we approach the difficult passage about the 'seed' in 3.16 in the light of the quite clear reference in 3.29, where (as in 3.15–18) it is found within a discussion of the Abrahamic 'inheritance', we might suggest that the singularity of the 'seed' in v.16 is not the singularity of an individual person contrasted with the plurality of many human beings, but the singularity of one *family* contrasted with the plurality of families which would result if the Torah were to be regarded the way Paul's opponents apparently regard it. The argument of vv.15–18 would then run: it is impossible to annul a covenant;[30] the covenant with Abraham always envisaged a single family, not a plurality of families; therefore the Torah, which creates a plurality by dividing Gentiles from Jews, stands in the

[29]It seems clear (despite e.g. Betz 1979, 184 f.) that Paul is deliberately echoing the synagogue prayer in which God is thanked for not making the worshipper a Gentile, a slave or a woman (Singer ed., *Authorised Daily Prayer Book*, 6 f.).

[30]Although Paul is clearly regarding this 'covenant' as a 'will' or 'testament', it is quite wrong (despite many exegetes: e.g. Betz 1979, 154) suddenly to abandon the covenantal theme which has been so strong throughout the chapter so far.

way of the fulfillment of the covenant with Abraham; and this cannot be allowed.[31]

This way of reading the passage, I submit, makes excellent sense of vv.15–18. But it has to meet three possible objections. First, is this meaning of σπέρμα justified? Second, why would Paul say 'many', and not 'two', if the problem was that the world, and the people of God, were now split permanently between Jew and Gentile? Third, what is to be done with the last phrase of the verse, ὅς ἐστιν Χριστός?

It is clear that the great majority of occurrences of σπέρμα in the LXX are collective, so that a plural would not make sense. However, precisely because this usage is so familiar, the word comes to be used, following the gradual extension of the Hebrew זרע for 'family' or 'nation'. Brown, Driver and Briggs list eight passages with this sense, three of which have parallels elsewhere, most referring to 'the king's seed', i.e. the royal family.[32] Two quite late passages, both from books which had considerable influence in the Judaism of Paul's day, are particularly significant for our purposes. In Ezra 2.59 (paralleled in Nehemiah 7.16) certain of the exiles 'were unable to show their father's house, and their seed, whether they were of Israel': here the word is clearly used as a synonym for 'race'. In Esther 10.3 Mordecai is said to be 'seeking the good of his people and speaking peace to all his seed'. Again the sense, parallel with 'people', must be 'race' or 'nation'. And once this new singular meaning—the collective seen as one whole—is a possibility, there is also the possibility of a new meaning for the plural, namely, 'families' or 'races'. One can find later instances of the plural of זרע in this sense: for instance, Kiddushin 70b in the Babylonian Talmud, which states 'there are two families (זרעיות) in Nehardea, one called the House of Jonah and the other the House of 'Urbathi: and the sign thereof is, the unclean is unclean and the clean is clean'. It is therefore clear that, under certain circumstance, זרע and its regular translation σπέρμα could have a new singular sense, deriving from the regular collective one, of 'family'. This, I suggest, is exactly what our passage requires if it is to make sense.

Second, why does Paul say 'as of many', if what he is talking about is the potential *duality* created by the Torah, i.e. the split between Jew and Gentile?[33] One could reply to this that Paul is simply speaking in general terms: the contrast is between one and more-than-one. But it would perhaps be better, and more exact, to see under Paul's argument his real fear, which emerges into the light in 4.1–11: if ethnic origin, racial and geographical

---

[31] See the description of a similar line of thought in Burton 1921, 508 (b), citing Dalmer, Zahn and Bacon (*Journal of Biblical Literature* 1917, a mistake for 1897).

[32] See Brown, Driver and Briggs 1905, 457: compare Burton 1921, 505–6.

[33] I am grateful to Dr John Barclay of Glasgow University for raising this with me at the 1986 British SNTS meeting in London.

loyalties, and the like, are to be allowed to remain as the key factors in deciding who one is allowed to eat with, that is, in determining the boundaries of the people of God, then there will be far more than two 'families'. There will not only be Jew and Gentile, but Athenian and Roman, Galatian and Ephesian, African, Scythian, and so on *ad infinitum*. Concede the Torah its permanent validity, and any Gentiles who come to believe in Jesus will have no reason to abandon their ethnic loyalties. The στοιχεῖα will still rule the world.[34]

What about ὅς ἐστιν Χριστός? These words have been considered by some so problematical as to require excision. Certainly, if taken in the usual sense, they are very difficult, and would make the interpretation of σπέρμα just offered impossible.[35] Most interpretations of the verse, however, have begun at the end, with this difficult phrase; I suggest that if we read the verse from the beginning a different possibility offers itself. Here, as elsewhere, we meet Paul's use of Χριστός in a representative or corporate sense.[36] It is true that, for Paul, Χριστός always denotes Jesus of Nazareth (2 Corinthians 5.16 is a possible exception, but that would be controversial to argue). The word never becomes a mere cipher. But it is also true, as I argued in ch. 3 above, that Paul understands 'Christ' as 'Messiah', carrying the significance of the one 'in whom' the people of God is summed up precisely *as* the people of God; and Galatians 3.23–9 is in fact one of the most important bits of evidence for this.[37] Many of Paul's frequent 'incorporative' expressions cluster together in vv.26–9, in just that passage where the worldwide church is affirmed to be 'one' and therefore to be 'the seed of Abraham'. They are the children of God (as Christ is the Son of God); they are baptized into Christ, have put on Christ, they are one in Christ, they are 'of Christ'. It would not therefore be surprising to find that in vv.15–18, which look forward to just this conclusion, we should find the same point being made, albeit with characteristically Pauline brevity.

[34]The point is articulated precisely in Eph.3, esp.v.10. Despite my ignoring of hermeneutical possibilities in this volume, I cannot resist suggesting that Gal. 3.16, read in this way, deserves the closest attention by the contemporary church.

[35] Burton 1921, 508 rejects the above interpretation of σπέρμα on the grounds that the required sense of Χριστός is very difficult, and resorts (509–10) to the theory of interpolation. See, however, Ellis 1957, 70–73. Newman 1984 is strongly in favour of an 'individual messianic' referent, and says that the text 'cannot have reference to a corporate line of descent' (336).

[36] See above, ch. 3. See here particularly Moule 1977, ch.2; Barrett 1962, 77–78; Ellis 1957, 72; Lagrange 1942, 77–9; Bover 1923, 365–6—though Bover does not maintain the corporate sense throughout the passage. In this he is supported by a Vallisoleto 1932 and di Fonzo 1941.

[37]Against e.g. Watson 1986, 70. Dahl 1977, 130 f. rightly notes the messianic significance of Χριστός here, but fails to see the corporate overtones latent in precisely this meaning, which give the present passage its coherence. See too Wilcox 1979, 5, following Betz 1978, 12.

ὅς ἐστιν Χριστός could then perhaps be not so much an *exegetical* note, an attempt by Paul to read 'the Messiah' out of 'your seed' in Genesis 13.15, etc., but rather an *explanatory* note, informing his readers that the 'one family' spoken of in the promises is in fact (as he will prove) the family created in Christ.[38] Christ is the 'seed' because, and insofar as, the promised single family of Abraham is brought into being in and through him and him alone. It therefore finds its identity in him. He is its incorporation. This view of the phrase clearly suggests that Paul's use of Χριστός was more flexible, more capable of different levels of meaning, than is often supposed.[39]

In vv.15–18, then, Paul is not merely contrasting 'law' and 'promise' as mutually incompatible types of religious systems.[40] Nor is he merely establishing the chronological superiority of the promise over the law. He is arguing that God always intended, from the time of the promise to Abraham, that his people should be a single family: that all nations are to be blessed in Abraham (v.8, quoting Genesis 12.3); and that therefore the one family cannot be characterized by possession of the Torah, since that would create a plurality of families, with Jews and proselytes on the one hand and Gentiles, presumably believing Gentiles, on the other, and the latter moreover further subdivided by their various races. The Torah, if taken absolutely, would undercut the promise (v.18) not so much because of the difference between 'works' and 'faith', and the impossibility of perfection in the former area (that is nearer to the argument of vv.10–12, though as we saw in the last chapter there is more to that difficult passage than that; v.15 then begins a new point). It would undercut the promise by creating two or more distinct families. By exploiting the ambiguity of διαθήκη, 'covenant' or 'will', Paul is able to argue that the terms of the will, i.e. the covenant with Abraham, are not to be set aside by any later enactments. It would be wrong, in view of the Abrahamic context, not to hear the overtones of 'covenant' in διαθήκη in v.15: and indeed the 'human illustration' (κατὰ ἄνθρωπον λέγω, v.15a) may have been suggested to Paul's mind because he was already thinking in covenantal terms, where διαθήκη would be appropriate. Paul is deeply aware

[38]See Burton 1921, 182; and Sanders 1983, 175. Ridderbos 1975, 393 rightly says that although the idea of the body of Christ is not mentioned here, 'it is certainly present materially'; see too his pp. 62, 342, and Ridderbos 1953, 132 f. Ridderbos is in some respects close to the solution I propose here, but sees Paul's argument here as narrowing down the 'seed' of Abraham to one strain, in the manner of Rom. 9.6 ff., whereas here it is surely the broadening of the 'seed', to include Gentiles within the one family, that is the focus of thought.

[39]It is thus not so much the case that σπέρμα in Rom. 9.29 will bear a 'latent christological sense' for readers who also know Galatians (Hays 1989, 207), as that Χριστός in this passage and elsewhere will bear a latent ecclesiological sense, for readers who know its corporate overtones.

[40]Here I agree strongly, in general terms, with the whole drift of Watson 1986, while still disputing his analysis of Paul's arguments.

of the content of the promises to Abraham, and throughout the chapter is arguing precisely from them.[41]

The law is therefore to be understood not as a restriction of the Abrahamic promises to one race—that is the mistake Paul's opponents are making—but as a temporary measure introduced for certain specific purposes which, in the long run, would not prevent but would rather facilitate the creation of the single family spoken of in the promise. It is this theme which is then taken up in vv.19–22. When the scripture had done its work of demonstrating that all, Jew and Gentile alike, were sinners (and hence that there could not be two different 'families', because all needed the same remedy and the same way of salvation), the promise of a single family could be given ἐκ πίστεως... τοῖς πιστεύουσιν (v.22). The law holds temporary sway until the coming of the seed (v.19), of faith (vv.23, 25), of Christ (v.24). And, just as 'faith' is defined by its object (πίστις 'Ιησοῦ Χριστοῦ, v.22[42]), so 'the seed', the single family, can best be defined by reference to the one 'in whom' it has its unity: ὅς ἐστιν Χριστός.

Although this argument stands by itself, it is further reinforced by a consideration of Romans 4.13–17, which according to the usual view is at odds with Galatians 3.[43] Though Romans and Galatians are not to be forced into an unnatural 'harmony' as though both were written to say the same things, the discussions of Abraham and his family in Galatians 3 and 4 have several similarities in intention and detail with those in Romans 4 and 9. Thus, it may be suggested that Romans 4, like Galatians 3, argues (i) that the promises of Genesis 15, 17 and 18 always envisaged a worldwide family; (ii) that this family would be characterized by faith, not by circumcision or Torah; and (iii) that this family is to be identified with those who believe in Jesus Christ. Romans 4.13–18 in particular stands in very close relation to Galatians 3.15–29, while going on to make more of the specific nature of Abraham's faith, and while including within the line of thought other elements—wrath, grace, and the idea of God as the lifegiver—which find no place in the parallel passage in Galatians. Leaving these aside, the similarities are striking: Romans 4.13 is closely parallel with Galatians 3.16, 19, 21, 26–9, Romans 4.14 with Galatians 3.18, Romans 4.16 with Galatians 3.15–18 as a whole. There can be little doubt that the passages are both quarried from the same seam of thought in Paul's mind; and in Romans 4 the argument about Abraham and his 'seed' envisages that 'seed' as the single family, drawn from all nations and characterized by faith, which was promised to Abraham in Genesis. Paul makes this explicit with his quotation

---

[41]Against e.g. Betz 1979, 157: Paul pays 'no attention to the content of the promises'. Were my name Räisänen, I would perhaps add a (!) to this remark.

[42] *Pace* Hays 1983, 123. The point at issue here does not affect my present argument.

[43]See e.g. Hübner 1984, 53; Beker 1980, 96.

of Genesis 15.5 in Romans 4.18, using the passage as a means both of expounding Genesis 18.18, 22.17 f. and 17.5 (he quotes the latter two passages in vv.13, 17) and of returning to the starting-point of his argument, since it was Abraham's faith in *the promise concerning his 'seed'* that was 'reckoned to him as righteousness' (Genesis 15.6, quoted in vv.3, 9, 22 f.). The nub of this argument is found in Romans 4.16, which can best be understood as follows. The promise had to be by faith, so that it could be according to grace: otherwise there would be some who would inherit not by grace but as of right, by race. This is impossible, because the promise had to be valid for *all* the 'seed'—not Jews only, but also Gentiles who share Abraham's faith.[44] In other words, there is to be *one* seed, in accordance with the promise; that 'seed' cannot therefore be characterized by possession of Torah, but only by faith. In essence, the argument makes exactly the same point as that of Galatians 3.15–18, and in so doing lends strong support to the exegesis of that passage offered above.[45]

(iii) One God, One People, No Mediator: 3.19–22

We may therefore return to Galatians 3 and look at v.20, our other problematic verse, in the context of vv.19 ff. as a whole. This section follows naturally from vv.15–18: its opening question is occasioned by what has preceded, and it continues to refer to *the coming of* τὸ σπέρμα ᾧ ἐπήγγελται (the family to whom the promises had been made) as the event which would mark the end of the temporary reign of the Torah.

Certain fixed points about vv.19–22 may be made at once. The section asks the question 'why the Torah?', and gives the answer that the law was a necessary part of God's plan, but not his final word. This is explained, in a manner to be investigated, by v.20, which then raises the question of 21a, whether the law is then against the promises. Whatever we say about v.20, its meaning must be such as to raise this question. Paul then answers that it would be a mistake to oppose law and promise, since the law relates to the universally sinful human condition whereas the promise is given to faith. The sequence 'promise—law—Christ' is then further elaborated in vv.22–9.

[44]Rightly, Räisänen 1986a, 172.

[45]I have become aware, in various discussions about Gal. 3.16, that the normal reading of the verse, according to which Paul is then regularly charged with fanciful or 'Rabbinic' exegesis in which we cannot ourselves follow him, has played a large and important role within many different discussions both of Paul's theology and of the New Testament as a whole (see, for instance, Barton 1988, 28; Dunn 1987, 109 f.). This problem is a particular instance of that discussed above in ch. 1: we should beware of arguments whose *real* force is 'we know that Paul was craggy and inconsistent; here is an apparent craggy inconsistency; therefore this is the right way to read the passage'.

The line of thought we have observed in 3.15–18 suggests the following approach to v.20.[46] To begin with, it is grammatically preferable to see the definite article in the phrase ὁ δὲ μεσίτης not as introducing a generalization, but as anaphoric: 'the mediator just mentioned'. The article can of course be used generically, but this usage normally employs the plural, with the exception of the occasional ὁ ἄνθρωπος.[47] But if a specific reference to *the* mediator, i.e. Moses, is intended, where does that take Paul's argument? Bring, as we saw, suggested that Paul is asserting that Moses is not the mediator of one race only, i.e. Israel, but offers the god-given Torah to all the world. But this ignores the discussion which both precedes and follows our passage.[48] In the light of 3.15–18, and in particular of 3.19 ('until the time when there should come the seed to whom the promises had been made'), the natural way of reading ἑνός, 'of one', is as a reference to the one family, the single 'seed', promised to Abraham and now fulfilled in Christ. Paul's point is then this: that Moses is not the mediator through whom this promised 'one seed' is brought into existence.[49] He cannot be, since he (Moses) is the mediator of a revelation to Israel only, οἱ ἐκ νόμου. This offers a quite satisfactory reading of ἑνός, understanding only a typically Pauline ellipse: 'the mediator is not [the mediator] of one'.[50] We can simply cut out the manifold theories about mediatorship implying a plurality of parties on one side or the other. That is not the point. Paul is saying that Moses, to whom the Galatians are being tempted to look for membership in the true people of God, is not the one through whom that single family is brought about.[51]

[46] The only anticipation of this view of which I am aware was the article of Davidson 1888, of which no notice was taken. I came across this after having formulated the theory independently. Rendall 1912, 172 came formally, though not materially, close to this view when he suggested the meaning that Moses was the mediator, not of the single family promised to Abraham, but of the many Jewish families at the time; Burton 192 was perhaps overly harsh in his criticism of Rendall.

[47] See Moulton and Turner 1963, 180–1. This rules out any need for the superfluous reference to angels in v.20 itself.

[48] Gaston 1982, 74–5 suggests 'the Mediator (in question) is not one (of a kind)': i.e. the angel is not alone, but is accompanied by 70 others through whom the Gentiles are also 'under the law'. This, it seems to me, creates far more problems than it solves.

[49] We may perhaps hear echoes at this point of an implicit contrast between Moses, seen in some Jewish circles of the time as a royal figure, and the royal 'seed', i.e. the true Messiah, Jesus, and his people. See Meeks 1967, 214, etc.

[50] Supplying the second 'mediator' as in AV, RV.

[51] This is where the contrast between my suggestion and that of Bring (1966, 309, etc.) becomes most apparent. See the criticisms of his view in Mauser 1967, e.g. that Paul could not have said 'Moses is not of Israel'. Mauser, however, fails to see that Gal 3.6–14 also deals with the Jew-Gentile problem; he seems to think (268) that God's unity depends on the universality of salvation, whereas for Paul the argument works the other way around; he suggests (268–9) that what divides humanity is the *mis*understanding of Torah as an 'invitation to works', whereas in my view (cf. vv.19, 21–3) the division of humanity is in fact the paradoxical *intention* of the law. This latter problem also prevents Mauser (269 n.1) from grasping what in my view

This solution is, I believe, quite satisfactory as it stands. But it can be further improved if the grammatical structure is lined up a little differently.[52] This does not alter the suggested overall meaning, but rather makes it even clearer. The ellipse mentioned above is not a real problem, but the thought would be smoother without it. There is also another question-mark over this reading of v.20a: why is there no article before ἑνός? If the word refers, as I have suggested, to 'the one family' which has been the underlying theme of the passage so far, it would be natural to expect the article, especially when μεσίτης has one. If, however, we read μεσίτης as complement, not subject, leaving the resumptive ὁ δέ as the complete subject of ἐστιν, the phrase μεσίτης ἑνός is natural, following the regular pattern: the *nomen regens* (μεσίτης) loses its article in conformity with Hebrew idiom, and, as is required by Greek, the *nomen rectum* (ἑνός) follows suit.[53] 20a would then read 'Now he (i.e. the mediator referred to in v.19) is not mediator of one'; i.e. is not (the) mediator of (the) single family. This, I think, is easier and clearer than the other way of taking the verse suggested above.[54]

The problem of v.20b can be solved quite easily once 20a is read in this way. Moses is not the mediator of the 'one family', *but God is one*, and therefore desires one family, as he promised to Abraham. The presupposition of Paul's argument is that, if there is one God—the foundation of all Jewish belief—there must be one people of God. Were there to be two or more 'peoples', the whole theological scheme would lapse back into some sort of paganism, with each tribe or race possessing its own national deities. This may be, in fact, the point at which the argument of the present passage interlocks with the στοιχεῖα passages in ch.4: the Torah is seen in the guise of a local or tribal deity. Monotheism demands as its corollary a single united family; the Torah, unable to produce this, cannot therefore be the final and permanent expression of the will of the One God. Paul has used the first article of the Jewish creed (monotheism) to modify,

---

is the correct interpretation of 3.16 (see above).

[52]This is the point at which my case goes further than that of Davidson 1888; he also suggests (300 n.1) that his position would work as well even if ὁ μεσίτης were after all read as generic: 'a mediator is only concerned for those he represents'. This, however, would be a far weaker point in the context of Paul's argument, and is certainly not the natural reading of the Greek.

[53]See Blass-Debrunner-Funk 259. For a similar construction, involving the article expressing the subject and the noun being complementary, see Rom. 2.28–9: οὐ γὰρ ὁ ἐν τῷ φανερῷ Ἰουδαῖός ἐστιν οὐδὲ ἡ ἐν τῷ φανερῷ ἐν σαρκὶ περιτομή, ἀλλ᾽ ὁ ἐν τῷ κρυπτῷ Ἰουδαῖος...κτλ. The resumptive ὁ δέ is of itself common enough, e.g. Mk. 6.50.

[54]ἑνός may be read as masculine, referring to Christ (so Mauser 1967, 270 n.1: this would of course also work if Χριστός were, as in my view, incorporative), or, with most commentators, as neuter. Exegetically there is no real difference (rightly, Davidson 1888, 380 n.1).

drastically, the second (election). The irony of this position—in which Paul in effect uses the *Shema* to relativize the Torah which it summarizes—is at once reflected in the question and answer of v.21.

Once more a parallel passage in Romans helps to reinforce the exegesis. Romans 3.30–31 makes, *mutatis mutandis*, the same points as Galatians 3.20–1.[55] In the context of his argument that 'boasting' is excluded by the doctrine of justification, because faith is the same for Jew and Gentile alike, Paul uses the *Shema* in exactly the same way that, according to my argument, he has done in Galatians 3.20b. This time the middle term of the compressed argument is spelt out clearly:

> Is God the God of the Jews only? Is he not of gentiles also? Yes, of Gentiles also—since God is one, who will justify circumcision on the basis of faith and uncircumcision through faith.

In Romans, this argument is part of the discussion of God's righteousness; in Galatians, of the (closely related) discussion of the temporary validity of Torah. And in Romans 3.31, just as in Galatians 3.21, Paul is driven by the irony of his own argument to ask whether the law is therefore nullified, and to answer in the negative. God is one; therefore he desires one people; therefore the law cannot be the means of bringing his people into existence; but this does not mean that the law is not God's law, or that it is rendered null and void, because the law all along was intended to take precisely this secondary and paradoxical role within God's overall purposes. This obviously requires further explanation, and Paul provides such a discussion in Romans 7 and 9.30–10.13, where the ambiguities of the law in the plan of God are explored in more detail.[56]

The force of Galatians 3.19–22 is therefore as follows:

(a) Beginning with the question raised by vv.15–18, namely, 'why then the law?', Paul states that it was 'added' (sc. to the plan of God which, beginning with the promise to Abraham, was to culminate in the 'one family') 'because of transgressions'.[57] This can be taken either in a strong sense—the law was

---

[55] Davidson 1888, 383 suggests that 1 Tim. 2.5 can be included here as well, since there the writer is making the same universalistic point.

[56] See below, ch. 13.

[57] On this last troublesome phrase see Betz 164–165. Räisänen 1986a, 140–45, discusses the phrase at some length, but I am not convinced that he has got to the bottom of the meaning: in the light of Rom. 5, it is misleading to say that the law causes 'sinning', since there the point is precisely that sin is already in the world ἄχρι νόμου (5.13). Gaston's support (1987, 30, 198 n.50, 201 f. n.43) for the reading of P46 (...νόμος τῶν πράξεων, and omitting τῶν παραβάσεων χάριν προσετέθη) is, to say the least, unusual. The brief similar argument of Eshbaugh 1979, 62 f., does nothing to persuade me that P46 is likely to be original.

given to turn ἁμαρτία into παραβάσις, as in Rom 5.12–14, 20[58]—or in the weaker sense, that Israel as a physical entity could not, because of sin, be the 'one family', and needed the Torah to keep her from going totally astray prior to the coming of the Messiah and the creation of the promised 'seed'.[59] My case, fortunately, does not depend on making a decision on this issue (though I incline to the former due to the thrust of v.22).[60] The problem, on either account, is the all-pervasiveness of sin, which means that no human race, not even Israel, can of itself establish a claim on God's grace.

(b) The Torah was given, then, by God, via the angels and the Mediator, Moses. It is at this point, i.e. v.19, rather than in v.20, that there is perhaps a hint of the law's indirectness, being given to the people at two removes; the mention of angels in v.19 makes its own point, and does not need to spill over into v.20, where it has frequently produced havoc. The fact that 20a begins with the reference to Moses, the mediator, rather than to the angels, provides extra confirmation of this, as does the awkwardness of 20b on any reading which continues the implicit reference to the angels.

(c) Paul then explains further, in v.20, how it is that the law cannot be God's final word: God, being himself one, desires a single family, but the Mosaic law was given to one race only and therefore cannot put this plan into operation.[61] This does not set the law against the promises; each has its proper place, and the fact that the law has the effect of shutting up the entire human race under sin (compare Romans 11.32) does not mean that it is not a good law, but simply that all human beings are sinful and can therefore find membership in the people of God only through faith in Jesus Christ (21–22). It is exactly this point that is then expanded in vv.23–29: the temporary status of the Torah has given way to the permanent creation, in Christ, of a worldwide people characterized by faith. This people is the single family promised to Abraham. We may compare Romans 8.3 f.: what the law could not do, being weak because of human sinfulness, God has done in Christ and by the Spirit.[62]

---

[58]The point here being that παραβάσις is what happens when miscellaneous sin (ἁμαρτία) is confronted by a specific command. So, rightly, Barrett 1985, 33. It is remarkable how many exegetes simply fudge this issue. See, e.g., Hübner 1984, 78: 'the Law was added because of sins, (i.e. to provoke sin)' (German original, 71: Um (der Provokation) der Sündentaten willen wurde das Gesetz hinzugefügt). But παραβάσις is far more specific than *Sündentaten*.

[59]So Wilckens 1981, 171 (summarized in Wilckens 1982, 22): the law was added to condemn transgressions, not to cause them. Martin 1989, 37–9, tries to keep both senses by distinguishing between the 'ostensible intention' of the law (to restrain sin) and the 'real intention' (to increase it, so that humans come to realize the impossibility of saving themselves. I do not think that this quasi-scholastic distinction advances understanding.

[60]See also Dunn 1990, 262.

[61]Perhaps Paul says 'he' and then repeats 'mediator' ('he, however, is not the mediator of the one') so as to avoid aligning Moses himself, whose role goes far beyond what is here discussed (see ch. 9 below) with the temporariness and inadequacy here spoken of.

[62]See below, ch. 10.

(iv) Conclusion

A few remarks are in order by way of conclusion. In addition to clarifying the detail of 3.16, 20, my argument suggests certain points of wider application about the letter as a whole. It supports, for instance, the view (which seems to be gaining ground fast, though not without some opposition) that the real problem is not 'legalism' as usually conceived within traditional Protestant theology, but rather the question of whether one has to become a Jew in order to belong to the people of God.[63] The law in this passage is not an abstract generalized entity, but is the Mosaic Torah, given to Jews and Jews only, which relates to Gentiles simply in that it forms a barrier to keep them out of the covenant. Paul is mounting his (comparatively) familiar argument, that the Torah is not necessary for membership in the covenant; but the means by which he mounts it in this passage is, if I am correct, not usually recognized.

In particular, my argument supports the view of Paul's theology, which has come under considerable attack in recent years, that for Paul there was only one way of salvation, namely, faith in Jesus Christ.[64] Unless I am totally mistaken, the argument of Galatians 3 actually hinges on the divine purpose to create not two families, as in much recent theology, but one. This, I submit, makes much better sense of the rest of Galatians, and for that matter of Romans, than does its alternative, though to argue this point in any detail would take me way beyond the scope of the present chapter and indeed book. It is however probably necessary to add the comment that my position in no way commits Paul to being anti-Semitic, or even anti-Judaic. He does not wish to prevent the Jews from practising their ancestral religion. Indeed, he himself continues to attend synagogue. He merely wants to present his fellow Jews with the gospel as the fulfillment of God's purposes for Israel, his promises to Abraham. His opposition to Judaism is simply an opposition to its being absolutized; and the basis for this is the fact, implied throughout, that Jews are, in the matter of sin, on the same level as the Gentiles. To that extent, Paul's opposition is precisely *not* specific to the Jewish race, but relates to sinful humanity as a whole. The whole post-Auschwitz determination to discover 'anti-Judaism' under every possible New Testament bush is no doubt a necessary reaction to the anti-Judaism endemic in much previous New Testament scholarship, but at the moment it is,

[63]See particularly, of course, Sanders 1977.
[64]See e.g. Stendahl 1976; Richardson 1969, 99–102; Gaston 1987; etc.

frankly, shedding just as much darkness on serious historical understanding as did its predecessor.[65]

A further point that should be emphasized is that this passage, understood in the way I have suggested, lends strong support to the way of reading Paul for which I was arguing in chs. 2 and 3 of the present volume. Central to this passage, I have suggested, are the covenant, the Messiahship of Jesus, and the corporate nature of that Messiahship. When these categories are invoked, texts which before were obscure and disjointed come together and attain a new coherence. 'Christ', in this passage, while (of course) *denoting* Jesus, *con*notes the one in whom the promises are fulfilled, in whom the people of God are summed up. In particular, the word indicates the one in whom that people are a single family, composed not of Jews only but of Gentiles also. Why this line of thought has been ignored, and how it is that Paul can mount such an argument, must be considered further elsewhere. One might venture the suggestion that it has been downplayed this century due to the interests of the two dominant schools of thought in history-of-religions research. The first, wishing to make Paul a Hellenist, did not want to find such thoroughly Jewish material in him. The second, not wishing to find him making claims in opposition to Judaism, did not expect him to see these Jewish concepts finding their fulfillment in Jesus. It may be that both approaches are wrong, and that Paul, like some other writers in the New Testament, believed that what the Gentile world needed was precisely a Jewish message, and that what Israel needed was the news that she had been condemned and brought to new life in the person of her representative Messiah (see Galatians 2.15–21).

One indication of the latter point may be suggested here: in interpreting the promises to Abraham, Paul quietly passes over the concept of the *land*. What has happened to it? It has been transformed: Abraham, as in Romans 4.13, is to inherit the *world*.[66] At points like this we can see clearly enough that Paul's missionary work, of which his writing of Galatians forms a part, was grounded not merely in the half-suppressed workings of his own psyche,[67] nor merely in a sociological agenda for which 'theology' was a mere pretext,[68] but in his theology and christology. His preaching, and his writing, are aimed at one thing: the glorification of God through the effective announcement in all the world that the promises to Abraham have come true in Jesus Christ.

[65]This comment applies perhaps particularly to Gaston 1987, and to Gager 1983 who acknowledges his debt to Gaston. See too the important collections edited by Davies 1979 and Richardson 1986.

[66]See Davies 1974, esp. 176–9.

[67]Against Räisänen in particular, e.g. 1986a, 133.

[68]Against Watson 1986.

Chapter Nine

REFLECTED GLORY: 2 CORINTHIANS 3.18[1]

(i) Introduction

'There is always the nagging thought... "Yes, but what about 2 Corinthians 3?"'[2] Though most of the discussion of Paul and the Torah focusses inevitably, and rightly, on Romans and Galatians, one can easily be lulled by this into thinking that the task is more or less complete when those two letters are dealt with. But Second Corinthians, a noble and remarkable writing worthy of close consideration in itself and not merely as a footnote to other letters, raises in its third chapter, though from a different angle, several of the central issues.

2 Corinthians 3 is all about glory. But what precisely does it say about this glory? And how does glory, as a theme, fit within the overall argument of the wider unit (2 Corinthians 2.14—4.6, or indeed 2.14—6.13)? In particular, what does Paul mean by the verse (18) with which ch.3 reaches its triumphant conclusion? Has he 'proved too much' at this point?[3] Do Christians 'reflect', or 'behold as in a mirror', the glory of the Lord? If the latter, what is the mirror? And what is the 'glory' itself? There is no agreement on any of these points.[4]

---

[1]This chapter was originally published in the *The Glory of Christ in the New Testament: Studies in Christology in Memory of George Bradford Caird*, ed. L.D. Hurst and N.T. Wright, Clarendon Press, Oxford, 1987, pp. 139–150. I have made some revisions, clarifications and additions for this version. Caird's own discussion of the passage may be found in Caird 1944, 234 ff.; 1959, 391 f.

[2]Gaston 1987, 14: cf. Cranfield 1979, 853. The virtual absence of discussion of 2 Cor. 3 from Hübner 1984 inevitably leaves a sense of an important lacuna.

[3]So Barrett 1973, 126, quoting Lietzmann. The habit of detaching v.18 from the rest of the argument has even been given a hypothetical history-of-religions rationale by Jervell 1960, 173 f. My solution will render this quite unnecessary.

[4]Among recent literature on the subject, see Barrett 1973; Collange 1972, 114–125; Furnish 1984, 173–252, with extensive bibliographical listings; van Unnik 1963 (= 1980, 194–210); Dunn 1970; Moule 1972b; Hickling 1974–5; Hanson 1980; Hooker 1980–1; Richard 1981; Kim 1981, 11–14, 140–4, 233–9, etc.; Lambrecht 1983; Gaston 1987, ch. 10; Hays 1989, ch. 4. The history of the early interpretation of this chapter is discussed by E. Prümm in several articles in *Biblica* vols. 30–32.

(ii) 2 Corinthians 3.1–11 in Context

It is now generally agreed that the overall theme of the section of which 3.18 forms a central part is Paul's defence, not of his apostolic ministry in itself, but of the particular style or character of that ministry.[5] It is a ministry of sincerity (2.17), of confidence (3.4), of glory (3.8–11), of great παρρησία (3.12), and one in which the minister need not lose heart (4.1, 16). This theme falls, in turn, within the wider argument of the chapter: that Paul does not need 'letters of recommendation', because the Corinthian church is itself his 'letter' (3.1–3). The idea of 'commendation' is a major theme, in fact, in the letter as a whole (as it stands, i.e. without taking sides at present in the debate on the unity of the letter): see 4.2, 5.11 f., 6.4, 10.12, 18, 12.11. These arguments form the basic structure of the passage, within which the rest of the complicated discussion must find its place. (The nature of Paul's ministry continues as the main subject right through to 6.13: this is clear from 5.11–15, where v.12 in particular echoes ch.3 in several ways, and from 5.20 f., 6.1–13.) Paul's defence of his style of ministry includes as one important feature the demonstration that the human weaknesses and frailties which characterize it do not undermine its credibility but, on the contrary, reveal precisely its Christlike character (4.7–12, 16–18, 6.3–10). This theme is strengthened further by Paul's emphasis that he is not sufficient of himself to be a minister of Christ, and that his 'sufficiency' is from God (2.16, 3.5–6).[6]

If the main thrust of the argument is thus a defence of Paul's ministry, both in that he does not need 'letters of recommendation' and in his paradoxical apostolic boldness and confidence, the main weapon with which he begins this thrust is the concept of the new covenant. Though mentioned explicitly only in 3.6, this is clearly in mind in the language of 3.3, with its echoes of Ezekiel 36 and Jeremiah 31;[7] and it dominates the subsequent discussion (3.7 ff.). Paul's 'sufficiency', which comes from God, consists in this: that he is a minister of the new covenant, which operates by means of the Spirit's work in the hearts of his hearers. The two conclusions Paul draws from this within the present argument are (1) that the Corinthians in

[5]See, among recent commentators, Barrett and Furnish, ad. loc.

[6]3.6 carries, I believe, echoes of Paul's reflections on a Christian hermeneutic of the Jewish scriptures, but this is the first-order subject neither of this chapter in Corinthians nor of this chapter in the present book. On the theme see now Westerholm 1988, 209–216, Hays 1989 *passim*, especially ch. 4.

[7]Compare Rom. 2.29, 7.6 (see ch. 10 below). Echoes of Jer. 31, acknowledged by e.g. Wilckens 1981, 162, Kim 1981, 234, Davies 1984, 129, and Martin 1989, 32, are denied by e.g. Gaston and Räisänen: see below. It would be quite wrong to think that such an idea could have come to Paul only through a tradition, perhaps that of the Lord's Supper. A Jew who longed for the restoration of Israel, and believed that this had paradoxically happened in the events concerning Jesus the Messiah, would come independently to the same conclusion.

themselves, because of the Spirit's work, are his 'letter of recommendation' (3.2 f.), and (2) that he himself can properly adopt a 'bold' style of ministry, can speak the truth in Christ without fear or reserve: 'because we have this hope, we use great boldness' (3.12).[8] Both of these, I shall suggest, are present in the climax of v.18, and to recognize this is to achieve fresh understanding of that verse.

It is in this light that the difficult discussion of Moses and his veil may be understood (3.7–16). Although it is sometimes suggested that Paul's opponents were already using Moses as a model of true ministry (and contrasting him with Paul, to the latter's disadvantage), such explanations are not needed if we recognize the importance of the covenant theme throughout the passage.[9] The argument falls naturally into two sections, 3.7–11 and 3.12–18.

It is not difficult to assess Paul's purpose in 3.7–11.[10] He wishes to argue that his ministry possesses δόξα, glory—presumably to counter any suggestion that an itinerant preacher with a poor speaking style and a prison record is not fit to be an apostle of the Lord of glory. He argues, not by means of demonstration ('what I mean by glory is *x*: you can see that I possess *x* because...') but, in the first instance, with an *a fortiori*: the ministry of the old covenant had δόξα, so that of the new must have even more.[11] He makes this point in three different ways:

(a) Vv. 7–8: The ministry of the old covenant was that of the 'letter', written on stone, and was an administering of death (Paul is obviously

[8]Hanson 1980, 23 sees the second of these points, but for the first he substitutes 'it is a ministry which is centred on Christ'—an idea which he has, I believe, imported into the context: see below.

[9] In connection with the debate over Paul's opponents in this passage, see now the wise comments of Furnish 1984, 242–5. We do not need elaborate hypotheses, either of the theology of Paul's opponents or of the textual pre-history of our passage, to make sense of the argument. See too Käsemann 1971, 149; Watson 1986, 85–7, and Hays 1989, 141 f.: Georgi 'fills the intertextual space with elaborate creatures of the imagination.' Gaston's reliance on Georgi here (1987, 151 ff.) effectively undercuts his denial that this chapter 'has anything to do with law or scripture,' but rather attacks a 'divine man' understanding of Moses—a view difficult enough anyway in the light of the arguments advanced below.

[10]Despite Richard 1981, 358, who sees it as a 'parenthetical clarification' of v.6, and Gaston 1987, ch. 10, who sees Paul's contrast as being between his own ministry and that of a 'divine man' type of charismatic ministry, which, as in 1 Cor. 13.8, is due for abolition. This seems to me simply fanciful, only explicable in fact by reference to Gaston's determination that Paul shall say nothing whatever derogatory about Moses, Torah, Jews, etc. The irony is that in fact Paul here, despite the common exegesis, is in fact speaking positively of Moses. Sanders 1977, 485, 551; 1983, 138 f., is right to see that Paul is here talking about the Torah, though it is dubious whether we should press this passage for information about how he arrived at his view of the law.

[11]So Caird 1944, 236 f.

picking up the themes of vv.3, 6); that of the new is of the lifegiving Spirit.[12] We may compare Romans 8.10, 1 Corinthians 15.45.

(b) V.9, explaining this (γάρ): The ministry of the old covenant was one of condemnation (Paul does not here say why this is so, nor does he substantiate the previous claim that the old mode of administration was one of death); that of the new is one of justification.[13] This point is then amplified in v.10: it is as though, by comparison, the old has come to have no glory at all.

(c) V.11, offering further explanation (εἰ γάρ): The old covenant was destined to be abolished; the new is destined to remain. Thus, if Paul's readers acknowledge that he is a minister of the new covenant, they must see that his ministry possesses δόξα, however surprising that may be.[14]

It is within this (of itself quite clear) argument that Paul refers to the glory of Moses' face. In v.7, by way simply of indicating how great Moses' glory was as a minister of the old covenant, he writes that his glory was such 'that the Israelites could not look steadily at the face of Moses, because of its glory—which glory was to pass away' (my translation). The reason why the Israelites could not look at Moses was not, here, because the glory was passing away, but because it was at present so bright. The reference to its impermanence (τὴν καταργουμένην) is simply introduced as a foretaste of Paul's third *a fortiori* (v.11), much as his reference to the 'ministry of death' (v.7) is a foretaste of the second *a fortiori* (v.9).

(iii) The Reason for Boldness: 3.12–17

So far, so good. The final paragraph, however, is of course the most problematic. Almost every verse presents fresh difficulties. What was it that the children of Israel were not supposed to look at (τὸ τέλος τοῦ καταργουμένου, v.13)? Why does Paul suddenly mention their hardness of heart, and how can he move the veil from Moses' face to their understanding (v.14) or to the hearts of his Jewish contemporaries (v.15)?[15] Is v.16 an

---

[12] I choose 'administering' over 'dispensation' in deference to Gaston's point (1987, 158 f.) that the latter is lexicographically indefensible. However, although I think the sense of 'dispensation' to which he principally objects, that of a sharp antithesis between law and gospel, is not present in this chapter, there might still be senses of 'dispensation' which fitted the theme here. Sanders' use of the word (1977, 512; 1983, ch. 4, etc.) seems perfectly proper.

[13] Although justification is not normally associated directly with covenant theology, I shall elsewhere advance arguments to show that, for Paul, it should be. The use of δικαιοσύνη in the present context is itself quite telling.

[14] So surprising, in fact, that some exegetes cannot believe that Paul really meant this: e.g. Gaston 1987, 161, 165.

[15] Or for that matter his pagan ones, or perhaps to the gospel (4.3–4).

adapted quote from Exodus 34.34, or is it a general statement? Does 'the Lord' in v.17—and in v.18—refer to the Spirit *as* Lord, to Yahweh as Spirit, or to Jesus—or, by implication at least, to more than one of these three? Finally, in v.18, what precisely does κατοπτριζόμενοι mean (looking intently? seeing as in a mirror? reflecting?); why does Paul say that 'we are being changed into *the same* image'? The same as what? Must ἀπὸ δόξης εἰς δόξαν remain ambiguous and perhaps rhetorical, 'from glory to glory'? And how can we cope with the final four words, καθάπερ ἀπὸ κυρίου πνεύματος? How do they fit into the overall thought?

To analyse, let alone to answer, all of these questions would require a longer chapter than this. I propose to look at the problems of v.18 in particular; and one of the ancillary arguments for the position I shall adopt is that it goes with a way of reading vv.12–17 also which at least suggests plausible answers to the questions raised by those earlier verses.

We may begin by repeating a point which, though it should be quite obvious, is often forgotten. The argument, as we have seen, is twofold: it concerns the 'letter of recommendation' written in the hearts of the Corinthians, and, within that, the nature ('boldness') of Paul's ministry. Having established that this is a ministry of the new covenant, which involves the writing on the heart by the Spirit (vv.1–6), and having argued that, precisely as a new covenant ministry, his work has δόξα far exceeding that of Moses, Paul is now making the further point that, 'because of the hope',[16] he is able to use much παρρησία, freedom of speech. This is the specific point of the new section (vv.12–17): Paul can be *bold* in his dealings with Christians, not least those in Corinth. He has no need to veil the glory. He can let it be clearly seen. 'With the decline of democracy, *parrhesia* meant the courage to speak out when social pressures were against it.'[17] If this is his main point in this section, its obvious conclusion is v.17b: where the Spirit of the Lord is, there is freedom—freedom, that is, not in the vague sense of release from any constraints at all; not even in the more precise sense of freedom from the Jewish law, though that idea is both thoroughly Pauline and quite closely related to the present passage; nor yet 'liberty to conform to Christ';[18] freedom, rather, in the sense of freedom of speech, boldness, openness and honesty in proclaiming and defending the gospel (cf. 2.17, 4.1 f.)[19] This point is then picked up again in 4.1–2 as the beginning of the

---

[16]I.e. the hope of life, guaranteed by the gift of the Spirit in the present, as in v.5. He does not say, as one might have expected, because of this ministry: this shows that the δόξα in question is eschatological, as in Rom. 8.30.

[17]Young and Ford 1987, 95.

[18]Davies 1984, 105.

[19]So, rightly, Furnish 1984, 277, against, e.g., Hickling 1974–5, 394; though Furnish obscures the issue with his alleged parallels from Philo, which give a quite different sense of both 'freedom' and 'boldness' from that which Paul here develops. For the background of παρρησία see the various articles of van Unnik (1962, 1963, and the 1980 collection), who

next subsection: we renounce any practice that might look like dressing up the unvarnished truth, and simply go ahead and state it clearly.

It then becomes apparent that the main contrast in the passage is not that between Paul and Moses, nor that between Christians and Moses, but that between the Christians—even those in Corinth!—and the Israelites, both of Moses' day and of Paul's.[20] Paul can use boldness not because he is different from Moses but because those who belong to the new covenant are different from those who belong to the old. Moses is actually, here, in one sense a *precursor* of the new covenant people in 3.18, since he, alone among the Israelites, is able to look at the divine glory with unveiled face. This is the point of vv.14 f.: Moses had to use the veil, because the hearts of the Israelites were hardened (unlike those of the new covenant people; this is the point of the ἀλλά, 'but', at the start of v.14[21]). The Israelites come, that is, in the negative category indicated in vv.3, 6: they are those who belong to the covenant on tables of stone, the covenant of the 'letter'. The argument is not so much allegorical, or even (as current fashion would have it) 'midrashic', but follows the line of thought in Galatians 3.15–22, or even Mark 10.2–9. Difference in style of ministry is occasioned by difference in the spiritual condition of the hearers: Paul's overall point is that his boldness correlates with the new covenant membership of the Corinthians, according to which they are themselves his 'letter of recommendation'. The contrast, then, is between the necessary style of Moses' ministry to Israel and the proper and appropriate style of Paul's ministry to Christians who, as in vv.1–3, are themselves the 'letter' written by the Spirit. This shows that vv.14–15 are not

---

argues that the Semitic background of the word points of itself to the idea of 'barefacedness'. Whether or not this will stand, there is clearly a very close link between v.12 and vv.17–18. Lack of emphasis on Paul's defence of his 'boldness' has allowed exegesis to go off course here: e.g. Gaston 1987, 159, etc., arguing that the idea of 'glory' is something that, since Paul would not have wanted to talk about it, must have been introduced into the conversation by his opponents. On another point, Dr. George Johnston suggests to me that ἐλευθερία here may be another deliberate 'Exodus' motif.

[20]So Bultmann 1976, 93 f., Furnish 1984, 213–4, against e.g. Caird 1944, 236 f.; Hickling 1974–5, 393, who thinks that Moses is contrasted with the Christians; Richard 1981, 364 n.82, who, following Georgi in some ways, advances the extraordinary claim that Paul makes Moses 'a precursor of his Christian rivals and the antithesis of the true Christian minister'; and Kim 1981, 233–9. So, too, J. Jeremias is not strictly accurate when he says (1967, 869 n.230) that here 'Moses represents the OT community': rather, he stands over against them. Hays 1989, 142 f., reads the passage as though a submerged parallel between Moses and Paul breaks out from under the argued contrast. I think this puts it, if anything, the wrong way round, and helps to explain why Hays does not, in my view, give sufficient weight to Paul's argument about 'boldness', which does not appear (for instance) in his otherwise fine summary of the thrust of the passage (153).

[21]It hardly means 'furthermore', as suggested by Kim 1981, 238.

an aside, but a development of Paul's main point throughout the chapter.[22] It also explains, incidentally, why Paul's argument in vv.7–11 does not result in his having to wear an even thicker veil, to hide the even greater glory.[23] His hearers do not need protecting from it as Moses' did.

Christians, then, are those upon whose hearts the Spirit of the living God has written the 'letter of recommendation', so that they can be known and read by all (vv.2–3). Paul's ministry is therefore a ministry in which God equips him by the Spirit to minister to those who are receiving the Spirit (vv.5–6), and who, as he will now show, are able to look upon the glory with unveiled face. This clears the way for a proper reading of vv.13–15.

V.13 makes the (by now obvious) contrast between Paul's ministry and that of Moses. Moses, he says, had to veil the glory because it was temporary. Furnish is, I believe, correct in seeing (p.203) that vv.7, 13 speak, not of a glory which gradually fades from Moses' face, but of a glory which, because it is part of the old covenant, is to be annulled as is that covenant.[24] Exactly as we found in Galatians 3 (above, ch.8), the Torah is given for a specific period of time, and is then set aside—not because it was a bad thing now happily abolished, but because it was a good thing whose purpose has now been accomplished. The παλαία διαθήκη was always *intended* to be a temporary mode of administration. The veil means that the Israelites cannot see the glory, foreshadowing as it does the glory of the gospel (compare 4.4).[25] This leads in to v.14 by means of an explanatory contrast, signalled by the ἀλλά at the start of v.14: *their* hearts, however, that is, the hearts of the Israelites, were hardened, whereas yours, that is, the Christians', have been changed by the Spirit.[26] The ἀλλά thus explains the οὐ καθάπερ Μωϋσῆς at the start of v.13: *we* use great boldness in relation to you, unlike Moses before the Israelites, because your hearts are not like those of the Israelites, in whose presence Moses had to veil the glory.

Vv. 14b–15 then fill out the point: Jews are still, from the perspective of the new covenant, in the same condition of 'veiledness' when faced with the glory of the Mosaic revelation. Paul transfers the veil from Moses' face to

[22]*Contra* Furnish 1984, 233, 236, 243.

[23]*Contra* Hooker 1980–1, 297 f.; Gaston 1987, 159.

[24] With e.g. Hays 1989, 133–6, *contra* e.g. Hooker 1980–1, 291, 303–4: see the discussion in Hanson 1980, 13 f. Gaston 1987, 161 is thus right in what he denies, even if he may be wrong in what he affirms.

[25]This means that τέλος can be read as 'goal' or 'final destination' rather than 'cessation', even though τοῦ καταργουμένου indicates that the idea of the conclusion of the Torah's temporary dispensation is also present within the argument. See Ridderbos 1975, 219 n.28; Davies 1984, 129 f. ('Paul does not oppose Sinai, but a particular understanding of it'); Hays 1989, 136–8; against, e.g., Räisänen 1986a, 56.

[26]This shows that the suggestion of a *non sequitur* here (Gaston 1987, 162, following Hooker) is unwarranted.

the 'reading' of Torah in the synagogue,[27] in order to be able to say that the 'reading of the old covenant' remains a hidden thing. The person reading aloud comes to be (in some ways, not all) in the same position as Moses faced with the Israelites. The implication is that the old covenant itself is glorious still, but that those who hear it read in the synagogue (and the reader himself, presumably, hence the qualification a moment ago) cannot see that glory. The fact that Moses is no longer among those present, in other words, does not alter the state of affairs, since the reason for Moses' veil in the first place was the spiritual condition of his hearers, which has not changed with the passage of time in the Israelite community. The veil in question remains in place, he says, because only in Christ is it abolished. It is not the Torah itself that is abolished, but the veil which lies between Torah and its hearers. In other words, what goes when the covenant is renewed is the inability to understand Torah; or, to remove the double negative, when someone is in Christ he or she can understand Torah properly (even though the Torah-dispensation is itself, as in Galatians 3, to be done away).[28] Romans 10.3–4 comes readily to mind as a close parallel: the Jews, being ignorant of God's righteousness, and seeking to establish their own, did not submit to God's righteousness, τέλος γὰρ νόμου Χριστὸς εἰς δικαιοσύνην παντὶ τῷ πιστεύοντι (see below, ch. 12). The contrast between the two glories, of Torah and the gospel, in vv.7–11 is subsumed under the truth that both are indeed revelations of glory; and those who are in Christ, it seems, can receive the glory, whether the glory of Torah or the glory of the gospel. Torah and gospel are not the same, but nor are they here antithetical.[29]

The ἀλλά at the start of v.15 introduces what is simply, in the present context, an assertion (in other words, not an argument):[30] in contrast to the taking-away of the veil in Christ, whenever Moses is read in the synagogue, the veil lies on their hearts. All through the chapter, the condition of the heart has been one of the major focal points, and here Paul brings out the force of 14a in relation to the developed idea of veiledness. Thus, although the idea has come quite a long way from the picture of Exodus 34, Paul's development of it grows naturally out of his own reading of the passage, in

---

[27]Perhaps reflecting the practice of wearing the *tallit* in the synagogue? So, at least, is suggested by Le Déaut 1961, 47.

[28]This is one of those points where Paul has been accused of self-contradiction: is the Torah abolished (Gal. 3) or maintained (2 Cor. 3)? (Sanders 1983, 162 n.1.) This is a false dichotomy. The Christian no longer lives *under* the Torah, but this is not because the Torah is a bad thing now happily done away. Part of membership in the new covenant family, which is not *demarcated* by Torah, is (what Paul would consider) the true *understanding* of Torah, precisely as a God-given deliberate temporary dispensation.

[29]Sanders 1983, 102, rightly notes that the effect of removing the veil is that Christians can now understand the Torah. The 'new covenant' does not involve a new, that is a different, law.

[30]See above, ch. 1.

which the crucial factor was the reason for the veiling of Moses' face, namely, the state of the Israelites' hearts (14a).

It is in this light that the direction of thought in vv.16–17 becomes comprehensible:

(a) Paul desires to show that the new covenant people whom he has described briefly in vv.1–3, 6 are capable of receiving the glory of that new covenant, and therefore that the appropriate style of new covenant ministry is 'boldness' as opposed to a veiled secrecy.

(b) To this end he uses Exodus 34.34, not as an exact quotation, but as a deliberate allusion, in order to make the transition between Moses, who in the Exodus narrative was the one who went back into the presence of the Lord and so removed the veil, and the people, *whether apostles or their hearers*, who now possess the freedom which allows 'boldness'. The context of the Exodus passage is significant (Paul refers to it again, in a related passage, at Romans 9.15): Israel has committed idolatry, and is under divine judgment. In this context the point of the Exodus quotation includes the contrast between Moses and the people, and its thrust is clearly that when Moses returned into the Tent of Meeting he removed the veil; having been face to face with the Israelites, and so veiled, he is now once again face to face with the glory, and so unveiled. Paul, in quoting this verse, expands it, because his argument throughout is precisely that someone—anyone, not just Moses—who is not hard-hearted does not need the veil. Moses thus quite properly stands as a model for anyone who, like the Corinthians according to 3.1–6, is not hard-hearted.[31]

(c) This reinforces, therefore, the basic point of the chapter: those who are in Christ, the new-covenant people, are *unveiled* precisely because their hearts are *unhardened* (3.1–3, 4–6). Paul wants *both* meanings to resonate (the Exodus meaning and the contemporary one), or he would presumably have added τις here to make it clear that the subject of ἐπιστρέψῃ is no longer 'Moses', but 'one' or 'someone'.[32] He wants to include a reference to all those who 'turn to the Lord' and therefore possess 'freedom'. The current equivalent, he is saying, of Exodus' reference to 'turning to the Lord', the moment when the veil is removed, is openness to the work of the Spirit—in other words, that condition which, as he has argued from the beginning of the chapter, characterizes the church.[33] This means, too, that ὁ δὲ κύριος at the

[31]So, rightly, Dahl 1977, 138 n.3.

[32]This double reference may also be helped by an echo of the Targum on Ex. 33.1–6, in which those Israelites who are penitent return to the Tent to confess their sins: so Le Déaut 1961, 45.

[33]Sanders 1983, 177 is right to draw attention to the fact that the verb ἐπιστρέψῃ has the sense 'convert'.

start of v.17 can bear its natural anaphoric sense: '"the Lord" in this passage refers to the Spirit'.[34]

(d) V.17, therefore, draws on the categories of vv.1–6 (new covenant membership, signalled by the Spirit's writing on the heart), in the light of the discussion of Moses in vv.13–16 (old covenant 'veiledness' because of hardness of heart), to provide a Q.E.D. to the initial statement in v.12: since we have this hope, we use great boldness (on this specific meaning of 'freedom', ἐλευθερία, see above). 'The reason we have boldness is this: you, unlike the Israelites before whom the glory (even of the old covenant) had to be veiled, possess the Spirit because you are within the new covenant, and you are therefore able to bear the bold, direct revelation of God's glory.' The point Paul is making is that the open-faced style of ministry he employs is *appropriate* because of *the condition that he and his hearers share*, that is, unhardened hearts and the consequent Spirit-given ability to behold the glory of God. The result is that when (vv.16–17) someone turns to the Lord-who-is-the-Spirit, the veil is removed. Precisely as in 3.1–6, Paul and the congregation see the Spirit's work manifest in one another.

Vv. 12–17 thus follow a typical Pauline format (see above, ch. 1, on Paul's styles of argument). He opens with an initial statement (12: we use great boldness) which is explained in an initial fashion (13: our boldness is a matter of open-facedness, in contrast with the practice of Moses). This then is itself explained (14a: the reasons for Moses' practice), and a further comment is added (14b–15: such a practice is still in effect in the synagogue). He then turns round to begin the approach to his final statement of the point to be proved (the transition from 15 to 16 thus corresponds to that between Romans 8.8 and 9, on which see ch. 10 below), with an initial statement about how the Mosaic condition is alleviated (16); he then affirms that these conditions are met in Christian experience (17a), and can at once produce the Q.E.D. for the argument of 12–17: since these conditions are met, the result is 'freedom', i.e. boldness (17b). This whole paragraph then functions as the argument which leads up to the Q.E.D. for which we have been waiting since the first paragraph of the chapter, which is delivered in v.18.

---

[34]See Dunn 1970, Moule 1972b, against Furnish 1984, 210 ff. Furnish is right, however, to reject the christological interpretation of e.g. Hanson (see below). Kim 1981, 12 f. argues that Moule and Dunn have failed to notice the parallel with v.14; but Kim himself has given little if any weight to the argument of the whole chapter about the work of the Spirit. This means that his frequent references to 2 Cor. 3.16–18 as evidence for Paul's view of the glorious Christ (e.g. 108; 137 and frequently, claiming 3.18 as evidence for 'image' as a christological title) are called into question.

(iv) The Glory and the Mirror: 3.18

If this exegesis is correct—and it seems to make very good sense of an otherwise difficult passage—it raises a possibility for the interpretation of v.18 which has not, to my knowledge, so far been explored. Paul is dealing not merely with his own ministry but with the state of heart of his hearers. This is clearly reinforced by the 'all' which emphasizes that the 'we' at the start of the verse is not merely the 'royal we', or 'Paul and his fellow-workers', but refers to each Christian.[35] This, and not a self-reference, is Paul's main point.

There is general agreement that linguistic evidence favours the meaning 'behold as in a mirror' for κατοπτριζόμενοι.[36] But the question, the lack of satisfactory answers to which has driven scholars to seek less frequent meanings, is—what is the mirror? I suggest that the 'mirror' in which Christians see reflected the glory of the Lord is not, in this passage at any rate, the gospel itself, nor even Jesus Christ. *It is one another.* At the climax of Paul's whole argument, he makes (if I am right) the astonishing claim that those who belong to the new covenant are, by the Spirit, being changed into the glory of the Lord: when they come face to face with one another they are beholding, as in a mirror, the glory itself.[37] Though the verb could therefore have its alternative sense of 'reflect', since the one in whom the glory is seen as in a mirror could himself be said to be 'reflecting' the glory, that is not the point Paul is making.[38] Unlike the Israelites, those in the new covenant can look at the glory as it is reflected in each other. If we were to visualize the point pictorially, we might imagine Paul and the Corinthians each as an angled mirror, in which the other sees, reflected, the glory of the Lord:

[35]The omission of πάντες in P46 may safely be ignored. My reading of this verse makes it highly unlikely that Paul intends here a reference to his own conversion, or, by analogy, to that of anyone else. He is talking about relations now within the church, not in this verse about how people become members of it (*pace* Kim 1981, 71, 79, 231, etc.).

[36]See e.g. Philo *Leg. Alleg.* 3.101—an interesting passage, with echoes of 2 Cor. 4.18 as well, though ones of which Paul would not have approved. For the alternative, 'reflect', see e.g. Knox 1939, 131 ff. (See the discussion in Collange 1972, 116 ff.) My argument renders this solution unnecessary.

[37]Lambrecht 1983, 250 seems to want to include this possibility as an extension of his main idea, that the gospel is the mirror in question. But his argument is very vague at this point; and his suggestion that this 'seeing' is itself indirect is hardly compatible with the emphasis of the passage. Gaston 1987, 165, denies any glory to Paul or his hearers—in line with his constant refusal to admit the possibility that Paul might think of a *present* glory. This seems to me simply to cut clean across the text.

[38]*Contra* van Unnik 1963, 167. Caird, 1944, 1959, argued that 'reflect' makes better sense of the passage as a whole and in particular its underlying christology. I submit that these arguments point more to 'behold', not in the sense that Caird rightly rejected (a contrast between Moses and Jesus), but in a sense consonant with his main emphasis (that Paul and the Corinthians are being changed into the glory of God).

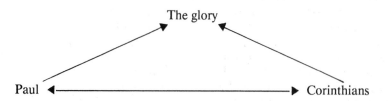

This is the final proof that the Corinthians themselves are Paul's 'letter of recommendation'. And, if this is so, 'the Lord' in the phrase 'the glory of the Lord', the object of κατοπτριζόμενοι, need not be identified as either 'God' or 'Christ', but may, perfectly consistently within the thought of the chapter as a whole, refer to the Spirit. It is the peculiar glory of the Spirit that is seen when one looks at one's fellow-Christians.[39]

V.18, if this is correct, thus picks up quite precisely the thought of vv.1–3. It does not 'prove too much',[40] or introduce 'an entirely new idea',[41] or leave behind the purpose of the earlier part of the chapter.[42] The new covenant people are a letter, written by the Spirit, to be known and read by all—'a letter of Christ, ministered by us' (v.3). The 'turning to the Lord' spoken of in the allusion to Exodus 34.34 is a turning to, an openness towards, the Spirit—who is operative in the ministry of Paul and also in the new covenant community. The phrase need not be taken in the general sense of 'turning to Christ', i.e. becoming a Christian, though this is no doubt implied. It is more specific: when one looks at the work of the Spirit, the veil is unnecessary. It is taken off—this is the point of the passage—not in private communion with God, but in the boldness with which Paul proclaims the gospel to the Corinthians.

Two different emphases in ch.3 as a whole come, therefore, to full and parallel expression in v.18, and can be seen in the participle and verb around which the sentence is structured:

(a) If we focus on μεταμορφούμεθα, the emphasis that appears is: the Christians in Corinth are Paul's 'letter', because the Spirit has written the new covenant on their hearts through his ministry: 'we are being changed' by the work of the Spirit.

(b) Focussing on κατοπτριζόμενοι, we discover the emphasis that Paul's ministry is 'bold', 'unveiled': 'we all, with unveiled face, behold as in a mirror the glory of the Lord'.

---

[39]This means that Kim's attempt to read the entire passage as basically about Paul himself, with the ἡμεῖς πάντες in v.18 as the sole exception, shows that he has missed the point of the whole chapter, in his eagerness to find material about Paul's conversion (Kim 1981, 235, etc.).

[40]See above, n.3.

[41]Furnish 1984, 238.

[42]Hickling 1974–5, 393.

What is the logical relation between these two? It is possible to let the emphasis fall on (b), translating in some such way as: 'it is *as we behold* the glory of the Lord as in a mirror—i.e. in one another—that we are being changed...'. This would emphasize the participle κατοπτριζόμενοι rather than the indicative μεταμορφούμεθα, and it may be for this reason that P46, partially supported in A and elsewhere,[43] reverses the grammatical order, exchanging the participle and indicative and reading κατοπτριζόμενοι οἱ τὴν αὐτὴν εἰκόνα μεταμορφούμενοι κτλ. This throws the weight of the sentence even more clearly in this direction: 'we all, with unveiled face, behold the glory of the Lord—we, that is, who are being changed into the same image from glory to glory'. The participle could then have explanatory force: it is precisely because 'we are being changed... into glory' that 'we all behold the glory of the Lord as in a mirror' in the course of Christian ministry.[44]

The majority reading, however, throws the weight of the sentence on to the indicative μεταμορφούμεθα; and this is probably to be preferred. It is here, after all, that we find the climax of the underlying discussion: Paul does not need 'letters of recommendation', because he and the Corinthian church alike are being 'changed' so that they, the church, *are* his 'letter'. The relation between the two verbs is therefore straightforward, even though the meaning is striking: as we behold the glory in one another, we are being changed into the same image. The parallel with Moses here is that, just as Moses gazes at the Lord, with the result that his face is changed, so Christians gaze (as in a mirror) at the Lord, the Spirit—in one another: and so they are changed, as the Spirit writes the 'letter', the new covenant, on their hearts. The reading of P46 may, perhaps, have come about through a scribe's being so taken up with the subsidiary argument of the chapter (that Paul's ministry is one of 'boldness') as to forget the more fundamental one (that he does not need letters of recommendation).

One of the strengths of the view of v.18 I am proposing is the sense it is able to make of the otherwise troublesome phrase τὴν αὐτὴν εἰκόνα, 'the same image'.[45] First, the word εἰκών is introduced suddenly; although Paul will make an important further use of it in 4.4, that seems insufficient to

---

[43]E.g. in some occurrences of the phrase in Origen.

[44]This reading cannot be lightly dismissed. It explains the other readings well: κατοπτριζόμεθα οἱ could easily have been contracted into κατοπτριζόμενοι, which yields the odd reading in A (and 614, a thirteenth-century minuscule) of two participles without a main verb. Having arrived at that reading, one of the natural corrections open to a scribe would be to turn μεταμορφούμενοι into μεταμορφούμεθα, particularly in view of the greater Patristic interest in transformation, even deification, than in the boldness of apostolic ministry. Finally, the reading of the ninth-century MS 33, which has both verbs in the indicative, can be explained as a copying error from either source.

[45]See Furnish 1984, 215, discussing, among other things, the apparently awkward accusative.

explain why he brings it in here, especially since the uses are not quite the same. There it refers to Christ; here, to (the work of) the Spirit. It seems much better to take it very closely with κατοπτριζόμενοι, understood, as I have suggested, as 'beholding as in a mirror'. That which one sees in a mirror is an εἰκών, a reflection.[46] Of course, Paul is quite well aware of the other overtones that might be heard (of Genesis 1.26, for example) in what he is saying; but his present use is simply part of the overall metaphor of this particular verse (so Barrett, Furnish). Second, the force of τὴν αὐτήν, 'the same', at last becomes clear. Paul is not saying that one is changed into the same image as Christ (except in the broad sense that the glory remains ultimately that of Christ; but that is not his main point[47]). He is asserting that Christians are changed into the same image as each other. This is why he can be so bold: he and his audience have this in common, that each of them is being changed into the same image, and so is able to behold the glory of the Lord reflected in the other.[48] Thirdly, in terms of its relation to the rest of the sentence, τὴν αὐτὴν εἰκόνα is perhaps best read as in apposition to δόξαν: 'beholding the glory—the same reflection!—as in a mirror'.

The rest of the sentence presents less of a problem, though of itself it is still at first sight ambiguous enough.[49] Although ἀπὸ δόξης εἰς δόξαν could simply mean 'from one degree of glory to another', the thought of the verse as a whole, and the ἀπό-phrase which immediately follows, suggests that ἀπὸ δόξης refers to the source of the glory, that is the Spirit who is producing it in Christian lives, and εἰς δόξαν to the resultant glory which is actually possessed by believers.[50] Alternatively, the contrast between the glory of the old covenant and that of the new in vv.7–11, and the idea of transition from one to the other in vv.16–17, might indicate that the two 'glories' were that of Torah and Gospel.[51] Of these two options (there are of course others noted in the commentaries) I prefer the first, but either goes well with my main argument.

The final phrase, καθάπερ[52] ἀπὸ κυρίου πνεύματος, then has the force of a 'that is': 'from glory to glory—that is to say [*or* as one would expect] from the Lord, the Spirit'. In addition, it is quite likely that Paul intends an

[46]E.g. Euripides, *Medea*, 1162, Plato, *Republic*, 402 B. I am not persuaded that Wisdom 7.26 forms part of the intended background of this verse: εἰκών is the only word in common between the two passages. This is not, of course, to say that 'Wisdom' ideas are totally absent from the passage; as we have seen in earlier chapters, Paul can make good use of them when he wants to.

[47]The objection of Hays 1989, 220 f. is therefore not damaging to my case.

[48]This solution is similar to, but stronger than, that of van Unnik 1963, 167 f.

[49]See particularly Moule 1972b.

[50]So Collange 1972, 122 f. Barrett 1973, 125 notes that Schlatter takes this view.

[51]See Furnish 1984, 242.

[52]Or καθώσπερ (B); this reading, if correct, would make the point a shade stronger again, but would spoil the possible allusion to v.12: see below.

allusion to, and hence a contrast with, v.13: we use boldness, οὐ καθάπερ Μωϋσῆς... [ἀλλὰ] καθάπερ ἀπὸ κυρίου πνεύματος.[53] In any case, the words κυρίου and πνεύματος should be taken in apposition: '"the Lord", that is the Spirit' (compare v.17). The chapter has come full circle. The Spirit (who is not to be separated in a Marcionite fashion from the Lord with whom Moses spoke)[54] has now written the new covenant on the hearts of all those who believe in Christ (v.3). This has come about through the paradoxical and bold ministry of Paul, because Christians are transformed by beholding, in each other, the glory of the Lord (that is, the Spirit) as in a mirror. This interpretation ties the threads of the chapter together more tightly than any other known to me.

(v) Conclusions

The exegesis I have offered is strikingly confirmed, and firmly located within Paul's christology, in the continuation of the argument in ch. 4.

First, it is clear from 4.1 ff. that Paul, at least, has not been sidetracked from the discussion of his ministry. That, obviously, is why he introduced the subject of glory, and of Moses, in the first place. He continues now by answering the objection that, since not all believe his gospel,[55] it must, like Moses' ministry, be veiled. He repeats the shift already made between the veil on Moses' face and that on the hearts of the people (3.14 f.): 'those who are perishing' have their minds blinded by the god of this world, so that they may not see the light which consists of the gospel of Christ's glory (4.4). Paul's ministry is therefore not called into question by the phenomenon of continuing unbelief.

Second, 4.5–6 explains further just what is involved in the 'beholding' of 3.18. The creator God has shone 'in our hearts' (4.6, picking up 3.3; in other words, the act referred to is that which brings people into the new covenant), with the result that the knowledge of the glory of God, now seen in the face of Jesus Christ, can shine as a light to all around.[56] This, in other words, explains the mutual beholding of 3.18: God shines, with the light of the

[53]So Hays 1989, 144; in redrafting this chapter (August 1990) I thought I had come to this view independently, but on re-reading Hays I begin to suspect that it may have been an unconscious echo of his own suggestion.

[54]Indeed, it is the pre-existent *Spirit*, not the pre-existent Christ as Hanson suggests, that is the striking feature of vv.13–18: compare 4.13. Hanson, in his review of the volume where an earlier version of this chapter appeared (*Journal of Theological Studies* n.s. 39, 1988, 584), questions quite properly whether Paul distinguished the pre-existent Christ and the pre-existent Spirit; I think this passage itself gives some reason to suppose that he did.

[55]See Rom. 10.16 for a similar objection.

[56]See Barrett 1973, 135 for this sense of πρὸς φωτισμόν.

gospel of Jesus Christ, into the hearts of his people, who then reflect his light, becoming mirrors in which others can see God's glory.

Finally, and most strikingly, this glory, into which Christians are being changed, because of which they reflect God's glory to one another and so enable an honest and open-faced ministry to take place, is indeed seen in the face of Jesus Christ—the Jesus who suffered and died and rose again.[57] In 4.7–11 Paul shows how it is that he, at least, is being changed into glory:

> But we have this treasure in jars of clay to show that this all-surpassing power is from God and not from us. We are hard pressed on every side, but not in despair; persecuted, but not abandoned; struck down, but not destroyed. We always carry around in our body the death[58] of Jesus, so that the life of Jesus may also be revealed in our body. For we who are alive are always being given over to death for Jesus' sake, so that his life may be revealed in our mortal body...[59]

In other words, the glory which is seen, as in a mirror, in Paul's ministry is the glory which shines through suffering. This glory consists in the fact that Paul does not despair in his sufferings, is not abandoned although persecuted, is not destroyed even when struck down. It is not a glory which enables him to avoid the suffering, just because it is the glory of the Messiah who is Jesus, the one who was crucified and raised. The pattern Paul is acting out is the pattern of Philippians 2.6–11 or Romans 8.17–25, and it gives him confidence that God will in the end vindicate both him and his ministry (4.13–15). Although in one sense the full glory is yet to be revealed (4.14, Romans 8.18, 23–5), in another sense it is already being accomplished by God in his people: that is the force of the present tense (κατεργάζεται) in 4.17, which is not to be reduced to 'is preparing'.[60] It is precisely this inaugurated eschatology which is then picked up in 5.5: God worked this very thing in us,

---

[57]This is the sense in which Dunn's point (1975a, 320), that the mark of the eschatological Spirit is that relationship 'which makes the believer more like Jesus', ceases to be (as he says) 'simple, pietistic language' and takes on the typical character of Pauline paradox. The glory is actually seen in the present (*pace* Gaston 1987, 160, 165)—but it is precisely the glory that shines through suffering and death.

[58]Barrett (1973, 139 f.) suggests that νέκρωσις in v.10 should be understood as 'killing'; see, however, Hanson in *Journal of Theological Studies* n.s. 39, 1988, 584.

[59]NIV translation. I take v.12 ('So then, death is at work in us, but life is at work in you') as ironic: Paul is issuing a characteristic rebuke to those who, boasting in a life which has risen above suffering, are ashamed of him or consider him unworthy of apostolic status because of *his* suffering.

[60]*Contra* Arndt and Gingrich 1979, 421, who cite only this reference in Hellenistic Greek; the classical parallel suggested in Herodotus vii.6.1 is not to the purpose, since there χρόνῳ δὲ κατεργάσατό τε καὶ ἀνέπεισε Ξέρξην ὥστε ποιέειν ταῦτα is surely best taken in the sense 'in time he *succeeded in* persuading Xerxes to do this': see Liddell and Scott 1953 *ad loc.*, also citing the other classical passage adduced in Arndt and Gingrich (Xenophon *Mem.* ii.3. 11).

giving us the Spirit as a down-payment. And this, I suggest, gives us the full meaning of 3.18: that the glory of God, at which Christians look with unveiled face when they behold their fellow-Christians in whom God is inaugurating the new covenant by the Spirit, is seen precisely in the paradoxical pattern of Christ, that is, the pattern of suffering and vindication.

On the one hand, then, Paul is defending the boldness, the straightforward proclamation of the truth, which characterizes his ministry. On the other hand, he is demonstrating that suffering and persecution do not pose question-marks against his apostolic claims, but on the contrary vindicate them. It is enough that the servant be like the master. The Corinthians, looking at the Spirit's work in Paul and seeing there the revelation of God's Christlike glory, are being changed into 'the same likeness': that is why they are themselves Paul's 'letter of recommendation'. Paul thus issues both a rebuke and a challenge, anticipating the final challenge of 13.5–10: if this is how the new covenant glory is revealed, perhaps your attitude towards my suffering and ministry shows that you have never shared in that glory at all.[61] The glory of God is seen in the face of Jesus Christ, the crucified and risen Messiah: where the Spirit renews the covenant, this glory will be seen in the lives of Christians. To have the face unveiled does not mean that the glory is, like that on Moses' face, the sort of thing that can (so to speak) be seen with the naked eye. That is the mistake the Corinthians, or those amongst them whom Paul is opposing, are tempted to make (5.12). The true glory is in the heart, and provides the real apostolic commendation (3.1–3, 5.12). This is the theme which is expressed compactly in 3.18, and it is this theme too that is picked up at the climax of the whole section (6.3–10):

> As servants of God we commend ourselves in every way... by purity, knowledge, forbearance, kindness, the Holy Spirit, genuine love, truthful speech, and the power of God... as unknown, and yet well known; as dying, and behold we live.

One or two final remarks are in order as we look from 2 Corinthians 3 to the wider concerns of this volume as a whole. First, we have again seen the central importance of covenantal categories within Paul's handling of a debate concerning the law.[62] Second, the picture of Torah which emerges

---

[61]There are no doubt many ways in which this reading could be fitted into an analysis of who Paul's opponents were, but this lies beyond my present concern. The possibility that Paul is attacking a view which included an exalted figure of Moses, perhaps as king, cannot be excluded in the light of the evidence for such a view presented by Meeks 1967, 1968.

[62]*Contra* e.g. Gaston 1987, 156, 224 n.59, 236 n.17, claiming that the covenantal language is borrowed from Paul's opponents; this depends on Gaston's *a priori* on p. 156, that 'the concept of covenant is characteristic not of Paul's gospel to the Gentiles but of Jewish Christianity', which seems to me to assume what is to be proved. See too Räisänen 1986a, 242–245, claiming that there is no reference to Jer. 31 in 2 Cor. 3. Gaston's own point (236 f., n.23), that in 1QH 4 there is a frequent link of covenant renewal and the illumination of the face, tells

from 2 Corinthians 3 is that of a deliberately temporary dispensation, much as we saw in Galatians 3.[63] Third, this dispensation resulted in a decidedly ambiguous state of affairs, not because there was anything wrong with Torah (or with Moses, its mediator) but because of the condition of the hearts of its recipients. The Torah itself, it seems, is for Paul good, and even glorious, but in the event can only condemn its recipients, because of their state of heart.[64] It is only, finally, when the work of Christ and the Spirit has been accomplished that the glory which shone in Torah can shine once more, this time effectively. And if these conclusions mean that 2 Corinthians 3 fits perfectly into the overall scheme of thought we discovered in Galatians 3, they also mean that we now have a high road straight into our next passage. What the law could not do, God has done in Christ and by the Spirit.

---

quite strongly against this. Sanders 1977, 514 argues differently: the new creation transcends covenantal categories. This is true in a sense, but to transcend a category is not to deny or exclude it.

[63]Rightly, Westerholm 1988, 130.

[64]This is perceived as a tension by e.g. Sanders 1983, 138 f., but within Paul's overall account of the divine purpose, as in Gal. 3 or Rom. 9–11, it makes sense, as we have now seen.

Chapter Ten

THE VINDICATION OF THE LAW: NARRATIVE ANALYSIS AND ROMANS 8.1–11[1]

(i) Introduction

Romans 8.1–11 raises in a more precise and specific form several of the questions which have dominated discussion of Paul's theology in general, and his view of the Torah in particular.[2] We could itemize the key ones as follows:

a. What is the meaning of νόμος in this passage, especially in 8.2? This touches the debate between (e.g.) Hübner and Räisänen as to whether νόμος refers to Torah (Hübner) or not.

b. What role does the law play here? Is it positive or negative, or both, or what? In particular this relates to 8.3 f., which is often taken as viewing the law in a disparaging light.

c. What, in particular, is the meaning of τὸ δικαίωμα τοῦ νόμου in 8.4? Is it 'the righteous behaviour which the law desires'? Or what?

d. What is the relation between the Spirit and the law in this passage? Is it antithetical, much as the Spirit-flesh antithesis in vv.5–8, or complementary, or what?

e. How is the discussion of law, and the apparently forensic language in vv.4, 10, to be integrated with the incorporative christology of the passage as a whole?[3]

[1]An earlier version of this chapter was given as a paper at the 1986 annual meeting of the Canadian Society of Biblical Studies, in Winnipeg. I am very grateful to friends and colleagues there for their comments and questions.

[2]As I said in the Introduction, it is impossible to document this chapter as fully as some of the others, and in any case less necessary, because of the detailed recent commentaries that are available, e.g. by Wilckens, Zeller, Dunn and Ziesler. I shall concentrate instead on the exposition of a new line of argument, namely, the narrative analysis of Rom.8.1–11, which will then by implication enter the debate with these writers, and of course with Sanders, Räisänen, Hübner, Westerholm, Martin and other recent writers who have dealt with the passage in their monographs.

[3]These questions are all raised, in one way or another, by Moule 1974. I think my arguments will strengthen and fill out the case he there began to advance.

I propose to come at these questions in two related ways. After an introduction in which I shall offer some preliminary observations, and a section setting out in rough summary my view of Romans 7, I shall examine the logical structure of 8.1–11, and draw some conclusions from that, and then study the narrative structure which underlies 8.3–4, and draw some further conclusions from that. This will lead to some final suggestions on a wider front.

Among the many interesting things about Romans 8.1–11 two stand out for the present discussion. Here we appear to find Paul's positive and negative views of the law side by side, not only in the same passage but even in the same pair of verses (8.3–4). And, second, though we are accustomed to finding discussions of the law surrounded with debate about justification, we both do and do not find this here. There is language about justification, to be sure: the root δικ- is found in δικαίωμα (v.4) and δικαιοσύνη (v.10). But these are themselves often felt to be problematic, since the discussion seems to be about something other than 'justification', namely, new life in Christ and the work of the Spirit.[4] This prompts the reflection: how is it that we have accepted so happily the watertight compartments into which Schweitzer bundled up Paul's theology, reflecting merely his perception of the different sorts of ideas in, say, Romans 1–4 and Romans 5–8? A glance at the parallels in Galatians to both sections would indicate that no such division is warranted.

This leads to a thesis I wish to suggest about Romans 5–8 in general: that it is not an aside between Romans 1–4 and 9–11, any more than it is the 'real centre' of the letter, to which those other sections are merely ancillary. It is the continuation of the same argument, the necessary bridge between the discussion of the family of Abraham defined by faith in Jesus Christ (3.21—4.25) and the family of Abraham defined by grace not race (9–11). This suggests, what might have been obvious from chs. 5–8 itself, that the subject-matter of those chapters cannot be generalized into a discussion of 'man under the law', 'men made new', or whatever. The subject remains principally the question of God's righteousness, i.e. his covenant faithfulness, which includes as its central component the question of the covenant itself, and hence of Israel, and hence of Torah. I take the basic line of thought in chs. 5–8 to be as follows. Those who are declared to be members of Abraham's family on the basis of faith (as in 3.21—4.25) are to rest assured that the problems which remain, that is, the problems of how God can be righteous in making this declaration over people who still face sin and death,

[4]See Moule 1974, and the discussion which followed.

have been dealt with in Christ and through the Spirit. By these means God has inaugurated the new covenant, and thus creates these people as his true humanity.[5] As the climax of this argument, Paul demonstrates that those who are thus members of the new covenant family inherit the sonship, the glory, and the promises, particularly that of the resurrection which, itself the sign of the new covenant, will precipitate that renewal of all creation for which Israel in her apocalyptic visions had longed, and which was to be brought about because Israel herself was to be the new Adam, ruling over the new Garden (8.12–25).

If it be asked why Paul is writing all this to a predominantly Gentile church, my reply, necessarily tendentious like much else in this particular chapter, is that the Roman church consisted largely of ex-proselytes who were, in a sort of mirror-opposite of the Galatian situation, thankful to be relieved of the burden of Torah—and who were in danger of rejoicing too happily over its apparent demise. This accounts for the skillful defence (as I understand it) of the Torah in ch. 7 as well as the attack on antisemitism in ch. 11, and also explains the purpose of the letter: to prepare the way for Paul's intended use of Rome as his new base of operations for a mission whose *modus operandi* was always 'to the Jew first, and also to the Greek'. If the Roman Christians are to give their backing to a mission with this theological shape it is vital that they understand that the covenant, though apparently redrawn, redefined, rethought or whatever, has been fulfilled rather than abrogated. They must not lapse into Marcionism, though they should not be given a chance to topple back into the philoJudaism of the Galatians.

It should not come as a surprise, then, to find that the Torah and the covenant are still central categories in Romans 5–8. It could even be argued that Romans 5.20 is the climax of the whole Adam-Christ passage, explaining the position of the law within the entire scheme of divinely ordered history: νόμος δὲ παρεισῆλθεν ἵνα πλεονάσῃ τὸ παράπτωμα. Certainly it is to that verse that the discussion of Torah in 7.1—8.11 looks back quite obviously, via the hints—which fit happily into the same scheme of thought—in 6.14–15. The position Paul is arguing, just as in Galatians 3, is that the Torah has not alleviated, but rather has exacerbated, the plight of Adamic humanity. This can only mean that the recipients of Torah, i.e. Israel, have found themselves to be under its judgment because of their participation in Adamic humanity. Since therefore Christians have left the realm of the παλαιὸς ἄνθρωπος in baptism, they have also left the realm of Torah, coming out from the place where it could exert a hold over them.

[5]For the latter theme, see ch. 2 above. Fuller exposition of this reading of Rom.5–8 is found in Wright 1980a, ch.3.

This, indeed, is the place where one of Paul's central themes, which is usually totally ignored, comes to fullest expression (see also above, pp. 39, 154). Within the apparently negative effect of Torah, stated in 5.20 and amplified in 7.7–20, there lies the extraordinary positive purpose explained in 8.3. God has deliberately given the Torah to be the means of concentrating the sin of humankind in one place, namely, in his people, Israel—in order that it might then be concentrated yet further, drawn together on to Israel's representative, the Messiah—in order that it might there be dealt with once and for all: οὗ δὲ ἐπλεόνασεν ἡ ἁμαρτία, ὑπερεπερίσσευσεν ἡ χάρις (5.20b). This, I think, is perhaps the most significant point to be made about Paul and the law in current debate.[6] But this is to run a little ahead of the argument.

(ii) Romans 7: A Tendentious Sketch

Before launching in to Romans 8 itself, it is necessary to say something about the view of Romans 7 that I shall presuppose. The passage is, of course, notoriously difficult, and here I can only offer a brief sketch of a case that should really be argued in far more detail. I have set out the outline of the whole passage as I see it in an Appendix.[7]

Paul now develops the picture of those who come out from under Torah. For this he uses one of his most misunderstood analogies (Romans 7.1–3). Various points should be noted at once. The husband in the illustration is not the Torah. Nor should it present great difficulties to find that the same person ('you') first 'dies' and is then 'married to the one who was raised from the dead' (v.4). The key is to be found in the whole line of thought of the preceding chapters, particularly in 5.20 and 6.6. The former husband is the παλαιὸς ἄνθρωπος, the old 'you' which died in baptism, the self over which, because of the Torah's condemnation of Adamic humanity, the Torah exercised a hold. It is not, then, the Torah, but the 'old man' that dies, leaving the self—who clearly plays the part of both husband and wife in the illustration—to be married to the new man, i.e. Christ, through participation in whose death and resurrection (7.4) she has herself been enabled to die and rise. The doctrine of resurrection was always a 'new covenant' idea, as we can see by setting Ezekiel 37 and the Maccabean resurrection passages (e.g. 2 Maccabees 7) in their historical as well as literary contexts, and the echoes of 2 Corinthians 3 in Romans 7.6 indicate clearly enough that what Paul is talking about here is indeed the inauguration of the new covenant, whose

[6]This solves in principle the problem raised sharply by Sanders 1991, 92 f.

[7]Below, pp. 217-219. The literature on Rom.7 is of course vast: good listings are found in Dunn's commentary *ad loc.*

boundary-marker is Christ and Spirit and not Torah. This theme is to be picked up in 8.1 ff.

The inevitably controversial passage 7.7–25 fills out the picture Paul has expounded thus far.[8] I here summarize my own view of the section, which will be further supported by the subsequent exegesis of 8.1–11. The passage, I suggest, divides designedly into three quite clear sections:

> *a.* 7.7–12: the law is not sin, but its arrival, in Sinai as in Eden, was sin's opportunity to kill its recipients
>
> *b.* 7.13–20: the law was not the ultimate cause of 'my' death: it was sin, working through the law and in 'me', unwilling though 'I' was, and thus swelling to its full size
>
> *c.* 7.21–25: the result in terms of Torah: it bifurcates—and so do 'I'.

7.7–25 is basically a defence of Torah against the imputations that it is identified with sin and that it is ultimately responsible for the death which results from its presence. Paul answers the first objection with reference to the initial arrival of the Torah in Israel, at which time Israel recapitulated the sin of Adam: this allows for the echoes both of Gen. 3 and of Israel's plight in 7.7–12. The primary emphasis of the argument is on Israel, not Adam: what is being asserted about Israel is that when the Torah arrived it had the same effect on her as God's commandment in the Garden had on Adam.[9] The 'fit' of 7.7–12, read this way, with 5.20, quoted above, serves as an initial confirmation.

Paul then faces the harder question, the relation between the Torah and the death which results from its sentence of condemnation (7.13–20).[10] His basic answer is that it is sin once again, not Torah, which is responsible for death, and that the fact that sin has made its base of operations in the very Torah itself, holy and just and good as it is, shows how exceedingly sinful sin in fact is. The result of this argument is that in fact not only the Torah, but also the ἐγώ, is exonerated, 7.17–19 (so far removed are we from Bultmann's view of the passage as the analysis of the problem of the cloven ἐγώ). There was nothing wrong with wanting to keep Torah; it was merely impossible to do it, because Israel too (who I take as the principal referent of the ἐγώ, as in Galatians 2.19–20; Paul's theological, not psychological, autobiography is included in this picture as a result, but Paul is not seeking to draw attention

---

[8]See further below, the conclusion of ch. 11; and also ch. 12. In addition, see the Appendix at the end of the present chapter.

[9]It is possible that Paul here has the Golden Calf episode in mind, as he evidently does in 9.14 ff.

[10]On this passage see also ch. 12 below.

to his own 'experience') is in Adam, is σάρκινος. The vindication of the ἐγώ, closely bound up here with the vindication of Torah itself, thus stands very close to the vindication of Israel in 3.1 ff.

The further result of 7.13–20 is that 5.20a is expanded, on its way to the resolution of 8.3. Sin has now been concentrated in Israel. As in the earlier passage, the ἵνα-clauses (7.13, twice) indicate the underlying divine purpose: *so that* sin might be seen as sin, *so that* sin might become exceedingly sinful, might as it were be piled up in one great obvious heap. The perplexity of the 'I' in Romans 7, and the puzzle of the Torah in the same passage, is the reflex of the strange plan of God to deal with sin by collecting it in one place and condemning it there. The 'I' does not understand what is happening, since its real desire is the right and proper one of obeying Torah. But Torah has the effect, when applied to Israel-in-Adam, of focussing a bright spotlight precisely on the Adamic character of the people of God, showing sin up in its true colours. The reason for this will become clear in 8.3: only so can sin be properly dealt with.

The conclusion which Paul draws (εὑρίσκω ἄρα τὸν νόμον, v.21, which I would read as 'this then is what I find to be true about Torah', somewhat parallel to the use of εὑρέθη in 7.10) is that Torah takes on a strange double role.[11] Even here νόμος can have the meaning 'Torah': what Paul finds, as he asks questions about the Torah, is that he is driven to an analysis of himself *qua* Jew and his (theologically analysed, not emotional or in that sense 'autobiographical') internal tensions. From this analysis he can draw the conclusion that the law is good, and holy, and that insofar as the Jew is called to be part of God's people and entrusted with his oracles he delights in it and is quite correct to do so. But the fact that he is in Adam, is 'fleshly', means that the Torah cannot help but condemn him; and in this role it seems to take on a sinister aspect, enslaving and imprisoning him despite his, and its, right aspirations. This is the ἕτερος νόμος, the Torah as it has been taken over and used by sin operating through the foothold which is the flesh. The Torah, unable to do what it would have wished because of sin and the flesh, cannot but stand over against, and accuse, the very people whose covenant membership it appeared to mark out. Israel's paradoxical vocation, spelled out more fully in Romans 9–11, is that she should be the people of the covenant, even though that covenant condemns all those, Israel included, who are in Adam.

In the light of 5.20 and 7.13, however, it should become clear that even this negative side of Torah's work has its ultimately positive goal: this is how, in the purposes of God, sin is to be condemned and its effects undone. The

---

[11]Against e.g. Watson 1986, 226 n.51—cited here because, interestingly enough, it was Watson himself who first persuaded me of this view, in an unpublished paper written (I think) in 1977.

ἕτερος νόμος, then, is not really an anti-Torah, or a demonic Torah; it is held within the divine purpose, under the rubric of the ἵνα-clauses of 5.20, 7.13 and 8.3.

It is significant that at the end of the passage Paul does not ask 'who will deliver me from this Torah', or even 'from this ἕτερος νόμος', but rather 'from this body of death'. It is sin, in the humanity which the Jew shares with everyone else, that is the problem from which he or she needs to be delivered. Again we can offer here a single strand of support out of many possible ones. If we take Paul's highly rhetorical statement in 7.20–23, pass it through the conclusion of 7.24–25, and boil it down to its barest essentials, we have something almost exactly like Galatians 3.21–2:

> (21) ὁ οὖν νόμος κατὰ τῶν ἐπαγγελιῶν τοῦ θεοῦ; μὴ γένοιτο. εἰ γὰρ ἐδόθη νόμος ὁ δυνάμενος ζῳοποιῆσαι, ὄντως ἐκ νόμου ἂν ἦν ἡ δικαιοσύνη· (22) ἀλλὰ συνέκλεισεν ἡ γραφὴ τὰ πάντα ὑπὸ ἁμαρτίαν, ἵνα ἡ ἐπαγγελία ἐκ πίστεως Ἰησοῦ Χριστοῦ δοθῇ τοῖς πιστεύουσιν.[12]

I thus have no basic problem with seeing νόμος in vv.21–3—the crucial passage—as referring throughout to Torah.[13] Indeed, this reference seems to me utterly required by the context, and to suggest otherwise is to accuse Paul of making a play on words exactly when it is most likely to be confusing. To be sure there is tension. That is precisely what Paul is writing about. But to dissolve that tension by saying either that 'the law of God' in v.22 is something other, perhaps bigger, than the Torah; or that the ἕτερος νόμος of v.23 is not the Torah at all but something demonic; or that the two uses of νόμος in v.23b are not references to the same bifurcated Torah; or to suggest that νόμος in v.21, or anywhere else in the passage, means simply 'principle'—to do any of these things is to escape the deep rush of Paul's argument and paddle off into a shallow and irrelevant backwater. The plight of 7.25b—a clause which belongs where it is—is that of the αὐτὸς ἐγώ, significantly the same phrase as in 9.3. Paul has been describing the plight of the Jew from a Christian viewpoint: now this reaches its climax, as he looks at his 'flesh' (see 11.14) as the locus of sin and death, agonizing because the holy Torah itself has been used to bring this about, and yet rejoicing because God has, in Christ and by the Spirit, provided the exact remedy for this situation. Romans 7 concludes, then, with an analysis of Torah which does what Paul's interpreters have found it so hard to do: it holds together (a) the

---

[12]To insist that this passage cannot be used in support because it is in Galatians would be taking the assumption of Pauline incoherence—or significant changes of mind—to unacceptable extremes.

[13]For the details of the debate on this point, see Räisänen, Hübner (below, n.23), and the commentaries *ad loc.*

affirmation of the Torah as God's holy law, (b) the nuanced critique of the Torah which we find spelt out in so many ways in Galatians and elsewhere: it cannot give what it promised, because of sin and the flesh, and (c) the hint that even within this apparently 'negative' side of Torah there lies hidden one essential part of the positive, saving purposes of God.

(iii) Romans 8.1–11: Structure of the Argument

We now turn to Romans 8.1–11, and the first thing to notice is its shape. The basic argumentative structure of 8.1–11 is that of a syllogism whose conclusion precedes its minor premise:[14]

> *a*. The problem is caused by sin and death operating through Torah (ch. 7):
>
> *c*. Therefore there is no condemnation for those in Christ Jesus (8.1):
>
> *b*. For God has made provision for exactly this problem. (8.2–11)

We may now fill in the detail of this a little more. The most noticeable feature of the passage, from the point of view of structure, is the line of γάρs which stretches from v.2 to v.8, with only the occasional δέ to break the sequence, and then the line of δέs which brings the argument back up the slope from v.9 to v.11. This can be explained as follows.

Paul's basic assertion (*c* in the syllogism) is contained in 8.1, but he must at once explain it if it is not to be immensely and frustratingly paradoxical, relying only on 7.25a to rescue it from total absurdity. He therefore advances a preliminary explanation, a first statement of *b* in the syllogism, in v.2: for the law of the spirit of life in Christ Jesus has set you free from the law of sin and death. Paul knows that this is going to be a big idea to bite off at one go, so he at once explains it again (vv.3–4, to which we shall return in conclusion, since they form, not indeed Paul's conclusion, but still the driving force of the whole paragraph): for God has done what the Torah could not do, weak as it was because of σάρξ, i.e. he has condemned sin once and for all, and has enabled the δικαίωμα of the Torah to be fulfilled 'in us' through the death of his Son and the gift of his Spirit.

The string of γάρs which follow (5a, 6a, 7 twice—and the διότι with which 7 opens should really be considered part of the same logical chain) are aimed, it appears, at two things. First, they explain the negative analysis of σάρξ which dominated ch. 7 and was summed up in 8.3 (the law was 'weak

[14]See ch. 1 above.

through the flesh'). Second, and at the same time, they point out, in the first two stages of the explanation, the way in which the πνεῦμα enables these problems to be got round. They explain, in other words, the negative and positive sides of vv.3–4. This complex explanation comes in three stages, consisting in, respectively, vv.5, 6, and 7–8:

i. those who are κατὰ σάρκα think about τὰ τῆς σαρκός:
ii. thinking like that is death:
iii. because thinking according to the flesh is at enmity with God.

This sequence is like the larger unit 8.1–11 in that the middle term is the logical conclusion, for which the final explanation gives the reason; but the final explanation belongs where it is (i.e. it is not 'misplaced' in terms of Paul's actual argument), since it is this that forms the climax to this particular line of thought he is developing. And this climax consists once more of the vindication of the Torah, and the claim that it is the σάρξ that has caused the problem with it: the mind of the flesh is hostile to God, for it does not submit to God's law, for indeed it cannot, and *those who are in the flesh cannot please God*. This is the substance of ch.7, now repeated as part of the further stage in the argument.

In parallel with this is the sequence of thought that picks up the positive side of vv.3–4, but here there are only two members, the third being delayed until vv.9–11:

i. Those who are κατὰ πνεῦμα think about τὰ τοῦ πνεύματος:
ii. The mind of the spirit is life and peace...

The result of this analysis for our appreciation of where Paul's argument is going is that the passage seems to be emphasizing two things: the fact that it is the flesh that has caused the problem with the law (the problem, that is, of its resulting in death), and the fact that the spirit is God's answer to this problem. The first of these is Paul's expansion of 3a: the law was weak διὰ τῆς σαρκός. The second, logically, we should expect to be an expansion of v.4, and also of the first words of 3: 'what was impossible to the law... so that the δικαίωμα τοῦ νόμου might be fulfilled in us who walk according to the Spirit'. And if we work on with this expectation, we will find that fresh light may dawn on that very difficult passage.

From vv.2 to 8, then, Paul has been explaining, in sequence, first his bold conclusion of v.1 and then the various bits of the explanation itself. V.2 explains v.1. Vv. 3–4 explain v.2, setting out the bifurcation of flesh and spirit and showing how the Torah could do nothing with the one but could achieve its purpose through the other. Vv. 5–8 explain this bifurcation further, showing how life in the flesh leads to death (i.e. how being in the flesh rendered the Torah powerless to do what it wished, which as we shall see was to give life), and how life in the Spirit points to the covenant blessings of life and peace.

Finally, after all these explanations and explanations of explanations, Paul can begin to build once more towards his eventual conclusion. V.9 places his audience on the map he has drawn: 'you, however, are in the spirit-category', the category hinted at in 7.6, 8.4, 8.5b, 6b. He pauses only for a moment (9b) to assure them that all Christ's people do indeed have the Spirit; that is, he is not in 9a addressing a subgroup of the church. Having in this aside referred to the Spirit as 'the Spirit of Christ', he can now move a stage further in the argument: if Christ is in you, then, despite the sin-caused death which the body will still inherit, the spirit (presumably the human spirit, in parallel with 'body') is life διὰ δικαιοσύνην. This last phrase is notoriously difficult either to translate or interpret in context, but the sequence of thought we are examining will result in a suggestion presently. This statement of the present condition of the person in whom the Spirit dwells leads to a further point (hence the δέ at the start of v.11): well then, if you are indwelt by the Spirit of the God who raised Jesus, your own resurrection too will be assured. The variation in words denoting Jesus is extremely significant: 'Jesus' refers to Jesus as the man who was raised from the dead, whereas Χριστός carries the connotations of 'Messiah', the one who represents his people so that what is true of him is reckoned as true of them.[15]

Seeing the train of thought in 8.1–11 as a whole in this way leads to three initial conclusions in controversial areas, which we can suggest here before moving to a detailed consideration of vv.2–4.

First, the thing that 'the law could not do' in 8.3 was not to produce mere ethical behaviour, but to give *life*—that is, the life of the new age, resurrection life. That this is Paul's meaning is clear not only from the train of thought as a whole but also from the hints in 7.10 ('the commandment which was unto life') and Galatians 3.21 (cited above). This suggests that ἵνα τὸ δικαίωμα τοῦ νόμου in v.4 may also point in the same direction. At the same time, the train of thought we have observed running from 5.20 through 7.13 to 8.3 suggests that κατέκρινεν in 3b also represents something which God has done which the Torah could not do. (This is surely the most natural way, in any case, of reading the grammar of the sentence.) At first sight this looks odd. The Torah, it might seem, is actually quite good at condemning sin.[16] But at the level on which Paul is operating it seems that what the Torah actually does is to collect sin into one place, to allow it to show its true colours, so that it may *then* (though not by the Torah itself) be dealt its

[15]See above, chs. 2–3.
[16]So Hooker 1990, 32.

decisive death-blow.[17] This, then, corresponds—at the level of its theological structure at least—to the revelation of the righteousness of God in the death of Jesus, apart from Torah, in 3.21–26.

Second, the overtones throughout are *covenantal*, as they have been since 7.6. The Torah is not a miscellaneous collection of regulations; it is the covenant document, and its desire to give life is its basic intention when viewed in that way (in e.g. Deuteronomy 30.15, a passage not far from Paul's mind as he writes Romans). Though it is unfashionable to use covenantal categories in interpreting Paul, I believe, as is already clear in this book, that they are actually central; and, moreover, *they are habitually expressed in forensic language*, i.e. using the root δικ-. This point must be simply asserted here, since there is no room to spell it out as could be done; were I to amplify it, I would return at once to Galatians 3, and work back to Romans 8 via 2 Corinthians 3, Romans 2 and Romans 4. δικαιοσύνη, I suggest, can often be translated, more or less, as 'covenant membership' (when referring to the δικαιοσύνη of humans, of course); and δικαίωμα can perfectly properly bear the meaning 'the covenant decree', i.e. the decree according to which one who does these things shall live (e.g. Deuteronomy 30.6–20). This is the 'just decree' which belongs to the Torah, corresponding to the 'just decree' which is issued negatively and referred to in 1.32: they know the δικαίωμα τοῦ θεοῦ, that those who do such things deserve to die. This once more places the emphasis of 8.4 not on ethical behaviour as such, but on that which *results from* the work of the Spirit—which is, for the moment, *evidenced by* (what we call) ethical behaviour: those who are now made alive by the Spirit will live. This explains also the (at first surprising) διὰ δικαιοσύνην of 8.10. The spirit is life because of *covenant membership*, which is precisely the assurance of life. There is a close link between justification and resurrection in Paul, much closer than the traditional separation of categories (e.g. 'juridical' and 'ontological') would suggest. Both belong in the covenantal context: the idea of resurrection began as the hope of Israel that God would finally validate his covenant and rescue her from the death of exile, and the idea of justification properly belongs not in an individualistic soteriology but in the context of God's affirmation that this or that person is a member of his covenant family. Resurrection is therefore, as in much contemporary Jewish thought, the ultimate 'justification': those whom God raises from death, as in 8.11, are thereby declared to be his covenant people. This, indeed, is the future justification spoken of in 2.1–16, of which the present justification discussed in 3.21 ff. is simply the advance announcement. But to follow this line of thought would take us too far afield. Sufficient for the present point to note that the language of justification, far from being out of place in this passage,

---

[17] I was helped to this conclusion by an illuminating discussion with Christopher Palmer.

is very much at home, because the matrix of thought to which it belongs is precisely that which we have here, namely the theology of the renewed covenant.

Third, this covenantal context, which makes sense in terms of the overall drift of Romans as well as the detail of this passage, suggests strongly that Paul is making a positive connection between the Spirit and the Torah. Having asserted bluntly in 7.14 that the Torah is πνευματικός, he is now showing that the people created in Christ is a people who, as it were, fit the law (or perhaps, a people whom the law fits). The paradox of 8.1–11 is that God does, by the Spirit, what the law intended but could not do of itself. This points forward to the very similar argument in 9.30—10.13, in which Gentiles, without apparently even realizing it, succeed in fulfilling the Torah when they confess Christ and believe in his resurrection. (At the same time, the 'negative' side of Torah, as in 8.2b and the condemnation of 8.3, is picked up by Israel's stumble in 9.32–3.) This suggests that Hübner is right in asserting that ὁ νόμος τοῦ πνεύματος in v.2 is referring to the Torah itself, even if some of the meanings he attaches to that assertion, and the arguments with which he supports it, are not as strong as he hoped.[18] The new-covenant overtones found here by e.g. Cranfield are the key to the whole, though again Cranfield's reading of 7.1—8.11 as a whole is also called into question.[19] In fact, the analysis I have offered of 8.1–11 strongly supports the tendentious account of Romans 7 given in the previous section.

(iv) Romans 8.3–4: Narrative Analysis

I now wish to propose a narrative-style analysis of the two key verses of Romans 8.1–11. I take as my model that worked out by Richard B. Hays in his book *The Faith of Jesus Christ*, where he first argues for the appropriateness of using such techniques and then applies them to certain passages in Galatians.[20] I do not claim, any more than Hays does, that these methods are all-embracing—that, for instance, all narratives can fruitfully be submitted to such analysis. But the possibilities he has opened up are too inviting to leave untried, and I believe that in fact this kind of analysis will prove very interesting in our present passage. It is impossible to reproduce here the full statement of method that Hays offers (pp. 92–103): I shall attempt to summarize it without, I hope, losing clarity in the process.

[18]See Hübner 1984, 144 f., etc. This question is often rightly joined with the similar one regarding Rom. 3.27, but the present case can be made on its own just as well.

[19]Cranfield 1975, 330–392.

[20]Hays 1983, following the work of A.J. Griemas.

Hays describes the three normal *sequences* in a narrative: the *initial sequence*, in which the protagonist is given a task to perform and runs into problems in performing it, the *topical sequence*, in which the protagonist is enabled to overcome the problems which he/she faces, usually by the intervention of a new person or factor, and the *final sequence*, in which the initial sequence, originally aborted because the problems could not be overcome, is successfully accomplished. Each of these sequences can be analysed further, particularly in terms of a diagram in which the different actors or elements in the narrative are set out in their mutual relations:

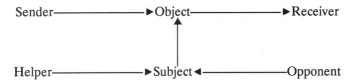

Thus the Sender commissions the Subject to accomplish the desired task, of communicating the Object to the Receiver; the Subject is hindered by the Opponent, and may or may not receive aid from the Helper. In the *initial sequence* the opponent will win, and the helper's aid be ineffective, otherwise there would scarcely be a story at all, but only a statement. In the *topical sequence*, however, the person who was the subject in the initial sequence, and will again most likely be the subject in the final sequence, becomes the Receiver, since the aim of the topical sequence is precisely to give him/her what he/she lacks, in terms of the initial sequence, to accomplish the task. The *final sequence* will then feature Sender, Subject, Object and Receiver in more or less the same places as in the initial sequence, but with the Helper being the means by which the subject has been able to overcome the outstanding difficulties.

Clearly, this bald summary does justice neither to Hays' far more carefully nuanced scheme nor to the great majority of stories. In even a quite simple novel there will be a great deal more to it than this: more mini-sequences within the topical sequence, for instance. But the rough shape still fits. We could give as an example an analysis of the fairy-tale *Jack the Giant-Killer*:

In the initial sequence, Jack, whose aim is to acquire wealth for himself and his mother, is frustrated in this desire by their circumstances (where the desire came from, i.e. who the 'Sender' is, is not specified):

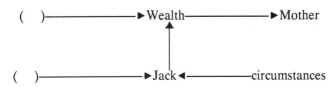

Having no 'helper', Jack's story would not get off the ground, metaphorically or literally. But in the topical sequence Jack is enabled to acquire the giant's gold by the magic beanstalk, despite his mother's anxiety and the giant's anger:

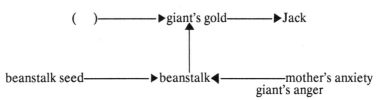

This results in the final sequence, in which Jack has successfully accomplished his initial object:

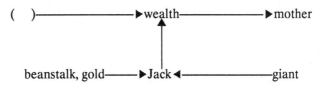

It will be clearly seen from this that Jack, who is the Subject in the initial and final sequences, is the Receiver in the all-important topical sequence. This will continue to be of importance as we turn back to Romans 8.[21]

Hays makes a good case for the use of such analysis in certain Pauline passages, where apparently Paul is alluding to a story of some sort—in Galatians 3–4, a story or stories about Jesus—in which certain things become much clearer once we have grasped the shape and dynamic of the underlying story. Thus, while it may be true that we can ultimately only get out of such an analysis what we put into it, it is also true that an exercise such as this serves to put a passage—especially a dense passage like Romans 8.3–4—under the microscope, so that the relations between the component parts may be studied and clarified. The proof of this pudding is of course in the eating, and to this we turn.

Romans 8.3 begins with a statement which turns quite easily into an initial sequence to form the basis for what follows:

[21]The absence of an explicit 'Sender' throughout is a characteristic of many stories (e.g. the overall plot of *The Lord of the Rings*). But other forms of analysis—e.g. psychological or sociological—might suggest the powerful implicit presence of a Sender, in this case perhaps Jack's dead father and his supposed expectation that Jack will care for the widowed mother. The ultimate satisfaction of these latent expectations may be part of the reason for the story's power.

τὸ γὰρ ἀδύνατον τοῦ νόμου ἐν ᾧ ἠσθένει διὰ τῆς σαρκός...
That which was impossible for the law, in that it was weak through the flesh...

In the light of our earlier argument, that what the law was unable to do was to give life, we may construct an actantial structure:

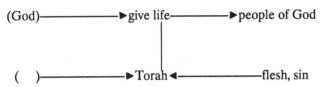

The sequence is abortive: the Opponent renders the Subject powerless to achieve the mission of the Sender, conveying the Object to the Receiver. There is at the moment no Helper in sight. There is presupposed here, and spelt out more clearly in Romans 7.10 and Galatians 3.21, a sort of *heilsgeschichtlich* scheme in which there is a divine purpose, that of giving life, which stands behind the role of the law. Behind the stated opponent, 'flesh', there is of course sin which has made its base in the flesh; but here Paul highlights flesh because that is the material the Torah has to operate on, and it is thus, as in 7.25b, the immediate cause of the problem.

The topical sequence, which follows in 8.3b, fits exactly into the model. Here God is named as the Sender; the Son is the Subject; what he achieves is the condemnation of sin in the flesh. The normal dictates of the model are that the Subject of the initial sequence should become the Receiver of the topical sequence, since the point of the topical sequence is to enable the (initial) Subject to accomplish his (previously impossible) task: this suggests that the law is the Receiver, though this is not explicit in 8.3b. We thus have:

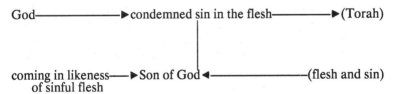

Stress is laid by Paul on Jesus' qualifications (here categorized as Helper) for his task. It is necessary for him to share the 'likeness of sinful flesh' (in whatever precise sense Paul intends that), since God's desire is to condemn sin in the flesh, which comes to pass in Jesus' death on the cross (not stated, but the clear referent of κατέκρινεν). Because Jesus is Son of God, Israel's royal representative (chs. 2, 3 above), he is able to draw on to himself Israel's paradoxical destiny, becoming in himself the 'place' where sin abounded (5.20, 7.13–20), the individual representative of Israel-under-Torah (cf. Galatians 4.4 f.), herself representative of the whole of Adamic humanity—in order that in his death sin as a whole might find itself condemned.

The point of the action, as becomes clear in 8.4, which forms the *final sequence*, is that the law might be set free from its being held back through the flesh, and sin, to do what it was originally meant to do, so that, as in 8.1, there might be now no κατάκριμα for 'those who are in Christ Jesus.' Thus we have the following final sequence in 8.4:

The opponents, flesh and sin, have been overcome; God achieves his purpose through the law, since the Son and the Spirit have come to its aid, enabling its δικαίωμα to be fulfilled for his people, 'those in Christ'.

Although in one sense this analysis has told us little that could not have been deduced by careful historical exegesis, the fact of spelling it all out in this way highlights several features of the structure of what Paul is saying which are normally overlooked. We may itemize them as follows.

(a) The Torah has an extremely positive role in the overall structure of thought, which is not diminished by the negative things said about it in vv.2,3. Were this a novel or even a short story, the Torah would have the place of protagonist, struggling against the odds to begin with but eventually, having received the necessary help, winning through and accomplishing the intended mission. This, of course, fits well with Romans 3.31, 7.12, and as we have seen with Romans 8.7. It does not, however, tally with the normal view of the passage, in which the law is brushed aside as an intruder. The normal translation of 8.3a, 'what the law could not do', is in fact misleading, suggesting a sharper antithesis between the law in 8.3a and God in 8.3b than is necessarily the case in the Greek. Indeed, the common translation 'what the law could not do' may itself throw the emphasis in the wrong way, since τὸ ἀδύνατον could equally well mean 'the powerlessness', an abstract quality rather than a concrete action.[22] Either way it is very clear that there is nothing wrong with the law in itself; it is only in its present anomalous position because sin, through the flesh, has rendered it so. When that obstacle is removed, as it is apparently by God's action in the death of Jesus,

[22]Liddell and Scott 1953, s.v.

the law again does happily what it was intended, and rightly intended (δικαίωμα) to do. The effect of this is that the 'problem of Romans 7', and for that matter Romans 8.1–8, is emphatically *not* that of 'man under the law' (even allowing for exclusive language), but of 'the law under man', or, more specifically, under flesh. The whole implied narrative sequence of 8.3–4 consists of a story about how God has enabled the law to escape from the chains of human flesh, sin and death, and do at last what it wanted to do—that is, of course, what God wanted it to do—all along.

(b) This enables us to see the relationship between the main verb (κατέκρινεν) and the ἵνα-clause (ἵνα ... πληρωθῇ). How does God's condemnation of sin facilitate the fulfillment of the Torah's δικαίωμα? At first sight they seem to have little to do with each other, the one looking as it were backwards, to the problem of sin, and the other forward, to the gift of life. The answer must be that sin, by causing death, stood in the way of the divine intention of giving life; when, on the cross, God condemns sin, heaped up as it has been in one place by the Torah, then sin is powerless to prevent the gift of life, at Easter and in the repetition of Easter that is yet to come (8.11; compare the similar train of thought in 1 Corinthians 15.17).

(c) This means that ὁ νόμος τοῦ πνεύματος τῆς ζωῆς ἐν Χριστῷ Ἰησοῦ in 8.2 may be understood quite comfortably as a reference to the Torah understood in one particular phase, specifically the final sequence. The law is the subject of both the initial and the final sequence, and in the latter capacity it is the law itself, 'helped' by the Spirit and the Son, that gives the required δικαίωμα to God's people. If we begin our thinking with this idea of the law, helped by Spirit and Son, giving life to God's people, we find, in fact, that this is expressed almost exactly in 8.2a: the law of the Spirit of life in Christ Jesus. 8.3–4, understood as I have suggested, thus makes it extremely likely that 8.2a is a reference to Torah itself.[23] If we press for further explanation of this, other passages (Romans 9.30—10.13, Galatians 4.1–6, etc.) would suggest the following scheme of thought. When God by his Spirit works to bring life to a person (Romans 8.9–11), the desire and purpose of the Torah is thereby being fulfilled. To put it the other way round, what we have here is Pentecost-theology: as the Jews celebrate the giving of Torah, so the church celebrates the giving of the Spirit, not to abolish but to fulfil the earlier gift and its final intention. It seems likely to me that 8.2a corresponds closely to the νόμος πίστεως of 3.27, though I would argue this point differently from Hübner.[24]

[23]See Hübner 1984 (1978) 164 n.211 for a list of those who take this view. Räisänen's opposition to the idea (1986a, 52 f.) seems to relate more to his determination that Paul shall be read as declaring the law abolished than to actual exegesis.

[24]See Hübner 1984, 139 f., etc.

(d) But if this is so, what about 8.2b, ὁ νόμος τῆς ἁμαρτίας καὶ τοῦ θανάτου? Two things begin to come clear.

1. It is extremely likely that this too is a reference to Torah, but now to Torah as it appears in the initial sequence, where it is prevented, precisely by the flesh which is dead through sin, from giving what it offered (see, again, Romans 7.10–11, 14–25, and Galatians 3.21–2). The qualifying phrase ('of sin and death') corresponds too closely with what is said clearly about the Torah in Romans 7 (7.7–12: the Torah is taken over and used by sin; 7.13–20: the Torah, thus taken over, produces death) and 1 Corinthians 15.56 ('the sting of death is sin, and the strength of sin is the Torah') for it to be even seriously likely that Paul would mean by νόμος here something other than the νόμος which had been his explicit and careful subject all through the previous chapter, i.e. the Torah. To be sure, this phrase, like that in 8.2a, is compressed, and hence, as it stands, cryptic. This, however, is typical of Paul. It is to be expected that such an abbreviated formulation would need to be further understood in the light of what immediately precedes (7, especially vv.23, 25b), which he is summing up, and of what follows (8.3–8), in which he explains his meaning further. Indeed, since in the latter passage he offers an unpacking of the compressed initial explanation (v.2) it is perhaps foolish to expound 8.2 as though the rest of 8.1–11, in which the Torah is still clearly the subject, did not exist. In short, the only reasons I can see for continuing to deny that both uses of νόμος in 8.2 refer to the Torah have to do with *a priori* assumptions about what Paul could and could not have said—either because we know him to be 'consistent' within a tight pre-given theological structure, or because we wish to prove him 'inconsistent' within an equally tight and arbitrary scheme. His own scheme corresponds to his own underlying subject-matter: the story of God and Israel, reaching its high point in Jesus and the Spirit, the climax of the covenant.

Paul's negative reference to Torah thus stands in a comprehensible relation to the neighbouring positive one: the riddle is solved by 8.3–4 as analysed above. The Torah of sin and death is the Torah taken over, prevented from doing what it really wanted, by sin, working through the flesh to produce death. Even this, however, is in this passage taken up within the strange long-term plan of God, as Paul also suggests in Galatians 3.19–22 and Romans 9.30 ff. Without this negative work of Torah sin would not be collected together, would not be hauled off to the scaffold for execution. Paul does not in this passage address the question, which surfaces in Galatians 3.19, 22 and Romans 9.30 ff., as to whether this function of Torah is not also itself part of the strange long-term plan of God. The Torah of sin and death, then, is the Torah *as it stands in the 'initial sequence'*, whereas the Torah of the Spirit of life in Christ Jesus is the Torah *as it stands in the 'final sequence'*; and even in the initial sequence, as we realize from its sequel, the negative work becomes a vital part of the positive purpose. The Torah, as it were, goes on trying to put God's will into operation, but because of the flesh and sin it has the opposite effect from that which it ultimately intended. Simply by issuing the double δικαίωμα (1.32, 8.4) the law results in death for those who are ensnared in sinful flesh (i.e. all human beings; though the law speaks especially 'to those who are under the law', i.e. Jews). This δικαίωμα is God's own decree (1.32). The law is simply enforcing it. But to those who are 'in the flesh' it thus has the effect of enslaving, trapping, accusing and condemning them. Thus it is that Paul can say such positive things about the Torah here while not needing to take back the negative things he said in, for instance, 5.20, 6.14 f., 7.1–6 and 7.23.

2. Though this way of looking at the Torah appears to offer a heavy indictment of it, we must continually remind ourselves that this can only be understood in the context of the vindication of Torah which takes place in 7.1–8.11 as a whole, and particularly of the nuanced statement which follows at once in 8.3a. The description of Torah *in malam partem* here corresponds very closely, in fact, to that of Galatians 3.22, quoted above, coming directly after a verse we have had occasion to cite several times as a parallel, and offered in explanation of how, though the Torah is not against the promises of God, and would have given life if it could, its effect was nevertheless thoroughly negative. This viewpoint is summarized exactly in Romans 7.23, which clearly refers to the same problem as 8.2b. It would be foolish to cry 'inconsistency' here of all places; Paul, it seems, is well aware that he is arguing for a strange new case, and is determined to hold on both to the positive and to the negative points he has made. Neither should be explained away in the interests of a simpler scheme, as Räisänen (1986a, 66) rightly sees; though Räisänen himself is of course among those who are too quick, here and elsewhere, to let both stand and then accuse Paul of self-contradiction.

(e) The meaning of τὸ δικαίωμα τοῦ νόμου is best explained as 'the just decree', i.e. the decree that gives life in accordance with the covenant. This is complex, because Paul evidently intends the word to carry two connotations: first, of a decree which is itself just, and second, of a decree which announces, justly, that certain people are in the right, i.e. a justifying decree. The first meaning is what aligns this usage with Romans 1.32; the second, with 5.16. In the present passage it is vital for Paul's argument that he means both, the former (the decree's own justice) because of his underlying argument about God's justice, and the suggestion that what has happened about Torah has somehow cast doubts on that, and the second because of the thrust of the passage in which δικαίωμα here is (as in 5.16) set in counterpoint with κατάκριμα.

In particular, then, this decree righteously gives the covenant verdict, that of 'life'. The place of τὸ δικαίωμα in the crucial final sequence, i.e. as 'object', corresponds to the 'object' in the initial sequence, which was the life that God wished to give to his people; and it is axiomatic in the model that the 'object' in initial and final sequence must be substantially the same, since otherwise the story simply would not work. The analysis offered in both sections of my argument, then, enables us to clarify further the conclusions of Keck and Benoit on this point[25] in such a way as to meet the objections that have been raised to their view, that δικαίωμα means 'right intent' or 'verdict'. The word is hardly ever found in the singular in the LXX, and Paul is quite capable of using it in its LXX sense, in the plural (e.g. Romans 2.26, where the meaning is clearly the performance of those things which the law commanded). It seems to me that commentators have been misled into treating the word as indicating performance of the law's demands by the apparent emphasis on ethical behaviour which immediately follows.[26] However, as we saw in our earlier analysis of 8.1–11, the real emphasis of the entire paragraph is not on how one behaves, whether as a Christian or as one still 'in the flesh', but on the analysis of sin, flesh and law which enables Paul to reach his conclusion in v.11, which is that God will give to those in Christ the *life* which the law promised (7.10) but could not itself produce. The discussion of behaviour is ancillary to this larger issue, and serves not as a new command, still less a new 'law', but simply as evidence for the proposal that a certain group of people are now not in the flesh but in the Spirit.

Seeing 'life' as the 'just decree of the law' has a similarity, but only a superficial one, to Bultmann's analysis of Romans 7–8.[27] The context within which I have set the question is that of covenantal theology, many a mile from Bultmann's existentialism. This again frees δικαίωμα from the necessity of being interpreted as something which has to be done or performed, even if we were to think of Paul reducing the total demand of the law to a single command (e.g. love), as some writers think. The structure of the verse as I have analysed it actually implies that δικαίωμα cannot be reduced to terms of τοῖς μὴ κατὰ σάρκα περιπατοῦσιν ἀλλὰ κατὰ πνεῦμα. It is, rather, the opposite of κατάκριμα in v.1: the decree that gives life, set over against the decree that gives death.

(f) The link of κατάκριμα in v.1 with κατέκρινεν in v.3 underlines the view of Jesus' death which has been implicit in the discussion so far (and see

[25]See Keck 1980, 52; Keck does not notice that the climax of the argument (8.11) gives this strong support; Benoit 1961, 30 f. See the discussion in Räisänen 1986a, 65 n. 113.

[26]E.g. Martin 1989, 145, 152. On this point, it seems to me, Hooker 1990, 32 is right in what she denies but wrong in what she affirms.

[27]See Sanders 1983, 89, pointing out the Bultmannian origin of Keck's view.

also ch. 7 above).[28] The κατάκριμα which hung over the head of Adamic humanity (5.16) has been meted out on the real culprit, namely, sin (7.17, 20). It is therefore true to Paul to speak of the punishment which all have deserved being enacted, instead, on the cross. But Paul has here nuanced this view in two ways which distance it from the cruder theories made familiar in some branches of theology. First, he is careful to say that on the cross God punished (not Jesus, but) 'sin', just as in ch. 7 he was careful to distinguish 'sin' as the real culprit, rather than 'I'. Second, his argument functions within the whole matrix of thought according to which the death of Jesus can be interpreted in this way because he represents Israel and Israel represents humankind as a whole. There is therefore nothing arbitrary about his death being interpreted in this way: once grant, with Paul, that he is Israel's Messiah, there is no other way in which it could be seen. The idea of vicarious representative suffering is itself quite well known in the period, as 2 Maccabees 7.37–8 and other passages testify clearly enough.

(g) The revealing use of νόμος in 8.7, where it is the 'law of God' as in 7.22, 25b, falls comfortably into place. The 'mind of the flesh' does not submit to God's Torah, indeed it cannot, and those who are 'in the flesh' cannot please God; this is a summary, clearly, of what has been said in ch. 7, and shows that the assent of the 'mind' to the Torah, and even the 'delight' in Torah, there expressed, cannot count as full 'submission', since the σάρξ, precisely the σάρξ, remains disobedient. The implied corollary is a startling addition to the exegesis of Romans 8.3–4 just offered. Paul implies that those who are *not* in the flesh, those who are 'in the Spirit', do now submit to Torah, in the sense of its righteous decree coming true in them. They are not 'under Torah'; they are not bound by 'works of Torah'; but they 'submit to it', in the sense of its deepest intention, and thereby, again by implication from v.8, actually 'please God'.[29]

(h) Is it possible to integrate this discussion of νόμος, and the mention of its δικαίωμα, and the reference to δικαιοσύνη in v.10, with the whole 'incorporative' train of thought that has normally been seen, following Schweitzer, in this section of Romans? The answer is that both systems of thought ('juristic' and 'participationist', as they have been analysed in modern discussion) are in fact part of Paul's overall covenantal theology, more specifically his *new* covenantal theology, of which Romans 7.1—8.11 forms a key section, to be integrated with 2 Corinthians 3, Galatians 3 and Romans

[28]Hooker 1990, 33 suggests that Paul 'does not explain... how it is that the sending of God's Son... frees men from condemnation'. I think, however, that he does, in the way that now follows.

[29]On this latter idea see 1 Cor. 7.32, 1 Thess. 4.1. This exegesis of νόμος in Rom. 8 would give a good viewpoint, were there time and space, from which to examine Rom. 2.13 f., 2.25–9, and particularly 3.27.

2.17–29. The Torah is the covenant boundary-marker, and, when its δικαίωμα is fulfilled through the work of the Spirit in the new covenant, it retains exactly the same function, of demarcating the people of God. δικαιοσύνη is, more or less, 'covenant membership', the status within the people of God of which 'righteousness' (in any of its senses from the Reformation to the present day) is merely one aspect. Faith is not mentioned in this passage at all. The implication, however, especially in the light of Galatians 3 and other closely related passages, is that faith is the result of the work of the Spirit, and thus the *evidence* of membership in the new covenant people of God, just as works of Torah were attempted not in order to earn salvation but in order to demonstrate one's membership in the Sinaitic covenant. This I take to be the real meaning of the classic Pauline statements of justification: God declares that those who believe the gospel are his covenant people. This declaration, in turn, is closely correlated with baptism, in which one becomes a member of that family in its historical life. This is clearly an enormous theme which cannot be taken further here.

(i) Going back, finally, to the actantial analyses of 8.3–4, we may suggest that there is a latent ecclesiology in the similarity and distinction between the Receiver in the Initial, and in the Final, sequences. The original intention of the Torah was to give life, presumably to those to whom it was given, i.e. Israel. The final sequence has the Torah enabled at last to give life, but this time, clearly, to those 'in Christ', those who walk according to the Spirit. This again is a matter far too large for discussion here.

(v) Conclusion

There are many areas of debate in Pauline Theology which are in principle affected by the arguments and conclusions I have advanced. I here simply mention three.

(a) The whole question of Paul and the law, as it has been discussed recently by Sanders, Hübner, Räisänen and others is still in need of a thorough re-working. Concentration on Romans 8.1–11 has led me in this chapter to develop what seems to me a positive view of Torah.[30] But it would be possible in principle to move from here into a nuanced discussion of the various other crucial texts in Romans, including those that speak in a negative way (5.20, etc.), and also to reinforce our earlier treatments of passages in Galatians, which as we have seen throughout offer significant parallels to the ideas which we have been discussing. Though there is no space here to go into details, I believe that Galatians and Romans, seen from

[30]See further Badenas 1985.

the perspective I have outlined, come closer together in a coherent framework (allowing, of course, for all kinds of differences due to the very different situations addressed) than is possible within most usual schemes today.

(b) The vital place of *story* in Pauline Theology, highlighted by Hays in relation to Galatians, is reaffirmed by our study. Although it is Romans 5.12–21 that most obviously 'tells a story' within this letter, the subsidiary story of the fortunes of the law is clearly of great importance. It comes, perhaps, as a sort of sub-category of *Heilsgeschichte*; and the complexity which it possesses indicates that *Heilsgeschichte* is not as simple a matter as has sometimes been thought. To require of Paul that he should always say exactly the same thing about Torah all the time would be like criticizing the story of Jack and the Beanstalk on the grounds that it was internally inconsistent, because Jack was sometimes going up the beanstalk and sometimes coming down. To reply that this makes Torah in Paul's thought a very strange thing, different from what it was in Judaism, would hardly be to the point. Paul does not claim total history-of-religions continuity with his Jewish background. He claims, implicitly and sometimes explicitly, to have rethought Judaism entirely, and now to be re-presenting it as need arises, as part of the fresh understanding he has of Israel's story, the world's story, and ultimately even God's story, on the basis of the death and resurrection of the Messiah and the gift of the Spirit. But this is looking too far afield for our present limited task.

To return to the other possible 'stories' in Romans: it might, in fact, be possible to draw up a narrative analysis of 5.12–21 similar to that we have suggested for 8.3–4, and then to enquire as to the role of the latter within the former. In such a scheme, the law would appear as an opponent, but not the principal opponent; that role would be taken by sin and/or death. The means by which this multiple opponent would be overcome, i.e. the topical sequence which would lead to the final sequence in which grace abounds for the 'many', would correspond at least obliquely to the 'story' we analysed under 8.3–4, in that the law would be neutralized as an opponent, thus making it clear that its status as opponent was more apparent than real. It is this point which Paul then picks up in 7.7—8.11.

(c) Finally, the relation of solution to problem, about which Sanders in particular has written so provocatively, may be approached in a different light.[31] To be sure, Paul came to his theological thinking on the basis of having believed the crucified and risen Jesus to be God's Messiah. He rethought the place of the law within the plan of God in that light. But what he has done is not to invent a 'problem of the law' from scratch. The

[31]Cf. Sanders 1977, 442–7, etc.; and the discussion in ch. 14 below.

problem which underlies the problem of the law is the problem of the righteousness of God: how can God be true to the covenant, granted the present (i.e. first-century Jewish) state of things? The cross and resurrection of the Messiah enabled him to redraw this problem and to offer a solution in both continuity and discontinuity with the solutions suggested among his contemporaries. What the Torah, the covenant document, could not do, in that it was weak through the flesh—human flesh, Jewish flesh—with which it had to work, God has done, thus declaring himself to be in the right in terms of his covenant. He has sent his Son to die, and given his Spirit to bring life, so that the righteous covenant decree of the law (and hence his own righteousness: the δικαιοσύνη θεοῦ stands behind the δικαίωμα τοῦ νόμου) might be fulfilled in the creation, and eventual salvation, of a new covenant community, those who are ἐν Χριστῷ ᾽Ιησοῦ.

Appendix

Outline of Romans 7.1—8.11

Though there is not space to argue for the view of Romans 7 presupposed throughout the preceding chapter, it may be useful or interesting to set out, without argument, the analysis to which I have been driven by years of puzzling over this text. One of the very interesting features of it is the careful organization of the argument, reflected in the succession of connecting words. This alone should make us wary of saying, with Sanders, that the passage is simply confused.[32]

A. 7.1–6 Two Marriages

    a. *Illustration*: 1–3
        1. negative 1–2a spelt out in 3a
        2. positive 2b   spelt out in 3b
    b. *Application*: 4–6
        1. negative (assumed from 5.20) spelt out in 5
        2. positive 4   spelt out in 6

B. 7.7–12 The law is not sin, but its arrival, in Sinai as in Eden, was sin's opportunity to kill its recipients

    a. *First question*: 7a: is the law sin?
    b. *Answer and basic concession*: 7b–8a
        (ἀλλὰ)   1. No: granted that it was through the law that I discovered sin (7b)
        (δὲ)   2. Sin used Torah as base of operations (8a)
    c. (γὰρ) *Explanation*: 8b–10
        1. Sin is powerless without Torah (8b)
        (δὲ)   2. 'My' story: the arrival of Torah, and 'my' death (9–10)
    d. (γὰρ) *Further Explanation*: 11
        1. sin used the law to deceive me and kill me
    e. (ὥστε) *Result*: 12: the Torah itself is good.

---

[32]Sanders 1983, 81, etc.

C. 7.13–20 The law was not the ultimate cause of 'my' death: it was sin, working through the law and in 'me', unwilling though 'I' was, and thus swelling to its full size

a. *Second question*: 13a: was it the law, then (οὖν), that caused death to come to me?

b. *Answer and basic concession* (ἀλλά): 13b: it is sin, which lives in 'me', and works *through* Torah

(ἀλλά)   1. No: granted that sin, the real culprit, was working *through* the Torah (13b(i))

2. The purpose of this was that sin might appear *as* sin, and might become 'exceedingly sinful' (13b(ii))

c. (γάρ) *Explanation*: 14: there is an ontological imbalance between the Torah and 'me'—spirit/flesh

d. *Further Explanation*: 15–16/17: analysis of 'my' action means exoneration of Torah from the charge of 13a—and, by implication, the blaming of 'sin'

(γὰρ)   1. basic: I do not understand my actions (15a)

(γὰρ)   2. explained: I do not do what I want (15b)

(εἰ δὲ)   3. result: I affirm the Torah (16)

(νυνὶ δὲ)   4. result: it is not me, but sin.

[17 is both the conclusion of this train of thought and the start of the next, though νυνὶ δέ etc. is regularly a new point]

e. *Further Explanation*: 17/18–19: analysis of 'my' actions means exoneration of the 'I'—and, explicitly now, the blaming of 'sin'.

(νυνὶ δὲ)   1. It is not me, but sin (17)

(γὰρ)   2. explained: no 'good' (see 13) in my flesh (18a)

(γὰρ)   3. explained: I cannot do what I 'will' (18b)

(γὰρ)   4. explained: I do the opposite of my willing (19)

f. (εἰ δὲ) *Result*: 20: therefore it is not me, but sin dwelling in me.

Result so far: Torah and 'I' exonerated, *sin* the real culprit, now concentrated in 'me', i.e. in Israel.

D. 7.21–25: The result in terms of Torah: Torah bifurcates—and so do 'I'

a. (ἄρα) *Basic Conclusion*: 21 This is what I find about Torah: that I want to do it and cannot

b. (γὰρ) *Basic Explanation*: 22–3

1. the two halves: 'I' delight in Torah of God (22)

(δὲ)   in my 'members' I see the Torah of sin (23)

c. (no connective) *Conclusion* (1): 24–25a

1. the lament: I need to be delivered from the 'body of death'

2. the anticipatory answer: this will be done through Jesus, the
Messiah/Lord

d. (ἄρα οὖν) *Conclusion* (2): 25b: αὐτὸς ἐγὼ, mind and flesh
corresponding to the 'two Torahs'.

E. 8.1–11: In Christ and Spirit, the life that the Torah could not give

a. (ἄρα) *Basic Conclusion*: 1: no condemnation
b. (γὰρ) *Basic Explanation*: 2: the redeeming Torah!
c. (γὰρ) *Further Explanation*: 3–4

    1. God has done what the Torah could not (3)

    2. He has *condemned sin, the real culprit*, in the flesh, the real location (3)

    3. He has enabled the favourable verdict ('life') to be given to his people

    (4). (In terms of 7.13–20, this means that both the 'I' and the Torah are

    to be vindicated: this is what is stated in 8.1–4 and explained in 8.5–11)

d. (γὰρ) *Further Explanation*: 5–10

    1. the two states (5)

(γὰρ)   2. explained: the consequences of the two states (6)

(διότι)   3. explained: the two states in relation to God and Torah (7–8)

(δὲ)   4. 'you' on this map (9–10)

        i. you belong in the πνεῦμα category (9)

(εἰ δὲ)   ii. you therefore have covenant life (10)

e. (εἰ δὲ) *Conclusion*: 11: the final verdict, corresponding to the present
one issued over faith: resurrection by the Spirit.

Chapter Eleven

THE MEANING OF ΠΕΡΙ ʹΑΜΑΡΤΙΑΣ IN ROMANS 8.3[1]

The intention of this chapter, which really functions as an extended footnote to the last one, is to offer a new argument, based on the context, for taking περὶ ἁμαρτίας in Romans 8.3 to mean 'as a sin-offering'.

(i) Introduction

Many commentators today accept that when he wrote καὶ περὶ ἁμαρτίας in Romans 8.3 Paul may very well have meant 'and as a sin-offering'.[2] Equally, about as many again reject it.[3] And since neither see any contextual reasons why Paul should introduce the idea of the sin-offering here the case usually turns on the commentator's view of Paul's Septuagint allusions in general.[4]

Before we can proceed, however, we should note a third view which has been supported by a minority at various stages of the history of interpretation. This view takes the phrase καὶ περὶ ἁμαρτίας not with the preceding πέμψας but with κατέκρινεν, which follows it.[5] While it is true that 'περί with the genitive to mean "on the charge of" or "on the grounds of"

---

[1]An earlier version of this chapter was originally given as a paper at the Sixth International Congress on Biblical Studies, in Oxford, in April 1978, and published in *Studia Biblica 1978*, ed. E.A. Livingstone, J.S.O.T. Press, Sheffield, 1980, 453–459. In the original version I ventured some concluding remarks about Romans 7 about which I had already changed my mind by the time the paper was published; the last paragraph of the present chapter, together with ch. 10 above, indicates my present view.

[2]E.g. Bruce 1963, 161; Moule 1882, 139; Vaughan 1885, 149f.; more recently Käsemann 1973, 208; Wilckens 1980, 127; Dunn 1988, 422; cautiously, Ziesler 1989, 204 f. Cf. too Kittel and Friedrich 8.383 f. (E. Schweizer) and 6.55 (E.H. Riesenfeld). Among EVV this meaning is taken by RV, RSV mg., and NEB.

[3]E.g. Barrett 1957, 156 (Barrett says the general sense is 'more probable'); Cranfield 1975, 382; Kuss 1959, 493f.; Lagrange 1916, 193; Michel 1966, 190; Sanday and Headlam 1902, 193; Zeller 1984, 152 f. This general sense if followed by AV, RV mg., RSV, NEB mg.

[4]The omission of the phrase in 110 *pc* is clearly due to homoioteleuton, though Jülicher 1917, *ad loc.*, regarded it as a gloss. The Jerusalem Bible appears to treat the phrase as superfluous.

[5]So Chrysostom, in *PG* 60.514; Theodoret of Cyrrhus, in *PG* 82.129 A; 'Ambrosiaster' in *PL* 17.123 C; Bengel 1862, 528; recently Thornton 1971, 515ff. Cranfield (*loc.cit*) cites Calvin as taking this view, but this is misleading, since, while Calvin translated the last clause of v.3 *etiam de peccato damnavit peccatum in carne*, when expounding the text he clearly supported the sacrificial meaning, taking περὶ ἁμαρτίας to represent חַטָּאת. See Calvin 1961, 156, 159f.; for the original, *Corpus Reformatorum 77* (*Calvini Opera* 49), 137, 139f.

in a judicial setting is common in the New Testament',[6] it appears to be straining the force of the καί to make it emphatic in this context, and by no means all the early commentators took the phrase in this sense.[7] In addition, it is one of the presuppositions of this view that neither of the regular options is really open; so if we can find a good reason for either in the context, the need for this alternative suggestion is greatly reduced. We may therefore return to the main argument.

The case for the general meaning ('to deal with sin') depends likewise on the assumption that there is no contextual reason why Paul should have referred to the sin-offering, and thus falls if such a reason is given. In addition, as Thornton has pointed out,[8] the general view 'gives the isolated preposition περί a burden of meaning to carry in a way which is unprecedented in the New Testament, and unusual, if not unprecedented, elsewhere'. The way is therefore open for arguments, both old and new, on behalf of the sacrificial interpretation.

(ii) The Background: LXX Usage

We must begin with the old (and strong) argument from the LXX background. It is well known that חטאת is taken by the LXX, rightly, to mean on some occasions 'sin' and on other occasions 'sin-offering', in such a way that we could construct a sliding scale of usage, from the meaning 'sin' to the meaning 'sin-offering', in which nevertheless the meaning 'sin' in the phrase 'for sin' would still have inescapably sacrificial associations. At the 'sin' end of the scale comes the phrase περὶ τῆς ἁμαρτίας, which usually translates על-חטאת and sometimes לחטאת, and which normally means 'for sin', as in the phrase περὶ τῆς ἁμαρτίας αὐτοῦ ἧς ἥμαρτεν.[9] Near this end of the scale (though this is more difficult) comes ἁμαρτία by itself. Though it may well mean 'sin-offering', it might be argued that the LXX translators here took חטאת to mean 'sin', identifying the sacrifice with the sin.[10]

---

[6]Thornton 516: see Jn. 8.46, 15.22, 16.8f.; Ac. 23.6, 24.21, 25.9, 20; Jude 15.

[7]E.g. Origen, *PG* 14.1093 ff. This, coupled with the awareness of Gennadius of Constantinople and Photius of Constantinople that the phrase could be taken both ways (Staab 1933, 375, 509), rules out any argument on the basis of early or Greek-speaking commentators. Perhaps Origen was more sensitive to the LXX background of the NT than Chrysostom and other Antiochenes.

[8]*Loc. cit.*

[9]See Lev. 4.3 (twice); 4.14, 28; 5.6 (twice); 5.7, 9; 8.2; 8.14; 9.15; 10.16; 16.6, 11, 15, 27 (twice); Num. 15.25.

[10]See the various forms in Ex. 29.14, 36; Lev. 4.8, 20, 24, 25, 29, 32, 33, 34: 5.12; 6.17 (LXX/MT 6.10); 6.25 (LXX/MT 6.18); Num. 6.14.

At the other end of the scale comes the phrase τὸ περὶ τῆς ἁμαρτίας, which means simply 'the sin-offering'. This is frequent and undisputed.[11] Our problem is the location on the scale of περὶ ἁμαρτίας, the phrase we find in Romans 8.3. It occurs 54 times in the LXX, of which no fewer than 44 stand parallel to phrases such as εἰς ὁλοκαύτωμα, εἰς θυσίαν σωτηρίου, and the like.[12] περὶ ἁμαρτίας regularly translates לְחַטָּאת or simply חַטָּאת where εἰς ὁλοκαύτωμα translates לְעֹלָה or simply עֹלָה. This makes it clear that περὶ ἁμαρτίας, in the great majority of cases, must mean 'as a sin-offering', parallel to 'as a burnt-offering', etc. It is, in other words, simply the anarthrous equivalent of τὸ περὶ τῆς ἁμαρτίας. Of the remaining ten occurrences, one is Isaiah 53.10, the only place where περὶ ἁμαρτίας stands for אָשָׁם in the MT. It could conceivably be argued that the other nine[13] should be put further down the scale, nearer to the meaning 'for sin', but even if this were so the phrase would still have strong and unavoidable sacrificial associations. We may conclude that, whereas περὶ τῆς ἁμαρτίας usually means 'for sin', and τὸ περὶ τῆς ἁμαρτίας means '*the* sin-offering', περὶ ἁμαρτίας should almost always be translated either 'sin-offering'[14] or 'as a sin-offering'.

The characteristic sentence in which περὶ ἁμαρτίας occurs is well exemplified by Leviticus 9.2: λαβὲ σεαυτῷ μοσχάριον ἐκ βοῶν περὶ ἁμαρτίας καὶ κριὸν εἰς ὁλοκαύτωμα. This form, with a verb of sacrificing or taking for sacrifice, a direct object of the creature to be sacrificed, followed by περὶ ἁμαρτίας, is exactly parallel to Romans 8.3: ὁ θεὸς τὸν ἑαυτοῦ υἱὸν πέμψας ... περὶ ἁμαρτίας. The LXX evidence therefore provides a strong argument in favour of the translation: 'God, sending his own son...as a sin-offering'. Even if this were not accepted, it could not be denied that at the very least the phrase means 'for sin' with all the overtones of the sacrifices of Leviticus and Numbers.

This argument, however, has only convinced about half the commentators, while the other half reject it on the grounds that the context provides no reasons why Paul should have wished to speak specifically of the sin-offering here. It is this view which I now wish to challenge.

---

[11]See Lev. 5.8, 6.25 (LXX/MT 6.18), 6.30 (LXX/MT 6.23), 7.7, 9.7, 10, 22, 10.17, 19 (twice), 14.13 (twice), 19, 16.25; Num. 29.11; 2 Macc. 2.11. Note also the variants τὸ περὶ ἁμαρτίας in Num. 6.16; Ezek. 42.13; and τὸ ὑπὲρ ἁμαρτίας, etc., in Ezek. 40.39, 44.29, 45.22, 25, 46.20.

[12]See Lev. 5.7, 7.37, 9.2, 3, 12.6, 8, 14.22, 14.31, 15.15, 30, 16.3, 5, 23.19; Num. 6.11, 7.16, 22, 28, 34, 40, 46, 52, 58, 64, 70, 76, 82, 87, 8.8, 12, 15.24, 28.15, 22, 29.5, 11, 16, 19, 22, 28, 31, 34, 38; 2 Kgs. 12.17 (EVV 12.16); 2 Esdr. 8.35; Ps. 39.7 (EVV 40.6; MT 40.7).

[13]Lev. 5.6, 11 (twice), 16.9; Num. 15.27; 2 Esdr. 6.17; 2 Chron. 29.21; Ezek. 43.21; 2 Macc. 12.43.

[14]As in Ps. 39.7; compare Heb. 10.6, 8.

(iii) Unwilling and/or Ignorant Sin

The context in which the sin-offering is to be used, as laid down in Leviticus and Numbers, is not merely any sin. It is particularly unwilling sins or sins of ignorance. This emerges clearly in the use of the root שׁגג in the relevant texts,[15] translated in the LXX by ἀκουσιαζεῖν,[16] ἀκουσίος,[17] and ἀκουσίως.[18] The sin-offering covers sinful actions which the sinner either did not know he was committing, or did not know were sinful; in principle he wanted to keep the law, but through ignorance, or against his will, he failed.[19] The opposite of such unwilling sins is the sin committed 'with a high hand',[20] for which there is no sacrifice: the man responsible for such sins is to be 'cut off from among his people'. This same division of sins into 'unwilling' and 'deliberate', with the sin-offering as the remedy for the first, is clearly reflected in later Judaism,[21] and in one important passage in the New Testament. In Hebrews 10.26 the writer says that for the man who sins willingly there is no further sin-offering, but rather the prospect of judgment: Ἑκουσίως γὰρ ἁμαρτανόντων ἡμῶν μετὰ τὸ λαβεῖν τὴν ἐπίγνωσιν τῆς ἀληθείας, οὐκέτι περὶ ἁμαρτιῶν ἀπολείπεται θυσία, φοβερὰ δὲ τις ἐκδοχὴ κρίσεως ... κτλ. This evidence from LXX, Mishnah and New Testament[22] leads us to suspect that if Paul used a phrase like περὶ ἁμαρτίας, the context might well refer to sins committed unwillingly or in ignorance. This, in fact, is precisely what we find in the context of Romans 8.3.

The first four verses of ch. 8 show how God is doing 'what the law could not do', so as to deal with the problem described in 7.7–25.[23] In the context of the questions about the law which give 7.7–25 its structural outline, vv.13–20 describe a man who sins in a particular way, summed up in 7.15: ὃ γὰρ κατεργάζομαι οὐ γινώσκω. οὐ γὰρ ὃ θέλω τοῦτο πράσσω, ἀλλ᾽ ὃ μισῶ

---

[15]שׁגג Lev. 5.18; Num. 15.28; שׁגגה, Lev. 4.2, 22, 27, 5.15, 18, 22.14; Num. 15.24, 25 (twice), 26, 27, 28, 29; שׁגה, Lev. 4.13; Num. 15.22.

[16]Num. 15.28.

[17]Num. 15.25 (twice), 26.

[18]Lev. 4.2, 13, 22, 27, 5.15; Num. 15.24, 27, 28, 29.

[19]Compare also Lev. 5.18 (περὶ τῆς ἀγνοίας αὐτοῦ) and 22.14 (κατὰ ἄγνοιαν). The particular meaning of the sin-offering is noted by Sanday and Headlam, *loc.cit.*, but they do not see it as relevant to Rom. 8.3. Many commentators, failing to see the precise reference of this sacrifice, argue as though only a general sacrificial meaning could be implied if the phrase were taken to mean 'sin-offering'.

[20]Cf., e.g. Num. 15.30f. (ביד רמה: LXX ἐν χειρὶ ὑπερηφανίας). Compare also mKer. 1.2; 2.6; 3.2.

[21]Cf. mShab. 7.1; 11.6; mSanh. 7.8; mHor. 2.1–6; and see the notes of Danby 1933, 111 n.3, 562 n.16.

[22]Apart from those listed in n.6 above, the NT passages in which περὶ ἁμαρτίας or its equivalents occur are: Heb. 5.3, 10.6, 8, 18, 13.11; 1 Pet. 3.18; 1 Jn. 2.2, 4.10. Gal. 1.4 should be added if the v.l. is to be read, but this is very unlikely: see Burton 1921, lxxx, 13.

[23]See ch. 10 above.

τοῦτο ποιῶ. The sin described in these verses is precisely sin of ignorance, unwilling sin. The person who sins in this way delights in God's law (7.22), yet finds again and again that he fails to keep it. The remedy which the Old Testament offers for this very condition is the sin-offering, and when we meet, in the very passage where Paul is showing how God deals with the condition of 7.14–25, the phrase which elsewhere in the Greek Bible regularly means 'as a sin-offering', there can no longer be any suggestion that the context does not support the sacrificial interpretation. Though Paul can view Christ's death in various other ways (in, for instance, Romans 3.24 ff., 1 Corinthians 5.7) he here draws attention to that death seen in one way in particular, the way relevant for dealing with sin precisely as it is committed in 7.13–20.

This view, I think, holds good whatever decision is made about the interpretation of 7.13–25. If these verses were taken to refer to the Christian, they could be held to make good sense of the meaning I have suggested for 8.3: the Christian thus described can see that his or her predicament does not ultimately matter, since God has dealt with it in the death of Christ. The Christian would thus be in the position of the man in Leviticus 4, or Numbers 15, that is, a member of the people of God, desiring to live according to God's law, finding none the less that he or she sins as it were by mistake, either out of ignorance or despite better judgment.[24] If, however, the very strong arguments against this position are found too weighty—as I now find them myself—then the sin-offering will refer to the death of Christ insofar as that death rescues the one who is in the plight described specifically in 7.13–20, which as I have suggested in the previous chapter is the plight of the Jew under Torah, delighting in it yet still finding sin against it inescapable.[25] It is part of the astonishing feat of 7.1—8.11 that Paul has woven into his complex argument this strand too, which prepares the ground for 10.2–3 and hence for 11.11 ff. The plight of the Jew is not irremediable, as some Gentiles in the church may well have been suggesting.[26] The sin of the Jew is

[24]This is the view I held at the time of this chapter's original preparation, though not its publication (Wright 1980b). See also Nygren 1949, 265–303; Packer 1964; Cranfield 1975, 330–370; Dunn 1975b, and 1988, 374–412.

[25]Among the strong arguments against the 'Christian' position is 7.14, which scarcely fits Paul's view of the Christian; but the strongest argument of all is the coherence of the passage as a whole seen as a discussion of the Jewish Torah. It should be noted that, among the many mutually exclusive alternative ways of reading the passage as referring to pre-Christian existence, one which simply will not work is that advocated by Bultmann, Käsemann and others (e.g. Käsemann 1971, 16; 1980, 209), seeing 'sin' throughout as referring, not to acts of sin *per se*, but to the problem of 'nomism', the attempt to establish a claim on God by *good* works. I pointed this out in the original version of this chapter (1980b, 459 n.26); see now also Räisänen 1986a, 111.

[26]See below, ch. 13.

one of 'ignorance' (10.3), and as such can be dealt with.[27] The death of Jesus, precisely as the 'sin-offering', is what is required. Within this argument, I submit, there can no longer be any room for doubt that when Paul wrote καὶ περὶ ἁμαρτίας he meant the words to carry their regular biblical overtones, i.e. 'and as a sin-offering'.

[27]For more specific analysis of this in Rom. 7 and 9–11, see the next two chapters.

Chapter Twelve

ECHOES OF CAIN IN ROMANS 7

(i) Introduction

The present chapter is really another extended footnote to ch. 10 above. Although I consider the analysis of Romans 7 there to be in principle sound as it stands, there is a further possibility which helps, I think, to clarify the meaning of 7.13–20 in particular, and which fits very well with the theme of 'sins of ignorance' at which we glanced in ch. 11. I wish to propose that, just as Adam can be discerned under the argument of 7.7–12, so his wayward son Cain can be seen under the argument of 7.13–20.

At first sight this must appear as an exegetical *tour de force*. It invites, perhaps, the gentle scorn of Julian Barnes: how submerged does a reference have to be before it drowns altogether?[1] Actually, I think that the reference is not as submerged as all that, and certainly no more so than many others which have not only been proposed but widely accepted—the identification of Adam in Romans 1, for instance.[2] What count in a case like this are (1) the *verbal* echoes which would awaken ideas in the mind of either writer or reader, or both, in a culture much more attuned to orality than our own, (2) the *thematic* echoes which create a similarity of overall picture, and (3) the *greater coherence* that results in the text under scrutiny when the 'echo' is allowed to be heard in this way.[3] A good example is again the discovery of Adamic reference in 7.7–12 (see below), and for that matter Philippians 2.6–8 (see ch. 4 above); in both instances the exegesis is clarified by the hypothesis, and things about the passage which might have appeared obscure start to fall into place. No-one would deny that Romans 7.13–20 is one of Paul's more obscure paragraphs, and if we can hereby shed more light on it I shall be content.

---

[1]Barnes 1985, 17.

[2]See Hooker 1959–60 (= Hooker 1990, ch. 5). Hooker replies briefly in 1990, 6 to the criticisms of Wedderburn 1980.

[3]See particularly Hays 1989, ch. 1 for a discussion of these and related points.

(ii) Cain in Romans 7?

We may begin with Romans 7.7–12. It has become common to see Adam under the argument here, and I am persuaded that this is right.[4] Though this has recently been contested on the grounds that the reference is to the arrival of Torah in Israel,[5] I am sure that this is a false either-or: Paul's whole point is that when the Torah arrived in Israel she recapitulated the sin of Adam. The passage simply spells out what is said in compressed form in 5.20: νόμος δὲ παρεισῆλθεν ἵνα πλεονάσῃ τὸ παράπτωμα. We can best understand 7.7–12 if we allow its echoes of Genesis 3 full weight (see particularly 7.11, where 'sin deceived me and so killed me' picks up Genesis 3.13). Israel, Paul is saying, is in Adam too—and the Torah proves it. The overall thought is thus not far removed from that of 2.17–24 as a sharpening up of 1.18–32.

But if this reference to Adam is allowed, demonstrating that Israel recapitulated the Fall with the arrival of Torah (referring perhaps to the Golden Calf incident, the beginning of Israel's sin under the Torah), what are we to say about the passage which describes the settled state that results from this sorry beginning? If 7.13–20 moves into the present tense after the aorists of 7.7–12, as has often been observed, one natural way of taking this is as a reference in the first place to Israel's continuing life under Torah, not as actual autobiography[6] but as phenomenology described retrospectively with Christian hindsight. This point of view has some affinities with the line proposed by Kümmel and Bultmann, and followed by (e.g.) Jewett and Käsemann, but instead of suggesting that the problem is 'nomism' it fully allows for the tension between the proper demand of the Torah and the inability of Israel to keep Torah.[7] Instead of trying to broaden the reference so as to include all of humanity, it keeps the discussion very Israel-specific. Israel, after all, was the nation to whom Torah had been given. If it is thought that this makes the passage of less value hermeneutically, so be it; I would not agree, but this is not the place to pursue the question.

If, then, we (a) allow for a double reference (Israel and Adam) in 7.7–12, and (b) suggest that the primary reference of 7.13–20 is Israel continuing to live under Torah, this would still allow, in parallel to 7.7–12, for an allusive reference to a figure under the argument who would give depth to the analysis as Adam did in the earlier paragraph. Such a figure is Cain. He plays quite a prominent role in Jewish (and early Christian) thinking and writing, and for that matter art, and his story was the subject of various

---

[4]See e.g. Dunn 1988, 379.
[5]Moo 1986.
[6]*Pace* Gundry 1980, etc.
[7]See the discussions and bibliographies in the commentaries, e.g. Dunn 374 f.

Targumic expansions and elaborations.[8] In particular, there are nine elements of the Cain story, not least as elaborated in later Jewish writings, which suggest that he is the hidden partner of Israel in this passage.[9]

(a) Cain is seen as the archetypal possessor of the evil inclination, the יצר הרע. This passage has often been seen as a Pauline expression of the same idea.[10]

(b) Cain is warned by God (Genesis 4.7) that, when he is in a position to do good, 'sin is lurking at the door; its desire is for you, but you must master it'. In Romans 7.18 Paul summarizes the description of 7.13–20 as follows: when I want to do what is right, evil lies close at hand to me.[11]

(c) Cain is seen in some traditions as the archetypal 'double-minded' man, the man with two hearts (לב ולב). This is a not unnatural description of the person in 7.13–25.[12]

(d) Cain is portrayed in the Targumim and elsewhere as conducting an argument with Abel as to whether the world was made by a God of justice and love. The question of the justice and love of God are precisely the subjects at issue in the letter to the Romans, and ch. 7 is a closely integral part of these arguments, facing the problem of God's justice in his dealings with Israel—the problem which will then, though solved at one level in ch. 8, re-emerge in chs. 9–11. At the heart of the latter passage we find a description of Israel which could be an exact description of the Cain of the Targumim: 'being ignorant of the justice of God, and seeking to establish his own, they did not submit to God's justice' (Romans 10.3)[13]

(e) Cain's response to God's question about Abel (Genesis 4.9 f.) is one of professed ignorance as to what he has done: ὁ δὲ εἶπεν Οὐ γινώσκω... καὶ εἶπεν ὁ θεός Τί ἐποίησας; So too the description of the plight in Romans 7.13–20 gets under way with v.15: ὁ γὰρ κατεργάζομαι οὐ γινώσκω· οὐ γὰρ ὃ θέλω τοῦτο πράσσω, ἀλλ' ὃ μισῶ τοῦτο ποιῶ.[14]

[8]See e.g. Aptowitzer 1922, Mellinkoff 1979. The relevant Targums in particular are set out helpfully in Vermes 1975, 92–126. See also Josephus, *Ant.* 1.52–66; Philo *Quaest. Gen.* 1.59–75, and in the NT Heb. 11.4, 1 Jn. 3.12, Jude 11. Among various mentions of Cain in the Pseudepigrapha we may mention Apoc. Ad. Ev. 40. For Cain in the so-called NT Apocrypha see the index to Hennecke-Schneemelcher, s.v.

[9]The story of Cain, as elaborated in various Jewish writings, is conveniently available in Ginzberg 1937 <1909>, 1.103 ff.

[10]E.g. Davies 1980 <1948>, 20–31. On Cain see Vermes 1975, 95 f.

[11]The LXX translation of Gen. 4.7 is so peculiar that nothing can be made of the fact that there are no obvious verbal echoes in the Greek. In Apoc. Abr. 24.5 Cain is said to have been 'led by the adversary to break the law'.

[12]See Hanson 1978–9. The Symmachus translation of Gen. 4.12 has ἀκατάστατος for נע (fugitive); the same Greek word in James 1.8 clearly means 'double-minded'. See too Philo *Cher.* 67, *Post.* 42.

[13]Cf. Targumim on Genesis 4.8: Vermes 1975, 96–100.

[14]Contrast the description of Adam and Cain in Philo, *Post.*, 10, according to which Adam is the one who acts involuntarily while Cain acts voluntarily and thus sins more seriously.

(f) The result of the whole episode is that Cain is cursed, and laments his plight: his sin has meant that he cannot escape, now, the constant threat of death (Genesis 4.14, and the Targumim thereon). Even so, Romans 7 ends in the well-known lament: 'wretched man that I am, who will deliver me from this body of death?'[15]

(g) Cain's problem in the first place was that his sacrifice was unacceptable to God (Gen. 4.3–8; this, in the Targumim, is the reason for the debate between Cain and Abel about the justice and love of God). If the suggestion of my previous chapter is correct, Paul's matching of the death of Christ, seen as the perfect sin-offering, with the plight described in 7.13–20 means that 'Cain' has at last found an acceptable sacrifice.[16] This prepares the way for Paul's prayer for salvation for those in Cain's position, in 10.1–3.

(h) In the Pseudo-Clementine *Homilies* (3.42.7)[17] Cain's name is analysed etymologically to mean 'zeal'. This is the word used by Paul in that same passage (Romans 10.2) to characterize Israel under Torah, in an analysis which, as we shall see in ch. 13 below, depends quite closely on Romans 7.

(i) Finally, the Cain story is linked by the Targumim very closely with the story of Adam's fall.[18] If my reading of Romans 7 is correct, Paul has moved in the same way from a consideration of Israel as the place where Adam's trespass is worked out to a demonstration that Israel in her continuing existence is also the place where Cain's plight is now lived out to the full.

All these considerations suggest to me that we are right to see the same kind of allusion to Cain in Romans 7.13–25 as to Adam in 7.7–12, and with the same kind of intent. Death, the result of sin, is not escaped by Torah, but is merely exacerbated. The thought of this passage is very close to that of 2.17–24, 3.19–20, 4.15, 5.20 and 7.1–6; but now it is given the sharp edge of an analysis, a retrospective phenomenology of Israel under the Torah, by means of the rhetorically vivid 'I'. And, this analysis gains part of its depth and evocative power from its echoes of the figure of Cain. The wandering son of Adam becomes the model for the wandering Jew. The Torah is not the cure for doublemindedness, but simply intensifies it.

If this is in any way correct—and I would like to stress that my view of Romans 7, as sketched two chapters ago, does not depend at all on this analysis, but is merely filled out by it—then, as hinted in (g) above, a possibility emerges of a new reading of 10.2–3. It has often been observed

---

[15]On the plight of Cain see also Philo *Det.* 119; on his fate, Jub. 4.4–6, 31–2, Test. Benj. 7.3–5 and many similar references. There is quite a close parallel between the Cain/Abel contrast in *Post.* 39 and Rom. 6.23.

[16]According to Pseudo-Jonathan on Gen. 4.3, Cain and Abel brought their original sacrifices on 14 Nisan—the date of Passover.

[17]Hennecke and Schneemelcher 1965, 552.

[18]Vermes 1975, 104 f.; in the Neofiti Targum, the Targum Yerushalmi, and the Fragmentary Targum it almost looks as though Cain's murder of Abel is the real 'fall'.

that there is a close connection between Romans 7 and Romans 9.30–10.21, but articulating that link has proved extremely difficult. Though this is only one of many strands in the complex double argument, it should not, I think, be lightly dismissed. According to the Jewish traditions embodied in the Targumim, Cain argued that the world was not created by a god of justice, and tried thereby to prove himself in the right. Even so, says Paul, Israel has been ignorant of God's justice, the δικαιοσύνη θεοῦ, and has been seeking to establish her own δικαιοσύνη instead of submitting to God's. If we read this account of Israel's 'ignorance' in the light of Romans 7.13–20, and of the provision of the sin-offering in 8.3 for precisely this condition, then 10.2–3 take on overtones not normally audible. As well as putting forward a charge against Israel (and against 'sin'), the verses are already looking towards the solution to the problem: Israel has acted ignorantly,[19] and so the charge is not final. The same Lord is Lord of all, Jew and Gentile alike, rich in mercy to all who call upon him (Romans 10.12). If sins of ignorance can be pardoned by the sin-offering, then Cain and his spiritual descendants can be pardoned. This, however, takes us towards the subject of the next chapter.

[19]Compare Ac. 3.17, 13.27; and see ch. 11 above.

Conclusion: The Climax of the Covenant

Chapter Thirteen

CHRIST, THE LAW AND THE PEOPLE OF GOD: THE PROBLEM OF ROMANS 9–11[1]

(i) Introduction

The singular 'problem' in the chapter-title is deceptive. Romans 9–11 is as full of problems as a hedgehog is of prickles. Many have given it up as a bad job, leaving Romans as a book with eight chapters of 'gospel' at the beginning, four of 'application' at the end, and three of puzzle in the middle.

Yet it is at the singular 'problem' that we must look if we are to make any headway with understanding, not to mention using, Romans 9–11. What is this section of Romans all about, i.e. what is its basic *subject-matter*? And what, if we can answer that, is it saying *about* this subject-matter? And how can the section, thus understood, be handled in the twentieth century, so as to be the word of God for today?

This problem can only properly be approached as a subset of two other problems, namely, (1) what is Romans itself all about? and (2) how can any of Paul's theology, called forth as it was by particular and actually unique situations in the first century, be the word of God for today? These questions are of course being addressed in new ways in the present day, and it is impossible even to review the range of available answers.[2] I shall simply note here certain classic positions, and proceed to expound my own.

---

[1]This chapter began as an article for the periodical *Ex Auditu*, but failed to appear owing to a muddle on my part about dates. As with the other chapters on Romans, I am only too aware of the possibility of doubling its length by interacting with even a few of the scholars currently writing in this area. Fuller statements on several points may be found in Wright 1980a, ch. 4.

[2]See the recent commentaries, including full bibliographies, by Dunn, Wilckens, Ziesler and Zeller; the survey article of Räisänen 1988; and the contributions of, and debates engendered by, Sanders (see his summary in 1991, ch. 9), Räisänen, Hübner (1984a), Gaston and others. To discuss the interesting contribution of Cranfield to the debate would, unfortunately, take us too far afield.

(ii) Romans 9–11 Within Romans and Within Pauline Theology

Why does Paul write Romans 9–11 after 1–8? The answer will depend, naturally, on one's view of 1–8 and of the letter as a whole. If the letter is perceived as a treatise simply on individual salvation from sin, the section cannot but be seen as an aside or appendix, dealing with a different problem, that of the Jews. (In some older treatments, it was regarded as a doctrinal section dealing with the abstract doctrine of predestination; but this would find few advocates today.) Perhaps the best-known statement of this view is that of C.H. Dodd: the section is an old sermon, carried around by Paul in case of need, and inserted here without relevance to the rest of the letter, which runs on from 8.39 directly to 12.1.[3] If we are to avoid this—and most exegetes would now, rightly in my view, regard such a conclusion as a *reductio ad absurdum*—there are other options available. The section has been seen as the discussion of a possible counter-example to the thesis Paul has just proposed: if God is so reliable (1–8), what about the promises he made to Israel?[4] Käsemann sees the section as exemplary, with Israel as the type of *homo religiosus*: 'religious man' has been a key theme in the first section, and now Israel is discussed as an example of this condition.[5]

If the section is seen, instead, as an important integral part of the argument of the letter itself, there is still a wide range of possibilities open. Some see it as pointing towards the 'two-covenant' theology popular in some quarters in our own century, in which God's covenant with Christ and the church in no sense replaces, but simply parallels, his continuing covenant with physical Israel.[6] Some, following F.C. Baur, see it simply as addressing the problem of Jewish-Gentile relationships within the church, specifically the church in Rome.[7] All kinds of nuances have been built into these and other options, of which one of the more interesting is that of E.P. Sanders: Paul believed that Jews had to convert to Christianity in order to be saved, but if he were still alive today he would have modified that view towards the two-covenant one.[8] This points to the importance, for almost all writers on the topic, of the hermeneutical cash-value, perceived or real, of the exegesis. If the section is ignored or downplayed, there is an open and often-travelled road towards anti-semitism. A case can be made out, in fact, for saying that the standard Protestant exegesis of Romans, in which 9–11 was marginalized,

[3]See Dodd 1959, 161–3.
[4]E.g. Barrett 1957, 175; Zeller 1984, 170; Ziesler 1989, 37 ff. Ziesler's formulation, admitting that the subject-matter was problematic for Paul but implying that it is no longer so, still leaves chs. 1–8 as the real heart of Romans.
[5]Käsemann 1980, 253 ff.
[6]Stendahl 1976; Gaston 1987; etc.
[7]See, for a modern variation on this, Wedderburn 1988.
[8]Sanders 1978; and see 1983, 197 f.

robbed the church of the best weapon it could have had for identifying and combating some of the worst evils of the Third Reich. But when Romans 9–11 has been taken seriously as part of the letter, this has often been combined with the view (which of these is cause and which effect is perhaps hard to say) that Paul holds open either a fully-blown universalism in which all humans will be saved or at least a Jewish covenant of salvation which is apart from the Christian gospel. 11.25–7 is the key passage here: 'all Israel will be saved'.

Upon this passage, too, there have been built numerous theologies of the future of ethnic Israel; and indeed many treatments of Paul's theology have used this passage, interpreted as predicting a large-scale, last-minute salvation of ethnic Jews, as a fixed point around which to build other less secure material, and often as a key point to be played off against other early (or indeed contemporary) Christian theologians. This, unusually, has been something on which mainline critical exegesis and mainline fundamentalism has been at one. The former usually suggest that this is part of Paul's avoiding the Scylla of apparent Marcionism at the cost of the Charybdis of being proved wrong (the world did not end and the Jews did not convert *en masse*); the latter sometimes suggest that this last-minute salvation of Jews will have something to do with the pre-millennial fulfillment of prophecy. Either way, Paul is believed to have predicted a great event which is as yet unrealized, and which involves salvation, with or without faith in Jesus Christ, for a large number of ethnic Jews. And this belief is on the one hand held in a certain amount of tension with other passages in Romans as well as the other Paulines (e.g. Galatians, 1 Thessalonians 2.14–16), and on the other hand a matter of considerable hermeneutical importance for the appropriation of Paul's message for today. Either Paul is an apocalyptic dreamer, fantasizing about a future ingathering of the Jews, or he is the New Testament prophet of the modern state of Israel; or, perhaps, he is something in between, which justifies the church in abandoning a 'mission to Jews' on the grounds that ethnic Israel and the church are joint heirs, as they stand, of the promised salvation, with 'conversion' either way being unnecessary and inappropriate. No-one who has followed the main movements of modern theology will need reminding of how important these issues have been in the post-holocaust re-evaluation of the church's relationship to Judaism.[9]

These larger issues, however, cannot and must not be addressed at once, if we want to retain any hope of hearing what Paul himself was talking about. Instead, I want to suggest, in a nutshell, my own (no doubt tendentious) view of what Romans is all about, and the place of 9–11 within it, and then move in to look at the chapters in more detail.

[9]See, for instance, the discussions at Vatican II, and at the 1988 Lambeth conference.

Romans is written, I believe, not simply to sum up Paul's theology at the end of his main activity, nor simply to sort out problems within the Roman church, but in a measure both of those and more.[10] Paul wants to use Rome as a base of operations in the Western Mediterranean, much as he had used Antioch (originally) as a base in the East. But it is therefore vital that the Roman church should understand the underlying theology of his missionary endeavours, lest, like the church in Antioch, they effectively stab him in the back by adopting a different line, with different practical consequences. The problem which Paul foresees in Rome is in fact the mirror-image of that which he met in Antioch. There, the church was pulled in the direction of maintaining the distinctiveness of Jews and Gentiles within the Christian church: there was an 'inner circle' of Jewish Christians, and if gentile Christians wanted to belong to it they would have to get circumcised. In Rome, however, Paul foresees the danger of the (largely gentile) church so relishing its status as the true people of God that it will write off ethnic Jews entirely as being not only second-class citizens *within* the church, still maintaining their dietary laws when the need for them has past, but also now beyond the reach of the gospel *outside* the church, heading for automatic damnation. Paul, anxious about these possibilities, wishes to argue for two things: total equality of Jew and Gentile within the church, and a mission to Gentiles which always includes Jews as well within its scope.[11] This, arguably, was always his policy in the East; it is his intention to follow the same policy in the West. Romans is the letter in which he plants this goal of the mission and unity of the church in the firmest possible theological soil, i.e., the exposition of the righteousness of God—which I take to mean essentially the covenant faithfulness, the covenant justice, of the God who made promises to Abraham, promises of a worldwide family characterized by faith, in and through whom the evil of the world would be undone.

Within this overall purpose Romans 9–11 functions, I believe, as the climax of the theological argument[12] and the bringing into focus of the practical aim. The whole of Romans 1–11 is, in one sense, an exposition of how the one God has been faithful, in Jesus Christ, to the promises he made to Abraham: and this exposition must of necessity reach its climax in the historical survey of how these promises have worked out (note the way in which Romans 9.6 ff. begins with Abraham and works through to the prophets, in typically Jewish style, before then moving forward to Christ (10.4) and the mission of the church (10.9 ff.)). And it is only on the basis of

---

[10]The most recent discussion of the purpose of Rom., apart from in the commentaries, can be found in Wedderburn 1988. I find myself still in a fair amount of disagreement with him, and with the other views currently on offer.

[11]Against Sanders 1983, *passim*, and Watson 1986, chs. 5–9.

[12]So, rightly, Hooker 1990, 3.

234

the whole of Romans 1–11 that the warning of 11.13 ff.—to gentile Christians who are tempted to the arrogance of saying that Jews are now cut out of the covenant family permanently—can be understood. The theology which produces this understanding of mission in 10.14 ff. and 11.13 ff. is then, in 12–16, made the basis of the appeal for unity in the church itself: in particular, the strong must bear with the weak, and not please themselves. One of the exegetical strengths of the view I am proposing is that not only 9–11 but also 14.1—15.13 find new coherence with the argument of the letter as a whole, and the climax of the latter passage (15.7–13) can be seen in fact as the climax of the entire epistle. With this (extremely tendentious) sketch we have prepared the way to ask: what, then, is Romans 9–11 actually about?

(iii) Romans 9–11 In Itself

Some older writers saw Romans 9-11 as 'about' predestination or election, or as offering Paul's 'philosophy of history'. Modern scholarship has rightly focussed on the main subject: the Jews' failure to believe the gospel. But it has not so often been noticed that the reason Paul is discussing this, and the terms in which he is discussing it, have to do not merely with Israel but with God; and that the discussion about God focusses on the question of God's righteousness. Although the term δικαιοσύνη θεοῦ itself does not occur within this section until 10.3, this should not blind us to the fact that the question throughout has to do with the character and purposes of God, and particularly his faithfulness to his promises, and hence the justice of his dealings with Israel and the world. Thus the opening claim in 9.6 has to do with the unfailing character of God's word; 9.14 raises the question of whether God is unrighteous; 9.19, that of why he still finds fault; 9.19–23 of the rights of the potter over the clay, a metaphor taken directly from the discussions in Isaiah and Jeremiah of God's covenant behaviour with Israel.[13] After the central and climactic statement of 10.3 f., the argument of ch. 11 remains focussed not merely on the future of the Jews but on the character of God, as 11.22, 29 and 32 bear witness, and as is celebrated in 11.33–6. And the tools of thought Paul uses are those developed already in the letter: in the first eight chapters he has set out the revelation of God's righteousness which has been made in and through Jesus the Messiah, specifically, through his cross and resurrection, and through the Spirit. 10.4 is not an isolated statement, but draws together the theme of the section as a whole.

This conclusion is further confirmed by the numerous echoes, within the section as a whole, of Jewish writings in which the question of God's

---

[13]These questions are all organically related to those at the start of ch. 3—a fact which was one of the first things I noticed when studying Romans as a doctoral student in the early 1970s.

faithfulness to his covenant is uppermost. We cannot pursue these parallels here, but the themes of God's forbearance, his delay of judgment to allow space for repentance, his hardening meanwhile of those who refuse his grace, and the idea of an historical survey in which his strange purposes are seen and understood, are all clearly reminiscent of Jewish apocalyptic writings such as 4 Ezra or 2 Baruch, and share with such works common roots in the literature of the exile.[14]

The main subject-matter of Romans 9–11, then, is the covenant faithfulness of God, seen in its outworking in the history of the people of God. And what is Paul saying *about* this? He is arguing, basically, that the events of Israel's rejection of the gospel of Jesus Christ *are* the paradoxical outworking of God's covenant faithfulness. Only by such a process—Israel's unbelief, the turning to the Gentiles, and the continual offer of salvation to Jews also—can God be true to the promises to Abraham, promises which declared *both* that he would give him a worldwide family *and* that his own seed would share in the blessing. It is by understanding this paradoxical process, and their place within it, that the Roman church will be on the one hand ready to support Paul fully in his own mission and on the other hand willing to unite across racial barriers in the way indicated (building on 9–11) in chs. 14–15.

The problem about the content of Romans 9–11 then becomes one of *integration*. Put simply, the issue is this: if Paul rejects the possibility of a status of special privilege for Jews in chs. 9 and 10, how does he manage, apparently, to reinstate such a position in ch. 11? It is this apparent inconsistency that has led many to suggest that the section contains a fundamental self-contradiction, which is then explained either as a resurgence of patriotic sentiment (Dodd) or the vagaries of apocalyptic fantasy (Bultmann). As we have already hinted, the real crux of the issue lies not so much in 11 as a whole, but in 11.25–7: the regular interpretation of that passage as predicting a large-scale last-minute 'salvation' of Israel, worked out in terms of the chapter as a whole, leads to this charge.[15] And the only way in which this problem can be addressed is by working through the exegesis of the passage as a whole. To do this properly is, obviously, an enormous undertaking. Here we have only space for a further tendentious sketch of what seems to me the main line of thought.

[14]See also Wisd. Sol. 10 ff., especially chs. 12 and 15.

[15]See Plag 1969. Plag's solution (that 11.25 ff. is an interpolation, albeit also by Paul) is unacceptable; but he shows well that it is only this small passage, read in the usual way, that creates the real 'contradiction'.

(iv) Romans 9.1–5

Three features of 9.1–5 are important for our present purposes. First, Paul's evident grief at the failure of the Jews to believe must always be kept in mind. This shows on the one hand that their failure is not, in his mind, a mere accident which only appears to cut them off from salvation, but does not do so really; and, on the other hand, that his approach to the issue is not that of the armchair theologian calmly dissecting someone else's fate, but that of the vitally involved human being, with all his natural sympathies alert and operative. The hints of parallels with 7.7–25 reinforce this point: Paul looks at 'his flesh' in rebellion against the gospel, and in himself (αὐτὸς ἐγώ, 9.3) he identifies with them.

Second, the list of Jewish privileges in 9.4 f. is not arbitrary, but echoes precisely those privileges which, throughout Romans up to this point, Paul has shown to be transferred to the Jews' representative Messiah, and, through him, to all those who are 'in him', be they Jewish or Gentile. Sonship, glory, covenants, law, worship, promises, patriarchs: all has become the glory of the church in Christ. This intensifies the irony—and, for Paul, the agony—of the present situation.

Third, the climactic privilege is that from the Jewish race, according to the flesh, is the Messiah.[16] Just as 1.3–4 provides a programmatic christological statement for the rest of the letter, especially chs. 5–8, so 9.5 stands programatically at the head of 9–11. The Jews are the people of the Messiah, but they are this according to the flesh. And the Messiah to whom they belong is not merely 'theirs', but is also 'God over all, blessed for ever'. Attention has naturally focussed on the ascription of θεός to Jesus, which, following Metzger and Cranfield, I endorse.[17] The real emphasis of the phrase, however, lies elsewhere, and is picked up in (e.g.) 10.12: the Jewish Messiah is God over *all*, Jew and Gentile alike. Within the very heart of the Jewish privilege there lies the vocation which proves the Jews' apparent undoing: that the Messiah, who encapsulates her destiny in himself, is God's means of salvation not for her alone but for the whole world. More specifically, as we have seen in earlier chapters, the Messiah in his death brought to a head the sorry tale of Israel's own acting out of the sin of Adam (see also below). As long as Israel clings to the fact of ancestral privilege, she cannot but miss out on God's intended universal salvation. She is denying its premise. And behind this whole picture there stands Israel's own fundamental doctrine: creational and covenantal monotheism. The God who made promises to Israel is also the creator of the whole world; but if that is

[16]On the meaning of Messiahship see chs. 2–3 above.
[17]Metzger 1973; Cranfield 1975, 464 ff., *pace* Moule 1977, 137. The ascription is of course filled out with the christological passages studied in chs. 4–6 above.

so his promises cannot be confined to Israel alone, and to imagine that they are is to deny his very character.

(v) Romans 9.6–29

How then is God faithful to the covenant? What is the righteousness of God all about? Did God after all have two plans, and has he changed in the middle of history from the first to the second? This is not an abstract question about the reliability of God in general, but a particular problem about the apparent failure of God to remain true to specific and fundamental promises upon which all else depends. Nor does this mean that Romans 9–11 is a 'practical' question to illustrate or focus a 'theoretical' discussion; the whole letter is thoroughly 'practical', aimed at a particular situation—though not for that reason any the less 'theological'. To answer the problem, Paul goes back, in good Jewish style, to the beginning: to the story of Abraham, where he has already been in ch. 4. And he argues that what God has done is what he always said he would do. God has not been unfaithful to the promises that were actually made.

Thus, in 9.6–13, he argues that the succession from Abraham to Isaac (not Ishmael), and to Jacob (not Esau) was in line with the promises actually made. God never promised Abraham that *all* his physical offspring would be within the covenant. There is already a 'double "Israel"': in 6b there is an 'Israel' that is so merely according to the flesh, and there is an 'Israel' that is a 'true Israel', the Israel of promise. This is an important initial move in the argument. What counts, exactly as in Romans 3.21–4.25 or Galatians 3–4, is grace, not race. And the cross-reference to Romans 4 in particular shows how unwise it is to imagine that the true 'seed' of Abraham in 9.7 is simply a subset of ethnic Israel. In 4.16 it is already clearly a worldwide family.

Then, in 9.14–18, Paul faces the question of whether this progressive narrowing down of the 'seed' of Abraham means that God is unjust. We may notice that in Jewish thought of the period vv.6–13 might find agreement: nobody would speak up for Ishmael or Esau. What becomes the bone of contention is Paul's insistence that the same principle continues to operate. But to address this problem Paul moves on in history to the time of the Exodus, and specifically to the Golden Calf incident.[18] At that time, Israel as a whole stood condemned, with only Moses pleading to God on her behalf (the parallel may well have been in Paul's mind in 9.1–5). Israel, it appears, is not a *tabula rasa* upon which God writes an abstract decree, but a rebellious and sinful nation, the people of God maybe but a people, in the

---

[18]Which, as we saw in chs. 10 and 11, may have been in his mind in Rom. 7.7–12.

bad sense, *according to the flesh*. God's dealings with her—which is what is at issue, not an abstract question of God's way with individual humans *per se*—are just; and the justice is that of the judge who must judge sin properly, and of the covenant God who must act to glorify his great name despite the failure of his people. We may compare 2.17–29, with its echoes of Ezekiel and, behind that, Deuteronomy.

This leads to 9.19–29. Here we see, fully blown, Paul's version of the Jewish doctrine of God's righteousness. God will judge; he will save a people for himself; but at the moment he is patient, restraining his proper and righteous wrath, in order that more may be saved; and, throughout his actions, he is impartial, having no respect of persons. Throughout, Paul is deliberately drawing on Old Testament imagery in order to make the point that what has happened in his own day is not outside the purposes of God as foretold in Jewish scripture, but is precisely what was prophesied. God has not been unfaithful to his promises, but has—precisely in the present apparent disaster—fulfilled them completely. Scripture always envisaged that Israel could not be affirmed as she stood, that there would need to be a process of judgment and mercy, of exile and restoration. It is not God who has failed, but Israel. That is the emphasis of 9.6–29.

In particular, the line of thought from 5.20, through 7.13, to 8.3 (ch. 10 above) gives a new force to the difficult passage about the 'vessels of wrath' in 9.19–24.[19] The point is not that the creator decides, arbitrarily, to save some and condemn others. Rather, he sees that the only way of rescuing his world at all is to call a people, and to enter into a covenant with them, so that through them he will deal with evil. But the means of dealing with evil is to concentrate it in one place and condemn—execute—it there. The full force of this condemnation is not intended to fall on this people in general, but on their representative, the Messiah. But, insofar as they become the place where sin is thus initially focussed (5.20), Israel necessarily becomes the 'vessel of wrath'. And insofar as Israel clings to her privileged status, and to the Torah as reinforcing it, refusing to recognize the crucified Messiah as the revelation of God's covenant faithfulness, she is bound to remain in that condition.

(vi) Romans 9.30—10.21

The central section of 9–11 (i.e. 9.30—10.21) is not making a different point (as many exegetes and translators have imagined) but exploring the same one further. Its basic theme remains the fall of Israel, and the paradoxical fact

[19]This passage has been much criticized; for a recent example, see Sanders 1991, 119.

that this is in accordance with the promises and warnings of scripture. The difference is that here Paul shows, alongside this, that Gentiles are thereby being brought into the covenant family; and that he reveals the paradoxical role that the Torah played throughout the process.[20] The passage is not about 'human responsibility' as such, nor simply about 'Israel's unbelief'.[21] It is about the way in which, through the Messiah and the preaching which heralds him, Israel is transformed from being an ethnic people into a worldwide family—and about the fact, once more, that this was what God always said that he would do.

Thus, in 9.30–33, Gentiles are said to be attaining membership in the people of God, while Israel is missing out, through pursuing the Torah in the wrong manner. This, strange though it sounds in normal Protestant ears, is exactly what Paul means, as becomes apparent in 10.5 ff. The Torah really is the νόμος δικαιοσύνης, the boundary marker of covenant membership; but it is so in a paradoxical fashion, since it can only be fulfilled by faith, not by the 'works of the law', the badges of Jewish membership (Sabbath, dietary laws, circumcision) which kept Jews separate from Gentiles. The result is that Israel has stumbled over the stumbling stone, which in one sense is clearly the Torah and in another is clearly the Messiah, or the preaching about him. Israel's rejection of Jesus as Messiah simply *is* the logical outworking of her misuse of the Torah, her attempt to treat it as a charter of automatic national privilege. But this 'fall' was itself, it appears, part of the plan of God, who gave the Torah (there is no suggestion here that the Torah is a bad thing) and who, after all, sent the Messiah. Here is the irony of Romans 9–11, foreshadowed indeed in Galatians 3 and Romans 5–8 but now spelt out in detail: Israel's disobedience is already actually part of the covenant plan, part of God's intention from the beginning. The Torah has indeed concentrated sin in Israel, and now we see its full extent. As well as 'ordinary' sin—the *breaking* of God's law—which was the problem in ch. 7, Israel is now shown to be guilty of a kind of meta-sin, the attempt to confine grace to one race.[22] The result of this idolatry of national privilege is that Israel clings on to the terrible destiny—of being the place where sin was concentrated—which she was meant to allow her Messiah to bear on her behalf. Once again, 9.5 is visible as the real foundation stone of the whole section.

[20]One of the fascinating features of this section, which we have not space to explore here, is the way in which Paul develops themes from chs. 2 and 7.

[21]As is suggested by the heading in the NIV, which drives this interpretation through the text by, for instance, making the unpardonable addition of 'the Israelites' in 10.16.

[22]This is the truth behind the Kümmel/Bultmann/Käsemann view of Romans 7, masked because that tradition of exegesis (a) sees it as 'nomism' rather than 'national righteousness' and (b) attempts to read it into Rom. 7, where, however it is described, it does not belong.

This cryptic initial statement (9.30–3) is spelt out further in 10.1–13, which explains the divinely appointed covenant way to salvation.[23] Israel, already charged in 7.13–20 with ignorant *sin*, is now also seen to be ignorant of the δικαιοσύνη τοῦ θεοῦ, 10.2—that is, of God's own covenant faithfulness and its nature and shape, in other words of what God was righteously, justly and faithfully doing in her history. She was bent, instead, on pursuing τὴν ἰδίαν δικαιοσύνην, that is, a status of covenant membership which would be for Jews and Jews only.[24] In doing so, she did not submit to God's own covenant plan: because Christ all along was the secret goal of Torah, the τέλος νόμου, so that her rejection of Christ and her abuse of Torah, turning it into a charter of racial privilege, were really one and the same thing. The notorious crux of 10.4[25] can, I think, be reduced to these terms: that the Torah is neither abolished as though it were bad or demonic, nor affirmed in the sense in which the Jews took it. It was a good thing, given deliberately by God for a specific task and a particular period of time. When the task is done and the time is up, the Torah reaches its goal, which is also the conclusion of its intended reign, not because it was a bad thing to be abolished but because it was a good thing whose job is done. In terms of the Luther-Calvin debate which has dominated discussion of this issue, we can put it like this. The Lutheran wants to maintain the sharp antithesis between law and gospel; so does Paul, but within the context of a single plan of God, and with no suggestion that the Torah is itself a bad thing. The Calvinist wants to ensure that God did not change his plan, or his mind, in the middle of history; so does Paul (that, indeed, is what Romans 9–11 is all about), but he insists that *the single plan always involved a dramatic break*, a cross and a resurrection written into the very fabric of history. The Messiah is the fulfillment of the long purposes of Israel's God. It was for this that Torah was given in the first place as a deliberately temporary mode of administration. In the Messiah are fulfilled the creator's paradoxical purposes for Israel and hence for the world. He is the climax of the covenant.[26]

[23]The time is more than ripe for a re-assessment of what precisely 'salvation' meant for Paul. I have a suspicion that his thought was closer to the Jewish idea, which had very little to do with an other-worldly state of bliss and a great deal to do with a renewed space-time universe, than we usually imagine. But we cannot pursue this here.

[24]This view has now become quite popular (e.g. Gager 1983, 224; Dunn 1988, 595; Sanders 1991, 121 f.; more cautiously, Ziesler 1989, 256 f.). I first suggested it in 1978 (Wright 1978, 83, and 1980a, 98).

[25]On 10.4 see now Badenas 1985, and the (somewhat shallow) discussion of views in Martin 1989, 129–54.

[26]It was in conversation with Richard Hays that I first thought of the title for this book, and his instant reaction was to ask if I were suggesting this phrase as a translation of τέλος νόμου. My only possible reply was that until that moment I had not been conscious of doing so.

There is therefore something brought to an end by Christ. The cross brings to a halt any suggestion of Jewish national privilege, as Paul says with characteristic brevity in Galatians 2.21 ('if covenant membership were through Torah, Christ died in vain'). This is the 'scandal of the cross', which prevents Israel from hearing the message about Jesus, and which lies at the heart of the revelation of God's covenant faithfulness and justice in 3.21 ff. For the long-awaited Messiah to die at the hands of pagans meant that the moment of vindication had appeared to be, instead, a moment of black tragedy. But, within this bringing to an end of Jewish national privilege, he also brings to an end the process of concentrating *sin* within Israel (see above). This means that the παντί of 10.4b can be given its full weight. If he has fulfilled God's purpose for Israel (that she should be the means of dealing with the world's sin), then Gentiles can now be welcomed into the covenant family. But if he has brought it to its goal, and hence its terminus, Israel's ambiguous vocation to be the people in whom sin was to be concentrated in order that it be dealt with, then Israel too is free, when she acknowledges him as Messiah, to enjoy covenant membership without, any longer, the former ambiguity.[27]

But if Christ is the 'end' of the Torah in terms of the use of 'works' (Sabbath, food, circumcision) to bolster national privilege, this must not be taken to mean that the Torah itself was, after all, a bad thing now happily got rid of. Even when the Torah has clearly been abused in a particular direction, Paul does not imagine for a moment that it is other than God's law, holy and just and good. Rather (and this is the mystery at the heart of Paul's theology, the reason why a quintessential verse like Romans 10.4 is so amazingly difficult to unravel) the Torah as Israel's covenant document, even as the covenant charter for Israel according to the flesh, *even as that which incites Israel to 'national righteousness'* and then condemns her because her sin makes the boast groundless, this Torah is also, and far more importantly, *vindicated* when Israel's king dies Israel's death outside the walls of Israel's capital. It is not simply that the Torah, the covenant charter, always warned that God would do exactly this, and so is naturally vindicated when it comes to pass, true though that is (see 9.6a: it is not as though God's word had failed). There are two deeper strands of thought which come together in Romans 9–11 and which show that the whole Torah is vindicated in Christ, even as God is vindicated in Christ.

First, there is the purpose of the covenant itself, now realized. The covenant was made in the first place in order that, through Israel, the creator might give to his world the life which it had lost through Adam and the Fall. Israel was to be the means of that life, the means of Adam's restoration,

[27]This, I think, is the thrust of Phil. 3.2–11.

and the Messiah was to bring this national destiny to its triumphant conclusion. He was—precisely in the flesh!—to do and be what Israel according to the flesh was called to do and be. And that calling, Paul now indicates clearly, drawing on the line of thought from 5.20 onwards, was that Israel, and her Messiah, should be *cast away* so that the world might be saved.[28] The Torah, therefore, precisely in that it *condemns* Israel, and, with her, her Messiah (Galatians 3.13), is vindicated: it had to do this, so that the sin of the world might be borne. Christ on the cross is thus the *goal* of Torah.

Second, therefore, the means by which Torah did this is seen to be vindicated. The Torah was bound to declare to Israel that she was the chosen people, the creator's special possession. This was true, and Israel needed to be constantly reminded of it, and given signs to help her to remain faithful. But, being at the same time a people in Adam, according to the flesh, Israel was bound to misuse her high calling, turning her privilege into a boast and her safeguarding symbols into badges of superiority. What we see here, in fact, is the outworking, at the level of 'national righteousness', of the analysis of Torah given in Romans 7 at the level of sin. Here at last is the passage where Paul comes to the full analysis of Israel's meta-sin which, wrongly analysed in the first place by those who saw the problem as 'nomism' or Pelagian self-righteousness, was then wrongly superimposed on to Romans 7 by the majority view of that passage.[29] The 'meta-level' of Israel's problem with the Torah is 'national righteousness', and it is here, not in ch. 7, that it is dealt with.[30] So, just as in ch. 7 the Torah was good, eventually vindicated (8.4 is the equivalent, there, of 10.4 here), and at the same time deadly because of Israel's σάρξ—and yet even in that respect was doing what God intended (Galatians 3.21 f.)—so here the Torah is good, vindicated by Christ as its goal, and within its actual good purpose tripping up Israel, enticing her into 'national righteousness', becoming the place where Adam's pride found its full outworking, in order that the long saving purposes of Israel's God, for the world and also for Israel herself, might thereby be brought to fruition. Thus the means by which the Torah condemned Israel at this meta-level are vindicated as part of the strange purposes of the creator, that he should have a covenant people who would die and be raised so that the world might be saved. In this sense also, then, Christ, the dying Messiah, is the goal of Torah, including the Torah when seen as the necessary means of Israel's condemnation, the Torah which entices her into national righteousness. And

---

[28]That this is the correct reading of this passage is indicated by the fact that Paul uses exactly this idea in Rom. 11.11 ff.; moreover, because the Messiah has taken Israel's destiny upon himself in Israel's place, Israel, though she must go through the same death, will also be able to experience the same resurrection (11.14 f.). For all this, see below.

[29]See above, chs. 10–12.

[30]We may note, as a tell-tale indication of this, that ἁμαρτία, sin, is entirely absent from the discussion in Rom. 9–11—until all the threads are drawn together in 11.27.

the sense of cessation which remains—the Lutheran view is not without its merit, it simply needs setting in a wider context—is contained within the sense of climax, of 'goal'. When I reach my goal I stop travelling; not because my journey was a silly idea but because it was a good idea now fully worked out.[31]

There is therefore in this passage, just as in 7.1—8.11, a *double Torah* under the argument. Now, however, the two, for all that their functions are so different, are more obviously integrated. There is, first, the Torah seen as the νόμος δικαιοσύνης (9.31): it really is affirmed as the covenant-document, and Israel's fault is not that she pursued it but that, pursuing it in the wrong way, she did not attain to it (9.31-2). In consequence, we have the Torah as the means whereby God becomes a stumbling-block to Israel.[32] 9.32b, which (oddly in Paul) has no connecting word to 32a, seems all the same to be explanatory: to pursue the Torah through works *is* to stumble over the stumbling stone. The Torah is therefore, in a sense, the stone over which Israel has now stumbled, just as in another sense it is the crucified Messiah over which she has now stumbled. Once more, these are not two but one. And the 'one' that these two are is actually *the covenant plan of the one God*, which, expressed in Torah, was enacted in the Messiah. That is why the stumbling-stone, and the object of faith, in 9.32 f., are systematically and properly ambiguous (do they refer to God, Christ, or Torah?). Israel's fault was her rejection of God's plan; which manifested itself in her 'national righteousness' (which was invalidated by her Adamic sin); which expressed itself in her rejection of the crucified Messiah. Even so, 'faith' within this context is (a) the acceptance of the crucified Messiah as the risen Lord (10.9); (b) the 'fulfillment' of Torah in faith, and consequent membership in the worldwide family (10.5-8, 3.27); and (c) the acknowledgement of, and appropriation of benefits from, the covenant faithfulness of the one God as expressed in promise, Torah and finally in Christ (10.3, 3.21-31). It is only after Israel's failure, therefore, that the first Torah can come into its own: because, with the help of the gospel, a worldwide family can attain to Torah, the Torah which is now paradoxically fulfilled whenever anyone confesses that Jesus is Lord and believes in the God who raised him from the dead. The twin topics of the present volume—Christ and the Law—reach their richest joint expression in Romans 10.4, which itself states our single theme, the climax of the covenant.

The next turn of the paradox is immediately apparent in Romans 10.5-8. This passage is regularly regarded as an arbitrary piece of exegesis on Paul's

[31]This means that I am close in form, though not in substance, with the view of R. Bring, summarized in Martin 1989, 65 f.

[32]Isa. 8.14, quoted here, indicates that it is God himself who is to be seen as both the sanctuary and the stumbling stone for Israel.

part, choosing to treat Leviticus 18 as a statement of a pre-Christian view of Torah and its accomplishment and Deuteronomy 30 as a 'Christian' view of its fulfillment. But, not least in the light of our reading of Galatians 3 in ch. 7 above, I suggest that this is actually unwarranted. Paul's whole theme thus far has been the covenant purpose of God. He has traced it from Abraham, Isaac and Jacob (9.6–13) through Moses and the prophets to the exile (9.14–29), and has now stated that it has reached its climax in the Messiah. What more natural move than that he should now draw on a classic Old Testament passage (Deuteronomy 30) which, certainly from a first-century perspective, would inevitably be read as a prophecy of the return from exile, that is, of the renewal of the covenant, to express that which results from the climactic work of the Messiah? This is further supported by the clear 'new covenant' overtones of Joel 3.5 (quoted in 10.13) and Isaiah 52.7 (10.15).[33]

The best way to read Romans 10.5–8 is then as follows. The 'doing of Torah', spoken of by Leviticus, is actually fulfilled, according to Deuteronomy, when anyone, be they Jew or Gentile, hears the gospel of Christ and believes it. Each of the three verses in Deuteronomy quoted here end with the phrase 'so that you may do it'; *this*, Paul is asserting, is the true 'doing' of the Torah, of which Leviticus speaks. This is how God will give her a new heart, so that she will find the Torah 'on her lips and in her heart': and, just as with the stumbling stone of 9.33, Christ and Torah are fused together, so that when Christ is preached and believed, Torah is being paradoxically fulfilled.[34]

This leads, of course, to the establishment of the gentile mission (10.14–18) and the demonstration of Jewish recalcitrance (10.19–21), which closes the section as it began (compare 9.30 f. with 10.20 f.). Again, Paul's point is to argue for the nature of the gentile mission on the firmest possible theological basis (this is one more indication that his mind is working on the theme of return from exile/renewal of covenant: the ingathering of Gentiles was a stock idea within this theme).[35] He aims to show that the rejection of Israel is not an oddity but rather that which had been predicted all along within the Old Testament itself (specifically, the covenant warnings of Deuteronomy 32 and Isaiah 65), and that it is organically, if paradoxically, linked to the promised ingathering of Gentiles. To this end he builds in (v.19) the key note of 'jealousy', which will be vital for the argument of ch. 11.

Before we turn to examine ch. 11, however, we must note that Paul has made it clear beyond any doubt, and completely in line with Galatians, 1 Thessalonians 2, 2 Corinthians 3, Philippians 3, and the whole of Romans

[33]See the discussion of Rom. 10 in Hays 1989, chs. 2 and 5.

[34]The details, of course, require a great deal of working out for which there is here no space. See particularly now Hays 1989, 163 f.

[35]E.g. Isa. 2.2–4, Tobit 14.6 f., etc.

1–8, that there is no covenant membership for Israel on the basis of racial or 'fleshly' identity. She cannot be the people of God simply by clinging to ancestral privilege; that privilege reached its intended goal in her being the place where sin became concrete and concentrated. Israel, rather, is cast away, as was her Messiah, so that the world might be brought into the family of God. It is *within* that destiny, not by somehow avoiding it, that the clue may be found to the puzzle that remains. If Israel is the people of the crucified Messiah, she can also be raised to new life. The cross and resurrection is the clue to the consistency of Romans 9–11.

(vii) Romans 11

It is usually held that, in Romans 11, Paul predicts a large-scale entry of Jews into the Kingdom in fulfillment of the ancestral promise, after the Gentiles have been saved. There are, of course, numerous variations on this theme. Some see this sudden event as happening immediately before the Parousia, while others see it as concurrent. Some see it as involving actual conversion to Christ, while for others it is a salvation which takes place apart from Christ. Some see it as involving all Jews living at the time, others as including a large number but not all. Whatever the variation, this basic view always seems to fit very badly with Romans 9–10, where, following Galatians and Romans 1–8, Paul makes it abundantly clear that there is no covenant membership, and consequently no salvation, for those who simply rest on their ancestral privilege. This tension is then explained either as a reassertion of an illogical patriotism, or as mere apocalyptic speculation about the sequence of events in the end-time, or as a 'new mystery' (cf v.25) suddenly revealed to Paul during the writing of the letter,[36] or as a textual corruption whereby 11.25–7 has been inserted into a chapter about something else, so colouring the whole.[37]

This last proposal is helpful to this extent: that it draws attention to the fact that 11.25–7 is the only passage in the whole of ch. 11 which seems to demand to be read in the way just outlined. For this reason it seems best to leave it until the end, and to read the rest of the chapter first, remembering that, structurally at least, it forms the climax not only of 9–11 but of the whole letter. It is of course possible that Paul, in so carefully crafted a piece of writing, suddenly went off at a tangent, just when he *thought* he was drawing the threads together: but it is *a priori* more likely that 'the text has a

[36]E.g. Bruce 1963, 221.
[37]E.g. Plag 1969.

central concern and a remarkable inner logic that may no longer be entirely comprehensible to us'.[38]

11.1–10 raises, and answers, the question: can *any* Jews then be saved? Paul answers with his own case. He is a Jew, part of the remnant that is saved in the present.[39] He emphasizes, however, that this is a remnant chosen by grace, not by race or by the 'works' that were the badges of Jewish privilege (11.5–6). It is not, in other words, a small number for whom 'national righteousness' avails after all, but those who, like Paul himself, have died and risen with Christ (compare Galatians 2.19–21, where 'grace' is a shorthand for this whole action). The 'rest', meanwhile, are hardened. Again we must remember that within normal Jewish apocalyptic thought-forms 'hardening' is what happens when people refuse the grace and patience of God, and is the prelude to a final judgment which will be seen to be just (compare Paul's own reworking of this theme in 2.1–16).

11.11–24 then asks the consequent question: can any *more* Jews be saved? It may be the case that some Jews have somehow come in to the Christ-family, but (Paul expects a predominantly gentile church to suggest) surely now there will be no more? Surely they are now all hardened permanently, so that after the first generation the church will be an entirely gentile phenomenon? It is at this point, I believe, that Paul addresses one of the key issues of the entire letter. His mission, he has emphasized from the outset, is 'to the Jew first and also to the Greek'. He suspects that the Roman church—who apparently need the warning in chs. 14–15 that the strong must bear with the weak and not please themselves—is only too eager to declare itself a basically gentile organisation, perhaps (this can only be speculation, but it may be near the mark) in order to clear itself of local suspicion in relation to the capital's Jewish population, recently expelled and more recently returned.[40] But a church with a theology like that would not provide him with the base that he needs for his continuing mission, in Rome itself and beyond. It would result, as Paul sees only too clearly in the light of his Eastern Mediterranean experience, in a drastically split church, with Jewish and Gentile Christians pursuing their separate paths in mutual hostility and recrimination. Instead, in this section and in vv.17–24, he argues with great force that Jews *can* still be saved, and indeed that it is in the interests of a largely gentile church not to forget the fact.

Paul therefore makes two basic points in 11.11–16. First, he emphasizes the point he has made in various ways ever since 5.20: it is by Israel's acting

---

[38]Käsemann 1980, viii.

[39]We should not miss the deliberate 'echo' in 11.2 of 1 Sam. 12.22, in which another Saul, from the tribe of Benjamin, was in himself the evidence that 'God had not forsaken his people'. Hays 1989, 68–9, notes the echo but not this (surely significant) point.

[40]I therefore read Rom. in the opposite direction to that of e.g. Stuhlmacher 1985, who, following a long tradition, sees it basically as a fuller and more considered version of Gal.

out of Adam's sin that the world has been saved.[41] Second, if this (rather than the simple reversal or abandonment of election) is the reason for Israel's 'fall', there is no reason why she should not herself be subsequently saved, and indeed every reason why she should. All she has to do is relinquish her frantic grip on the Torah (cf. Galatians 2.19–21). The submerged allusions to Romans 5 here are extremely telling: Israel acts out the sin of Adam (compare 5.12–21 with 11.11–12), but also the pattern of the Messiah (5.10 with 11.15).

This is the context within which the details of vv.12, 14, 15–16 are to be read. They are not to be interpreted in the light of a reading of vv.25–7 which, as I shall shortly suggest, is misguided. The key is found in v.14: Paul's aim is 'to make my flesh jealous and save some of them'. Paul treats the entire gentile mission, which is his primary vocation, as a means to a further end: that Jews should see 'their' privileges (9.4 f.) being taken up by Gentiles (cp. 9.30 f.), and so should be made 'jealous' (10.19) and decide to come in themselves. One is inescapably reminded of the Prodigal Son, and the elder brother looking on jealously at the party which he might claim as his by right but now could only enter by an act of great humility. (And, to anticipate the hermeneutical conclusion, one cannot but reflect that the church has as a rule celebrated the party in such a way that few Jews would be likely to be jealous of it.) This sets the context for the natural meaning of 11.15: when a Gentile comes into the family of Christ, it is as it were a *creatio ex nihilo*, but when a Jew comes in it is like a resurrection (compare 4.17, in context).

The 'olive tree' allegory then makes exactly the same point. Gentile Christians must not boast of their superiority to Jewish non-Christians (not to Jewish Christians: Paul is referring to branches that are broken off), because to do so would be to set up an inverted 'national righteousness', which would incur the same sentence as the original (Jewish) sort (v.21). And the possibility that is always held out (continuing the answer to 11.11) is not a large-scale last-minute restoration of 'all Jews', irrespective of Christian faith, but the chance that Jews, during the course of the present age, will come to Christian faith and so be grafted back in. The crucial verse here is 23: 'if they do not remain in unbelief'. Paul clearly sees the salvation of Jews in the future as dependent on their coming to Christian faith. His major concern is that the Roman church must not regard Jews as being beyond the reach of the gospel of Jesus. To do so would be to exhibit gentile arrogance, implying that the one God, into whose family they, the Gentiles, had now come by grace, was no longer intending to save any other than Gentiles.

Omitting 11.25–7 for the moment, we may press on to 11.28–32. Here, in Paul's summary of the divine plan of salvation, he draws together the threads

---

[41]11.11, 12a, 12b, 15, forming a climactic sequence.

248

of the entire three chapters, which together form the climax of the theme of the letter, i.e. the righteousness, the covenant faithfulness and justice, of the one God. God's plan, the righteous plan which he had always indicated he would follow, and therefore in which (9.6) his word has not failed, was always to cast Israel away that the world might be saved (here again we see the christological pattern of the whole thought). This, however, cannot be taken to mean that when God promised a family to Abraham it would *exclude* physical Jews. Rather, Jews, as well as everybody else, had to discover in practice that they were 'in the flesh', children of Adam in need of salvation by grace. All must come by the way of death and resurrection. And the way by which Jews are to be brought back in (v.31) is 'by your mercy',[42] in other words, by the process of jealous observation and emulation already described. This process takes place 'now'.[43] Paul is envisaging a steady flow of Jews into the church, by grace through faith. God wanted a family from all nations, saved without favouritism and hence by grace alone. Only such a family, of Jews and Gentiles, together, would fulfil all the aspects of the promises made to Abraham (compare Romans 4). This, the process of vv.28–32, is how he has achieved it. It would be quite intolerable to imagine a church at any period which was simply a gentile phenomenon, just as it would ultimately impugn the covenant justice of God if his family consisted only of Jews.

What, then, of 11.25–7? Does it actually intrude into this sequence of thought with a different idea, a large-scale, last-minute salvation of Jews with, perhaps, no suggestion of Christian faith? The answer is emphatically no.

11.25a clearly belongs closely with what has gone before: gentile Christians are not to vaunt themselves over Jews. The reason is given in the 'mystery', which is not a new revelation suddenly made to Paul (and contradicting not only the rest of the immediate context but the rest of Paul's theology). The 'mystery' consists of this: that, instead of immediately judging the people that rejected his Son, God has allowed a period of hardening, within which his salvation will spread to the ends of the earth, but at the end of which there will be judgment (this is always the point of 'hardening' within the apocalyptic context).[44] During this period of time, the Gentiles are to come in to the people of God: and *that is how* God is saving 'all Israel'. Despite repeated assertions to the contrary, the meaning of οὕτως is not 'then' but 'thus', 'in this manner'.[45] Paul's meaning is not a temporal

---

[42]Taking τῷ ὑμετέρῳ ἐλέει with what follows, rather than with what precedes.

[43]The reading νῦν in אBD, etc., is (in my view) certainly to be preferred.

[44]There is therefore a close link, despite what is often thought, between this passage and 1 Thess. 2.14–16.

[45]Compare Gal. 6.2: 'and in this way'. See Liddell and Scott, Arndt and Gingrich, s.v. The latter take this reference to be an example of οὕτως...καθώς. This could be so, but since the καθώς in 11.26 is part of the regular formula καθὼς γέγραπται it is more likely that the two do

sequence—first the Gentiles, *then* the Jews. Rather, it is the interpretation of a particular process *as* the salvation of 'all Israel'. And in this context 'all Israel' cannot possibly mean 'all Jews'. It is impermissible to argue that 'Israel' cannot change its referent within the space of two verses, so that 'Israel' in v.25 must mean the same as 'Israel' in v.26: Paul actually began the whole section (9.6) with just such a programmatic distinction of two 'Israels', and throughout the letter (e.g. 2.25–9) as well as elsewhere (e.g. Philippians 3.2–11) he has systematically transferred the privileges and attributes of 'Israel' to the Messiah and his people. It is therefore greatly preferable to take 'all Israel' in v.26 as a typically Pauline polemical redefinition, as in Galatians 6.16 (though that is of course also controversial), and in line also with Philippians 3.2 ff., where the church is described as 'the circumcision'. What Paul is saying is this. God's method of saving 'all Israel' is to harden ethnic Israel (cp. 9.14 ff.), i.e., not to judge her at once, so as to create a period of time during which the gentile mission could be undertaken, *during the course of which* it remains God's will that the present 'remnant' of believing Jews might be enlarged by the process of 'jealousy', and consequent faith, described above. This whole process is God's way of saving his whole people: that is the meaning of καὶ οὕτως πᾶς Ἰσραὴλ σωθήσεται.

What then is predicted in the composite scriptural quotation in 26b–27? It has been customary to see this as a prediction of the Parousia, the event at which (so it is supposed) the great ingathering of Jews will suddenly take place. But the text itself not only does not bear this out. It actually points explicitly in a very different direction.

The quotations used by Paul here come from Isaiah 2.3, 27.9, 59.20 f. and Jeremiah 31.34. All have to do with God's action the other side of judgment. Paul has combined Isaiah 59.20 f. with Isaiah 2.3 (and/or Micah 4.2) to create the new prediction that the redeemer (not the Torah) will come out from (not 'on behalf of') Zion. These are all passages which speak of the final great renewal of covenant, the overcoming of exile, and the blessing which will then flow to the nations as a result of the vindication of Israel. Within the Old Testament, this blessing could be thought of in terms of Torah going out to the nations (e.g. Micah 4.2 f.); for Paul, what the Torah could not do is now done in Christ and the Spirit. Hence the replacement of Torah's outgoing by that of the Redeemer. We are here very close to 9.30—10.13, and this increases the probability that what Paul is here referring to is not the Parousia but the gentile mission; v.26b is *explaining* v.26a, and is doing so with reference to covenantal promises of gentile

---

not belong together. Sanders 1991, 123 rightly acknowledges the meaning 'thus', but still draws (to my mind) the wrong conclusion.

inclusion in the blessings of the people of God. The reference to Jeremiah 31 invokes that which has arguably been under Paul's discussions in so much of Romans—the new covenant. This new covenant, which God makes with his people the other side of exile and death, is the real reaffirmation of the Abrahamic promises, and is therefore the final vindication of the righteousness of God. And the new covenant is emphatically not a covenant in which 'national righteousness' (which, as Paul has already demonstrated, was not envisaged even in the initial promises to Abraham) is suddenly affirmed. It is the covenant in which sin is finally dealt with. This was the purpose of the covenant all along: now at last, as in Jeremiah 31.34, it is realized. Isaiah 27.9, whose context is full of allusions to similar sequences of thought, not to mention to the olive tree allegory of 11.17 ff., is not about the vindication of ethnic Israel as she stands but about forgiveness of sins the other side of cataclysmic judgment on the temple. And the ὅταν ἀφέλωμαι in 11.27b enables Paul to include the idea of a recurring action. 'Whenever' God takes away their sins, i.e. whenever Jews come to believe in Christ and so enter the family of God, in that moment the promises God made long ago to the patriarchs are being reaffirmed. The Roman Gentile Christians must not stand in the way of this fulfillment, for in it there is at stake nothing other than the covenant faithfulness and justice of the one God. It is that which is celebrated in the paean of praise which concludes the chapter (11.33–6).

There is, therefore, no justification for taking Romans 11, as a whole or in its parts, as a prediction of a large-scale, last-minute salvation of Jews. With that, the case for finding fundamental contradiction within Romans 9–11 falls to the ground. These chapters, taken together, bring to their proper climax the series of themes which Paul has been developing throughout the letter: the righteousness of God, revealed in Jesus the Messiah, not in Torah (though the Torah bears witness to this revelation), and the discovery of the true definition of the people of God within the paradoxical promises to Abraham and their working out in judgment and mercy, in cross and resurrection. And these themes, in reaching this sustained climax, result in the clear message to the Roman church: here, and nowhere else, is the basis of the mission of the church, the mission in which Paul is engaged and for which he now enlists their support. Paul could see that, in Rome, the temptation would always be for a largely gentile church to downplay or forget its Jewish roots. But if the church heeds his argument, such a possibility will never be realized. The way is now clear for chs. 12–16, in which—though there is no space here to explore this further—Paul applies the whole theology of Romans 1–11 to the church in itself. The spotlight falls particularly on the unity and mission of the church, and this becomes most clear in 14.1—15.13, arguably the final main emphatic thrust of the letter.

(viii) Hermeneutics and Theology

How can Romans 9–11 have anything to say to the church or world today?[46] This is of course a subset of the larger question, as to how the Bible as a whole, or at least the New Testament, can 'speak'—whatever that might mean—to church and world.[47] It is clear that with Romans we are dealing with a specific situation addressed by Paul, and this must have an initial effect of restraining the urge to absolutize everything he says, to make it the word for all time. It is a different word (though, I suggest, happily compatible) to that spoken in Galatians, where the issue is not how to avoid the risk of antiJudaism but how to avoid the risk of philoJudaism. Hermeneutics cannot be attempted in the abstract at this point, but must be earthed in the historical particularity and peculiarity of the original context.

That said, the historical context of Romans is (I believe) that it is written in order to further the mission of the church in a new area, and to that end it also seeks to further the unity of the church that will undertake and/or support that mission; and that it claims, at least by implication, to carry apostolic authority. From that point of view, it is to be expected that the church in subsequent generations will look for significant continuities between Paul's agenda and its own, and will try to show how the tasks to which it believes itself called can be plotted on a map which is, effectively, the extension of that which we find in Romans.

In such a quest the unity of the church remains high on the list of priorities. It is a measure of how far the church has travelled from Paul's vision that Romans has often been read as a book about individual salvation rather than as a treatise on the nature of the people of God.[48] It is not surprising that, in such a misreading, highly significant passages (chs. 4, 5.12–21, 9–11) have been effectively marginalized or reduced to the status of 'examples' or 'proofs from scripture'—often with the patronizing implication that they are not very *good* examples, or not very *persuasive* 'proofs'. And when Paul speaks of the unity of the church he means specifically a unity which crosses racial barriers. This has immediate implications for the

---

[46]I have forsworn hermeneutical and theological reflections so far in this book. But (a) I showed earlier how such issues have influenced the study of Rom. 9–11, and it may be only fair to complete the picture with my own view—which has actually changed, over the last twenty years, chiefly because of the demands of the exegesis of this passage; and (b) there may be some benefit—lest it be thought that I am ignoring the calls of scholars like Käsemann and Stuhlmacher that our exegesis be in the service of the church—in showing something at least of the wrestling that goes on at the interface between historical exegesis and would-be Christian proclamation.

[47]On this subject see my paper 'How can the Bible be Authoritative?', to be published in *Vox Evangelica*, April 1991.

[48] See Kaylor 1988. This book deserves more interaction among scholars than it has yet received.

mission which Paul envisages. The gospel is 'to the Jew first and also to the Greek'. I submit that if all we had to go on were the text of Romans, no-one would have dreamt for a moment that Paul was not still engaged in a mission which, though its geographical sphere was of course the gentile world, habitually embraced Jews as well as Gentiles, much on the pattern of Acts.

This is probably the most controversial point of application in the modern world. Shrill voices from all sides denounce Christian 'missions' to Jews, whether the strident 'Jews for Jesus' movements or the more restrained and traditional mission movements from within mainline denominations. Many Christians have come to agree with most Jews that, since the Holocaust, the church has no right to engage in evangelism towards Jews, since to say that Jesus is the true Messiah for Jews as well as for Gentiles is to be implicitly antisemitic or at least antiJudaic, hinting that Judaism is somehow incomplete. Within scholarly circles, this concern has emerged particularly as the 'two-covenant' theory, which suggests that God has on the one hand maintained his covenant with ethnic Israel intact, and on the other hand has inaugurated the Christian 'covenant' as his regular way of saving Gentiles. In this scheme, Paul is sometimes cast as the hero who anticipated two-covenant theology, sometimes as the villain against whom it makes its vital point.

We must note by way of introduction to this question that it is clearly not the issue Paul is addressing in Romans. We cannot read an answer to the modern post-holocaust discussions straight off the pages of this (or any other) letter. And we must of course recognize fully that there can be no complacency about the past. It was not merely neo-paganism, but Christian complicity with neo-paganism, that sent millions of Jews to their deaths in our own century. Christian arrogance must be renounced entirely.

But, ironically, it is against Christian arrogance—specifically, gentile Christian arrogance—that Romans 9–11 is explicitly directed. Paul is writing, with all the weight of eleven chapters of theology behind him, in order to say that 'gentile Christians' have not 'replaced' Jews as the true people of God. The church has not become an exclusively gentile possession. Precisely because the gospel stands athwart all ethnic claims, the church cannot erect a new racial boundary. The irony of this is that the late twentieth century, in order to avoid anti-semitism, has advocated a position (the non-evangelization of Jews) *which Paul regards precisely as anti-semitic.*[49] The two-covenant position says precisely what Paul here forbids the church to say, namely that Christianity is for non-Jews. To this extent, it actually agrees in form with the German Christian theology of the 1930s—while of course disagreeing in substance, because it denies that Christianity is the only way of salvation.

[49]See the wise words of Prof. C.F.D. Moule in a letter to *Expository Times* 102, 1991, p. 115.

But what does 'salvation' mean in this context? It is my impression that in these discussions it is usually left vague. As soon as we try to make it more precise, however, we will run into difficulties. As is often pointed out, the 'Christian' and the 'Jewish' doctrines of salvation are (to say the least) rather different.[50] Will we then say, if we follow the two-covenant model, that 'Christian' salvation is what Jews will finally experience? Probably not (that looks again like covert imperialism); but, if not, then what? It appears that the two-covenant doctrine is still in fact clinging to a scheme of religion based on race, which is exactly what Paul is renouncing and opposing with his whole theology of the new humanity in Christ. With the two-covenant model the Powers are not challenged, but merely regrouped.

This does not mean, of course, that in Paul's theology the Jews are any worse off than Gentiles. That could only be imagined within a scheme that saw Gentiles as belonging automatically to the new people of God. This is not at all Paul's position. When a Gentile becomes a Christian, he or she has to renounce his or her ancestral and tribal gods (this, of course, is seldom recognized, let alone acted on, in the Western world today, but it is Paul's view for all that). All must come, and can only come, by the painful and costly route of death and resurrection, by a faith in the one God which demands the abandonment of idols. It is thus within Paul's theology itself, not through some modern mutation of it, that genuine multi-racial religion is to be found. Saying 'all roads lead to God' has of course been the trend in the West since (at least) the eighteenth century, but this facile view, in which the recognition and critique of idolatry becomes very difficult, is not Paul's. In practice, the god to whom all roads lead is not Paul's god, but that of eighteenth-century Deism. Suggesting that people who do not profess Christianity may be 'anonymous Christians' may itself be a form of imperialism, but in avoiding it we should beware of claiming New Testament support for a view that makes all people, Christians included, anonymous Deists.[51]

What is at stake in this debate is not the privileged position of this or that race or religion. It is the nature of monotheism itself. The two-covenant model claims the high ground of monotheism: all roads lead to the one god.[52] But this is not the God of the Old Testament, who (in order to rescue his world) made an exclusive, binding and highly paradoxical covenant with Israel, nor the God of the New, who revealed himself fully and finally in the sending, 'giving up' and raising of Jesus Christ and in the sending of the

---

[50]See, e.g., Loewe 1981.

[51]See now the exposition of a view like this in Hick 1988, 233–246.

[52] Or is it only two roads that lead there? Why only two? Is the two-covenant idea not inherently unstable, offering simply a half-way house on the road to a fully-blown relativism? That would scarcely commend itself to mainline Judaism, either.

Spirit. It is, as I have just suggested, a Deist god—as we would expect from what is basically a modern version of an eighteenth-century view; and, like other versions of Deism, this theology is supplemented by a fideism in which 'my religious experience' becomes the sole criterion of truth (since the Deist god is too remote to be accessible). Over against this stands Paul's argument throughout Romans: the one true God has revealed his paradoxical righteousness, his strange covenant faithfulness and justice, in Jesus. This revelation reaches its fullest exposition in Romans 9–11; and it appears that the two-covenant theory is bound not only to misunderstand this climactic section but, in support of this, to misunderstand Romans 1–8 as well. Small wonder if, as a result, it is unable to sustain the bracing agenda of chs. 12–16.

Paul is thus offering a doctrine of God, and of the people of God, which is built firmly on Christ and the Spirit, and in which the people of God are known, not by race or moral behaviour, but by Spirit-inspired faith in the God revealed in Jesus. Here is the doctrine of justification, as it appears in Romans 9–11: Christian faith alone is the index of membership (10.4 ff., 11.23).[53] Here, too, is the potential resolution of the debate which still perplexes Pauline scholars anxious to systematize Paul within this or that framework. 'Salvation history' and 'apocalyptic', which are in this context very much twentieth-century words, both find their referents in Paul's thought at the same point, namely, the belief that God has acted within history to bring the old age to an end and inaugurate the new. Pauline monotheism—which means creational and covenantal monotheism, not the Deism of the eighteenth century or the pantheism of neo-paganism—remains the basis of his whole theology. It is his argument in Romans that this monotheism is vindicated in the cross and resurrection and the sending of the Spirit, and that it must (if his authority is to be claimed) be implemented in the mission and unity of the church.

We may therefore be in a position to point towards further and wider applications of Romans 9–11 in the modern world. We have explored thus far the contemporary meaning of Paul's actual argument, and have reaffirmed his call that a humble, paradoxical mission of Christians to Jews is still both mandatory and appropriate. But, once this point is grasped, we realize that in the modern world it is not only the failure of Israel to believe that calls the righteousness of God into question. The problem of Romans 9–11 is but the sharp edge of the problem of evil as a whole. This is obviously not the place to begin an exposition of this problem, let alone to offer a solution to it. But it seems to me that reflection on, and extrapolation from, Romans 9–11 might well be a good place to start such a task. At its

---

[53] This is seen quite clearly by Sanders 1978, in opposition to the two-covenant theory of Stendahl. Sanders then makes the large hermeneutical leap to a more characteristically C20 position: if Paul were alive today he would by now have changed his mind.

centre would be the cross; and at its leading edge would be the passionate concern of the church, led by the Spirit, that the loving justice of the one creator God, now revealed in the gospel, must be made known in the world. God's dealing with the failure of his own people to see his justice and respond appropriately would thus become the model for our understanding of how he wishes to deal with the failure of humankind as a whole to do the same. Käsemann's insight—that Israel is paradigmatic for humankind in general—may yet have something to teach us, even if not exactly in the way he imagined.

And when the church really turns to face this task, as it must if it is to be true to its vocation, it will find (as Paul saw in 2 Corinthians particularly) that its role is Christ-shaped: to bear the pain and shame of the world in its own body, that the world may be healed. And with this we realize (in case it were not already apparent) that there is no room in this hermeneutic for a Christian or ecclesial triumphalism, which is precisely what Paul is opposing in Romans 11. The church is called to do and be for the world what the Messiah was and did for Israel. All that has been said so far must therefore call into question a good deal that is done in and by the church in pursuit of its own security and self-importance. The church must find out the pain of the world, and must share it and bear it.

When that task is done, then Paul's theology suggests that what we call 'natural evil' will also, finally, be undone. God's covenant purpose was to choose a people in and through whom the world would be healed. That purpose, reaching its climax in the Messiah, is now to be worked out through his people. The creation itself will be set free from its bondage to decay and come to share the liberty of the glory of the children of God; and in the meantime the Church is to share the groaning of the world in the faith that her own groanings are in turn shared by the Spirit. The Spirit thus accomplishes within the church what, *mutatis mutandis*, the Torah accomplished within Israel. Just as the sin and death of the world were concentrated, by means of Torah, on Israel (see ch. 10 above), so now the pain and grief of the world is to be concentrated, by means of the Spirit, on the Χριστός, the family of the Messiah, so that it may be healed (Romans 8.18–30). This is the very antithesis of all Christian triumphalism or imperialism.

Paul thus offers in Romans in general, and in 9–11 in particular, not only a theology of Israel and her paradoxical fate and future, but also a theology of and for the world in its pain and longing for justice, and of and for the church in her vocation to share that pain and to work for that justice. It is a theology which, based on a clear view of the transcendent God now made known in and through Jesus of Nazareth and the Spirit, calls and drives the church towards the twin goals of mission and unity, that God may be all in all:

> And though the last lights off the black West went,
> Oh, morning, at the brown brink eastward, springs—
> Because the Holy Ghost over the bent
> World broods with warm breast and with ah! bright wings.[54]

[54]G.M. Hopkins, 'God's Grandeur'.

Chapter Fourteen

THE NATURE OF PAULINE THEOLOGY

(i) Introduction

I have argued in this book that Paul's christology can be understood in terms partly of an 'incorporative' idea of Messiahship and partly in terms of a redefinition of monotheism itself. That is, Paul's view of Jesus of Nazareth is directly, and apparently causally, linked to his major redefinition of the twin Jewish doctrines, election and monotheism. I have argued, further, that his view of the Jewish law was nuanced and carefully balanced, correlating closely with this redefinition of monotheism and election. It forms part of his complex critique of Israel, which is itself carefully balanced and nuanced. Underneath all this is the argument, which I have advanced at various stages, that Paul's whole view of Christ and the law can be understood in terms of the *story* of God and the people of God—a story which cannot be reduced to a single formula or proposition, but which when viewed whole can be seen to have the proper integration and coherence that a story ought to have. Christ and the law in Paul's theology form two closely related segments of the story of the covenant, and of how, in Paul's view, it reached its climax.

It would take a longer and more wide-ranging book than this to set these arguments in their larger context and show all the interconnections, exegetical, historical and theological, that remain to be explored.[1] But there are several provisional conclusions which can be drawn, if only by way of pointing tentatively and tendentiously towards work which remains to be completed.

(ii) Paul's Questions and Answers

I stressed in the opening chapter that it is vital to follow Paul's actual questions and answers, and not to presume that he was asking or answering the same questions that subsequent interpreters have brought to him. We are now in a position to see how the debate has continued to be bedevilled by this problem, even when new views of Paul have come to birth. Sanders and Räisänen dismissed the 'Lutheran' picture of Paul as historically and

---

[1] I have discussed the shape of Paul's theology briefly in the second part of Wright 1991, and intend to expand these suggestions elsewhere.

theologically inadequate. I have added exegetical reasons for drawing the same conclusion, without sharing their overall position. But, ironically, both writers still persist in foisting onto Paul questions that come from the Lutheran debate: was Paul for or against the Torah? Is it abolished or not? The charge of inconsistency which Räisänen in particular levels at Paul only works, logically, within the rather rigid dogmatic framework against which Räisänen himself is reacting (over-reacting, some might say).

But what questions, then, *was* Paul addressing? And where are they located on the map of his overall worldview? I think it is clear that Paul holds an overall worldview which is recognizably Jewish, and which has been recognizably Christianized from top to bottom. It concerns not only 'theoretical' but also 'practical' issues. (Another irony in modern Pauline scholarship is the post-enlightenment 'either-or' of theory and practice, of theological and pragmatic modes of thought and action, foisted frequently on to Paul in the name of historical scholarship.) It has to do with the Creator God, with his world, with his people, with his purposes for his world and his people, with his dramatic action in history in bringing those purposes to completion, and so on. The questions Paul asks arise within this worldview, not within that of the Fathers, the mediaevals, the reformers, or post-enlightenment historical scholarship. They are, *mutatis mutandis*, the questions that Paul's Jewish contemporaries were asking as well: how is God fulfilling the covenant? What is happening to Israel? How is evil being defeated? Why has God apparently done the opposite to what one would have expected? And, granted Paul's belief about Jesus and the Spirit as the inauguration of the renewed covenant, further questions were bound to arise, concerning the constitution and maintenance of the new covenant community itself: should Christians keep Torah, and why? What happens when different races come together in the people of God? What has happened to the Jewish dream of the ingathering of the nations? What happens when Christians sin? And so on.

Paul is thus driven to ask and answer (what we call) 'situational' and 'theological' questions at the same time, in the same breath, with the same words. I suggest—indeed, at this stage of a book like this I insist—that he would not have understood the difference between those two categories, would (perhaps) have sympathized with Beker's attempt to do justice to him by the categories of 'coherence' and 'consistency' but would have felt frustrated that his twentieth-century interpreters were unable finally to transcend the either-or imposed within modernism. When we read a letter like Galatians it simply makes no sense to split the contingent argument from the coherent centre of Paul's thought. The questions, should Christians get circumcised, and should Jewish and Gentile Christians eat at the same table, are thoroughly 'contingent' *and* thoroughly 'theological', and we cannot and must not reduce either to terms of the other. We must renounce on the one hand the reductionism that makes everything a matter of speculative theology, and sees the particularities of Paul's mission as merely the chance occasion for the real work of serious theological reflection which could be transplanted smoothly to different times and places; and on the other hand the reductionism that refuses to recognize a theological argument when (as in Galatians) it jumps up and bites the reader on the nose, insisting instead on everything in terms of sociological or cultural forces or agendas. *We* may believe, if we wish, that one or other reductionism is appropriate within the modern world and/or church. As historians, we must insist that Paul would not have split the world in two in that fashion.

Once we recognize this, we are free to do *both* historical exegesis *and* serious constructive 'Pauline Theology'. To take another example from this book, the particular situation of 2 Corinthians, and the ironic polemic of ch. 3 in particular, should not blind us to the fact that there Paul is arguing from the same basic theological premises as in both Galatians and Romans. We, hedged about with the worldview of post-modernism, have a difficult time explaining even within the guild of biblical scholarship how it is that a worldview can lie behind, or above, or beneath the things that are actually said on any one particular occasion. Another irony, this time self-referring.

So where was Paul's starting-point, and how did he move from that to his fully-blown theological position? Everything in this book points to a basically simple answer. Paul was a Pharisee who believed that Jesus of Nazareth, who had been crucified as a messianic pretender, had been vindicated by Israel's covenant God in being raised from the dead. He therefore rethought and reimplemented Jewish theology and the Jewish agenda in the light of this new belief, and (he would quickly have added) in the power of the Spirit of the creator God, made known as the Spirit of Jesus and let loose through the new covenant community into the world. So far, so good. But Paul did not need to pretend to argue from these premises when addressing this or that issue in this or that church. Nor does his 'failure' to follow this sequence of thought when discussing (say) the law in Galatians 3 mean that he is playing fast and loose, arguing upside down, or rationalizing from an *a priori*. His over-arching (or underlying) scheme of thought is large and subtle enough to provide him with many varied starting-points depending on the argument to be advanced and the audience to be addressed.

In particular, Paul did not move from 'plight to solution' or from 'solution to plight'. The antithesis between the views of Bultmann and Sanders is a false one.[2] Paul, like all first-century Jews, had a 'plight', though it is not to be identified with that of the puzzled existentialist, or for that matter that of

[2]See Sanders 1977, 474–511; 1991, 41; and Thielman 1989 *passim*.

the conscience-stricken Protestant. The 'plight' consisted of the sorry state of Israel, interpreted as a problem about the covenant faithfulness and justice of the creator God who had called her to be his chosen people. To the extent that this sorry state included the present sinfulness of Jews as individuals, the normal 'Lutheran' reading can be contained within this analysis. To the extent that many of Paul's contemporaries (not, I think, Paul himself) were aware of a crippling uncertainty as to what to believe and do, as to where their future might lie, the normal 'existentialist' reading can also find a home here. But neither will do as a total or complete account. Nothing less than the framework of covenant theology will do justice to the plight as perceived by Paul. It was real, indubitable, a fact of first-century life. As long as Herod or Pilate ruled over her, Israel was still under the curse of 'exile'. This was in no way a retrojection, imagined out of thin air as the reflex of a new theological belief or religious experience.

Equally, the 'solution' Paul believed he had received on the road to Damascus challenged the normal Jewish analysis and understanding of this plight at its root. If the creator had done for Jesus what he was supposed to be doing for Israel, then the solution to Israel's plight had arrived, but it was not in the form that Israel had expected. Paul's theology takes its particular characteristic from this: that he found himself compelled to understand Jesus' death and resurrection *as* the great event for which he had been longing—and thereby to relativize and redraw the categories, theological and practical, in which that great event could be understood. He moved, in short, to a fresh analysis of the plight:

Plight (1) ——————▶ Solution ——————▶ Plight (2)

And in this fresh analysis was contained, as a reflex of the 'solution' but, more radically, as a deepening of the first 'plight' itself, the critique of Israel and the Torah which Saul the Pharisee had not been able to see. Here, too, we must be careful. Near the heart of the critique we find the accusation that Israel is sinful, but the critique cannot be reduced to terms of 'human sin, with Israel as a special example'. Near the heart of the critique we find the analysis of Israel as double-minded, but the critique cannot be reduced to terms of existentialist muddle with Jews happening to play the leading role in the Sartrean drama. At the very heart of the critique we find the rebellion of Israel against the covenant purposes of God, *seen as* the acting out by Israel of the primeval sin of Adam, coming to its full flowering in 'national righteousness', the meta-sin against which the gospel of the cross struck with its scandalous force, and resulting in Israel's rejection of that gospel. And this rebellion, seen in these ways, was itself explained by Paul not simply as the greatest of all tragedies, but as the necessary if paradoxical outworking of God's plan, to save the world by focussing its problems, through the Torah, first on to Israel and then on to her Messiah. And Paul was careful to demonstrate that this whole critique and analysis was not merely a *novum*, a Christian invention. It was based on Torah, Prophets, and Psalms, read (he would have said) with eyes now at last unveiled.

(iii) Paul as a Theologian

Paul's qualification to be called a 'theologian' is not, therefore, that he wrote 'systematic theology'. Obviously he did not. His qualification lies in the way he went about obeying his vocation. His sense of purpose, call and mission demand to be understood in terms of a worldview which can only be called 'theological': the belief-structure which informed and directed his life and work, and through which he perceived the world, was itself thoroughly theological. I do not mean simply that it contained God, the World, and other 'theological' counters—lots of people have God and the World in their worldview without thereby being theologians. I mean that he thought through this worldview in such a way as to be in direct touch with the springs of his own activities. He had reflected on, and come to fresh conclusions about, God, God's people, the nations, and the whole created order, and he made those conclusions central to his actual life and work.

Turning to specifics, he was above all a theologian conscious of living at a particular moment within the purposes of the creator. Now, he said, is the day of salvation: he took the risk (as the Teacher of Righteousness had done) of identifying the present time as the crucial moment in the story of the covenant. The promised end of exile had arrived, but in a mysterious and unexpected fashion. Everything else followed from this. The renewed people of God *was* the new temple (failure to appreciate the huge significance of the temple within first-century Judaism has led to a gross downplaying of the 'temple' theme within Pauline ecclesiology and for that matter soteriology). The word of the Lord *was* now going out to the Gentiles. All this and more is to say: Israel's destiny is now fulfilled. And in the centre of this picture we find the corporate christology which we saw to be utterly characteristic of Paul; not just that he picks up one Jewish theme among many, that of the king who sums up his people in himself, but that he sees Israel's destiny, that of suffering at the hands of the pagans and then being vindicated by the creator, fulfilled precisely in this one man.

So, in the course of the gentile mission which Paul believed (as a matter of theology) must logically follow the climax of the covenant, and which he believed moreover (as a matter of vocation) must be undertaken by himself, Paul writes in order to call into being, and sustain in being, communities composed of men, women and children of every race and every class of society, believing that in so doing he is acting midwife (or even mother, as in Galatians 4.19) to the renewed covenant people of God, which can know no boundaries because it is precisely the renewed human race. These communities must never forget their basic continuity with the people of God from Abraham onwards; that way lies neo-paganism, the transformation of a fulfilled Judaism into a Hellenistic cult. It is astonishing, considering the exegetical *tours de force* that are required, how many Christian writers have claimed (as historians) that this is the way Paul himself went, and have congratulated him (as theologians or preachers) for doing so. Equally, these communities must never lapse into thinking of themselves as merely a sub-set of racial or geographical Judaism. If they are to be the renewed, and renewing, human race they cannot allow this muzzling of the essentially new message. It is perhaps less astonishing, in view of events this century, how many Christian writers have claimed Paul as an advocate of continuing Jewish privilege, and have congratulated him for it. The exegetical *tours de force* are required just as much here too.

Paul as theologian, then, is Paul drawing from the well of his thought-out worldview and belief-structure that which is needed to persuade this or that church to maintain and further its own vocation, against the pressures from one side or another. He is no less a theologian for being a tactician, a pragmatist, a rhetorician *malgré soi* ('I am no orator, as Brutus is'). Theology is what makes him all of these, and what makes all of these serve his vocation.

(iv) Paul as a Biblical Theologian

In particular, Paul is a *biblical* theologian, self-consciously so. There is no room at this stage of the present book to examine his use of the Jewish scriptures as fully as the subject deserves.[3] But the subject-matter of the present volume suggests a set of particular angles on this question, and it will be worth while at least to suggest ways of proceeding.

I have argued in the second section of this book that Paul's view of the Torah encompassed a variety of different emphases held together within a story-line which enables us to see how they could be thought compatible. But Torah is not something utterly distinct from the Jewish scriptures which Paul never tired of quoting, discussing, referring to both directly and indirectly.

[3]See Hays 1989 for a recent provocative discussion and up-to-date bibliography.

Does Paul then *use* the Jewish scriptures in a way which coheres with what he *says* about them? This is a question of some interest, both theoretical and practical—the latter in that it directly affects exegesis.

The nuanced view of Torah for which I have been arguing indicates that this question will not be a simple one. I propose to come at it obliquely in the first instance, by discussing the recent proposal of Richard Hays in his exciting book *Echoes of Scripture in the Letters of Paul* (1989). Paul, according to Hays, finds that scripture prefigures, metaphorically, the church of his own day: by his constant allusions to scripture, Paul creates a picture of a community in continuity with the Old Testament People of God, fulfilling God's basic intention for this people. This, Hays argues, is more central to Paul than the christological or christocentric hermeneutic which has often been found in the letters.

I find this basically convincing. We have seen time and again in this book that Paul does indeed draw on scripture to create a picture of the people of God which he then proceeds to apply to the church of his own day. We need only think of the single seed promised to Abraham (my argument in ch. 8 is another indication of an ecclesiocentric hermeneutic in Paul where exegetes have traditionally seen a christocentric one) or the glory on Moses' face (where Moses, as we saw in ch. 9, prefigures the position of the whole church). And the whole emphasis on the corporate Messiah points in the same direction, as well as suggesting a reason why exegetes who did not notice the nature of Paul's incorporative language settled for christological rather than ecclesiological interpretations.

But I still find Hays' picture incomplete, and leaving Paul looking more arbitrary in his handling of the Jewish Bible than I think exegesis actually suggests. On the basis of almost all of the chapters above, I suggest that Paul saw scripture as story and as prophecy, *not* in the abstract sense of mere typological prefigurement between one event and another, according to which in principle the two events could stand in any chronological relation to each other, but in the sense of a very specific story functioning in a very specific way.[4] For Paul, the story was always moving towards a climax; it contained within it, at specific and non-arbitrary moments, advance warnings and promises about that climax; it contained within it, again not at arbitrary moments, prefigurements of that climax (the story of Isaac, of the Exodus, and so forth); and, most importantly, it was a story whose climax, Paul believed, *had now arrived*. The resurrection of Jesus was, for Paul, the sure and certain sign, unmistakable if unexpected, that Israel's consolation had been given to her, that the Age to Come had therefore arrived, and at the

---

[4]Hays suggests to me, in conversation, that 'typology' allows for the distance between the events to remain, whereas allegory in principle collapses them. This may be so; but I still find his own reading of Paul in danger of such a collapsing of distance. See below.

same time the sure and certain sign that Israel—and he, Paul, in particular!—had up until that point been looking in the wrong direction.

He therefore read the Jewish scriptures as the covenant book whose final key had now been supplied. From this point of view there is a formal, though not a substantial, parallel between Paul's exegesis and that of Qumran. Both believed that the Jewish scriptures had been written to point forward, in story and prophecy, to a great day of Israel's redemption that lay in the future. Both believed that that day had in principle arrived, secretly and unexpectedly, unrecognized by the majority of Israel. Both therefore re-read scripture in the light of this belief. But, whereas Qumran worked through books of prophecies and discovered detailed predictions about individual events in the life (say) of the Teacher of Righteousness, Paul characteristically took passages from Israel's *story*, passages in which the covenant was inaugurated, enacted, discussed in detail—and argued that the promises all along, historically considered, envisaged the chain of events that was now taking place in the death and resurrection of Jesus, the sending of the Spirit, the welcome of Gentiles into the people of God. His arguments hinge on the fact of the meanings not being hidden, not being like the book of Habakkuk sealed up for future generations to discover.[5] He goes back to Genesis 15, or Deuteronomy 30, to argue that what has come to pass actually is what God promised to Abraham, and to appeal to that in the public domain and not by means of an esoteric secret which other contemporary Jews could not share. He does not, then, collapse the distance between Abraham, Moses, Isaiah and himself.[6] He claims to offer a historical reading in which the 'prefigurements' are part of the story that has now come to its climax.

Is Paul's use of scripture then consistent with his theologically-argued view of Torah? We would need a book at least as long as the present one to address this question properly, but a preliminary answer can be given. His view of Torah, we have seen, is that it was God's law, holy and good; that it could not give the life it promised; that therefore, if absolutized, it became a demonic gaoler; that precisely in its negative mode it remained the agent of the divine saving purpose, drawing sin on to Israel in order to deal with it in the Messiah; that what it itself could not do God had done by Christ and the Spirit, so that Torah itself was both reaffirmed and relativized, and all within the unifying framework of the covenant story. We can see at once that there are important parallels between this multi-faceted view of Torah and Paul's multi-faceted use of scripture. He treats it as authoritative, and yet as relativized in Christ and the Spirit. He appeals to its promises and warnings while categorically setting aside the features of it which marked Israel out

[5]Cf. 1QpHab 7.1 ff. (Vermes 1987, 286).
[6]Against Hays 177.

from other nations.[7] But this is not simply playing fast and loose with a sacred text. We are here up against the same complex but coherent ambiguity that we met in looking at Paul's view of Torah itself, and behind that of Israel. From Paul's perspective, the Torah was *intended* as a temporary measure; Israel according to the flesh was *intended* as the advance guard of the eschatological people of God, to be relativized when that people finally came into being; and it should therefore not be surprising to find him using Scripture in a way which implies that it is *intended* as the paradoxical pre-announcement of the climax of the covenant. His re-reading of texts like Deuteronomy 30 (Romans 10) or Isaiah 59 and Micah 4 (Romans 11) is not arbitrary, but reflects his underlying theological belief, that what God had said he would do for Israel he had done for Jesus. Jesus therefore properly (from Paul's point of view) takes on the role of Torah, relativizing Torah itself in the process by setting aside the temporary dispensations of land, circumcision, and food laws, whose tasks are now complete. Though we have no space to produce the full argument that is really needed, I suggest that Paul's use of scripture is comprehensible and coherent—within the covenant story as he understood it.

(v) Conclusion

I have argued that christology is, for Paul, a means of redefining the people of God, and also a means of redefining God himself. Correlated exactly with this double redefinition is his rethinking of Torah. For Jews of his day (and many other days), Torah was at one and the same time the charter of the people of God and the full and final revelation of God himself. If, then, Jesus has taken on this double role, it is no surprise to find him taking on precisely the role of Torah in Paul's understanding of the plan of the one God. It is as though the Torah was made in order that, one day, the anointed representative of God's people should come to do and be what Torah apparently was and did, only this time to do it successfully and to be it fully. As we saw particularly in ch. 10, it is important to stress that Torah is thereby reaffirmed, however paradoxically. As both God and the people of God are redefined, so the reaffirmation of Torah takes on the form of radical redefinition. No longer can the Torah keep the people of God as a single ethnic or geographical unit, with all the taboos that maintain such a system. It must now become—and, in the plan of God, has now become—the new charter for the renewed people.

This means, of course, that there is a large gap in the argument of the present book, inevitable in a study of this sort in which we have taken

[7]The best example of this is the highly ironic 1 Cor. 7.19.

exegetical soundings rather than expounding a subject systematically. Christ, for Paul, does not fulfil the role of Torah alone. It is always Christ and the Spirit together who redefine the people of God; it is frequently Christ and the Spirit together who redefine God himself. We have said little about the Spirit, but the picture will not be complete until this gap is made good. Equally, we have in much of this book been circling round the subject of justification: if Christ and the Spirit redefine the people of God, it is clear that the mark of that redefinition is not the possession or keeping of Torah, but the faith which is evoked by the work of the Spirit and which is defined specifically as πίστις Ἰησοῦ Χριστοῦ. But that is another story, to do with the boundaries of the covenant and their maintenance rather than with the climax of the covenant itself.

Bibliography

a Vallisoleto, X. M. 1932. "'Et Semini Tuo Qui Est Christus' (Gal. 3.16)." *Verbum Domini* 12:327–332.

Aletti, J.-N. 1981. *Colossiens 1,15–20: Genre et Exégèse Du Texte; Fonction de la Thématique Sapientielle*. Analecta Biblica. Rome: Pontifical Biblical Institute Press.

Alford, H. 1865. *The Greek Testament: With a Critically Revised Text...* 4th ed. London/ Oxford/ Cambridge: Rivingtons.

Allegro, J. M., ed. 1968. *Discoveries in the Judaean Desert of Jordan*. Vol. 5. Oxford: Clarendon Press.

Aptowitzer, V. 1922. *Kain und Abel in der Aggada, den Apokryphen, der hellenistischen, christlichen und mohammedanischen Literatur*. Wien/Leipzig: Löwit.

Arndt, William F., and F. Wilbur Gingrich. 1979. *A Greek-English Lexicon of the New Testament and Other Early Christian Literature*. Rev. F. W. Gingrich and F. W. Danker. 2nd ed. Chicago: University of Chicago Press.

Attridge, Harold W. 1984. "Josephus and His Works." In *Jewish Writings of the Second Temple Period*, ed. Michael E. Stone, 185-232. Compendia Rerum Iudaicarum ad Novum Testamentum, Section Two: The Literature of the Jewish People in the Period of the Second Temple and the Talmud, vol. 2. Assen/Philadelphia: Van Gorcum/Fortress Press.

Badenas, Robert. 1985. *Christ the End of the Law: Romans 10.4 in Pauline Perspective*. Journal for the Study of the New Testament Supplement Series. Sheffield: J.S.O.T. Press.

Badham, F. P. 1907–8. "Philippians ii.6: ἁρπαγμὸν." *Expository Times* 19:331–333.

Balchin, J. F. 1985. "Colossians 1:15–20: An Early Christian Hymn? The Argument from Style." *Vox Evangelica* 15:65–94.

Bammel, E. 1961. "Versuch Kol 1 15–20." *Zeitschrift für die neutestamentliche Wissenschaft* 52:88–95.

Barclay, John M. G. 1988. *Obeying the Truth: A Study of Paul's Ethics in Galatians*. Studies of the New Testament and its World. Edinburgh: T. & T. Clark.

Barclay, W. 1958. "Great Themes of the New Testament, I: Phil. 2:1–11." *Expository Times* 70:40–44.

Barnes, Julian. 1985 <1984>. *Flaubert's Parrot*. London: Pan Books.

Barrett, C. K. 1957. *A Commentary on the Epistle to the Romans*. Black's New Testament Commentaries. London: A. & C. Black.

268

------. 1962. *From First Adam to Last: A Study in Pauline Theology*. London: A. & C. Black.

------. 1964 /5. "Things Sacrificed to Idols." *New Testament Studies* 11:138–153.

------. 1971 <1968>. *A Commentary on the First Epistle to the Corinthians*. 2nd ed. Black's New Testament Commentaries. London: A. & C. Black.

------. 1973. *A Commentary on the Second Epistle to the Corinthians*. Black's New Testament Commentaries. London: A. & C. Black.

------. 1985. *Freedom and Obligation: A Study of the Epistle to the Galatians*. Philadelphia: Westminster Press.

Barth, Karl. 1936–1969. *Church Dogmatics*. Edinburgh: T. & T. Clark.

------. 1947. *Erklärung Des Philipperbriefes*. Zürich: Zollikon.

Barton, John. 1988. *People of the Book? The Authority of the Bible in Christianity*. The Bampton Lectures for 1988. London: S.P.C.K.

Bassler, Jouette M., ed. 1991. *Pauline Theology: Toward a New Synthesis*. Vol 1. Minneapolis/Philadelphia: Augsburg/Fortress.

Bauckham, R. 1980–81. "The Worship of Jesus in Apocalyptic Christianity." *New Testament Studies* 27:322–341.

Baugh, S. M. 1985. "The Poetic Form of Col. 1:15–20." *Western Theological Journal* 47:227–244.

Beare, F. W. 1959. *A Commentary on the Epistle to the Philippians*. Black's New Testament Commentaries. London: A. & C. Black.

Beasley-Murray, G. R. 1962. "Philippians." In *Peake's Commentary on the Bible*, eds. M. Black and H. H. Rowley, 985–989. London: Nelson.

Beasley-Murray, P. 1980. "Colossians 1:15–20: An Early Christian Hymn Celebrating the Lordship of Christ." In *Pauline Studies: Essays Presented to Professor F. F. Bruce on His 70th Birthday*, eds. D. A. Hagner and M. J. Harris, 169–183. Exeter/Grand Rapids: Paternoster/Eerdmans.

Beet, J. A. 1887. "Thought It not Robbery to Be Equal with God." *The Expositor* 3d series 5:115–125.

------. 1891 –2. "Some Difficult Passages in St. Paul's Epistles: I." *Expository Times* 3:307–308.

------. 1894. "Harpagmos. Philippians II.6: A Reply." *Expository Times* 6:526–528.

Beker, J. C. 1980. *Paul the Apostle: The Triumph of God in Life and Thought*. Philadelphia: Fortress.

Bengel, J. Albrecht. 1862 <1773>. *Gnomon Novi Testamenti*. 3rd ed. London: Williams and Norgate.

Benoit, P. 1961. *Exégèse et théologie II: La théologie de Saint Paul*. Paris: Cerf.

------. 1975. "L'hymne christologique de Col i,15–20. Jugement critique sur l'état des recherches." In *Judaism, Christianity and Other Greco-Roman Cults: Studies for Morton Smith at Sixty*, ed. J. Neusner, vol. 1, 226–263. Leiden: E.J. Brill.

Bentzen, A. 1955. *King and Messiah*. London: Lutterworth.

Berger, K. 1984. *Formgeschichte Des Neuen Testaments*. Heidelberg: Quelle & Mayer.

Betz, Hans-Dieter. 1979. *Galatians: A Commentary on Paul's Letter to the Churches in Galatia*. Hermeneia. Philadelphia: Fortress Press.

Betz, Otto. 1978. "Die Heilsgeschichtliche Rolle Israels bei Paulus." *Theologische Beiträge* 9:1–21.

Blass, F., A. Debrunner, and R. W. Funk. 1973 <1961>. *A Greek Grammar of the New Testament and Other Early Christian Literature*. Chicago/London: University of Chicago Press.

Bligh, John. 1970. *Galatians: A Discussion of St. Paul's Epistle*. London: St Paul Publications.

Bonnard, P. 1950. *L'Epître Aux Philippiens*. Commentaire du Nouveau Testament. Neuchâtel/Paris: Delachaux & Niestlé.

Bornkamm, Günther. 1969. *Early Christian Experience*. Trans. P. L. Hammer. London: S.C.M. Press.

Bousset, Wilhelm. 1970 <1913>. *Kyrios Christos: A History of Belief in Christ from the Beginnings of Christianity to Irenaeus*. Trans. John E. Steely. Nashville: Abingdon Press.

Bouyer, L. 1951–2. "ΑΡΠΑΓΜΟΣ." *Recherches de Sciences Réligieuses* 39:281–288.

Bover, J. M. 1923. "'Et Semini Tuo, Qui Est Christus' (Gal. 3.16)." *Verbum Domini* 3:365–366.

Bring, Ragnar. 1966. "Der Mittler und das Gesetz: Eine Studie zu Gal. 3,20." *Kerygma und Dogma* 12:292–309.

------. 1968. *Der Brief des Paulus an die Galater*. Berlin/Hamburg: Lutherisches Verlagshaus.

------. 1969. *Christus und das Gesetz*. Leiden: E.J. Brill.

Brown, A., S. R. Driver, and G. A. Briggs. 1905. *A Hebrew-English Lexicon to the Old Testament*. Oxford: Oxford University Press.

Bruce, F. F. 1963. *The Epistle of Paul to the Romans: An Introduction and Commentary*. Tyndale New Testament Commentaries. London: Tyndale Press.

------. 1982. *The Epistle to the Galatians: A Commentary on the Greek Text*. Eds. I. H. Marshall and W. W. Gasque. The New International Greek Testament Commentary. Grand Rapids: Eerdmans.

------. 1984. *The Epistles to the Colossians, to Philemon, and to the Ephesians*. New International Commentary on the New Testament. Grand Rapids: Eerdmans.

Brunt, J. C. 1985. "Rejected, Ignored or Misunderstood? The Fate of Paul's Approach to the Problem of Food Offered to Idols in Early Christianity." *New Testament Studies* 31:113–124.

Bultmann, Rudolf. 1951-5. *Theology of the New Testament*. 2 vols. Trans. Kendrick Grobel. London/New York: S.C.M. Press/Scribner's.

------. 1976. *Der Zweite Brief an die Korinther*. Ed. E. Dinkler. Göttingen: Vandenhoek und Ruprecht.

Burney, C. F. 1925. "Christ as the APXH of Creation." *Journal of Theological Studies* 27:160–177.

Burton, E. de W. 1921. *A Critical and Exegetical Commentary on the Epistle to the Galatians*. International Critical Commentary. Edinburgh: T. & T. Clark.

Caird, George B. 1944. *The New Testament Conception of Δόξα*. Unpublished D.Phil. Thesis, Oxford University.

------. 1959. "Everything to Everyone: The Theology of the Corinthian Epistles." *Interpretation* 13:385–99.

------. 1968. "The Development of the Doctrine of Christ in the New Testament." Ed. N. Pittenger. In *Christ for Us Today*, 66–80. London: S.C.M. Press.

------. 1976. *Paul's Letters From Prison*. New Clarendon Bible. Oxford: Oxford University Press.

------. 1978. "Review of Sanders 1977." *Journal of Theological Studies* 29:538–43.

Callan, Terence D. 1976. *The Law and the Mediator: Gal. 3:19b–20*. Ph. D. Dissertation. Yale University.

------. 1980. "Pauline Midrash: The Exegetical Background of Gal. 3:19b." *Journal of Biblical Literature* 99:549–567.

Calvin, Jean. 1961. *The Epistles of Paul the Apostle to the Romans and to the Thessalonians*. Trans. R. Mackenzie. Edinburgh: Saint Andrew Press.

Campbell, J. Y. 1965 <1932, 1947, 1948>. *Three New Testament Studies*. Leiden: E.J. Brill.

Carmignac, J. 1971–2. "L'Importance de la Place D'une Négation: OYX 'APΠAΓMON 'HΓHEΣATO (Philippiens II.6)." *New Testament Studies* 18:131–161.

Cassuto, U. 1961a–64. *A Commentary on the Book of Genesis*. 2 Vols. Jerusalem: Magnes Press.

------. 1961b. *The Documentary Hypothesis and the Composition of the Pentateuch*. Trans. I. Abrahams. Jerusalem: Magnes Press.

Cavallin, H. C. C. 1978. "'The Righteous Shall Live by Faith': A Decisive Argument for the Traditional Interpretation." *Studia Theologica* 32:33–43.

Cerfaux, L. 1951. *Le Christ dans la Théologie de Saint Paul*. Lectio Divina. Paris: Cerf.

Chamberlain, J. S. F. 1892–3. "The Kenosis." *Expository Times* 4:189–90.

Charlesworth, J. H. 1982. "A Prolegomenon to a New Study of the Jewish Background of the Hymns and Prayers in the New Testament." *Journal of Jewish Studies* 33:265–285.

Cholmondeley, F.G. 1895–6. "Harpagmos. Philippians ii.6." *Expository Times* 7:47–48.

Clements, R. E. 1967. *Abraham and David: Genesis XV and Its Meaning for Israelite Tradition*. London: S.C.M. Press.

------. 1976. *A Century of Old Testament Study*. London: Lutterworth.

Collange, Jean-François. 1972. *Énigmes de la Deuxième Épître de Paul aux Corinthiens*. Society for New Testamnet Studies Monograph Series. Cambridge: Cambridge University Press.

------. 1979 <1973>. *The Epistle of Saint Paul to the Philippians*. Trans. A. W. Heathcote. London: Epworth Press.

------. 1987. *L'épître de Saint Paul A Philémon*. Commentaire du Nouveau Testament, 2nd series, Geneva: Labor et Fides.

Conzelmann, Hans. 1975 <1969>. *1 Corinthians: A Commentary on the First Epistle to the Corinthians*. Trans. James W. Leitch. Hermeneia. Philadelphia: Fortress Press.

Coppens, J. 1965. "Phil., II,7 et Is., LIII,12: Le Problème de la 'Kénose'" *Ephemerides Théologiques Louvanienses* 41:147–150.

------. 1967. "Une nouvelle Structuration de l'Hymne Christologique de l'Epître aux Philippiens." *Ephemerides Théologiques Louvanienses* 43:197–202.

Craig, W. L. 1980. "The Bodily Resurrection of Jesus." In *Gospel Perspectives*. 6 Vols., eds. R. T. France and D. Wenham, vol. 1, 47–74. Sheffield: J.S.O.T. Press.

Cranfield, C. E. B. 1975 , 1979. *A Critical and Exegetical Commentary on the Epistle to the Romans*. 2 Vols. The International Critical Commentary. Edinburgh: T. & T. Clark.

------. 1990. "Giving a Dog a Bad Name: A Note on H. Räisänen's *Paul and the Law*." *Journal for the Study of the New Testament* 38:77–85.

Cullmann, Oscar. 1963 <1959>. *The Christology of the New Testament*. Revised ed. Trans. Shirley C. Guthrie and Charles A. M. Hall. Philadelphia: Westminster Press.

Dahl, N. A. 1964. "Christ, Creation and the Church." Eds. W. D. Davies and D. Daube. In *The Background of the New Testament and Its Eschatology*, 422–43. Cambridge: Cambridge University Press.

------. 1974. *The Crucified Messiah and Other Essays*. Minneapolis: Augsburg.

------. 1977. *Studies in Paul: Theology for the Early Christian Mission*. Minneapolis: Augsburg.

Danby, Herbert. 1933. *The Mishnah, Translated from the Hebrew with Introduction and Brief Explanatory Notes*. Oxford: Oxford University Press.

Danieli, J. 1955. "'Mediator Autem Unius Non Est' (Gal. 3.20)." *Verbum Domini* 33:9–17.

Davidson, W. L. 1888. "The Mediator-argument of Gal. III.19, 20." *The Expositor* 3(7):377–386.

Davies, Alan T., ed. 1979. *AntiSemitism and the Foundations of Christianity*. New York/Ramsey/Toronto: Paulist Press.

Davies, W. D. 1974. *The Gospel and the Land: Early Christianity and Jewish Territorial Doctrine*. Berkeley: University of California Press.

------. 1980 <1948>. *Paul and Rabbinic Judaism*. 4th ed. Philadelphia: Fortress Press.

------. 1984. *Jewish and Pauline Studies*. London/Philadelphia: S.P.C.K./Fortress Press.

de Jonge, M. 1986. "The Earliest Christian Use of *Christos*. Some Suggestions." *New Testament Studies* 32:321–343.

Deichgräber, R. 1967. *Gotteshymnus und Christushymnus in der Frühen Christenheit*. Studien zur Umwelt des Neuen Testament. Göttingen: Vandenhoek und Ruprecht.

Demarest, B. 1980. "Process Theology and the Incarnation." In *Pauline Studies: Essays Presented to F.F. Bruce on His 70th Birthday*, eds. D. A. Hagner and M. J. Harris, 122–142. Exeter/Grand Rapids: Paternoster/Eerdmans.

di Fonzo, L. 1941. "De Semine Abrahae, Promissionum Herede, Iuxta S. Paulum in Gal 3." *Verbum Domini* 21:49–58.

Dinkler, E. 1962. "Die Taufterminologie in 2 Kor. i 21 f." In *Neotestamentica et Patristica. Eine Freundesgabe, Herrn Professor Dr. Oscar Cullmann zu seinem 60. Geburtstag Überreicht*, 173–91. Supplements to *Novum Testamentum*. Leiden: E.J. Brill.

Dodd, C. H. 1959 <1932>. *The Epistle of Paul to the Romans*. London: Collins/Fontana.

Donaldson, T. L. 1986. "The 'curse of the Law' and the Inclusion of the Gentiles: Galatians 3.13–14." *New Testament Studies* 32.

Drane, J. W. 1975. *Paul, Libertine or Legalist? A Study in the Theology of the Major Pauline Epistles*. London: S.P.C.K.

Driver S.R, and A. Neubauer. 1876–77. *The Fifty-third Chapter of Isaiah According to the Jewish Interpreters*. Oxford and London: Oxford University Press.

Duncan, George S. 1934. *The Epistle of Paul to the Galatians*. Moffatt New Testament Commentary. London: Hodder and Stoughton.

Bibliography

Dunn, J. D. G. 1970. "2 Corinthians III.17—'The Lord is the Spirit'" *Journal of Theological Studies* n.s. 21:309–320.

------. 1973. "1 Corinthians 15.45—last Adam, Life-giving Spirit." In *Christ and Spirit in the New Testament: In Honour of Charles Francis Digby Moule*, eds B. Lindars and S. S. Smalley, 127–41. Cambridge: Cambridge University Press.

------. 1975a. *Jesus and the Spirit: A Study of the Religious and Charismatic Experience of Jesus and the First Christians as Reflected in the New Testament*. London: S.C.M. Press.

------. 1975b. "Romans 7.14–25 in the Theology of St. Paul." *Theologische Zeitschrift* 31:257–273.

------. 1980. *Christology in the Making: A New Testament Inquiry into the Origins of the Doctrine of the Incarnation*. London/Philadelphia: S.C.M./Westminster Press.

------. 1982. "Was Christianity a Monotheistic Faith from the Beginning?" *Scottish Journal of Theology* 35:303–36.

------. 1987. *The Living Word*. London: S.C.M. Press.

------. 1988a. *Romans 1–8*. Word Biblical Commentary. Waco, Texas: Word Books.

------. 1988b. *Romans 9–16*. Word Biblical Commentary. Waco, Texas: Word Books.

------. 1989. "Foreword to Second Edition of Dunn 1980."

------. 1990. *Jesus, Paul and the Law: Studies in Mark and Galatians*. London: S.P.C.K.

Ellingworth, P. 1961–2. "Colossians I.15–20 and Its Context." *Expository Times* 73:252–253.

Ellis, E. E. 1957. *Paul's Use of the Old Testament*. Edinburgh: Oliver and Boyd.

Elmslie, W. A. L. 1911. *The Mishnah on Idolatry*. Trans. J. A. Robinson. Texts and Studies 8.2. Cambridge: Cambridge University Press.

Emerton, J. A. 1958. "Son of Man." *Journal of Theological Studies* 9:225–42.

Erhardt, A. 1964. *The Framework of the New Testament Stories*. Manchester: Manchester University Press.

Ernst, Josef. 1974. *Die Briefe an die Philipper, an Philemon, an die Kolosser, an die Epheser*. Regensburger Neues Testament. Regensburg: Friedrich Pustet.

Eshbaugh, Howard. 1979. "Textual Variants and Theology: A Study of the Galatians Text of Papyrus 46." *Journal for the Study of the New Testament* 3:60–72.

Eskanazi, Tamara C. 1982. "Paul and the Dead Sea Scrolls on the Law." In *Proceedings of the Eighth World Congress of Jewish Studies, Jerusalem, August 16–21, 1981*, vol. 1, 119–24. Jerusalem: World Union of Jewish Studies.

Eusebius. 1926-32. *Historia Ecclesiae*. Trans. Kirsopp Lake and J.E.L. Oulton. Loeb Classical Library. Cambridge, Massachusetts/London: Harvard University Press/ William Heinemann.

Fairweather, E. R. 1959. "Appended Note: The 'Kenotic' Christology." In *A Commentary on the Epistle to the Philippians*, by F. W. Beare, 159–174. London: A. & C. Black.

Fee, Gordon D. 1980. "Εἰδωλόθυτα Once Again: An Interpretation of 1 Corinthians 8–10." *Biblica* 61:172–197.

------. 1987. *The First Epistle to the Corinthians*. Ed. F. F. Bruce. The New International Commentary on the New Testament. Grand Rapids: Eerdmans.

Fernandez, M. P. 1983. "El numeral εἷς en Pablo como titulo cristologico: Rom 5,12–19; Gal 3,20; cfr. Rom 9,10." *Estudios Biblicos* 41:325–340.

Feuillet, A. 1942. "L'Homme-Dieu considéré dans sa condition terrestre de serviteur et de rédempteur (Phil. II, 5 ss. et texts parallèles)." *Révue Biblique* 51:58–79.

------. 1962 –3. "La Profession de Foi Monothéiste de I Cor VIII, 4–6." *Liber Annus (Studii Biblici Franciscani)* XIII:7–32. Jerusalem.

------. 1965a. "La Création de L'Univers 'dans le Christ' D'après L'Epître Aux Colossiens (i.16a)." *New Testament Studies* 12:1–9.

------. 1965b. "L'Hymne Christologique de l'épître aux Philippiens (ii:6–11)." *Révue Biblique* 72:352–380, 481–507.

------. 1972. *Christologie Paulinienne et Tradition Biblique*. Paris: Desclee de Brouwer.

Foerster, W. 1930. "οὐχ ἁρπαγμόν ἡγήσατο bei den griechischen Kirchenvätern." *Zeitschrift für die neutestamentliche Wissenschaft* 29:115–128.

------. 1964 <1933>. "ἁρπάζω, ἁρπαγμός." In *Theological Dictionary of the New Testament*, ed. G. Kittel, vol. 1, 472–4. Grand Rapids: Eerdmans.

Fox, Robin Lane. 1987. *Pagans and Christians*. New York: Alfred A. Knopf.

France, R. T. 1982. "The Worship of Jesus: A Neglected Factor in Christological Debate?" In *Christ the Lord: Studies in Christology Presented to Donald Guthrie*, ed. H. H. Rowdon, 17–36. Leicester: Inter-Varsity Press.

Frankowski, J. 1983. "Early Christian Hymns Recorded in the New Testament: A Reconsideration of the Question in the Light of Heb 1,3." *Biblische Zeitschrift* 27:183–194.

Fung, Ronald Y. K. 1988. *The Epistle to the Galatians*. Ed. Frederick F. Bruce. The New International Commentary on the New Testament. Grand Rapids: Eerdmans.

Funk, Robert W., revised and trans. 1973 <1961>. *A Greek Grammar of the New Testament and Other Early Christian Literature*. 5th ed. Chicago and London: The University of Chicago Press.

Furness, J. M. 1957–8. "ἁρπαγμός... ἑαυτὸν ἐκένωσε." *Expository Times* 69:93–94.

------. 1959–60. "The Authorship of Philippians ii.6–11." *Expository Times* 70:240–243.

------. 1967–8. "Behind the Philippian Hymn." *Expository Times* 79:178–82.

Furnish, Victor P. 1984. *II Corinthians*. Anchor Bible. New York: Doubleday.

Gabathuler, H. J. 1965. *Jesus Christus, Haupt der Kirche—Haupt der Welt*. Abhandlung zur Theologie des Alten und Neuen Testaments. Zürich-Stuttgart: Zwingli-Verlag.

Gabris, K. 1968. "Zur Kraft der Verheissungen (Zum Gal 3,15–22)." *Communio Viatorum* 11:251–264.

Gager, John G. 1983. *The Origins of Anti-semitism*. Oxford: Oxford University Press.

Gaston, Lloyd. 1982. "Angels and Gentiles in Early Judaism and in Paul." *Studies in Religion/Sciences Religieuses* 11:65–75.

------. 1987. *Paul and the Torah*. Vancouver: University of British Columbia Press.

Georgi, Dieter. 1964. "Der vorpaulinische Hymnus Phil. ii.6–11." In *Zeit und Geschichte: Festschrift für R. Bultmann*, ed. E. Dinkler, 263–293. Tübingen: J.C.B. Mohr (Paul Siebeck).

Getty, M. A. 1985. "The Primacy of Christ." *Bible Today* 23:18–24.

Gewiess, J. 1963. "Der Philipperbriefstelle ii.6b." In *Neotestamentliche Aufsätze: Festschrift Fr J. Schmid*, eds J. Blinzler, O. Kuss, and F. Mussner, 69–85. Regensburg: Verlag Friedrich Pustet.

Gibbs, J. G. 1970. "The Relation Between Creation and Redemption According to Phil. ii.5–11." *Novum Testamentum* 12:270–283.

------. 1971. *Creation and Redemption: A Study in Pauline Theology*. Supplements to Novum Testamentum. Leiden: E.J. Brill.

Giblin, C. H. 1975. "Three Monotheistic Texts in Paul." *Catholic Biblical Quarterly* 37:527–547.

Gifford, E. H. 1911 <1897>. *The Incarnation: A Study of Philippians II:5–11 and a University Sermon on Psalm CX*. Ed. H. Wace. London: Longmans, Green and Co.

Gilbert, M. 1984. "Wisdom Literature." In *Jewish Writings of the Second Temple Period*, ed. M. E. Stone. In *Compendia Rerum Iudaicarum Ad Novum Testamentum*, eds. W. J. Burgers, H. Sysling, and P. J. Tomson, 283–324. Assen/Maastricht/Philadelphia: Van Gorcum/Fortress.

Ginzberg, L. 1937 <1909>. *The Legends of the Jews*. Trans. H. Szold. 14th ed. Philadelphia: Jewish Publication Society of America.

Glasson, T. F. 1967. "Colossians 1.18, 15 and Sirach 24." *Journal of Biblical Literature* 86:214–216.

------. 1974–5. "Two Notes on the Philippians Hymn[2.6–11]." *New Testament Studies* 21:133–39.

Gnilka, J. 1980a. *Der Kolosserbrief*. Herders theologischer Kommentar zum Neuen Testament. Freiburg/Basel/Wien: Herder.

------. 1980b <1968>. *Der Philipperbrief*. 3rd ed. Herders theologischer Kommentar zum Neuen Testament. Freiburg/Basel/Wien: Herder.

Goldin, J. 1968. "'Not by Means of an Angel and not by Means of a Messenger'" In *Religions in Antiquity: Essays in Memory of Erwin Ramsdell Goodenough*, ed. J. Neusner, 412–424. Leiden: E. J. Brill.

Gordon, T. David. 1987. "The Problem at Galatia." *Interpretation* 41:32–43.

Grässer, E. 1981. "'Ein einziger ist Gott' (Röm 3,30): Zum christologischen Gottesverständnis bei Paulus." In *"Ich will euer Gott werden": Beispiele biblischen Redens von Gott*, eds. Norbert Lohfink et al, 177–205. Stuttgarter Bibelstudien. Stuttgart: Katholische Bibelwerk.

Grelot, P. 1971. "La traduction et l'interpretation de *Ph*. 2, 6–7: Quelques Eléments d'enquète Patristique." *Nouvelle Révue Theologique* 9–10:897–922, 1009–1026.

------. 1973. "La Valeur de οὐχ... ἀλλά... dans Philippiens ii. 6–7." *Biblica* 54:25–42.

Griffiths, D. R. 1957–8. "ἁρπαγμός and ἑαυτὸν ἐκένωσεν in Philippians ii.6,7." *Expository Times* 69:237–239.

Gundry, Robert H. 1980. "The Moral Frustration of Paul Before His Conversion: Sexual Lust in Romans 7.7–25." In *Pauline Studies: Essays Presented to Professor F.F. Bruce on His 70th Birthday*, eds. Donald A. Hagner and Murray J. Harris, 228–245. Exeter/Grand Rapids: Paternoster/Eerdmans.

------. 1985. "Grace, Works, and Staying Saved in Paul." *Biblica* 66:1–38.

Guthrie, Donald. 1974. *Galatians*. New Century Bible. London: Oliphants.

Hahn, Ferdinand. 1976. "Das Gesetzesverständnis im Römer- und Galaterbrief." *Zeitschrift für die neutestamentliche Wissenschaft* 67:29–63.

Hammerich, L. L. 1966. "An Ancient Misunderstanding (Phil. 2:6 'robbery')." *Historisk-filosophiske Meddeleser udgivet af Det Kangelige Danske Videnskabernes Selskab* 41(4). Copenhagen.

Hanson, Anthony T. 1978–9. "The Use of the Old Testament in the Epistle of James." *New Testament Studies* 25:526–527.

------. 1980. "The Midrash in II Corinthians 3: A Reconsideration." *Journal for the Study of the New Testament* 9:2–28.

Harper, George. 1988. *Repentance in Pauline Theology*. Ph.D. Dissertation, McGill University, Montreal.

Harvey, A. E. 1970. *The New English Bible: Companion to the New Testament*. Oxford and Cambridge: Oxford University Press/ Cambridge University Press.

------. 1982. *Jesus and the Constraints of History: The Bampton Lectures, 1980*. London: Duckworth.

Harvey, J. 1964–5. "A New Look at the Christ Hymn in Philippians 2.6–11." *Expository Times* 76:337–339.

Hawthorne, Gerald F. 1983. *Philippians*. Word Biblical Commentary, vol. 43. Waco, Texas: Word Books.

Hays, R. B. 1983. *The Faith of Jesus Christ: An Investigation of the Narrative Substructure of Galatians 3:1–4:11*. S.B.L. Dissertation Series. Chico, California: Scholars Press.

------. 1989. *Echoes of Scripture in the Letters of Paul*. New Haven and London: Yale University Press.

Hengel, Martin. 1974. *Judaism and Hellenism: Studies in Their Encounter in Palestine During the Early Hellenistic Period*. Trans. John Bowden. 2 vols. London: S.C.M. Press.

------. 1976. *The Son of God: The Origin of Christology and the History of Jewish-Hellenistic Religion*. Trans. John Bowden. Philadelphia: Fortress Press.

------. 1979. *Acts and the History of Earliest Christianity*. Trans. John Bowden. Philadelphia: Fortress Press.

------. 1983. *Between Jesus and Paul: Studies in the Earliest History of Christianity*. Trans. J. Bowden. London: S.C.M. Press.

------. 1989 <1961>. *The Zealots: Investigations Into the Jewish Freedom Movement in the Period from Herod 1 Until 70 A.D.*. Trans. D. Smith. Edinburgh: T. & T. Clark.

Hennecke, E., and W. Schneemelcher, eds. 1965 <1964>. *New Testament Apocrypha*. Trans. and ed. R. McL. Wilson. Philadelphia: Westminster Press.

Henry, P. 1950. "Kénose." In *Supplément Au Dictionnaire de la Bible*, 7–161. Paris.

Héring, Jean. 1966 <1962>. *The First Epistle of Saint Paul to the Corinthians*. Trans. A. W. Heathcote and P. J. Allcock. London: The Epworth Press.

Hick, John. 1988. *An Interpretation of Religion*. Basingstoke: MacMillan.

Hickling, C. J. A. 1980. "Paul's Reading of Isaiah." In *Studia Biblica 1978*, ed. E. A. Livingstone, 215–23. Journal for the Study of the New Testament Supplement Series, vol.

3. Sheffield: J.S.O.T. Press.

------. 1974–5. "The Sequence of Thought in II Corinthians, Chapter Three." *New Testament Studies* 21:380–395.

Hill, David. 1982. "Galatians 3.10–14: Freedom and Acceptance." *Expository Times* 93:196–200.

Hofius, O. 1976. *Der Christushymnus Philipper 2.6–11: Untersuchungen Zu Gestalt und Aussage Eines Urchristlichen Psalms.* Wissenschaftliche Untersuchungen zum Neuen Testament. Tübingen: J.C.B. Mohr <Paul Siebeck>.

Hooke, S. H. 1961. *Alpha and Omega: A Study in the Pattern of Revelation.* London: James Nisbet.

Hooker, Morna D. 1959–60. "Adam in Romans 1." *New Testament Studies* 6:297–306.

------. 1967. *The Son of Man in Mark.* London: S.P.C.K.

------. 1971. "Interchange in Christ." *Journal of Theological Studies* n.s. 22(2):349–61.

------. 1973. "Were There False Teachers in Colossae?" In *Christ and Spirit in the New Testament: Essays in Honour of Charles Francis Digby Moule,* eds. B. Lindars and S. S. Smalley, 315–331. Cambridge: Cambridge University Press.

------. 1975. "Philippians 2.6–11." In *Jesus und Paulus: Festschrift Für Werner Georg Kümmel Zum 70 Geburtstag,* eds. E. E. Ellis and E. Grässer, 151–64. Göttingen: Vandenhoek und Ruprecht.

------. 1979. *Pauline Pieces.* London: Epworth Press.

------. 1980–1. "Beyond the Things That Are Written? St Paul's Use of Scripture." *New Testament Studies* 27:295–309.

------. 1982. "Paul and 'Covenantal Nomism'" In *Paul and Paulinism: Essays in Honour of C. K. Barrett,* eds. M. D. Hooker and S. G. Wilson, 47–56. London: S.P.C.K.

------. 1990. *From Adam to Christ: Essays on Paul.* Cambridge: Cambridge University Press.

Hoover, R. W. 1971. "The Harpagmos Enigma: A Philological Solution." *Harvard Theological Review* 56:95–119.

Horsley, Richard A. 1978a. "The Background of the Confessional Formula in 1 Kor 8 6." *Zeitschrift für die neutestamentliche Wissenschaft* 69:130–135.

------. 1978b. "Consciousness and Freedom Among the Corinthians." *Catholic Biblical Quarterly* 40:574–589.

------. 1980. "Gnosis in Corinth: I Corinthians 8.1–6." *New Testament Studies* 27:32–51.

Houlden, J. L. 1970. *Paul's Letters from Prison.* Harmondsworth: Penguin.

Howard, G. 1977. "The Tetragram and the New Testament." *Journal of Biblical Literature* 96:63–83.

------. 1978. "Phil. 2:6–11 and the Human Christ." *Catholic Biblical Quarterly* 40:368–87.

Hübner, H. 1984 <German 1978>. *Law in Paul's Thought.* Trans. J. C. G. Greig. Studies of the New Testament and its World. Edinburgh: T. &. T. Clark.

------. 1984. *Gottes Ich und Israel. Zum Schriftgebrauch des Paulus in Römer 9–11.* Göttingen: Vandenhoek und Ruprecht.

Hudson, D. F. 1965–6. "A Further Note on Philippians ii:6–11." *Expository Times* 77:29.

Hunter, A. M. 1961 <1940>. *Paul and His Predecessors.* London: S.C.M. Press.

Hurst, L. D. 1986. "Re-enter the Pre-existent Christ in Philippians 2.5–11?" *New Testament Studies* 32:449–457.

Hurst, L. D., and N. T. Wright, eds. 1987. *The Glory of Christ in the New Testament: Studies in Christology in Memory of George Bradford Caird.* Oxford: Clarendon Press.

Hurtado, L. W. 1984. "Jesus as Lordly Example in Philippians 2:5–11." In *From Jesus to Paul: Studies in Honour of Francis Wright Beare,* eds. P. Richardson and J. C. Hurd, 113–126. Waterloo, Ontario: Wilfrid Laurier University Press.

------. 1988. *One God, One Lord: Early Christian Devotion and Ancient Jewish Monotheism.* Philadelphia: Fortress.

Isaacs, W. H. 1923–4. "Galatians iii.20." *Expository Times* 35:565–567.

Jaeger, W. W. 1915. "Eine Stilgeschichtliche Studie Zum Philipperbrief." *Hermes* 50:537–53.

Jeremias, Joachim. 1967. "Μωυσῆς." In *Theological Dictionary of the New Testament,* eds. G. Kittel and G. W. Bromiley, vol. 4, 848–873. Grand Rapids: Eerdmans.

Jervell, J. 1960. *Imago Dei: Gen. 1.26f. Im Spätjudentum, in der Gnosis und in Den Paulinischen Briefe.* Forschungen zur Religion und Literatur des Alten und Neuen Testaments. Göttingen: Vandenhoek & Ruprecht.

Johnston, George. 1957. *Ephesians, Philippians, Colossians, Philemon.* New Century Bible. London: Nelson.

Jülicher, A. 1917 <1907>. *Die Schriften des Neuen Testaments 2.* 3rd ed. Göttingen: Vandenhoek und Ruprecht.

Käsemann, Ernst. 1964 <1960>. "A Primitive Christian Baptismal Liturgy." In *Essays on New Testament Themes,* trans. W. J. Montague, 149–168. Studies in Biblical Theology vol. 41. London: S.C.M. Press.

------. 1967. *Exegetische Versuche und Besinnungen.* 5th ed. Göttingen: Vandenhoek & Ruprecht.

------. 1968. "A Critical Analysis of Philippians 2:5–11." *Journal for Theology and Church [=God and Christ: Existence and Province]* 5:45–88.

------. 1971 <1969>. *Perspectives on Paul.* Trans. Margaret Kohl. London: S.C.M. Press.

------. 1980. *Commentary on Romans.* Trans. and ed. Geoffrey W. Bromiley. Grand Rapids: Eerdmans.

Kaylor, R. David. 1988. *Paul's Covenant Community: Jew and Gentile in Romans.* Atlanta: John Knox Press.

Keck, Leander E. "The Law and 'the Law of Sin and Death' (Rom 8:1–4): Reflections on the Spirit and Ethics in Paul." In *The Divine Helmsman: Studies on God's Control of Human Events, Presented to Lou H. Silberman,* eds. J. L. Crenshaw and S. Sandmel, 41–57. New York: Ktav.

Kee, H. C. 1982. "Christology and Ecclesiology: Titles of Christ and Models of Community." Ed. K. H. Richards. *SBL Seminar Papers* 21:227–242.

Kehl, N. 1967. *Der Christushymnus Kol 1,12–20. Eine motivgeschichtliche Untersuchung zu Kol 1,12–20.* Stuttgart Biblische Mongraphien. Stuttgart: Katholisches Bibelwerk.

Kennedy, H. A. A. 1912. "The Epistle of Paul to the Philippians." In *The Expositor's Greek Testament,* ed. W. R. Nicoll, vol. 3, 397–473. London: Hodder and Stoughton.

Bibliography

Kertelge, Karl. 1984. "Gesetz und Freiheit im Galaterbrief." *New Testament Studies* 30:382–394.

Kim, Seyoon. 1981. *The Origin of Paul's Gospel*. Wissenschaftliche Untersuchungen zum neuen Testament 2. Tübingen/Grand Rapids: J.C.B. Mohr (Paul Siebeck)/Eerdmans.

Kittel, G., and G. Friedrich, eds. 1964-76. *Theological Dictionary of the New Testament*. Trans. G. W. Bromiley. Grand Rapids, Michigan: Eerdmans.

Klein, C. 1978. *Anti-Judaism in Christian Theology*. London: S.P.C.K.

Knibb, Michael A. 1987. *The Qumran Community*. Cambridge Commentaries on Writings of the Jewish and Christian World, 200 BC to AD 200. Cambridge: Cambridge University Press.

Knox, Wilfred L. 1939. *St Paul and the Church of the Gentiles*. Cambridge: Cambridge University Press.

Kramer, W. G. 1966. *Christ, Lord, Son of God*. Trans. B. Hardy. Studies in Biblical Theology vol. 50. London: S.C.M. Press.

Kreitzer, L. J. 1987. *Jesus and God in Paul's Eschatology*. Journal for the Study of the New Testament Supplement Series. Sheffield: J.S.O.T. Press.

Kuss, O. 1957 , 1959, 1978. *Der Römerbrief*. Regensburg: Verlag Friedrich Pustet.

Lacan, M. F. 1963. "Le Dieu Unique et son Médiateur: Galates 3, 20." In *L'Homme Devant Dieu. Mélanges Offertes Aux Père Henri de Lubac*, 113–125. Paris: Montaigne.

Lacoque, A. 1979. *The Book of Daniel*. Atlanta: John Knox Press.

Lagrange, M.-J. 1942 < 1918>. *Saint Paul Aux Galates*. 4th ed. Études Bibliques. Paris: Lecoffre.

------. 1950 <1916>. *Saint Paul: Épître aux Romains*. Paris: Gabalda.

Lähnemann, J. 1971. *Der Kolosserbrief: Komposition, Situation und Argumentation*. Gütersloh: Mohn.

Lambrecht, Jan. 1983. "Transformation in 2 Cor. 3,18." *Biblica* 64:243–254.

Langkammer, P. H. 1970-71. "Literarische und Theologische Einzelstücke in 1 Kor. VIII.6." *New Testament Studies* 17:193–197.

Larsson, Edvin. 1962. *Christus als Vorbild: eine Untersuchung zu den paulinischen Tauf- und Eikontexten*. Uppsala: Gleerup Lund.

Le Déaut, Roger. 1961. "Traditions Targumiques dans le Corpus Paulinien? (Hebr 11,4 et 12,24; Gal 4,29s; II C 3,16)." *Biblica* 42:28–48.

Lewis, C. S. 1943 <1933>. *The Pilgrim's Regress: An Allegorical Apology for Christianity, Reason and Romanticism*. 2nd ed. London: Bles.

Liddell, H. G., and R. Scott, eds. 1953 < 1940>. *A Greek-English Lexicon*. Revised and augmented by H. S. Jones and R. McKenzie. Oxford: Oxford University Press.

Lietzmann, Hans. 1969. *An die Korinther I.II*. Handbuch zum neuen Testament. Tübingen: J.C.B. Mohr (Paul Siebeck).

Lightfoot, J. B. 1876. *St Paul's Epistles to the Colossians and to Philemon*. 2nd ed. London: MacMillan.

------. 1868. *St. Paul's Epistle to the Philippians*. London: MacMillan.

279

Lincoln, A. T. 1981. *Paradise Now and Not Yet: Studies in the Role of the Heavenly Dimension in Paul's Thought with Special Reference to His Eschatology.* Society of New Testament Studies Monograph Series. Cambridge: Cambridge University Press.

Loewe, R. 1981. "'Salvation' is not of the Jews." *Journal of Theological Studies* 22:341–368.

Lohmeyer, E. 1961 <1927>. *Kyrios Jesus: Eine Untersuchung Zu Phil. 2,5–11.* 2nd ed. Sitzungsberichte der Heidelberger Akademie der Wissenschaften. Heidelberg: Carl Winter: Universitätsverlag.

Lohse, E. 1971 <1968>. *Colossians and Philemon.* Trans. W. R. Poehlmann and R. J. Karris. Hermeneia. Philadelphia: Fortress.

Longenecker, Bruce W. 1991. *Eschatology and the Covenant: A Comparison of 4 Ezra and Romans 1-11.* Supplements to J.S.N.T., vol. 57. Sheffield: Sheffield Academic Press.

Lührmann, D. 1978. *Der Brief an die Galater.* Zürcher Bibelkommentare. Zürich: Theologischer Verlag.

McCown, W. 1979. "The Hymnic Structure of Colossians 1:15–20." *Evangelical Quarterly* 51:156–162.

Manns, F. 1977. *Essais sur le Judéo-Christianisme.* Studium Biblicum Franciscanum Analecta. Jerusalem: Franciscan Printing Press.

------. 1979. "Col. 1,15–20: Midrash Chrétien de Gen. 1,1." *Révue de Sciences Religieuses* 53:100–110.

Marshall, I. H. 1968. "The Christ-Hymn in Philippians 2:5–11." *Tyndale Bulletin* 19:104–127.

------. 1982. "Incarnational Christology in the New Testament." In *Christ the Lord: Studies in Christology Presented to Donald Guthrie,* ed. H. H. Rowdon, 1–16. Leicester: Inter-Varsity Press.

Martin, Brice L. 1989. *Christ and the Law in Paul.* Supplements to Novum Testamentum. Leiden: E.J. Brill.

Martin, R. P. 1959. *The Epistle of Paul to the Philippians: An Introduction and Commentary.* Tyndale New Testament Commentaries. London: Tyndale Press.

------. 1972. *Colossians: The Church's Lord and the Christian's Liberty.* Exeter: Paternoster.

------. 1974. *Colossians and Philemon.* New Century Bible. London: Oliphants.

------. 1976. *Philippians.* New Century Bible. London: Oliphants.

------. 1983 <1967>. *Carmen Christi: Philippians ii.5–11 in Recent Interpretation and in the Setting of Early Christian Worship.* 2nd ed. Society of New Testament Studies Monograph Series, vol. 4. Cambridge: Cambridge University Press.

Mauser, Ulrich. 1967. "Galater III.20: Die Universalität des Heils." *New Testament Studies* 13:258–270.

Meeks, Wayne A. 1967. *The Prophet-king: Moses Traditions and the Johannine Christology.* Supplements to *Novum Testamentum*. Leiden: E.J. Brill.

------. 1968. "Moses as God and King." In *Religions in Antiquity: Essays in Memory of Erwin Ramsdell Goodenough,* ed. Jacob Neusner, 354–371. Studies in the History of Religions (Supplements to *Numen*). Leiden: E.J. Brill.

------. 1983. *The First Urban Christians: The Social World of the Apostle Paul.* New Haven: Yale University Press.

Bibliography

Mellinkoff, R. 1979. *Journal of Jewish Art* 6:16–38.

Metzger, Bruce M. 1973. "The Punctuation of Rom. 9:5." In *Christ and Spirit in the New Testament: In Honour of Charles Francis Digby Moule*, ed. Barnabas Lindars and Stephen S. Smalley, 95–112. Cambridge: Cambridge University Press.

Meyer, H. A. W. 1885. *Critical and Exegetical Hand-book to the Epistles to the Philippians and Colossians, and to Philemon*. Trans. and ed. J. C. Moore, W. P. Dickson, and T. Dwight. New York: Funk and Wagnalls.

Michael, J. Hugh. 1928. *The Epistle of Paul to the Philippians*. Ed. J. Moffatt. The Moffatt New Testament Commentary. London: Hodder & Stoughton.

Michel, Otto. 1966 <1955>. *Der Brief an die Römer*. 4th ed. Kritisch-Exegetischer Kommentar über das Neue Testament. Göttingen: Vandenhoek und Ruprecht.

Moo, Douglas J. 1986. "Israel and Paul in Romans 7.7–12." *New Testament Studies* 32:122–135.

------. 1987. "Paul and the Law in the Last Ten Years." *Scottish Journal of Theology* 40:287–307.

Moore, George Foot. 1927–30. *Judaism in the First Centuries of the Christian Era: The Age of the Tannaim*. 3 vols. Cambridge, Massachusetts.: Harvard University Press.

Moule, C. F. D. 1957. *The Epistles of Paul the Apostle to the Colossians and to Philemon*. The Cambridge Greek Testament Commentary. Cambridge: Cambridge University Press.

------. 1970. "Further Reflexions on Philippians 2:5–11." In *Apostolic History and the Gospel: Biblical and Historical Essays Presented to F.F. Bruce on His 60th Birthday*, eds. W. W. Gasque and R. P. Martin, 264–76. Exeter: Paternoster Press.

------. 1972a. "The Manhood of Jesus in the New Testament." In *Christ, Faith and History: Cambridge Studies in Christology*, ed. S. W. Sykes and J. P. Clayton, 95–110. Cambridge: Cambridge University Press.

------. 1972b. "2 Cor. 3:18b, καθάπερ ἀπὸ Κυρίου Πνεύματος." In *Neues Testament und Geschichte (Cullmann Festschrift)*, ed. H. Baltensweiler and B. Reicke, 233–237. Zürich: Theologischer Verlag.

------. 1974. "'Justification' in Its Relation to the Condition κατὰ Πνεῦμα (Rom. 8:1–11)." In *Battestimo e Giustizia in Rom 6 e 8*, ed. L. De Lorenzi, 177–187. Serie Monografica di 'Benedictina', no. 2. Rome: Abbazio S. Paulo Fuori le Mura.

------. 1977. *The Origin of Christology*. Cambridge: Cambridge University Press.

------. 1982. "Review of Dunn 1980." *Journal of Theological Studies* n.s. 33:258–263.

Moule, Handley C. G. 1882. *The Epistle of Paul the Apostle to the Romans*. The Cambridge Bible for Schools and Colleges. Cambridge: Cambridge University Press.

Moulton, J. H., and N. Turner. 1906–1963. *A Grammar of New Testament Greek*. Edinburgh: T. & T. Clark.

Moxnes, Halvor. 1980. *Theology in Conflict: Studies in Paul's Understanding of God in Romans*. Supplements to Novum Testamentum. Leiden: E.J. Brill.

Murphy-O'Connor, J. 1976. "Christological Anthropology in Phil. II:6–11." *Révue Biblique* 83:25–50.

------. 1977. *Becoming Human Together*. Wilmington: Michael Glazier.

------. 1978a. "I Cor. 8.6: Cosmology or Soteriology?" *Révue Biblique* 85:253–267.

------. 1978b. "Freedom or the Ghetto (*1 Cor.*, VIII,1–13; X,23–XI,1)." *Révue Biblique* 85: 543–74.

Mussner, Franz. 1974. *Der Galaterbrief*. Freiburg/Basel/Wien: Herder.

Nagata, Takeshi. 1981. *Philippians 2:5–11. A Case Study in the Contextual Shaping of Early Christology*. Dissertation, Princeton Theological Seminary.

Neill, Stephen C., and N. Thomas Wright. 1988 <1964>. *The Interpretation of the New Testament, 1861–1986*. 2nd ed. Oxford: Oxford University Press.

Newman, Barclay M. 1984. "'Seed' in Galatians 3.16, 19." *The Bible Translator* 35:334–337.

Noth, Martin. 1966. *The Laws in the Pentateuch and Other Studies*. Trans. D. R. Ap-Thomas. Philadelphia: Fortress.

Nygren, Anders. 1949 <1944>. *Commentary on Romans*. Trans. Carl Rasmussen. Philadelphia: Fortress Press.

O'Brien, Peter T. 1982. *Colossians, Philemon*. Word Biblical Commentary, vol. 24. Waco, Texas: Word Books.

O'Neill, J. C. 1975. *Paul's Letter to the Romans*. Harmondsworth: Penguin.

------. 1979. "The Source of the Christology in Colossians." *New Testament Studies* 26:87–100.

------. 1988. "Hoover on *Harpagmos* Reviewed, with a Modest Proposal Concerning Philippians 2:6." *Harvard Theological Review* 81:445–449.

Oepke, Albrecht. 1973 <1937>. *Der Brief Des Paulus an die Galater*. 3rd ed. Theologischer Handkommentar zum Neuen Testament. Berlin: Evangelische Verlagsanstalt.

Packer, James I. 1964. "The Wretched Man in Romans 7." *Studia Evangelica [Texte und Untersuchungen]* 2 [87]:621–627.

Petersen, Norman R. 1985. *Rediscovering Paul: Philemon and the Sociology of Paul's Narrative World*. Philadelphia: Fortress Press.

Plag, C. 1969. *Israels Wege zum Heil. Eine Untersuchung zum Römer 9 bis 11*. Stuttgart: Calwer Verlag.

Pöhlmann, W. 1973. "Die hymnischen All-Prädikationen in Kol 1 15–20." *Zeitzchrift für die neutestamentliche Wissenschaft* 64:53–74.

Pollard, T. E. 1981. "Colossians 1.12–20: A Reconsideration." *New Testament Studies* 14:572–577.

Prat, F. 1926–7. *The Theology of St. Paul*. London: Burns Oates and Washbourne.

Rainbow, Paul A. 1987. *Monotheism and Christology in I Corinthians 8.4–6*. Unpublished D. Phil. Thesis, Oxford University.

Räisänen, Heikki. 1986a <1983>. *Paul and the Law*. Philadelphia: Fortress.

------. 1986b. *The Torah and Christ: Essays in German and English on the Problem of the Law in Early Christianity*. Suomen Ekseegeettisen Seuran Julkaisuja. Helsinki: Finnish Exegetical Society.

------. 1987. "Römer 9–11: Analyse eines geistigen Ringens." *Aufstieg und Niedergang der Römischen Welt* 2.25.4:2891–2939.

------. 1988. "Paul, God, and Israel: Romans 9–11 in Recent Research." In *The Social World of Formative Christianity and Judaism: Essays in Tribute to Howard Clark Kee*, ed. Jacob

Neusner, Peder Borgen, Ernest S. Frerichs, and Richard Horsley, 178–206. Philadelphia: Fortress Press.

Reicke, B. 1951. "The Law and This World According to Paul." *Journal of Biblical Literature* 70:259–276.

------. 1962. "Unité Chrétienne et Diaconie: Phil. ii 1–11." In *Neotestamentica et Patristica: Eine Freundesgabe, Herrn Professor Dr. Oscar Cullmann zu seinem 60. Geburtstag überreicht.*, 203–212. Supplements to Novum Testamentum. Leiden: E.J. Brill.

Rendall, Frederic. 1912. "The Epistle of Paul to the Galatians." In *The Expositor's Greek Testament*, ed. W. Robertson Nicoll, vol. 3. London: Hodder and Stoughton.

Richard, Earl. 1981. "Polemics, Old Testament, and Theology: A Study of II Cor., III, 1—IV, 6." *Révue Biblique* 88:340–367.

Richardson, G. Peter. 1969. *Israel in the Apostolic Church*. Society of New Testament Studies Monograph Series. Cambridge: Cambridge University Press.

------. 1980. "Pauline Inconsistency: 1 Corinthians 9:19–23 and Galatians 2:11–14." *New Testament Studies* 26:347–62.

------, ed. 1986. *Anti-Judaism in Early Christianity*. Vol. 1. *Paul and the Gospels*. Studies in Christianity and Judaism/Etudes sur le christianisme et le judasme. Waterloo: Wilfrid Laurier University Press.

Ridderbos, Herman N. 1953. *The Epistle of Paul to the Churches of Galatia*. Trans. H. Zylstra. New International Commentary on the New Testament. Eerdmans: Grand Rapids.

------. 1975 <1966>. *Paul: An Outline of His Theology*. Trans. J. R. de Witt. Grand Rapids: Eerdmans.

Riesenfeld, H. 1979. *Unité et Diversité dans le Nouveau Testament*. Lectio Divina. Paris: Cerf.

Robertson, Archibald, and Alfred Plummer. 1914. *A Critical and Exegetical Commentary on the First Epistle of St Paul to the Corinthians*. International Critical Commentary. Edinburgh: T. & T. Clark.

Robinson, D. W. B. 1968–9. "ἁρπαγμός: The Deliverance That Jesus Refused?." *Expository Times* 80:253–254.

Robinson, J. A. T. 1973. *The Human Face of God*. London: S.C.M. Press.

Robinson, J. M. 1957. "A Formal Analysis of Col 1, 15–20." *Journal of Biblical Literature* 76:270–287.

Rohde, Joachim. 1989. *Der Brief des Paulus an die Galater*. Theologisches Handkommentar zum Neuen Testament. Berlin: Evangelische Verlagsanstalt.

Romaniuk, S. K. 1981. "Exégèse du Nouveau Testament et Ponctuation." *Novum Testamentum* 23:195–209.

Ross, J. M. 1909. "Ἁρπαγμός (Philippians ii.6)." *Journal of Theological Studies* (10):573–574.

Sampley, J. P. 1980. *Pauline Partnership in Christ*. Philadelphia: Fortress.

Sanday, W., and A. C. Headlam. 1902 <1895>. *A Critical and Exegetical Commentary on the Epistle to the Romans*. 5th ed. International Critical Commentary. Edinburgh: T. & T. Clark.

Sanders, E. P. 1977. *Paul and Palestinian Judaism: A Comparison of Patterns of Religion*. Philadelphia: Fortress Press.

------. 1978. "Paul's Attitude Toward the Jewish People." *Union Seminary Quarterly Review* 33:175–187.

------. 1983. *Paul, the Law, and the Jewish People*. Philadelphia: Fortress.

------. 1991. *Paul. Past Masters*. Oxford: Oxford University Press.

Schechter, S. 1961 <1909>. *Aspects of Rabbinic Theology: Major Concepts of the Talmud*. New edn. Introd. by L. Finkelstein. New York: Schocken Books.

Schenk, W. "Der Koloserbrief in der neueren Forschung (1945–1985)." In *Aufsteig und Niedergang der Römischen Welt*, vol. 2.25.4, 3327–3364.

------. 1984. *Die Philipperbriefe des Paulus*. Stuttgart/Berlin/Köln/Mainz: W. Kohlhammer.

Schillebeeckx, Edward. 1980 <Dutch 1977>. *Christ: The Christian Experience in the Modern World*. Trans. J. Bowden. London: S.C.M. Press.

Schlier, Heinrich. 1971. *Der Brief an die Galater*. 14th ed. Meyer Kommentar. Göttingen: Vandenhoek und Ruprecht.

Schoeps, H.-J. 1961 <1959>. *Paul: The Theology of the Apostle in the Light of Jewish Religious History*. Trans. H. Knight. London: Lutterworth.

Schumacher, H. 1914–1921. *Christus in seiner Präexistenz und Kenose nach Phil. 2:5–8*. Rome: Pontifical Biblical Institute.

Schürer, E. 1973–1987. *The History of the Jewish People in the Age of Jesus Christ (175 B.C.—A.D. 135)*. Revised and eds. G. Vermes, F. Millar, M. Black, and M. Goodman. 3 vols. Edinburgh: T. & T. Clark.

Schwartz, Daniel R. 1983. "Two Pauline Allusions to the Redemptive Mechanism of the Crucifixion." *Journal of Biblical Literature* 102:259–268.

Schweitzer, Albert. 1968 <1931>. *The Mysticism of Paul the Apostle*. Trans. William Montgomery. Preface by F. C. Burkitt. New York: Seabury Press.

Schweizer, E. 1970. "Kol 1,15–20." In *Beiträge zur Theologie des Neuen Testaments: Neutestamentliche Aufsätze (1955–1970)*, 113–1415. Zürich: Zwingli Verlag.

------. 1982 <1976>. *The Letter to the Colossians*. Trans. A. Chester. London: S.P.C.K.

Scott, C. A. A. 1935. *Footnotes to St. Paul*. Cambridge: Cambridge University Press.

Scroggs, R. 1966. *The Last Adam*. Oxford: Blackwells.

Seesemann, H. 1933. *Der Begriff ΚΟΙΝΩΝΙΑ im Neuen Testament*. Beihefte zur Zeitschrift für die Neutestamentliche Wissenschaft, vol. 14. Giessen: Alfred Töpelmann.

Staab, K. 1933. *Pauluskommentare aus der griechischen Kirche*. Münster.

Stanley, Christopher D. 1990. "'Under a Curse': A Fresh Reading of Galatians 3.10–14." *New Testament Studies* 36:481–511.

Stanton, Graham N. 1974. *Jesus of Nazareth in New Testament Preaching*. Society for New Testament Studies Monograph Series. Cambridge: Cambridge University Press.

Stauffer, E. 1955 <1941>. *New Testament Theology*. Trans. J. Marsh. London: S.C.M. Press.

Stendahl, K. 1976. *Paul Among Jews and Gentiles*. Philadelphia: Fortress.

Stolle, V. 1973. "Die Eins in Gal 3, 15–29." In *Theokratia: Jahrbuch des Institutum Judaicum Delitzschianum II, 1970–72*, 204–213. Leiden: E.J. Brill.

Stuhlmacher, Peter. 1978. "'Das Ende Des Gesetzes'. Über Ursprung und Ansatz der Paulinischen Theologie." *Zeitschrift für Theologie und Kirche* 67:14–39.

284

Bibliography

------. 1985. "Paul's Understanding of the Law in the Letter to the Romans." *Svensk Exegetisck Årsbok* 50:87–104.

------. 1986 <1981>. *Reconciliation, Law and Righteousness: Essays in Biblical Theology*. Trans. E. Kalin. Philadelphia: Fortress.

Talbert, C. H. 1967. "The Problem of Pre-existence in Philippians 2:6–11." *Journal of Biblical Literature* 86:141–153.

Thielman, Frank. 1988. "The Law or the Curse of the Law? The Object of Paul's Polemic in Galatians 3:10–14." Conference Presentation, Annual Meeting of the Society of Biblical Literature, Chicago, 1988.

------. 1989. *From Plight to Solution: A Jewish Framework for Understanding Paul's View of the Law in Galatians and Romans*. Supplements to *Novum Testamentum*. Leiden: E. J. Brill.

Thiselton, A. C. 1978. "Realized Eschatology at Corinth." *New Testament Studies* 24:510–25.

Thornton, T. C. G. 1971. "The Meaning of καὶ Περὶ ἁμαρτίας in Romans viii.3." *Journal of Theological Studies* n.s. 22:515–517.

Tomson, Peter J. 1990. *Paul and the Jewish Law: Halakha in the Letters of the Apostle to the Gentiles*. Compendia Rerum Iudaicarum ad Novum Testamentum, section Three: Jewish Traditions in Early Christian Literature, vol. 1. Assen/Minneapolis: Van Gorcum/Fortress Press.

Tremenheere, G. H. 1931. "Gal. iii.20. ὁ Θεός Εἷς ἐστίν.." *Theology* 22:35.

Trudinger, P. 1967–8. "ἁρπαγμός and the Christological Significance of the Ascension." *Expository Times* 79:279.

Tyson, Joseph B. 1973. "'Works of Law' in Galatians." *Journal of Biblical Literature* 92:423–431.

Urbach, E. E. 1987 <1975, 1979>. *The Sages: Their Concepts and Beliefs*. Trans. I. Abrahams. Cambridge (Mass.) and London: Harvard University Press.

van Dülmen, A. 1968. *Die Theologie des Gesetzes bei Paulus*. Stuttgarter Biblische Monographien. Stuttgart: Katholisches Bibelwerk.

van Unnik, W. C. 1962. "The Christian's Freedom of Speech in the New Testament." *Bulletin of the John Rylands Library* 44:466–488.

------. 1963. "'With Unveiled Face,' an Exegesis of 2 Corinthians iii 12–18." *Novum Testamentum* 6:153–169.

------. 1980. *Sparsa Collecta*. Supplements to *Novum Testamentum*. Leiden: E.J. Brill.

Vanhoye, A. 1978. "Un médiateur des anges en Ga 3,19–20." *Biblica* 59:403–411.

Vaughan, C. J. 1885 <1859>. *St Paul's Epistle to the Romans*. 6th ed. London: Macmillan and Co.

Vawter, B. 1971. "The Colossians Hymn and the Principle of Redaction." *Catholic Biblical Quarterly* 33:62–81.

Vermes, Geza. 1975. *Post Biblical Jewish Studies*. Studies in Judaism in Late Antiquity. Leiden: E.J. Brill.

------. 1987 <1962>. *The Dead Sea Scrolls in English*. 3rd ed. Harmondsworth: Penguin.

Vincent, M. R. 1897. *A Critical and Exegetical Commentary on the Epistles to the Philippians and to Philemon*. International Critical Commentary. Edinburgh: T. & T. Clark.

Vokes, F. E. 1964. "ἁρπαγμός in Philippians 2:5–11." In *Studia Evangelica*[Texte und Untersuchungen], ed. F. L. Cross, vol. 2 [87], 670–675. Berlin: De Gruyter.

Wanamaker, C. A. 1987. "Philippians 2.6–11: Son of God or Adamic Christology?" *New Testament Studies* 33:179–193.

Warren, W. 1911. "On ἑαυτὸν ἐκένωσεν, Phil. ii.7." *Journal of Theological Studies* (12):461–463.

Watson, F. B. 1986. *Paul, Judaism and the Gentiles: A Sociological Approach.* Society of New Testament Studies Monograph Series vol. 56. Cambridge: Cambridge University Press.

Wedderburn, A. J. M. 1971. "The Body of Christ and Related Concepts in 1 Corinthians." *Scottish Journal of Theology* 24:74–96.

------. 1973. "Philo's 'Heavenly Man'" *Novum Testamentum* 15:301–26.

------. 1974. *Adam and Christ: An Investigation Into the Background of 1 Corinthians XV and Romans V.12–21.* Unpublished Ph.D. Thesis, Cambridge, England.

------. 1980. "Adam in Paul's Letter to the Romans." In *Studia Biblica 1978: III. Papers on Paul and Other New Testament Authors*, ed. E. A. Livingstone, 413–430. JSNT Supplement Series, vol. 3. Sheffield: J.S.O.T. Press.

------. 1985. "Some Observations on Paul's Use of the Phrases 'in Christ' and 'with Christ'" *Journal for the Study of the New Testament* 25:83–97.

------. 1988. *The Reasons for Romans.* Studies of the New Testament and its World. Edinburgh: T. & T. Clark.

Wengst, K. 1972. *Christologische Formeln und Lieder des Urchristentums.* 2nd ed. Die Schriften des Neuen Testaments. Gütersloh: Mohn.

Westerholm, Stephen. 1988. *Israel's Law and the Church's Faith: Paul and His Recent Interpreters.* Grand Rapids: Eerdmans.

Wilckens, Ulrich. 1974. *Rechtfertigung als Freiheit: Paulusstudien.* Neukirchen-Vluyn: Neukirchener Verlag.

------. 1978 , 1980, 1982. *Die Brief an die Römer.* Evangelisch-Katholischer Kommentar zum Neuen Testament, vol. 6. Cologne/Neukirchen-Vluyn: Benziger/Neukirchener Verlag.

------. 1981. "Zur Entwicklung des Paulinischen Gesetzesverständnisses." *New Testament Studies* 28:154–190.

------. 1982. "Statements on the Development of Paul's View of the Law." In *Paul and Paulinism: Essays in Honour of C. K. Barrett*, eds. Morna D. Hooker and Stephen G. Wilson, 17–26. London: S.P.C.K.

Wilcox, M. 1977. "'Upon the Tree'—Deut. 21:22–23 in the NT." *Journal of Biblical Literature* 96:85–99.

------. 1979. "The Promise of the 'seed' in the New Testament and the Targumim." *Journal for the Study of the New Testament* 5:2–20.

Williams, A. L. 1907. *The Epistles of Paul the Apostle to the Colossians and to Philemon.* Cambridge Greek Testament. Cambridge: Cambridge University Press.

Willis, Wendell Lee. 1985. *Idol Meat in Corinth: The Pauline Argument in 1 Corinthians 8 and 10.* SBL Dissertation Series. Chico, California: Scholars Press.

Bibliography

Wink, Walter. 1986. *Unmasking the Powers: The Invisible Forces That Determine Human Existence*. The Powers, vol. 2. Philadelphia: Fortress Press.

Winter, S. C. 1987. "Paul's Letter to Philemon." *New Testament Studies* 33:1–15.

Wire, Antoinette Clark. 1974. *Pauline Theology as an Understanding of God: The Explicit and the Implicit*. Unpublished Ph.D. Dissertation, Claremont Graduate School.

Wolff, H. W. 1974. *Anthropology of the Old Testament*. London: S.C.M. Press.

Wright, N. T. 1978. "The Paul of History and the Apostle of Faith." *Tyndale Bulletin* 29:61–88.

------. 1980a. *The Messiah and the People of God: A Study in Pauline Theology with Particular Reference to the Argument of the Epistle to the Romans*. Unpublished D.Phil Thesis, Oxford University.

------. 1980b. "The Meaning of περὶ ἁμαρτίας in Romans 8:3." In *Studia Biblica*, ed. E. A. Livingstone, vol. 3, 453-59. Sheffield: J.S.O.T. Press.

------. 1983. "Adam in Pauline Christology." In *SBL 1983 Seminar Papers*, ed. K. H. Richards, 359–389. Chico, California: Scholars Press.

------. 1986a. "ἁρπαγμός and the Meaning of Philippians 2.5–11." *Journal of Theological Studies* n.s. 37:321–352.

------. 1986b. "'Constraints' and the Jesus of History." *Scottish Journal of Theology* 39:189–210.

------. 1986c. *The Epistles of Paul to the Colossians and to Philemon*. Tyndale New Testament Commentaries, new series. Leicester/Grand Rapids: Inter-Varsity Press/Eerdmans.

------. 1991. "Putting Paul Together Again: Towards a Synthesis of Pauline Theology." In *Pauline Theology: Toward a New Synthesis*, ed. Jouette M. Bassler. Philadelphia: Fortress.

Young, Frances, and David F. Ford. 1987. *Meaning and Truth in 2 Corinthians*. Biblical Foundations in Theology. London: S.P.C.K.

Zeller, Dieter. 1984. *Der Brief an die Römer*. Regensburger Neues Testament. Regensburg: Verlag Friedrich Pustet.

Ziesler, J. A. 1979. "Anthropology of Hope." *Expository Times* 90:104–9.

------. 1989. *Paul's Letter to the Romans*. S.C.M./ Trinity Press International New Testament Commentaries. London/ Philadelphia: S.C.M. Press/ Trinity Press International.

Zimmerli, W., and J. Jeremias. 1968. "παῖς Θεοῦ." In *Theological Dictionary of the New Testament*, ed. G. Friedrich, trans. and ed. G. W. Bromiley, vol. 5, 654–717. Grand Rapids: Eerdmans.

INDEX OF PASSAGES CITED

(indexes compiled by Dr Philip Hillyer)

EARLY CHRISTIAN TEXTS

GREEK AND LATIN TEXTS

INDEX OF MODERN AUTHORS

INDEX OF SUBJECTS

Gennadius of Constantinople 161, 221

Gentiles 143, 148, 162, 163, 164, 165, 166, 167, 168, 171, 173, 174, 195, 204, 224, 230, 232, 237, 248, 254, 262
  blessing for 153, 154, 156, 236, 250
  Christian mission to 195, 234, 245, 247, 248, 250, 253, 262, 265
  enter family of God 139, 154, 240, 242, 245, 246, 249-250
  Hellenistic-Jewish mission to 123, 124
  and Jews 15, 232, 234, 240, 248
  share in restoration of Israel 150-151
  and Torah 204, 240

glory 175, 177, 178, 179, 181, 182, 183, 185, 186, 187, 188, 189, 190, 191, 192, 195
  of church 237
  of the Lord 189

gnostic mythology and speculation 32, 70, 95, 96, 107

gnostics, gnosticism 19, 34, 123, 124, 160

God,
  and Christ 15, 55, 94, 97, 115, 117, 159
  knowledge of 123
  nature and character 55, 84, 86, 235, 254
    covenant faithfulness 109, 194, 234, 236, 238, 239, 241, 242, 244, 245, 249, 251, 255
    creator 108, 109, 110, 112, 117, 130, 133, 134, 189, 237, 242, 256, 259
    Father 30, 130, 133
    forbearance 236
    justice 211, 228, 230, 234, 239, 242, 249, 251, 255, 256
    lifegiver 167
    lordship 133
    love 59, 86, 124, 132, 228
    righteousness 35, 38, 171, 182, 194, 203, 216, 234, 235, 238, 239, 249, 251, 255
  people of *see* people of God
  promises of 238, 239
    see also Abraham, promises to; Israel, promises to
  redefined by Christ 133, 266, 267
  redefined by the Spirit 266
  Spirit of 87
  story of 258
  vindicated in Christ 242
  Wisdom of 110, 123, 131
  working of 53
  see also monotheism

Golden Calf 197, 227, 238

gospel 188
  glory of 182
  rejected by Israel 235, 236, 237, 244, 261
  and Torah 182, 241

grace 15, 167, 168, 172, 236, 240, 247, 248, 249

hardening 236, 249, 250

hardness of heart 183, 184

harpagmos,
  and meaning of Philippians 2.5-11 62-90
  summary chart 81

Herodotus 190

Hezekiah 24

historical scholarship 259

history of religions 42, 107, 115, 116, 117, 121, 135, 174

holiness 122

Holocaust 253

Holy Spirit *see* Spirit

hope 24

humanity 29-32
  new 49, 254

idols, idolatry 122, 124, 126, 128,